# The Education Doctorate (Ed.D.)

Issues of Access, Diversity, Social Justice,
and Community Leadership

Edited by Virginia Stead

PETER LANG
New York • Bern • Frankfurt • Berlin
Brussels • Vienna • Oxford • Warsaw

Library of Congress Cataloging-in-Publication Data

The education doctorate (Ed.D.): issues of access, diversity, social justice,
and community leadership / edited by Virginia Stead.
Pages cm. — (Equity in higher education theory, policy, & praxis; vol. 5)
Includes bibliographical references.
1. Doctor of education degree. 2. Education—Study and teaching (Graduate)—
Social aspects. I. Stead, Virginia, editor of compilation.
LB1742.E38    378.2'42—dc23    2014048957
ISBN 978-1-4331-2889-9 (hardcover)
ISBN 978-1-4331-2888-2 (paperback)
ISBN 978-1-4539-1529-5 (e-book)
ISSN 2330-4502 (print)
ISSN 2330-4510 (online)


Bibliographic information published by **Die Deutsche Nationalbibliothek**.
**Die Deutsche Nationalbibliothek** lists this publication in the "Deutsche
Nationalbibliografie"; detailed bibliographic data are available
on the Internet at http://dnb.d-nb.de/.

The paper in this book meets the guidelines for permanence and durability
of the Committee on Production Guidelines for Book Longevity
of the Council of Library Resources.

# Table of Contents

Preface...And a Call to Action................................................... ix
    Virginia Stead

**Section One: Ed.D. Program Access, Curriculum, and Pedagogy**

Chapter One: Ed.D. Program Candidate Recruitment and Admission
    Policy in the United States.................................................3
    Ann Toler Hilliard

Chapter Two: Online Ed.D. Program Delivery as a Medium for Enhanced
    Civic Engagement...................................................... 21
    Lara Willox

Chapter Three: Teaching Research Method Courses in a Hybrid Ed.D.
    Program: A Mixed Methods Study ....................................... 35
    Sunny Liu and M.D. Haque

Chapter Four: An Argument for the Ed.D. Project Study as an Alternative
    to the Dissertation ..................................................... 51
    Christina M. Dawson, Cheryl Keen, and Carol Philips

Chapter Five: Reforming Practitioner-Based Ed.D. Programs: Access,
    Diversity, and Impact................................................... 61
    Stephanie J. Jones

Chapter Six: A Mixed Methods Research Project: Combining Research, Evaluation, and Leadership Skills in Ed.D. Programs ........................ 71
Thomas W. Christ

Chapter Seven: Supervising the Educational Doctorate Dual Award (Ed.D.D.A.): Juggling Truth, Relevance, and Economic Development........ 85
Jude Chua and Yew-Jin Lee

Chapter Eight: Ed.D. Program Dissertation Research: Increasing the Odds of Completion .......................................................... 95
Kelly S. Hall

Chapter Nine: Perspectives from Morgan State, a Historically Black University: Rethinking Ed.D. and Ph.D. Education Programs ............... 111
Glenda M. Prime and Whitney Johnson

Chapter Ten: Fitness for Purpose: Is This a Problem for Professional Ed.D. Programs?........................................................... 123
Marnie O'Neill

## Section Two: Ed.D. Program Diversity and Social Justice

Chapter Eleven: Designing Educational Identity and Civic Courage: Using U.S.-Israeli Cross-National Dialogue to Transform the Ed.D. ................ 141
Carol Kochhar-Bryant

Chapter Twelve: Activating Graduate Teaching Experience to Challenge Microaggression in Evaluations of Minority Faculty........................ 155
Lerona Dana Lewis

Chapter Thirteen: Ed.D. Socialization Contexts: Origins, Evolving Purpose, Demographic Trends, and Institutional Practices........................... 171
Zarrina Talan Azizova

Chapter Fourteen: Promoting Social Justice Through the Indian Leadership Education and Development (I LEAD) Ed.D. Program .......... 187
Jioanna Carjuzaa, William G. Ruff, and David Henderson

Chapter Fifteen: The Authentic Ed.D. Program: Project-Based and Counter-Hegemonic...................................................... 197
Four Arrows, aka Don Trent Jacobs

Chapter Sixteen: Leveraging Multiplicity in the Ed.D. Cohort toward Transformation of Practice................................................. 211
Paris T. Priore-Kim

Chapter Seventeen: Critical Discourse Analysis of Ed.D. Program
    Narratives: Engagement with Academic Conferences and Publications.... 223
    Mariam Orkodashvili

Chapter Eighteen: Giving Voice Through the Practitioner-Based
    Ed.D. Program ......................................................... 237
    Jocelyn Romero Demirbag

Chapter Nineteen: The 100 Dinners Project: An Ed.D. Capstone Project
    Grounded in Conceptual Change Theory ................................ 247
    Audrey Hovannesian

Chapter Twenty: An Examination of the Intersecting Identities of Female
    Ed.D. Students and Their Journeys of Persistence........................ 261
    Amanda J. Rockinson-Szapkiw and Lucinda S. Spaulding

## Section Three: Ed.D. Program Power to Create Social Justice and Equitable Community Leadership

Chapter Twenty-One: Transforming the Ed.D. Program into a Force
    for Culturally Relevant Leadership ..................................... 275
    Michael L. Washington

Chapter Twenty-Two: Bridge Building: Can Ed.D. Program Redesign
    Connect Social Justice Scholars and Practitioners? ........................ 293
    Cynthia J. Macgregor and Michele Smith

Chapter Twenty-Three: The Ed.D. Program in Educational Leadership:
    Applying Principles of Human Appreciation ............................. 307
    Arnold Danzig and Elaine Chin

Chapter Twenty-Four: An International Survey of the Professional Ed.D.
    Program: Leading Reflective Research and Communities of Practice ...... 321
    Carla DiGiorgio

Chapter Twenty-Five: Professional Scholarship in an Ed.D. Program:
    Research and Writing for Real-World Contexts and
    Community Impact .................................................... 333
    Tara L. Shepperson and Jessica Hearn

Chapter Twenty-Six: Stepping Up: Tribal College Leadership and
    the Ed.D. Program .................................................... 349
    Sweeney Windchief

Chapter Twenty-Seven: The Doctorate in Educational Leadership for
   Social Justice: A Decade of Impact at Loyola Marymount University....... 365
   Jill Bickett, Karie Huchting, Ernest Rose, Mary K. McCullough,
   and Shane P. Martin

Chapter Twenty-Eight: Whose Knowledge Counts in an Ed.D. Program?
   Building Diverse Relationships to Illuminate Opportunities
   and Challenges ........................................................... 377
   Christopher Burke and Truman Hudson, Jr.

Chapter Twenty-Nine: Issues of Superintendent Preparation
   in Disadvantaged Areas: Considering the Usefulness
   of the Educational Doctorate (Ed.D.) ..................................... 389
   Chris Willis and Kay Brocato

Chapter Thirty: Reimagining the Education Doctorate (Ed.D.)
   as a Catalyst for Social Change........................................... 403
   David J. Siegel and Crystal R. Chambers

About the Contributors...................................................... 415

# Preface...And a Call to Action

*Virginia Stead*

This book is a response to the pandemic not of Ebola but of social alexithymia that permeates cultures such as ours and makes so many of us indifferent to the suffering of others. Finding avenues down which social justice leaders may travel undeterred is a daunting challenge but one that some Doctor of Education (Ed.D.) programs already count among their goals and one that others are working hard to implement.

The idea of Ed.D. programs as *educational crucibles* of any kind arose from the idea of the forging of heated contestations about how the academy currently functions, whom it serves, and whom it marginalizes. The more I thought about it, the more the metaphor seemed fitting.

The Carnegie Project on the Education Doctorate (CPED) distinguishes itself by the ways in which it offers affiliation and guidance to over 50 faculties of education as they conscientiously strive to address problems of elitism, racism, homophobia, and xenophobia. Many of the contributors to this book represent faculties of education that share CPED membership, and their insights have enormous value.

After much reflection about how the various chapters recommended themselves to collective themes, the following three sections emerged: (1) Ed.D. Program Access, Curriculum, and Pedagogy; (2) Ed.D. Program Diversity and Social Justice; and (3) Ed.D. Program Power to Create Social Justice and Equitable Community Leadership. Surprisingly, the authors who were first to respond to this book's call for chapters represented Australia, Canada, Singapore, and the United States. Over 70 chapter proposals were submitted for 30 chapter spaces within 3 days of the call.

It is our collective hope that this volume will serve as a beacon for social justice leadership through Ed.D. programs within all educational cultures and global communities.

# ED.D. PROGRAM
# ACCESS, CURRICULUM,
# AND PEDAGOGY

# CHAPTER ONE

# Ed.D. Program Candidate Recruitment and Admission Policy in the United States

*Ann Toler Hilliard*

## INTRODUCTION: WHAT IS THE DOCTORATE OF EDUCATION (ED.D.)?

A doctorate of education degree is based on educational research and its application in professional practices in an educational environment. Sometimes the doctorate of education degree is referred to as a practitioner's degree. Candidates will
seek the degree because they are professional practitioners or individuals who are
interested in becoming superintendents of schools or other school leaders at the
building, district, university, or community level. The doctorate of education degree
is likely to be the preferred qualification for many mid-career employees. Many
candidates in the Ed.D. program will already have master's degrees but may wish
to pursue studies at the doctoral level. Although the focus of doctoral programs
may vary, many programs emphasize instructional, organizational, public, and evidence-based leadership in state agencies and in public and nonpublic schools. They
also support educators as entrepreneurs within individual program specializations.

The original doctorate of education degree program was intended to prepare
experienced educational practitioners to serve as principals, directors, supervisors, and superintendents, as well as in other positions of leadership. These practitioners would be able to solve educational problems using best practices and
research-based strategies. The first doctorate of education degree program in the

United States was established at Harvard University in 1921 (Shulman, Golde, Conklin Bueschel, & Garabedian, 2006).

## ED.D. CANDIDATE RECRUITMENT

This discussion spans a broad array of issues ranging from the need to recruit future leaders to communication with potential candidates to digital marketing tools. It also takes into account the role of faculty members and the growing importance of international communities.

### In Search of Candidates Who Will Become Highly Qualified Leaders

The Ed.D.'s focus may vary from university to university. Because of the need for well-prepared educational leaders to serve in schools, it is important to have a pool of certified and highly qualified individuals to serve effectively in leadership positions in national and international educational communities. In order to assure that individuals are prepared for leadership positions, universities, colleges, and other organizations have assumed the task of educating and training candidates. Candidates are informed during the recruitment process that, when enrolled at the university, they are expected to engage in teaching and training and to jointly participate in project-based activities. The purpose of the doctoral degree is to ensure that educational systems have individuals who are qualified and ready to step into positions as leaders for the purpose of promoting high academic achievement for all students.

The recruiters for the doctoral degree program need to communicate to candidates how programs may differ in their focus or studies—that is, leadership, curriculum, technology, special education, policy studies, administration, organizational leadership, public and evidence-based leadership (Brungardt, Gould, Moore, & Potts, 1997). For over 3 decades, universities and colleges offering the doctorate of education degree have attempted to recruit underrepresented candidates. It is predicted that, by the year 2050, the underrepresented population in the United States will be approximately 50% of the total. Therefore, it is critical that members of this underrepresented population become participants in higher education so that they, too, can develop skills, knowledge, and the appropriate professional disposition to contribute to the growth of society educationally and economically.

However, the 10 years prior to 2012 in the United States were marked by a slight downturn in the number of candidates enrolling in Ed.D. programs. Since the fall of 2012, there has been just over a 1% increase in enrolled candidates in graduate programs. For the first time, there have been more than 461,000 enrolled candidates in the United States in graduate certificate, education specialist, masters, or doctoral programs (Canadian Association for Graduate Studies, 2011). The Council of

Graduate Schools is the only national organization that annually covers the enrollment of candidates in all fields of graduate studies in the United States.

## Recruitment Materials, Information, and Professional Practices

When soliciting Ed.D. candidates, recruitment teams must make every effort to be clear about when and where graduate fairs and open houses will take place and what the set agenda will entail. The recruitment team should use e-recruitment and other means of communicating with potential candidates as a strong link to the community (Gifford, 2010). The recruitment teams should discuss the quality of the program, its cost, the availability of financial aid, and how many graduates have ascended to positions of educational leadership. They should also talk about the strengths and benefits of the doctorate of education degree beyond potential financial gains. It is important for candidates to know that the recruitment management team is interested in keeping in contact with graduates after they complete the program. When recruiting candidates, it cannot be stated too often that all recruitment materials should be current, consistent, and clear about program cost and emphasize the typical return on the investment of the degree based on potential career opportunities.

The recruitment teams and office of enrollment management should also explain in an honest and tactical way that some outcomes are beyond the control of the college or university, such as guarantees of jobs or leadership positions. The teams should also explain that much depends on how favorable the economy may be at a given time. The recruitment teams should let potential candidates know where and when they may be contacted; further, if and when a potential candidate contacts the recruitment team, a team member should return calls or emails quickly and in a professional manner (Williams, 1993).

## What Do Graduate Recruitment Practices Look Like?

Further research is needed on what graduate recruitment practices should look like from a broader national and international perspective. To date, many studies have focused on individual college practices and strategies, but the risk is that the portfolio of activities at a few colleges or universities will neither describe the range of possibilities nor adequately assess the effectiveness of those activities as they pertain to recruitment. Recruitment is not a one-time approach. It must be done using a systematic approach to attracting and retaining graduating candidates. Today, a broad range of technology is used by recruitment teams to attract candidates to colleges and universities. However, the life cycle of technology based on best practices for graduate recruitment is likely to be very short.

The question, then, is this: What is the interplay between past practices of cultivating close personal contacts with prospects and faculty relationships and referring institutions and organizations with emerging technological tools and resources? In order to recruit candidates more successfully, the recruiters need to understand the thinking and needs of the adult learner (Aslanian & Giles, 2009). Graduate recruitment varies in planning and implementation. While print materials and open houses continue to be important, website information is the most frequently utilized recruitment tool. In this context, it is important to note that recruitment and marketing rarely exist as separate activities. Typically, the two use an integrated approach in the service of a common purpose. For example, recruiters should seek to reach minorities that are underrepresented in higher education but possess high performance ability. The goal at colleges and universities with low enrollments should be to recruit large numbers of candidates and build positive relationships within their communities (National Association of Graduate Admissions Professionals, 2001).

The literature identifies two notable changes in the field of graduate student recruitment. First, responsibility for recruitment appears to have shifted to a more shared collaborative model between academic units and graduate schools in the United States. Within the offices of financial aid, registrar, and enrollment management, graduate coordinators and faculty and other administrative staff work together to maintain or enhance graduate enrollment efforts. Second, while some practices continue to be important in a university's portfolio of recruitment activities, their effects must be enhanced by combining traditional practices with the use of technology (e.g., email, the institution's website, and social media) with emerging technology (e.g., social networks) as well as recruitment marketing tools. The blending of marketing initiatives and technology creates the best use of each resource for recruitment and may provide the highest possible return on the college and university's resources. Using technology tools is an asset, but recruiting teams at any college or university must be very sensitive to the rights and privacy of candidates' personal information. All communications to candidates must be professional and without future legal implications (Lindbeck & Fodrey, 2010).

Graduate recruitment must present a successful face. If it does not, the candidate population could decrease over time, and human and nonhuman resources could drop to a level at which the college or university will find it difficult to keep its doors open. Historically, the enrollment management team at colleges and universities has had to project an aura of success to national and international communities in order to be a strong competitor in the recruitment marketplace (Johnson, 2000). Recruiting candidates must be recognized as a major goal of the college or university's strategic plan. There is a need to have an adequate number of candidates enrolled at universities and colleges in order to maintain their ability to serve the public academically, socially, and culturally. Therefore, recruiting teams and the office of enrollment management must speak the same language in acquiring the number of candidates needed for the success of the college or university (Tucciarone, 2009).

## Program Expectations Should be Clearly Articulated to Candidates

Doctoral candidates recruited for the Ed.D. program should be aware of the importance of effective teaching, learning, leading, and field-based research with schools or district settings that support the schools. Emphasis should be placed on the importance of reflective practices in leadership behavior. During the recruitment effort, doctoral candidates should be given an overall view of program foci, standards, and expectations in coursework and clinical field experiences.

Doctoral candidates should be made aware of how most doctoral programs use a cohort group model in which candidates take courses together and work on project-based research activities. Candidates should be informed, too, about the benefits of the cohort model, which provides the opportunity for active, interactive, and engaging activities as a group. The cohort model can connect, in a meaningful way, a community of learners working together toward a common purpose (Maher, 2004). As adult learners, the doctoral candidates will be able to show their coursework initiative by creating educational study teams that can build the learning capacity to support learning communities and partnerships with local school districts in order to sustain realistic reform for school improvement (Irby & Miller, 1999). Recruited candidates will learn early on from the recruitment team that they will be connected with others in a learning community concept from Day One. This will add to the value of their experiences and should both motivate and bring comfort to them (Zhao & Kuh, 2014).

## Recruiters Must be Creative

Recruitment teams and the office of enrollment management must be collaborative and seek creative ways to recruit, retain, and graduate candidates in the doctorate of education degree program. It is important for recruitment teams and the office of enrollment management to realize that recruitment and retention go hand in hand (Johnson, 2000). If candidates have had positive experiences during their recruitment, retention, and graduation, this could carry over to the marketing success of the recruitment team and the office of enrollment management in their subsequent recruitment efforts. As the recruited candidates use media to share with friends their positive experiences at the university or college, so can the recruitment team use the highlighted information regarding outstanding features of the university and college programs to urge new candidates to enroll at that particular institution. Again, word of mouth and the use of social media technology can be powerful recruiting tools for those who have experienced success at the university or college (Astone & Nunez-Wormack, 1991).

## Benefits of Using Digital Marketing Tools

In order for university recruitment teams to stay current and take advantage of the many benefits of using digital marketing tools for recruitment, team members should encourage candidates to apply to the university or college directly through Facebook. The recruitment teams can analyze metrics to review how the Facebook pages are being used. They can identify how to benchmark candidates from other universities and balance the number of postings by faculty on the university or college's Facebook page, as well as the number of postings by other participants in this social media connection (Thostenson, 2011). The recruitment team should provide the webpages with eye-catching graphics aimed at those requiring financial assistance, as well as special interest groups or underrepresented candidates.

During the recruitment session, candidates should be informed about the university or college's on- and off-campus support services. They should also receive current information about admission, curriculum, and tuition fees. For the convenience of their schedules, candidates need to know about courses that are offered in a blended learning or online format, on weekends, and in summer sessions (Ntiri, 2001). Recruiting team members should telephone potential candidates or use other media to stay in touch and continue to build positive relationships with them. Smart recruiters will maintain contact with school districts, principals, and others, because at some future time, potential candidates from those districts may wish to enroll in the doctorate of education degree program (Tapscott, 2000).

## Recruitment Must be Strategic, and There Must Be a Plan

The recruiting of candidates for the Ed.D. program is a collaborative effort on the part of the recruitment team and the office of enrollment management. Recruitment by Colleges of Education or Schools of Education in the United States, for example, must work together to assess the strengths, weaknesses, opportunities, or threats to the recruitment of the university or college recruitment agenda. Developing a strategic plan provides the recruitment team with structure, goals, and direction during the recruitment process.

In order to improve the recruitment operation, there is a need to seek feedback from individuals in the Ed.D. program that will be passed on to potential students. Candidates could be asked about their level of satisfaction during the recruitment experience or admissions policy, procedures, and process. Feedback would help the recruitment team members to improve their own recruitment practices (Kaufman, Watters, & Herman, 2002).

At U.S. educational institutions, the doctorate of education degree program is generally located in the College of Education or the School of Education. The recruitment team and the office of enrollment management play a key role in persuading candidates to enroll at the university or college. Therefore, it is essential that the recruitment team and the office of enrollment management design and implement a purposeful strategic plan to attract and maintain groups of candidates that are underrepresented in doctoral programs. Methods used for recruitment today usually include Internet bulletins and media, national newspapers, research conferences, direct mail, open house sessions, television, educational partnership organizations, e-recruiting, and alumni support groups (Tapscott, 2000). Being strategic is essential to the recruitment effort. Before going out to recruit potential candidates, the recruitment teams and the office of enrollment management need a recruitment strategic plan. At this point, the recruitment team must be strategic thinkers.

Some considerations for recruitment teams may be modelled in different formats; however, the teams should take some matters into consideration before beginning the recruitment process. For example: (1) Where are we now as a committee or team with the recruitment effort? (2) What is the vision and mission of the School of Education or College of Education regarding recruitment? (3) What are the major obstacles, if any, to the recruitment effort? (4) What resources do we have at hand to do the job of recruitment? (5) What will be the key strategies to proceed in the direction in which we need to go? (6) What is a realistic timetable and method of accountability for the recruitment efforts? (7) How will recruitment be monitored and measured? (8) Who will be specifically responsible for all action tasks within the plan? (9) How will the success of the recruitment effort be measured? (Hayes, Ruschman, & Walker, 2009).

There are many definitions of a strategic plan. The most common one focuses on the process for establishing priorities in terms of what the college and/or university plans to accomplish in the future, as well as what it will do and what it will not do. The strategic plan pulls the entire college together around a single game plan for support in the recruitment effort. The plan must be based on the needs of the college or university regarding leadership engagement, diversity, international connection, and resources, and the strategic plan for candidate recruitment must be communicated effectively to the entire campus community.

## Marketing Best Practices in Recruitment

After the recruiters have made initial contact with potential students, it is essential to get back in touch with those candidates as soon as possible. The recruitment manager should make sure that all team members are on the same page (Mahan, 2012) and that they explain how the enrolees in the doctoral program are drawn from a diverse group; share information about the success rates of graduates; send emails to potential candidates; keep the college or university's website updated, and show photos, with permission, of faculty members and candidates' activities in the program; cite current research publications and awards received by faculty and candidates in the School of Education or College of Education; make every effort to provide information to potential candidates in an easy, accessible manner; use mass-marketing strategies to attract additional candidates to the program (Powers, 1990); and make the websites and contact numbers easy to access in order to answer questions that potential candidates may have. To attract international students, they must enlist the efforts of current students who are visiting their home countries or who could help market the program locally or regionally; use the Internet to advertise the doctorate of education program in the international educational marketplace; and use the ideas of graduate students or alumni to telephone or email their friends and coworkers. Finally, the recruitment manager will do well to assign recruiters with the skills, knowledge, and professional demeanor to represent the university in ways that will make the best impression on the public; and keep data on the pros and cons, outcomes, and results of the recruitment efforts made by all members of the recruiting team within the national and international community (National Association of Graduate Admissions Professionals, 2001).

## International Communities and Recruitment

A number of countries show no evidence of a well-organized office, team, or committee for recruiting graduate candidates for the doctorate of education degree program. For example, in Canada, most universities do not have an office or position dedicated to recruiting new candidates for various programs. For the past few years, Canada has utilized the Internet to create new opportunities to recruit candidates for graduate programs. However, the pace of recruitment has been relatively slow because the discipline-specific nature of graduate education programs at many of the universities is the same (Malaney, 1987).

## The Important Role of Faculty Members in Recruiting and the Use of Technology

Since faculty members will deliver instructional services to recruited candidates, they could help with the recruitment effort. Faculty members would have the unique ability to contact potential candidates and build positive relationships with those candidates. However, research shows that some faculty members feel that they already have too much to do, and recruitment should therefore be left to others. Paul Bryant has claimed that some faculty members believe that recruitment is beneath their dignity (Bryant, 1987). Nevertheless, Bryant contends that faculty should be encouraged to establish and maintain relationships with faculty from other schools, departments, and professions in order to help with the recruitment efforts at the university.

If they do become involved with recruitment, faculty members should be highly competent and have basic and specific knowledge regarding the entire recruitment process as well as the specifics of a college's programs. In addition to the use of brochures, letters, advertisements, phone calls, and conference displays, recruiters should take time to use a variety of digital media technology to market and manage their recruitment efforts during the recruitment process (National Association of Graduate Admissions Professionals, 2001).

Not surprisingly, the primary means of promoting graduate programs online is the institution's website. Typically, this consists of entire websites—or large sections of websites—devoted to providing information to prospective candidates. Information commonly found on such websites includes academic programs (including admission requirements, program requirements, duration of study, etc.), tuition, scholarships/funding, student services, location and facilities, and research/career opportunities. In assessing the information that prospective candidates seek from graduate school websites, Poock (2005) found that admissions information, faculty research interests, financial aid, program information, and department contacts are most important.

## International Communities' Doctoral Recruitment Practices

The Ed.D. program is valuable to the extent that candidates gain new and improved skills and knowledge about effective leadership and practices through research and theorizing policy. The doctoral degree is considered an academic or professional degree. Internationally, the doctorate of education degree qualifies candidates to teach at the university level and to serve in district leadership positions in school systems. In the international community, the degree is often called a terminal degree or the highest academic degree in a given field of study.

Many European countries will recruit diverse groups of candidates to their universities. For example, France recruits candidates from Morocco, Algeria, China, Tunisia, Senegal, Germany, Cameroon, Lebanon, Italy, and Vietnam. France stresses that its graduate programs are cofunded by the Ministry of Foreign European Affairs and the French regional authorities, which finance exchange for research training and research of new curriculum, project-based researchers, and connections with Russia, Brazil, China, India, South Africa, East Europe, as well as with ten French regions. Sweden recruits candidates, for the most part, from within. The United Kingdom recruits candidates from the Middle East, Libya,

Egypt, Saudi Arabia, India, and Pakistan by emphasizing the attractive features of its programs, features such as language, reputation, and opportunities for quality research partnerships, as well as high completion rates and long-term career opportunities. Germany recruits candidates from Eastern Europe, China, Vietnam, Indonesia, Malaysia, Chile, Brazil, and Egypt. Germany emphasizes its funding sources for scholarships and work positions, English instruction, dissertation examination, and the use of applied research projects made possible by contracts with industry. These countries are marketing their graduate programs by emphasizing expected outcomes for candidates. The methods used by the management recruitment teams include research networks, websites, social media, scientific journals, and symposiums. A strong emphasis is placed on funding being available for graduate programs. Particularly in Germany, enrollment in graduate programs continues to increase because low tuition fees (or even free tuition), as well as post-study work opportunities for foreign candidates, can make Germany an ideal location for study. In order to study in Germany, however, all candidates must secure a blue card that is equivalent to the green card in the United States. Germany is expected to continue to expand its recruitment enrollment by 2020 by focusing on learning and research and providing scholarship funding for the best German and international candidates. German universities intend to raise their profile internationally and to expand their network of branch offices and information centers around the world. Germany plans to continue to educate staff to increase their knowledge of foreign cultures and educational systems to help build international partnerships that could boost their recruitment efforts.

## Recruiting Potential Candidates

When the recruitment committees and enrollment management teams seek potential candidates, it is essential that the teams encourage candidates to apply to the graduate program for the doctorate of education degree as soon as possible. It is important to try to find a way to justify reduced or no fees if the candidate applies for graduate admission before a certain date or in the case of financial need. Networking is important when seeking candidates for enrollment, because candidates may be inclined to enroll in the program if team members develop a positive relationship with them. Staying in touch is essential when developing the networking relationship. Using Facebook, email, telephone contact, and—if it is affordable—inviting potential candidates to an inexpensive lunch or early dinner may boost the recruitment effort. Social media are also an important means of recruiting candidates to the doctoral program. When candidates make inquiries, recruiters should be sure to follow up and return information promptly. Recruiters should behave in a manner that makes candidates feel that they value them and want them to attend the university or college. It is important to make a favorable impression during the recruitment effort. Recruiters should continue to connect with potential candidates; however, recruiters should not overwhelm potential candidates with their communication behavior (Williams, 1980).

The strategic use of regional and national databases to make contact with candidates who may be underrepresented in the Ed.D. program should be a common practice for recruiters. They should visit scholarly program activities at the graduate level within and outside the university and try to recruit candidates to the Ed.D. program. It is also important to attend events at various universities, talk with graduates about the doctoral program, speak to and collect the names of individuals, leave business cards, and quickly contact potential candidates as a follow-up (Fern, 2014).

## Comparing National and International Focus on Recruitment

Graduate schools in both Canada and the United States may wish to adopt a leadership role in planning, guiding, motivating, and assessing graduate recruitment activities on behalf of their institutions. However, professional staff must be trained to understand trends and changes in student recruitment efforts, adapt to change in order to survive, and take advantage of technological opportunities in a timely fashion. Linkages to faculty and alumni must continue to play an important role in candidate recruitment. Canadian institutions suggest that there must be more collaboration in their graduate student recruitment practices, both with one another and with national and international organizations that have an interest in graduate education (National Association of International Educators, 2011). In addition, graduate schools and departments must strive to be adventurous and entrepreneurial in taking advantage of sometimes-brief windows of opportunity, even when the exact direction they should take seems unclear.

Universities and colleges today must see social media as another tool that can be used during and after the recruitment process. Therefore, recruiters use social media as much as possible to recruit candidates to the Ed.D. program beyond borders (Mayers, 2013). The recruitment marketplace today is very competitive, and recruiters need to be creative and quick in order to secure desirable candidates from national and international communities for their colleges or universities. Using social media can help to facilitate the recruitment efforts to a broader audience globally (Hayes et al., 2009).

In Canadian universities, admission to a doctoral program requires a master's degree in a related field, sufficiently high grades, recommendations, writing samples, a research proposal, and, typically, an interview with a prospective supervisor. Requirements for a doctoral degree are often more stringent than those for a master's program. In Canadian universities, only in exceptional cases can a student holding an honors B.A. with sufficiently high grades and proven writing and research skills be admitted directly to a doctoral program without first completing a master's degree. Many Canadian graduate programs allow students who start in a master's degree program to "reclassify" into the doctoral program after satisfactory performance in the first year, thus bypassing the master's degree (Canadian Association for Graduate Studies, 2011).

Advanced-degree candidates must usually declare their research goal or submit a research proposal upon entering graduate school in Canada. In the case of master's degrees, there is some flexibility (that is, one is not held to one's research proposal, although major changes—for example, from premodern to modern history—are discouraged). In the case of the doctoral degree, the research direction is usually known, as it will typically follow the direction of the master's degree research study area at an advanced level (Canadian Association for Graduate Studies, 2011).

Some schools require samples of the student's writing as well as a research proposal. At English-speaking universities in Canada, applicants from countries where English is not the primary language are required to submit scores from the Test of English as a Foreign Language (TOEFL). Nevertheless, some French-speaking universities, such as HEC Montreal, also require candidates to submit TOEFL scores or to pass the university's own English test. Some financial aid comes from various public and private sources in the form of scholarships for candidates. However, in many universities, the tuition fees may be waived for doctoral candidates (Canadian Association for Graduate Studies, 2011).

At the Laurentian University in Sudbury, Ontario, the typical admission requirements include an online application, official transcript from the candidate's postsecondary institution, a curriculum vitae, a completed form detailing the candidate's achievements and projects, three reference letters, a letter of intent from a member of the program of study, a commitment by a faculty member who is willing to supervise the candidate during the research experience, and proof of language proficiency for non-Canadian applicants whose language skills are in neither English nor French. Photocopies of faxed documents are not accepted by the university.

The Office of Admissions at the university should receive the online application, which must be duly verified. Once that process is complete, the documents are forwarded to the program director and the selection committee. The program director has the responsibility of discussing the candidate's project to create clarity of intent on the part of the candidate regarding his or her area of interest. The deadline for submission of completed applications is March 31 for September admission. A final decision on admission is made by the Admissions Committee. If the potential candidate is not admitted in the year applied, the candidate may reapply the following year (Laurentian University, Sudbury, Ontario, Canada, 2013).

## ED.D. ADMISSION POLICY AND PRACTICE

The complex process of candidate admissions operates within frameworks that distinguish first and foremost between domestic and international students. This section explores these differences within United States universities and contrasts American practices with those in a sample of European universities.

### Admission to Typical United States Universities

Most Ed.D. program recruiters seek candidates who have completed at least a master's degree related to educational leadership, policy studies, instruction, and other related disciplines. Candidates accepted into the doctoral program are expected to have demonstrated service in a relevant leadership position and are committed to enhancing their ability to learn and lead the educational mission of a school district. Most candidates admitted to the doctorate of education program are admitted as a cohort in the United States (National Association of Graduate Admissions Professionals, 2001).

Some admissions have eight to fifteen candidates, depending on the size of the teaching faculty. In order to be admitted to the Ed.D. program at Western Kentucky University, for example, the candidate must be able to produce official documents such as:

- transcripts of all undergraduate and graduate coursework from all universities;
- documentation of all master's degrees (or other graduate degrees) from an institution accredited by a nationally recognized accreditation organization;
- a completed application;
- a current resume;
- a carefully prepared personal statement outlining qualifications, rationale, goals and research area of interest in the Ed.D. program;
- three current letters of recommendation from persons in a position to evaluate the applicant's potential for success in a doctoral program academically, socially, and culturally;
- a copy of official GRE scores that meet the minimum GRE and GAP scores for doctoral degrees as described in the Western Kentucky University Graduate Catalogue; and
- a writing sample, if applicants took the GRE without the Analytic Writing portion or if the Analytic Writing score falls below the stated minimum. If analytical writing is not available, the applicant or candidate must take the writing sample on site during the interview process. The WKU Graduate School has established minimum GRE scores for WKU doctoral programs. For the

new GRE, these are 145 on the verbal, 145 on the quantitative, and a writing score of 4.0. Required scores are specific.

## International Candidate Admission Policy in the United States

International candidates are encouraged to apply early because of the time involved in securing and submitting required documents for the Ed.D. program. Including the regular submission of documents, the following *additional* documents for admission consideration must be presented by international candidates: in-person, verbal evidence and/or documentation of ability to communicate in English (including a minimum score on the paper-based TOEFL, a minimum score on the iBT TOEFL, a minimum score on the IELTS, or a degree from an institution with English as the language of instruction).

Evidence of adequate financial resources to complete the doctorate of education degree at the university is also required. In order to boost enrollment, some universities have chosen to admit candidates twice a year. All candidates must note that for the fall cohort admission at Western Kentucky University, the application deadline is April 1; for spring cohort admission, the application deadline is October 1. However, some universities in the United States have only one admission date, which occurs in the fall of the year.

If a candidate qualifies for a graduate assistantship, that information should be made known to the candidate as soon as possible. Although the Educational Leadership Doctoral Program at WKU is designed for working professionals, there are a limited number of competitive GA scholarships for students seeking full-time study. The university seeks persons who have strong research and/or P–12 backgrounds for the GA scholarship. While some universities have only one admission date (generally in the fall of the year), in order to boost their enrollment, other universities have chosen to admit candidates twice a year from the international community (Western Kentucky University, 2014).

## Tuition

Tuition for the WKU doctoral program is based on other campus graduate tuition rates. In addition, there is a course fee per credit hour for candidates in the program. The typical course fee is competitive with that of other universities in the United States. The doctoral program fee is consistent for each class (cohort) admitted.

At most universities in the United States, candidates for the Ed.D. degree are given financial support that may include fellowships, scholarships, student loans, tuition waivers for credits obtained by P–12 teachers, and monetary compensation to others who provided candidates opportunities to gain internship experiences.

Further waivers may be granted to state employees, employer district matching contracts or professional development funds, contracted organizational incentive discounts, candidates' personal funds, and research grant participation. Most colleges and universities in the United States operate on a similar basis regarding tuition and admission policy matters; therefore, Western Kentucky University was chosen at random for the next part of this chapter.

## Leadership in Urban Schools Ed.D.

The WKU doctorate of education program develops leadership and research skills for teachers, administrators, and others committed to transforming urban and non-urban school districts. Key practices that are central to the effectiveness of new leadership techniques and abilities—such as working in teams in a collaborative manner and identifying and prioritizing problems—are key components of various courses. Candidates working in a collaborative manner are involved in developing solutions for multifaceted environments.

In candidates' coursework, balancing stability and change and using appropriate theoretical frameworks and research methodologies are the major tasks confronted. Coursework and research in the doctoral program focuses on schools as organizations rooted in political, historical, economic, and cultural contexts. In order to accommodate candidates, courses are offered in the evenings, on weekends, online, in a blended learning format, and during the summer. Most candidates seeking the doctoral degree are working adults. Therefore, programs are designed for mid-career professionals who wish to continue working while they pursue a doctoral degree (Western Kentucky University, 2014).

## Admission to International Universities in Europe

Admission practices may differ at various universities in Europe. Candidates need to visit particular universities' websites and then make contact with the coordinator of the program and express interest in a specific level of study. The potential candidate should also make sure that the master's degree is adequate for admission to terminal degree programs. The potential candidate needs to provide proper documents where needed with the Apostle of The Hague Accords or through diplomatic channels. In some European colleges or universities (Oxford University, for example), each candidate must participate in a criminal background check as part of the necessary documentation for admission under the Rehabilitation of Offenders Act of 1974.

The candidate needs to remember that it normally takes several weeks for all documents to be reviewed carefully and processed for authenticity. The specific documents that are needed in, for example, Spanish universities include copy of passport, completed application form, university degree properly verified or translated into Spanish, academic transcript of university degree hours per courses taken, proof of master's degree from the issuing state (unless there is an agreement with the country—for example, China). All documents being sent to Spanish universities should be original; if they are copied, they must have the university's stamp affixed. At the Universidad de Murcia in Spain, once the documents are validated with the university's official stamp, the candidate may forward them to the Postgraduate Office at the Universidad de Murcia or to the Spanish Embassy or Consulate in the potential candidate's country. Candidates may be offered a scholarship by the National Ministry of Education, which also offers scholarships in specific doctoral programs.

## SUMMARY AND CONCLUSIONS

Digital marketing tools can be effectively used to support the traditional techniques for recruitment at a much more rapid pace today. Social media are crucial to educational institutions, since many potential candidates may be spending most of their time in that environment. Social media are globally engaging, and potential candidates from around the world are using this convenient tool to learn about university and college program offerings. Therefore, recruitment teams should take full advantage of available social media tools (Reuben, 2008).

The future is unknown regarding new and better ways to recruit graduate doctoral candidates, but all recruiters for doctorate of education programs must stay current with the latest technology and continue to build relationships with broader communities for candidate recruitment. Effective recruitment practices can be used in a transferability manner in different graduate colleges or university programs. Recruiters should continue to look at how well some colleges or universities' recruiters are succeeding in their recruitment and admission efforts (Sevier, 2000). Recruiters must stay abreast of information for effective recruitment initiatives and admission practices and shape their efforts to virtual communities nationally and internationally in order to continue to reach their recruitment goals for colleges or universities (Frolich & Stensaker, 2010).

## REFERENCES

Aslanian, C., & Giles, N.G. (2009, August). *Hindsight, insight, foresight: Understanding adult learning trends to predict future opportunities.* Retrieved from http://www.educationdynamics.com/CMSPages/GetFile.aspx?guid=119845f5-ed25-4597-a32e-9761e930d300

Astone, B., & Nunez-Wormack, E. (1991). *Pursuing diversity: Recruiting college minority students.* Association for the Study of Higher Education. Retrieved from ERIC database. (ED333856).

Brungardt, C.L., Gould, L.V., Moore, R., & Potts, J. (1997). The emergence of leadership studies: Linking the traditional outcomes of liberal education with leadership development. *Journal of Leadership Studies, 4*(3), 53–67.

Bryant, P. (1987, December). *Graduate recruiting: New wine in old bottles.* Paper presented at the Annual Meeting of the Council of Graduate Schools, Washington, DC.

Canadian Association for Graduate Studies. (2011). Council on Graduate School, 2012. Retrieved from http://cags.ca/publications.php

Fern, J. (2014). *The evolution from old-school to digital recruiter.* Retrieved from http://www.seventhpoint.com/evolution-old-school-counselor-digital-saavy-recruiter/

Frolich, N., & Stensaker, B. (2010). Student recruitment strategies in higher education: Promoting excellence and diversity? *International Journal of Educational Management, 24*(4), 359–370. doi: 10.1108/09513541011045281

Gifford, J. (2010). Digital public relations: E-marketing's big secret. *Continuing Higher Education Review, 74,* 62–72.

Hayes, T., Ruschman, D., & Walker, M. (2009). Social networking as an admission tool: A case study in success. *Journal of Marketing for Higher Education, 19*(2), 109–124.

Irby, B., & Miller, W. (1999). An inquiry into the exigency of a beginning doctoral cohort in educational leadership. *College Student Journal, 33*(3), 358–363.

Johnson, A.L. (2000). The evolution of enrollment management: A historical perspective. *Journal of College Admission, 166,* 4–11.

Kaufman, R., Watters, K., & Herman, J. (2002). Educational planning: Strategic, tactical, and operational visions, strategic planning and quality—more than hype. *Educational Technology, 36*(5), 60–62.

Lindbeck, R., & Fodrey, B. (2010). Using technology in undergraduate admission: A student perspective. *Journal of College Admission, 208,* 10–17.

Mahan, S. (2012, August 6). What's working in graduate student recruitment and marketing? Web log post. Retrieved from http://blog.noellevitz.com/2012/08/06/working-graduate-student-recruitment-marketing/

Maher, M.A. (2004, July/August). What really happens in cohorts? *About Campus, 9*(3), 18–23.

Malaney, G.D. (1987). Efforts to recruit graduate students: An analysis of departmental recruiting practices. *College and University, 62*(2), 126–136.

Mayers, L.C. (2013, February 28). Beyond our borders international student recruiting: College fairs [Web log post]. Retrieved from http://services.intead.com/blog/bid/261656/Beyond-Our-Borders-International-Student-Recruiting-College-Fairs

National Association of Graduate Admissions Professionals (NAGAP). (2001). *The admissions process: What works, what doesn't?* Retrieved from www.nagap.org/downloads/Adm_Survey.pdf

National Association of International Educators (NAFSA). (2011, May 17). *Using social media for international recruitment: A live collegial conversation.* Retrieved from http://www.nafsa.org/resourcelibrary/default.aspx?id=26853

Ntiri, D.W. (2001). Access to higher education for non-traditional students and minorities in a technology focused society. *Urban Education, 36,* 129–144.

Poock, M. (2005). Determining the design of effective graduate school web sites. *College and University, 80*(3), 23–26.

Powers, M. (1990). Marketing and recruitment for graduate programs. *Council of Graduate Schools Communicator, 24*(3/4), 1, 5, 9–11.

Reuben, R. (2008). *The use of social media in higher education for marketing and communication: A guide for professionals in higher education.* Retrieved from http://doteduguru.com/id423-social-media-uses-higher-education-marketing-communication.html

Sevier, R.A. (2000). Building an effective recruiting funnel. *Journal of College Admission, 169*, 10–19.

Shulman, L.S., Golde, C.M., Conklin Bueschel, A., & Garabedian, K.J. (2006). Reclaiming education's doctorates: A critique and a proposal. *Educational Researcher, 35*(3), 26. doi: 10.3102/0013189x035003025

Tapscott, D. (2000). *Growing up digital: The rise of the net generation.* New York: McGraw-Hill.

Thostenson, A. (2011, May 17). Re: Using social media for international recruitment: A live collegial conversation. [Online forum comment]. Retrieved from http://www.nafsa.org/resourcelibrary/default.aspx?id=26853

Tucciarone, K.M. (2009). Speaking the same language. *College and University, 84*(4), 22–31.

Williams, J.K. (1993). *A study of promotional strategies and the perceived contributions to traditional recruitment in higher education.* Unpublished doctoral dissertation, Oklahoma State University, Stillwater.

Williams, W.G. (1980). *Enrollment strategy.* Charlottesville, VA: Share.

Zhao, C.M., & Kuh, G.D. (2014). Adding value: learning communities and student engagement. *Research in Higher Education, 45*(2), 115–138.

# CHAPTER TWO

# Online Ed.D. Program Delivery as a Medium for Enhanced Civic Engagement

*Lara Willox*

## INTRODUCTION

This chapter will explore how one education doctorate (Ed.D.) program's transition to an online delivery model encouraged enhanced civic engagement by promoting a strong social presence, diversifying the student pool, and providing structured support to increase completion rates. The Ed.D. in School Improvement was a face-to-face program for 11 years prior to transitioning to an online delivery model 4 years ago. The original intent of the transition was merely to attract more students and ensure viability moving forward. The unintended consequences led to a major transformation, affecting every aspect of the program and ultimately leading students toward greater civic engagement.

The methodology employed is a formative evaluation focused on the online delivery model both at the level of implementation and as a curricular process. The exploration is structured by the community of inquiry model (Garrison, Anderson, & Archer, 2010) and principles identified by the Carnegie Project on the Education Doctorate (CPED) (Perry, 2012). The community of inquiry model explores three dimensions of learning in an online platform: teaching presence, social presence, and cognitive presence. The interaction of these three elements is considered essential to an educational transaction (Archer, 2010). The CPED consortium identified principles applicable to the Ed.D. program, as well as some key design elements. These principles frame program development for the education doctorate (Carnegie Project on the Education Doctorate, 2009).

The findings offer a different perspective of the online delivery model, one that moves away from a focus on flexibility or credibility (Ghezzi, 2007) toward broadening conceptions of possibilities of greater civic engagement and participation.

## CONTEXT

The education doctorate (Ed.D.) can be traced back to the Harvard Graduate School of Education, which was established nearly 100 years ago. The degree was aimed at students who had teaching experience and sought a higher position within their school system (Cremin, 1978). The goal was to provide rigorous coursework to enhance students' knowledge and skills and to better prepare them to lead as school practitioners (Cremin, 1978). Beyond the school-related goals, there was also a strong interest in separating education from the arts and sciences (Powell, 1980). While the degree claimed to focus more on the practitioner than the scholar, few curricular differences were found between the Ed.D. and a Ph.D. from Teachers College (Powell, 1980). Since the inception of the education doctorate, the differences between an Ed.D. and a Ph.D. were never quite clear, and the issue became further complicated when Teachers College began to offer both an Ed.D. and a Ph.D. (Cremin, 1978). For 80 years after the creation of the Ed.D. program, studies were done exploring the outcomes of both the Ed.D. and the Ph.D., but few explored the ways in which one might distinguish between the two degrees (Perry, 2012).

It was not until 2007 that a consortium of 25 schools of education came together to consider the Doctor of Education degree from the viewpoint of the graduate. The committee asked one question: "What knowledge, skills, and dispositions should professionals working in education possess and be able to use?" (Perry, 2012, p. 42). This group worked—and continues to work—to differentiate the outcomes and purposes of the Ed.D. program and the Ph.D. and to strengthen the Ed.D. through established principles and design concepts. The consortium has defined the Ed.D. as "the professional doctorate in education [that] prepares educators for the application of appropriate and specific practices, the generation of new knowledge, and for the stewardship of the profession" (Perry, 2012, p. 43).

## THE ED.D. IN SCHOOL IMPROVEMENT

The Ed.D. in School Improvement was first proposed in the spring of 1999 at what was then called the State University of West Georgia. It marked the culmination of 3 years of work by the faculty of the College of Education, Committee on Graduate Studies, and Faculty Senate, which forwarded the first proposal for the Ed.D. in School Improvement to the University System Office in June 1997. After external review and several revisions, the final copy of the proposal was completed in the fall of 1999. As stated in the executive summary of the proposal, the Ed.D. in School Improvement was focused on preparing instructional leaders to initiate change and model effective teaching and learning. The program of study consisted of teaching and learning for a diverse student population, effective use of research data and student assessments, development of leadership abilities, and incorporation of effective instructional technologies.

Table 2.1. Comparison of Traditional Doctoral Programs with Proposed Program. (Sethna, 1999, p. 28).

| Traditional Ed.D. Program, such as in Curriculum and Instruction or Educational Leadership | Distinguishing Features and Uniqueness of the Ed.D. Program in School Improvement |
|---|---|
| Candidates could have any background. | Candidates will be school personnel. |
| Minimal grade point average and Graduate Record Examination scores are required. | The admission criteria will be flexible and broad to ensure a diverse and experienced pool of candidates. |
| Candidates usually complete the program during full-time on-campus residency. | Candidates on a part-time basis and as a cohort will complete the program in the evenings, on weekends, and during the summer. |
| The program is delivered on campus using traditional methodologies. | This program will be delivered using a variety of instructional methodologies including video-conferencing and on-line (Web-based) instruction. Technology will be a major strand throughout program. |
| Faculty from the College of Education deliver the program. | Faculty from the Colleges of Education, Arts and Sciences, and Business as well as from schools will deliver the program. |
| Successful completion of courses will be used to determine progress in program. | Throughout the programs, candidates will develop their portfolios, which will be assessed in comparison with expected learning outcomes at several intervals as a measure of learning. A variety of assessment will be used. |
| A traditional dissertation is required. | A school-based research project must be designed, implemented, and evaluated as the dissertation project. |
| Candidates can complete the program without involvement in schools. | Throughout the program, candidates will work in and with schools to effect instructional changes to improve student learning. |
| Graduates will be indistinguishable from graduates of other traditional programs. | These educators will return to their schools prepared to lead initiatives in instructional improvement for enhanced student learning. |

The doctoral program was unique in that its focus was on school improvement, which is not a traditional education-focused degree program, and at the time was the only one in the nation. More often, doctorates in educational leadership, instructional technology, curriculum and instruction, or content-specific areas such as reading, elementary education, or educational psychology are offered. Table 2.1 was included in the original proposal to further distinguish this degree from traditional Ed.D. programs.

Ten students were admitted to the inaugural cohort in the fall of 2000. The first eleven cohorts of the program participated in a traditional face-to-face doctoral program—participating in weekly classes, completing coursework, and creating a culminating portfolio all before beginning work on the dissertation. Nine members of the original cohort graduated. Over the next decade, the cohorts ranged in size from 6 to 20 students. Most students graduated within 6 years of beginning the program.

In 2009, an independent consultant was hired to do a program review of the Ed.D. in School Improvement in order to share ways to revise and improve the program with the university's stakeholders, the dean of the College of Education, the incoming program director, and the program's advisory committee (Jarosewich, 2009). The review indicated that the interdisciplinary nature of the degree was still unusual, with only three universities identified nationally as having a similar focus. At the time of the report, 133 students had been accepted into the 10 cohorts; 30 students had already graduated, while 87 were active and 16 were inactive or on leave.

In late 2009, a new program director was hired to revise the program and address some of the needs highlighted in the report. The program was struggling both internally (faculty support) and externally (community awareness). The cohorts were not filling up, and the quality of the candidates was substandard. During the review, an instructional technology faculty member suggested that the program move online. Planning began in the spring of 2010 to redesign the program into a 3-year online doctoral program, and an advisory committee was assembled and charged with this goal.

During the 2010–2011 academic year, subcommittees were formed to consider course migration, dissertation mentoring, program logistics, curriculum planning, marketing, and program assessment. The new program maintained the school improvement focus but provided dissertation mentoring and support during the program, affording students the opportunity to finish both coursework and the dissertation in 3 years. The new program was set to launch in the summer of 2011. Cohort 12 would be an entirely online cohort following the revised 3-year course of study. The program received over 125 applications for the cohort, compared to the 12 to 15 received in the past, and 29 students were accepted. There was a great deal of skepticism on the part of both faculty members and the administration. They were concerned about creating a community, providing quality teaching and learning, and maintaining program expectations with an entirely online program.

During the first 3 years of implementation, data were collected to explore the delivery of the program and the quality of its implementation. This formative evaluation method remains a process for ensuring continued improvement.

## METHODOLOGY

Formative evaluation is commonly completed during the development or implementation of a program or product (Muraskin, 1993). The evaluation is often conducted more than once and provides ongoing information that leads to program changes. The goal of any formative evaluation is to strengthen or improve the program being evaluated (George, 1999). The focus of this study was both the program delivery (online) and implementation (curriculum/activities). One question guides this ongoing inquiry: How well is the program being delivered and implemented?

### Framework Exemplars

In order to address this question, it was important first to identify exemplars to compare and analyze the program against. Several frameworks were considered, but since the focus was on the entire program, it was determined that the community of inquiry model and principles outlined by the Carnegie Project on the Education Doctorate were the best for this purpose.

**Community of inquiry** online (COI) program delivery is a relatively new platform, and in recent years, several ways to evaluate quality have emerged. There are sets of best practices for specific course delivery outlined by the International Association for K–12 Online Learning (iNACOL) (2011) or Quality Matters (Frey & King, 2011), but it was determined that a more global exploration would allow for the entire program to be explored as a whole instead of the sum of individual parts. For the purposes of this formative evaluation, it was determined that the use of the community of inquiry (COI) model would allow for a more holistic approach to the formative evaluation. The COI framework (Figure 2.1) is grounded in the higher education literature and was developed for analysing online discourse in computer conferencing (Garrison & Arbaugh, 2007).

The COI framework is comprised of three core elements: social presence, cognitive presence, and teaching presence. *Social presence* refers to the online social interactions that include affective expression, interactivity, and group cohesion. *Cognitive presence* is a "cycle of practical inquiry" through which learners construct meaning through a process of self-reflection and shared discourse over time. *Teaching presence* refers to course design, content expertise, and scaffolding of learners through the "direction of cognitive and social processes" (Anderson,

Rourke, Garrison, & Archer, 2001, p. 5). The interaction of these core elements contributes to the total education experience in both face-to-face and online environments (Akyol et al., 2009; Garrison, Anderson, & Archer, 2000; Shea et al., 2010). Research indicates that the multiple roles, behaviors, and activities associated with teaching presence in online learning environments affect students' perceptions and learning outcomes (Morgan, 2011).

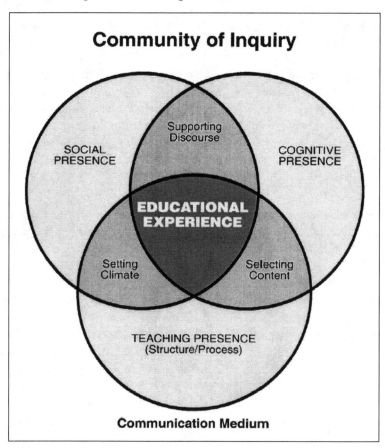

Figure 2.1. Community of inquiry framework.

The strength of the COI framework is its focus on interaction and process of teaching and learning in online learning, reflected in the overlap of the three main elements—teaching presence, social presence, and cognitive presence. The constructs of teaching presence, social presence, and cognitive presence are the three elements of the Community of Inquiry framework (Garrison et al., 2010), a useful explanatory model for understanding the educational experience in the online paradigm (Akyol & Garrison, 2011; Shea et al., 2010).

## CARNEGIE PROJECT ON THE EDUCATION DOCTORATE

In order to explore the actual implementation of the curriculum, the principles outlined by the Carnegie Project on the Education Doctorate (CPED) were used to benchmark program implementation. Created in 2007, the consortium sought to better distinguish the education doctorate by focusing on the outcomes while paying specific attention to graduates. Over 80 colleges and schools of education have used shared resources to critically examine the Ed.D. (Carnegie Project on the Education Doctorate, 2009). After ongoing dialog, experimentation, critical feedback, and evaluation, the CPED consortium provides working principles and design concepts that support the mission of a stronger Ed.D. The six working principles require that the Ed.D.:

(1) is framed around questions of equity, ethics, and social justice to bring about solutions to complex problems of practice;

(2) prepares leaders who can construct and apply knowledge to make a difference in the lives of individuals, families, organizations, and communities;

(3) provides opportunities for candidates to develop and demonstrate collaboration and communication skills to work with diverse communities and to build partnerships;

(4) provides field-based opportunities to analyze problems of practice and use multiple frames to develop meaningful solutions;

(5) is grounded in and develops a professional knowledge base that integrates both practical and research knowledge that links theory with systemic and systematic inquiry; and

(6) emphasizes the generation, transformation, and use of professional knowledge and practice. (Carnegie Project on the Education Doctorate, 2009, p. 1)

The recently released design elements offer specialized descriptions of program components that support the development of the scholar practitioner. The elements include descriptions of each of the following: scholarly practitioner, signature pedagogy, inquiry as practice, laboratories of practice, problem of practice, and dissertation in practice. The design elements were not used in this exploration but will be considered in the next iteration of the evaluation process.

## Data Sources

The formative evaluation process engages multiple data sources, program materials, assessment data, student survey results, advisory groups' meeting minutes, and additional anecdotal evidence. The program materials consist of the program sheets, course syllabi, mission, vision, and program marketing materials. The program gathers multiple assessment materials from current students and faculty, including course evaluations, dispositional data, and student projects and assignments. Students complete surveys at two different points in the program—after orientation weekend and after dissertation boot camp. While the program is entirely online, we do have students come to campus twice during the program, first for an orientation to the program and at least a year later to participate in dissertation boot camp. An advisory group meets monthly to support the program and consider program revisions and changes. Beyond these standardized measures, anecdotal evidence—including faculty, student, and administrative comments—is also collected.

## Findings

Using the aforementioned data sources in combination with the frameworks of COI and CEPD principles, we evaluated the program to determine how well it is being delivered and implemented. Beyond the results within each framework, additional findings provide comparative information between the previous face-to-face program and the current online iteration.

**Community of Inquiry (COI) framework.** This provides a way of evaluating the learning experiences in an online learning environment. The goal in an online environment is to create a community of scholars or a community of inquiry. This framework details three interdependent elements: social, cognitive, and teaching presences (Garrison & Arbaugh, 2007). The analysis first looks at each element and then explores the ways in which the elements overlap.

**Social presence.** Garrison and Arbaugh (2007) define social presence as "the ability of learners to project themselves socially and emotionally, thereby being perceived as 'real people' in mediated communication" (p. 159). Included under the rubric of social presence are expression, group cohesion, and open communication. This element is important because it facilitates the process of critical thinking and mediates between the teaching and cognitive presence (Garrison et al., 2010).

When considering the transition to an entirely online program, the factor that was most often raised as a concern was how the students would know (and trust) one another. Several program elements were considered to ensure a strong social presence. First, all students are required to attend a 3-day orientation that occurs immediately before the first courses begin. The main focus of the orientation is to allow cohort members to bond through specific, targeted activities for getting to know one another. Based on the survey results, the cohorts felt that the orientation was "a great opportunity to connect." Another student stated that "at first I didn't understand why an orientation with the cohort was so important since it was all online. Now I see that I was wrong. I'm so glad to have made these connections before interacting online for the next three years. Thank you!" We also encourage students to create a private page on a social media platform. The faculty and administrators do not have access to the group. Cohorts have created Facebook or Google groups to socialize outside of class. These program elements have succeeded in facilitating a social presence for our students.

**Cognitive presence.** The cognitive presence is heavily influenced by the instructor, who provides ways for students to construct meaning. This meaning is typically facilitated through sustained reflection and discourse (Garrison & Arbaugh, 2007). Garrison and Arbaugh (2007) describe the four phases of the inquiry model that develop cognitive presence: (1) identification of an issue, (2) exploration of the issue, (3) constructing meaning from the exploration, and (4) applying new meaning in other settings or contexts.

This cognitive presence is more difficult to evaluate because individual courses were not analyzed as part of the formative evaluation. Reflection and discourse are common elements across the entire program, and a 15-hour research strand is devoted to research and effective use of data. However, upon reflection of the strong influence of engaging inquiry consistently across courses, this is an area of ongoing growth and would require additional faculty development to ensure an inquiry-based, critical approach in each course.

**Teaching presence.** The teaching presence is best understood as the course framework in which the learning takes place. There are three important elements of teacher presence: (1) the design and organization of the course, (2) the engagement of students in the course, and (3) the intellectual leadership and feedback provided (Shea & Bidjerano, 2009).

Looking across each of the three elements of a strong teaching presence, our program is strong yet inconsistent. The learning management system allows faculty to establish well-organized and structured courses. There is a great deal of support provided to ensure that best practices are considered when designing an online course. As an additional means of support, the program has made a mentor available to faculty who are teaching in the program. Many instructors take advantage of the resources. Student engagement is also relatively consistent; students are working professionals who pay for their own education and are engaged with each of the courses, as evidenced by participation and grades. The most inconsistent element is the intellectual leadership and feedback received within each course. Based on course evaluations, faculty members teaching in the program are inconsistent in this area, and it causes the most frustration from students, who appreciate and expect timely feedback and consistent course engagement by the instructor. This is an area that is difficult to address because of academic freedom issues and lack of clear guidelines. This will be an area of ongoing growth.

**Presence interdependence.** While each presence was presented as an independent element, their depiction in the COI framework is one of overlapping circles. Each of the presences influences the other. Garrison and Arbaugh (2007) explain the relationship well: "social presence lays the groundwork for higher level discourse; and the structure, organization, and leadership associated with teaching presence creates the environment where cognitive presence can be developed" (p. 163).

## CPED Principles in Action

The specific principles detailed by the Carnegie Project on the Education Doctorate were listed above in the methods section. Using these principles as a guide, our program was analyzed to identify areas of strength and needed growth.

**Equitable solutions.** This principle focuses on the application of equity, ethics, and social justice when approaching solutions to complex problems. The mission states that the program is grounded in a commitment to diversity. However, there is only one course devoted entirely to diversity, and this course is often taught in the final semesters of the program, after students have completed much of their dissertations. A review of previous program dissertations shows that there is a focus on diversity, but that focus has yet to translate into solutions. This is partially because of the placement of the course, and it may need to be examined as an area that should be integrated across multiple courses.

**Leadership.** The principle of practitioner leadership is a strong theme in the school improvement program. Not only are 9 hours devoted to leadership-specific courses, but an additional course in the teaching and learning strand also focuses on instructional leadership. This is a stressed and valued aspect of the program, and students express a strong commitment to leadership efforts when completing the dispositions rubric.

**Collaboration and communication.** This doctorate is tailored to the working professional, and many of the projects required in different courses ask students to engage within their work settings and, in many cases, collaborate across settings with their fellow cohort members. The increased diversity of the cohort both racially and geographically has allowed for greater collaboration and communication.

**Field-based opportunities.** At least 60% of the courses require students to analyze problems in their own contexts and to consider multiple solutions. The strong cohort model also provides an additional framework for potential solutions, because many of the members share a similar work context. In many cases, therefore, they also share similar problems.

**Linking theory and practice.** The engagement highlighted above feeds directly into the linking of theory and practice. The students consistently remark that the most meaningful learning is the learning that they can immediately apply in their personal contexts. It has been the students themselves who have held instructors accountable to ensure that the coursework relates back to their professional practice.

**Professional knowledge use.** While the courses within the Ed.D. program emphasize "the generation, transformation, and use of professional knowledge and practice" (Carnegie Project on the Education Doctorate, 2009), this has yet to translate beyond coursework into the culminating expectations for the degree. The dissertation is still a traditional five-chapter dissertation, often reflecting professional practice elements and focusing on a traditional research paradigm.

## COMPARATIVE RESULTS

Beyond using the exemplars above during the evaluation process, there were additional results that arose specifically when considering program implementation for the first 11 years as compared to the current program. The two most salient differences were the diversity of the cohorts and their completion rates.

### Diversity

In the first 11 years of the program, all students came from within a nine-county area. Since moving the program online, the cohorts have become a great deal more diverse. The diversity extends beyond traditional racial diversity and includes geographic diversity, varied work environments, and ethnic and gender differences. Many practicing educators have had limited experience as a result of spending many years in the same school environment in the same region. Through contact with their fellow cohort members, they are able to reach beyond their current scope and engage in critical discussion about education across the globe. The most recent cohort includes members from Germany, California, and Maine.

### Completion

It is well known that doctoral education in the United States reports on average a 50% attrition rate (Church, 2009). Many doctoral candidates successfully reach the dissertation stage, but then many never complete the dissertation. This was also true during the first 11 years of the program, when there were 139 students but only 87 reached graduation as of the summer of 2014. To combat this phenomenon, it was decided to build the dissertation into the coursework. Our students take three two-credit courses aimed at writing a successful proposal. These courses are completed in the second year of the program. The expectation is that students will finish their dissertations during their third and final year. Only one cohort has had the opportunity to finish the first 3 years of the program, and 65%

of Cohort 12 graduated with a doctorate in the 3-year time frame. The seven students who did not complete their dissertations are still working on that phase. We are anticipating higher graduation rates as we continue to revise the program.

## Implications

The number of online programs is growing. When contemplating an advanced degree, potential students may consider the flexibility that online delivery provides while balancing that with the credibility of the program. As more and more degrees go online, the hope is for the discussion to shift away from flexibility and credibility to consider the broader aims of education and the potential development of a civically engaged cohort of scholars.

Civic engagement means working to make a difference in the civic life of our communities and developing the combination of knowledge, skills, values, and motivation to make that difference. It means promoting the quality of life in a community through both political and nonpolitical processes (Ehrlich, 2000). Thomas Ehrlich (2000) defines a civically responsible individual as one who "recognizes himself or herself as a member of a larger social fabric and therefore considers social problems to be at least partly his or her own; such an individual is willing to see the moral and civic dimensions of issues, to make and justify informed moral and civic judgments, and to take action when appropriate" (p. xxvi).

The key findings suggest that the Ed.D. in School Improvement is poised to continue graduating civically engaged scholars who will take with them a wealth of learning accumulated through interactions with one another, a critical reflection and discourse, a connection of theory and practice, and leadership training. We will continue to develop "educational professionals who initiate systemic and sustainable improvement in schools. Our graduates will strategically and collaboratively plan, design, implement, and document the impact of educational improvements that promote and increase the academic achievement and social development of all students" (University of West Georgia, 2014).

The findings suggest that we are working well within our mission when considering the Community of Inquiry framework, CPED principles, and national norms. There are areas of growth that the program will continue to improve upon, such as faculty development in online inquiry models and the development of critical thinking skills in an online platform. The program also requires a traditional five-chapter dissertation on a specific topic that may or may not be directly related to the student's professional practices. As suggested by the Carnegie Project on the Education Doctorate, it may be in the best interests of our students if the culminating experience were more focused on the needs of the scholarly practitioner.

# REFERENCES

Akyol, Z., Arbaugh, J.B., Cleveland-Innes, M., Garrison, D.R., Ice, P., & Richardson, J.C. (2009). A response to the review of the community of inquiry framework. *Journal of Distance Education*, *23*(2), 123–136.

Akyol, Z., & Garrison, D.R. (2011). Understanding cognitive presence in an online and blended community of inquiry: Assessing outcomes and processes for deep approaches to learning. *British Journal of Educational Technology*, *42*(2), 233–250. doi: 10.1111/j.1467–8535.2009.01029.x

Anderson, T., Rourke, L., Garrison, D.R., & Archer, W. (2001). Assessing teaching presence in a computer conferencing context. *Journal of Asynchronous Learning Networks*, *5*(2), 1–17.

Archer, W. (2010). Beyond online discussions: Extending the community of inquiry framework to entire courses. *Internet & Higher Education*, *13*(1/2), 69–69. doi: 10.1016/j.iheduc.2009.10.005

The Carnegie Project on the Education Doctorate, Inc. (2009). *Definition of and working principles for Ed.D. program design*. Retrieved from http://cpedinitiative.org/working-principles-professional-practice-doctorate-education

Church, S.E. (2009). Facing reality: What are doctoral students' chances for success? *Journal of Instructional Psychology*, *36*(4), 307–316.

Cremin, L.A. (1978). *The education of the educating professions*. Paper presented at the Annual Conference of the American Association of Colleges for Teacher Education, Washington, DC.

Ehrlich, T. (Ed.). (2000). *Civic responsibility and higher education*. Westport, CT: Oryx Press.

Frey, B.A., & King, D.K. (2011). *Quality Matters™ accessibility survey: Institutional practices and policies for online courses*. Retrieved from ERIC database. (ED520903).

Garrison, D.R., Anderson, T., & Archer, W. (2000). Critical inquiry in a text-based environment: Computer conferencing in higher education. *The Internet and Higher Education*, *2*, 87–105.

Garrison, D.R., Anderson, T., & Archer, W. (2010). The first decade of the community of inquiry framework: A retrospective. *The Internet and Higher Education*, *13*(1/2), 5–9. doi: 10.1016/j.iheduc.2009.10.003

Garrison, D.R., & Arbaugh, J.B. (2007). Researching the community of inquiry framework: Review, issues, and future directions. *The Internet and Higher Education*, *10*(3), 157–172. doi: 10.1016/j.iheduc.2007.04.001

George, J.W. (1999). *A handbook of techniques for formative evaluation: Mapping the student's learning experience*. London: Kogan Page.

Ghezzi, P. (2007). The online doctorate: FLEXIBLE, but credible? *School Administrator*, *64*(7), 30–35.

International Association for K–12 Online Learning (iNACOL). (2011). *National standards for quality online courses: Version 2*. Vienna, VA: iNACOL.

Jarosewich, T. (2009). The University of West Georgia doctorate. In T. Jarosewich (Ed.), *School improvement program review results* (pp. 1–50). Hinckley, OH: Censeo Group.

Morgan, T. (2011). Online classroom or community-in-the-making? Instructor conceptualizations and teaching presence in international online contexts. *International Journal of E-Learning & Distance Education*, *25*(1).

Muraskin, L. (1993). *Understanding evaluation: The way to better prevention programs*. Cambridge, MA: Westat, Inc.

Perry, J.A. (2012). To Ed.D. or not to Ed.D.? *Phi Delta Kappan*, *94*(1), 41–44.

Powell, A. (1980). *The uncertain profession*. Cambridge, MA: Harvard University Press.

Sethna, B. (1999). Executive summary for Ed.D. In Sethna, B. (Ed.), *School improvement college of education at State University of West Georgia* (pp. 1–32). Carrollton, GA: State University of West Georgia.

Shea, P., & Bidjerano, T. (2009). Community of inquiry as a theoretical framework to foster "epistemic engagement" and "cognitive presence" in online education. *Computers & Education, 52*(3), 543–553. doi: 10.1016/j.compedu.2008.10.007

Shea, P., Hayes, S., Vickers, J., Gozza-Cohen, M., Uzuner, S., Mehta, R., et al. (2010). A re-examination of the community of inquiry framework: Social network and content analysis. The *Internet and Higher Education, 13*(1/2), 10–21. doi: 10.1016/j.iheduc.2009.11.002

University of West Georgia. (2014). *Mission of the program*. Retrieved from http://www.westga.edu/eddsi/1246_1297.php

# CHAPTER THREE

# Teaching Research Method Courses in a Hybrid Ed.D. Program

## A Mixed Methods Study

*Sunny Liu and M.D. Haque*

## INTRODUCTION

The use of online instruction in higher education has grown substantially over the last few years, and all indicators suggest that the rate of growth in online enrollment will continue to evolve to incorporate emerging technologies. Nearly 60% of higher education institutions in the United States offer distance-based courses (D'Orsie & Day, 2006). About 30% of all institutions granting education-related degrees offer completely online programs (Allen & Seaman, 2008). Many doctoral programs are engaged in distance learning as well as blended learning, thus blurring the lines between in-class and distance for both the instructor's delivery and the student's participation (Dawson, Cavanaugh, Sessums, Black, & Kumar, 2011).

### The Effectiveness of Online Education

Given the steady increase in the availability of online courses, more and more higher education institutions acknowledge the need to examine how to offer their curriculum online in order to continue to attract students (Kirtman, 2009). However, the results of prior distance learning studies are mixed. In comparison to traditional face-to-face instruction, distance learning has been deemed to be less effective on some occasions. For example, graduate students in traditional face-to-face courses outperformed those in web courses (Logan, Augustyniak, & Rees, 2002; Urtel, 2008). Students in an online environment felt isolated, confused, frustrated, and less interested in the subject matter (Ni, 2013). In some cases it was deemed to be equally effective. For example, some conclude that distance learning is comparable to face-to-face instruction, or at least as effective as traditional classroom learning (Allen & Seaman, 2008; Freeman & Capper, 1999; Johnson, Aragon, Shaik, & Palma-Rivas, 2000; McFarland & Hamilton, 2005; Summers, Waigandt, & Whittaker, 2005). On other occasions, delivery of instruction in online environments was deemed to be more effective. For example, Means and colleagues (2010) found that learning outcomes for online courses, as compared to face-to-face courses, were more satisfactory. Lack (2013) expressed the similar opinion that online learning is more effective than face-to-face learning. Thus, the effectiveness of online learning remains inconclusive.

The use of technology in online education has undoubtedly had an impact on the instruction and learning process. However, some researchers disagree on whether the use of technology should be treated as a determining factor in deciding the effectiveness of online education. Bell and Federman (2013) suggested that delivery media do not necessarily impact learning but rather simplify the vehicles through which instructional content is delivered to the learners. They also noted that any form of instruction can be effective as long as it is able to create conditions conducive to student learning. To further explain the differences between online and traditional education, Dell, Low, and Wilker (2010) conducted a thorough literature review and found that one potential cause of a significant variance in the results across studies may simply lie in the diverse student populations and course contexts examined in each study. Therefore, focusing on the best strategies in offering curriculum online by investigating the benefits and challenges facing online learners will be an important topic of future studies.

## Blended or Hybrid Learning

The blended learning model builds upon and enhances current delivery methods, content, and technologies for distance learning. Several learning theories suggest that blended learning, a combination of distance and face-to-face learning, has the potential to produce even better results than face-to-face or online learning alone (Kerres & deWitt, 2003). According to Garrison and Kanuka (2004), blended learning is commonly defined as an integration of the traditional classroom-based approach and the best practices of online learning. Rovai and Jordan (2004) defined blended learning as a mix of "classroom and online learning that includes some of the conveniences of online courses without the complete loss of face-to-face contact" (p. 1). According to Allen and Seaman (2008), blended or hybrid instruction occurs when between 30% and 80% of a course's content is delivered online.

However, not many scholars support this notion, and the definition of blended learning remains mostly subjective. However, some scholars have provided a strong rationale for blended learning, stating that the major disadvantage of learning in an online environment is the lack of social interaction (as cited in Kistow, 2011). Blended learning promotes a social learning environment and helps to partially offset a primary drawback to totally online instruction (Jones, Moeeni, & Ruby, 2005). Driscoll and colleagues (2012) identified blended learning as a strategy for gradually moving learners out of more traditional classroom settings and into an online learning environment using incremental steps (as cited in Kerres & deWitt, 2003).

Furthermore, not all of the research on blended learning is positive. An experimental study conducted by Reasons, Valadares, and Slavkin (2005) showed that fully online courses were more effective than blended and face-to-face courses. A number of studies have investigated the role of the blended learning model and compared it to other modes of delivery, but much ambiguity remains regarding its utilization in different instructional situations (Singh, 2003).

Given the increase in online learning, it is particularly important to build knowledge about how academics should effectively incorporate blended learning into their programs in order to enhance student engagement (Alvich, Manning, McCormick, & Campbell, 2012). Alvich and fellow researchers further noted that blended learning programs are designed for working professionals who have a flexible and convenient online meeting schedule, while the interactive online discussions and face-to-face meetings offer students opportunities for professional networking and support. Therefore, future studies on the offering of blended learning should focus on the best strategies to maximize the benefits of combining online instruction and face-to-face meetings.

## Teaching Research Courses Online

A review of the literature reveals that the majority of articles dealing with online teaching have focused on undergraduate and graduate programs, while effective online teaching at the doctoral level—especially teaching online research methods courses—has been virtually ignored. According to Henriksen, Mishra, Greenhow, Cain, and Roseth (2014), online and blended doctoral studies represent a learning innovation that can accommodate practitioners who are unable to attend traditional, bricks-and-mortar courses and provide them with an opportunity to improve their teaching and learning while also leveraging their practical knowledge. A number of programs have begun offering fully online or blended models of doctoral education (Bolliger & Halupa, 2012) with the explicit purpose of opening up doctoral learning opportunities to more degree-seeking individuals beyond the traditional full-time, on-campus students (Henriksen et al., 2014).

Research methods courses are challenging to teach because of the technical complexity of the course materials (Ball & Pelco, 2006). Doctoral students generally find the content in research methodology courses rather demanding (Ewing, Mathieson, Alexander, & Leafman, 2012). Among the challenges that students face is a general lack of knowledge about research skills and a fear of statistics, reading academic journals, and evaluating research studies (Bailie, 2009). A study by Coleman and Conrad (2007) found that graduate students were less satisfied with research methodology courses as compared to courses with non-research-based content, even when the same instructor taught both courses. Acquiring research skills and completing required doctoral research projects in an online environment could be especially challenging for students. A study conducted by DeVaney (2010) showed that student anxiety caused by research-related coursework is more pronounced in an online learning environment. Also, persistence in an online environment may be more difficult in research methods classes (Ni, 2013).

Despite all the challenges, research courses are critical in helping doctoral students to progress to the dissertation stage and to successfully complete their dissertations (Henson, Hull, & Williams, 2010; Llamas & Boza, 2011). Since there is typically a smaller number of research courses in an Ed.D. program as compared to a Ph.D. program (Leech & Goodwin, 2008), the quality of the research courses in an Ed.D. program is especially important. Though studies on the subject of teaching research courses in an Ed.D. program in a blended or online setting have not yet been conducted, they are urgently needed.

## Purpose of this Study

Given the urgent need to study the best strategies to maximize the benefits of combining online and face-to-face instruction in teaching research courses in an Ed.D. program, the purpose of this mixed methods study was twofold: first, to determine the impact of demographics such as gender, ethnicity, and age on students' technology self-efficacy and course satisfaction and to determine the relationship between technology self-efficacy and course satisfaction; and second, to explore the benefits and challenges the students experienced in their blended research methods courses and to provide suggestions for improvement in teaching such courses. In arguing for better-focused and methodologically richer research into blended learning, this chapter adopts a definition of blended learning as follows: "Blended learning" describes learning activities that involve a systematic combination of co-present (face-to-face) interactions and technologically mediated interactions between students, teachers, and learning resources (Garrison & Kanuka, 2004).

## METHOD

### Sample

A total of 123 students enrolled in an Ed.D. program at a university in California were invited to participate in the study. Of the 123 students, 91 signed the consent form and participated in the study. This Ed.D. program was chosen because it is a typical 3-year professional doctoral program in educational leadership. The participants were first- and second-year students in the program, and they were required to enroll in a total of four research methods courses—two each year during the first 2 years of the program. All of the research courses were taught in a blended format with a combination of face-to-face meetings and online webinars.

Table 3.1. Participants Disaggregated by Demographics and Cohorts.

| Demographics | Year 1 ($n = 32$) | Year 2 ($n = 57$) | Total ($n = 89$) |
|---|---|---|---|
| Gender | | | |
| Male | 31.3% | 31.6% | 31.5% |
| Female | 68.8% | 68.4% | 68.5% |
| Ethnicity | | | |
| Asian | 9.4% | 5.3% | 6.7% |
| African American | 15.6% | 8.8% | 11.2% |
| Hispanics of any race | 18.8% | 24.6% | 22.5% |
| White | 50.0% | 52.6% | 51.7% |
| Age | | | |
| Younger than 29 years old | 15.6% | 8.8% | 11.2% |
| 30–49 years old | 71.9% | 71.9% | 71.9% |
| 50–64 years old | 12.5% | 19.3% | 16.9% |

*Note.* Two Year 1 students did not provide demographic information, so that total is 89 instead of 91.

Table 3.1 reports the participants disaggregated by demographics and cohorts. About two-thirds of the participants were female (68.5%). Half of the participants were White (51.7%), and one quarter of them were Hispanic (22.5%). Also, a majority of the participants were 30–49 years old (71.9%). The student profile matches the general population characteristics of an Ed.D. program in that area.

## Measures

Course satisfaction has been measured in many different ways in the literature—for example, students' overall satisfaction with the online courses as measured by the 21-item Course Satisfaction Questionnaire (CSQ) (Frey, Yankelov, & Faul, 2003); students' satisfaction with online interaction (Arbaugh, 2000); students' satisfaction with skills learned in the course (Alavi, 1994); students' course satisfaction in multiple dimensions such as pedagogies, resources, and delivery strategies (Hosie, Schibeci, & Backhaus, 2005).

Students' technology self-efficacy has been measured in many different ways as well. For example, the Online Technologies Self-Efficacy Scale (OTSES) was used to measure the technology self-efficacy of online learners (Miltiadou & Yu, 2000); the Computer Attitude Scale (CAS) was used to measure students' comfort level with computers (Loyd & Gressard, 1984); and the course anxiety scale was constructed to measure students' anxiety level with computers, the Internet, and online courses (Bolliger & Halupa, 2012). In the meantime, in regard to students' level of experience with technology, online learners were often asked to rank their online technology experiences (such as using a web browser) and online learning experiences (such as previous participation in self-paced online learning) from extremely inexperienced to extremely experienced (Artino, 2008).

To better measure the students' course satisfaction and technology self-efficacy with blended research methods courses (which were not measured in the previous literature), a 17-item satisfaction questionnaire and a 5-item technology questionnaire were developed. The satisfaction questionnaire is composed of 14 Likert-scale questions and 3 open-ended questions. The technology questionnaire is composed of four Likert-scale questions and one open-ended question.

To examine the internal consistency reliability of the two scales, Cronbach's (1951) alpha and the corrected item-to-total correlations were conducted. Based on each item's corrected item-to-total correlation, two items in the satisfaction questionnaire (#9: "It was easy to follow class discussions" and #11: "The extra learning resources provided to you [e.g., handouts, online resources, online discussion groups, online assessments] were helpful") were deleted, as their correlations were less than 0.40 (Cronbach, 1951). The resulting 15-item satisfaction scale has a Cronbach's alpha value of 0.91. None of the items in the technology survey was deleted, and the scale has a Cronbach's alpha value of 0.87.

## RESULTS

## Quantitative Data

To determine the impact of demographics such as gender, ethnicity, and age on students' technology self-efficacy and course satisfaction, and to determine the relationship between technology self-efficacy and course satisfaction, descriptive statistics, $t$-tests, analyses of variance (ANOVA), and correlation tests were conducted. The results are shown in Tables 3.2 and 3.3.

Table 3.2. Means and Standard Deviations for Course Satisfaction by Demographics and Cohorts.

| Demographics | Mean (SD) | T/F | $p$ |
|---|---|---|---|
| Gender | | | |
| Male | 5.62 (0.52) | | |
| Female | 5.27 (0.87) | 1.54 | >0.05 |
| Ethnicity | | | |
| Asian | 5.06 (0.73) | | |
| African American | 5.18 (0.43) | | |
| Hispanics of any race | 5.45 (0.84) | | |
| White | 5.42 (0.91) | 0.324 | >0.05 |
| Age | | | |
| Younger than 29 years old | 5.17 (1.43) | | |
| 30–49 years old | 5.44 (0.62) | | |
| 50–64 years old | 5.20 (1.06) | 0.56 | >0.05 |
| Cohort | | | |
| Year 1 | 5.25 (0.85) | | |
| Year 2 | 5.36 (0.80) | 0.27 | >0.05 |

Table 3.3. Means and Standard Deviations for Technology by Demographics and Cohorts.

| Demographics | Mean (SD) | T/F | $p$ |
|---|---|---|---|
| Gender | | | |
| Male | 5.43 (1.00) | | |
| Female | 5.29 (1.33) | 0.52 | >0.05 |
| Ethnicity | | | |
| Asian | 5.46 (0.71) | | |
| African American | 5.45 (1.07) | | |
| Hispanics of any race | 5.21 (1.27) | | |

| Demographics | Mean (SD) | T/F | $p$ |
|---|---|---|---|
| White | 5.37 (1.33) | 0.12 | >0.05 |
| Age | | | |
| Younger than 29 years old | 5.90 (0.97) | | |
| 30–49 years old | 5.32 (1.15) | | |
| 50–64 years old | 5.00 (1.64) | 1.62 | >0.05 |
| Cohort | | | |
| Year 1 | 5.20 (1.32) | | |
| Year 2 | 5.43 (1.19) | 0.81 | >0.05 |

The participants had very high levels of course satisfaction and technology self-efficacy. The average course satisfaction was 5.4 (s.d. = 0.79), which falls somewhere in between "slightly agree" and "agree." Therefore, on average, the participants slightly agreed or agreed that the blended research courses provided them with satisfactory learning experiences and increased their knowledge and/or skills. Similarly, the average technology experience and self-efficacy was 5.4 (s.d. = 1.24). Therefore, the participants were fairly familiar with technology and also felt rather confident in the use of technology in web-based learning.

The descriptive statistics on each individual item revealed that the individual item score distributions are similar to the average of all the item scores. The following two items, however, had the lowest means: #7: "Class discussions were more difficult to participate in than other courses" (reverse-coded mean = 4.74, s.d. = 1.67) in the satisfaction questionnaire and #3: "How experienced are you with self-paced, online learning (for example, courses like the online portion of this course)?" (mean = 5.02, s.d. = 1.7) in the technology questionnaire.

In general, males had a higher level of course satisfaction and technology experience and self-efficacy than females. Asian and African American students had a lower level of course satisfaction, and Hispanics had a lower level of technology experience and self-efficacy than other ethnic groups. Participants in the age group 50–64 had a lower level of course satisfaction and technology experience and self-efficacy than the younger age groups. Year 2 participants had a higher level of technology experience and self-efficacy than Year 1 participants.

However, none of the course satisfaction and technology experience and self-efficacy scores was significantly different across gender, ethnicity, age, or cohort (Year 1 vs. Year 2) based on the inferential statistical test results. The correlation between course satisfaction and technology experience and self-efficacy was positively correlated ($r = 0.27$, p<0.05). Not surprisingly, participants who had higher levels of technology experience and self-efficacy tended to have higher course satisfaction as well.

## Qualitative Data

The study has yielded interesting results that address questions about the benefits and challenges that students experienced in their blended research methods courses, as well as their recommendations for improvement.

**Advantages of online education.** There were several advantages to taking the research courses in a blended learning environment. One of the dominant advantages was flexibility and convenience. In addition, blended courses also provided the participants better accessibility and interaction, a lower stress level, and better instructor support.

**Flexibility and convenience.** For the online portion of the research courses, the participants appreciated the flexibility and convenience provided by the format. The participants saved time and transportation costs by not having to travel to the classroom. They received synchronous online instruction from home or work and engaged in online discussions with colleagues from various locations. In most of the cases, the flexibility afforded by such a setting became the only way for the participants to obtain a doctoral degree, as they were practitioners and had to juggle various commitments in their lives. As one participant stated: "One of the main advantages of taking research courses in a blended environment is the convenience it offers to the professional working adults in the program who are trying to balance their work, school and family life."

**Diversity and accessibility.** If designed properly, the blended research courses can truly provide the participants with more diversity and higher accessibility. The participants pointed out that there were a variety of learning tools available for online learning, and they had online access to all the resources for the courses. More diversity was promoted when students with different personalities, especially the introverts, were allowed to participate without feeling intimidated. For the participants with health issues, the blended learning format helped them minimize the challenges they might otherwise encounter in a face-to-face setting.

**Better interactions.** The participants appreciated the small-group instruction provided at the synchronous online instructional setting. Unlike a traditional classroom setting with a large group of students, each synchronous online session had a limited number of students, allowing them adequate opportunities for active engagement. One participating student also pointed out that honesty in interactions was fostered in a blended learning environment, as the student could express his or her opinions without worrying about confronting someone in a face-to-face situation.

**Lower stress.** The participants found it less intimidating to pursue research courses in a blended learning environment, thanks to the abovementioned advantages. Faculty provided the study materials such as the PowerPoint slides and handouts well ahead of the sessions. As a result, the participants could study the contents and prepare for classes at their own pace. One participant stated:

> I liked that I had my own screen to see/review the presentations and videos, as I am able to be more focused and engaged, whereas being in a face-to-face environment can be challenging with the distractions and interference of others in the room. I also liked the time allotted to the blended learning environment as it is usually well paced.

**Instructor support.** The participants also pointed out the importance of having an instructor who is accommodating, supportive, and patient. During the synchronous online meetings and at the asynchronous online discussions, the instructors should allow ample time for the participants to complete their work. It is also important to provide more than one meeting option for each instructional session so that students have the flexibility of choosing sessions based on their availability.

**Challenges of online education.** Undoubtedly, taking research courses in a blended environment has its unique challenges. The top challenges reported by the participants included technology difficulties, lack of communication, slower relationship building, and more demanding requirements for independent learning. The participants also acknowledged the difficulties instructors faced in controlling the discussion flow when some students dominated the conversation or spent too much time speaking.

**Technology difficulties.** Technology problems such as the loss of Internet and telephone connections, as well as weak signals, were an important reason for the reduced satisfaction of blended courses. When that situation occurred, the participants found it difficult to participate in online activities. Sometimes it was difficult to understand other people in a webinar because of noises, several people talking simultaneously, and so forth. In the meantime, there was a digital divide among participants. For the participants who were not good at using technology, the online tools provided in the courses became barriers instead of advantages. For example, one participant stated:

> I do believe that blended learning environment is a lot more challenging than traditional face-to-face learning. The challenges are using technology to help us learn. A lot of external factors can go wrong, like a slow Wi-Fi connection, phone background noise or get disconnected via phone line.

**Communication.** Communication through web technology did not offer the same experience as that of the face-to-face setting. The lack of access to instructors and peers in comparison to a face-to-face setting had an impact on the participants' experiences. They thought face-to-face learning invited more personal conversations; thus, a constant interpersonal connection was built. In a blended learning environment, no facial expressions or body language were communicated, and the online or phone conference interactions were impersonal in nature.

Also, not receiving immediate responses from the instructors and peers was a concern for the participants who experienced isolation as a result.. As one participant pointed out:

> Not having the social dynamic component to keep students engaged.... I also miss the socialization amongst my peers in the classroom and being able to bounce things off of them (ask them questions on items I may not understand or have missed).

Similarly, another participant stated:

> Sometimes discussions are difficult online because successful communication is aided by facial expressions and F2F interactions. Group work, in particular, can be challenging online because it is difficult for an individual to assert leadership in a project.

**Relationship building.** Because the participants did not see each other as often as they would in a traditional classroom setting, it took them longer to get to know each other and establish positive relationships. Some believed such relationships were developed by the end of their first year of study. Still, some felt they would never know the instructors and colleagues as well as they would in a face-to-face setting. As one student reported, that resulted in

> Lack of rapport with fellow students/peers and professors. It is more difficult to assess the skills of your students as a professor of blended courses; more difficult to establish a network of peers to reach out to when struggling as a student.

**Independent learning.** Learning in a blended learning environment required learners to be more accountable and to learn course materials on their own. For those who procrastinated and were not prepared, their peers thought they created roadblocks for online interactions. For example, a couple of participants indicated that:

> Some students procrastinate more than others and if we are this type of person, we may find that a blended course is much more difficult vs. face-to-face course...interacting with peers is not as productive especially when people are not prepared or take over the conversations.

**Suggestions for improvement.** Overall, the participants expressed their appreciation for the opportunity afforded by blended learning with the combination of face-to-face and online meetings. Many participants liked the question-and-answer sessions provided by the instructors, as they offered them an opportunity to ask individual questions. Some participants thought blended learning fit their needs, while others provided several suggestions for improvement based on the challenges they experienced with blended learning. To deal with the technology difficulties, some participants suggested that the program offer technology training, pre-meeting seminars, and an on-call technician; to deal with communication issues, some participants suggested adding visuals of instructors and peers and employing student check-in points during the online sections in order to make online discussions more interactive; to deal with procrastination and ill-preparedness, the participants suggested that instructors provide a summary of expectations at the beginning of the courses and the beginning of each webinar and provide additional scaffolding during the initial face-to-face sessions.

## DISCUSSION

Online instruction in higher education has grown rapidly over the last few years, and this growth will continue in the future. Online learning has also been the subject of increasing research interest, with several studies over the last decade examining its effectiveness. While the dominant trend in this area continues to be comparing online instruction with face-to-face instruction, it is unclear whether comparisons between distance programs and equivalent face-to-face programs are appropriate or useful. Given the urgent need to study the best strategies in maximizing the benefits of combining online instruction and face-to-face meetings in teaching research courses in an Ed.D. program, this mixed method study has revealed several interesting points.

First, it is clear that teaching blended learning research methods courses has its advantages and challenges. Thus, it is not appropriate to judge the pedagogical effectiveness of a program based on the mode of instruction. Several scholars have proposed that research should focus on an understanding of both online and face-to-face instruction and effective teaching and learning (Head, Lockee, & Oliver, 2002). Bell and Federman (2013) made clear that technology is nothing but a vehicle that delivers instruction, and that pedagogy—not technology—would affect student learning. They further noted that no single medium supports the educational experience in a manner that is superior in all ways to that supported by other media. Rather, characteristics of the instructional design such as the methods used, the feedback provided, and the degree of learner engagement create the conditions within which learning occurs. Given the state of research in the area of distance education, it is proposed here that research on the effectiveness of blended learning needs to shift its focus beyond comparisons with traditional education to exploring the most effective approaches, tools, technologies, and blends to deliver doctoral education. Based on the participants' suggestions for improvement, proposing clear expectations and a course outline at the beginning of the course, providing technology training and support along the way, offering timely feedback and being approachable, employing student check-in points during the online sections, and providing question-and-answer segments are essential components of promoting a successful blended or online course.

Second, Driscoll, Jicha, Hunt, Tichavsky, and Thompson (2012) noted that studies on both sides of the argument over the efficacy of online education generally use similar strategies to operationalize successful learning. The majority of such research relies on student performance on standard evaluations, student satisfaction, and final course grades. Since the use of technology in online or blended learning has surely brought new advantages and challenges in the teaching and learning process, an important question to ask is this: Should the students be evaluated differently from traditional settings as well? If so, what other indicators should be used besides the traditional measures of course satisfaction and course grades? For example, periodic checks on the students' progress are more important when the instructors and the students do not meet regularly on campus.

Third, this study was conducted on a single Ed.D. program from a university in California where the participants had a fairly high level of course satisfaction and technology efficacy. As a consequence, statistically significant results were not easily identified among demographic groups. Therefore, it would be better for future studies to recruit a larger sample and make sure that the sample is sufficiently diversified to replicate this study.

## REFERENCES

Alavi, M. (1994). Computer-mediated collaborative learning: An empirical evaluation. *MIS Quarterly*, *18*(2), 159–174.

Allen, I., & Seaman, J. (2008). *Staying the course: Online education 2008*. Boston, MA: The Sloan Consortium.

Alvich, D., Manning, J., McCormick, K., & Campbell, R. (2012). Hybrid doctoral program: Innovative practices and partnerships. *International Journal on E-Learning, 11*(3), 223–232.

Arbaugh, J.B. (2000). Virtual classroom characteristics and student satisfaction with Internet-based MBA courses. *Journal of Management Education, 24*(1), 32–54.

Artino, A.R. (2008). Motivational beliefs and perceptions of instructional quality: Predicting satisfaction with online training. *Journal of Computer Assisted Learning, 24*(3), 260–270.

Bailie, F. (2009). Proceedings from the Society for Information Technology & Teacher Education International Conference 2009: Charleston, SC: Association for the Advancement of Computing in Education (AACE).

Ball, C.T., & Pelco, L.E. (2006). Teaching research methods to undergraduate psychology students using an active, cooperative learning approach. *International Journal of Teaching and Learning in Higher Education, 17*(2), 147–154.

Bell, B.S., & Federman, J.E. (2013). E-learning in postsecondary education. *Future of Children, 23*(1), 165–185.

Bolliger, D.U., & Halupa, C. (2012). Student perceptions of satisfaction and anxiety in an online doctoral program. *Distance Education, 33*(1), 81–98.

Coleman, C., & Conrad, C. (2007). Understanding the negative graduate student perceptions of required statistics and research methods courses: Implications for programs and faculty. *Journal of College Teaching & Learning, 4*(3), 11–20. Retrieved from http://journals.cluteonline.com/index.php/TLC/article/download/1618/1598

Cronbach, L.J. (1951). Coefficient alpha and the internal structure of tests. *Psychometrika, 16*, 297–334.

Dawson, K., Cavanaugh, C., Sessums, C., Black, E., & Kumar, S. (2011). Designing a professional practice doctoral degree in educational technology: Signature pedagogies, implications and recommendations. *Journal of Distance Education, 25*(3). Retrieved from http://www.jofde.ca/index.php/jde/article/view/767/1317

Dell, C.A., Low, C., & Wilker, J.F. (2010). Comparing student achievement in online and face-to-face class formats. *Journal of Online Learning and Teaching, 6*(1), 30–42. Retrieved from http://143.43.221.130/coehs/ncate/standard_5_exhibits/wilker_candi.pdf

DeVaney, T.A. (2010). Anxiety and attitude of graduate students in on-campus vs. online statistics courses. *Journal of Statistics Education, 18*(1), 1–15. Retrieved from http://www.amstat.org/publications/jse/v18n1/devaney.pdf

D'Orsie, S., & Day, K. (2006). Ten tips for teaching a web course. *Tech Directions, 65*(7), 18–20.

Driscoll, A., Jicha, K., Hunt, A.N., Tichavsky, L., & Thompson, G. (2012). Can online courses deliver in-class results? A comparison of student performance and satisfaction in an online versus a face-to-face introductory sociology course. *Teaching Sociology, 40*(4), 312–331.

Ewing, H., Mathieson, K., Alexander, J.L., & Leafman, J. (2012). Enhancing the acquisition of research skills in online doctoral programs: The Ewing model. *MERLOT Journal of Online Learning and Teaching, 8*(1), 34–44.

Freeman, M.A., & Capper, J.M. (1999). Exploiting the web for education: An anonymous asynchronous role simulation. *Australian Journal of Educational Technology, 15*(1), 95–116.

Frey, A., Yankelov, P., & Faul, A.C. (2003). Student perceptions of web-assisted teaching strategies. *Journal of Social Work Education, 39*, 443–457.

Garrison, D.R., & Kanuka, H. (2004). Blended learning: Uncovering its transformative potential in higher education. *The Internet and Higher Education, 7*(2), 95–105.

Head, J.T., Lockee, B.B., & Oliver, K.M. (2002). Method, media and mode: Clarifying the discussion of distance education effectiveness. *Quarterly Review of Distance Education, 3*, 261–268.

Henriksen, D., Mishra, P., Greenhow, C., Cain, W., & Roseth, C. (2014). A tale of two courses: Innovation in the hybrid/online doctoral program at Michigan State University. *Tech Trends, 58*(4), 45–53.

Henson, R.K., Hull, D.M., & Williams, C.S. (2010). Methodology in our education research culture: Toward a stronger collective quantitative proficiency. *Educational Researcher, 39*(3), 229–240.

Hosie, P., Schibeci, R., & Backhaus, A. (2005). A framework and checklists for evaluating online learning in higher education. *Assessment & Evaluation in Higher Education, 30*(5), 539–553.

Johnson, S.D., Aragon, S.R., Shaik, N., & Palma-Rivas, N. (2000). Comparative analysis of learner satisfaction and learning outcomes in online and face-to-face learning environments. *Journal of Interactive Learning Research, 11*(1), 29–49.

Jones, K., Moeeni, F., & Ruby, P. (2005). Comparing web-based content delivery and instructor-led learning in a telecommunications course. *Journal of Information Systems Education, 16*(3), 265–270.

Kerres, M., & deWitt, C. (2003). A didactical framework for the design of blended learning arrangements. *Journal of Educational Media, 28*(2), 101–114.

Kirtman, L. (2009). Online versus in-class courses: An examination of differences in learning outcomes. *Issues in Teacher Education, 18*(2), 103–116.

Kistow, B. (2011). Blended learning in higher education: A study of a graduate school of business, Trinidad and Tobago. *Caribbean Teaching Scholar, 1*(2), 115–128.

Lack, K.A. (2013). *Current status of research on online learning in postsecondary education*. Retrieved from http://www.sr.ithaka.org/research-publications/current-status-research-online-learning-postsecondary-education

Leech, N.L., & Goodwin, L.D. (2008). Building a methodological foundation: Doctoral-level methods courses in colleges of education. *Research in the Schools, 15*(1), 1–8.

Llamas, J., & Boza, Á. (2011). Teaching research methods for doctoral students in education: Learning to enquire in the university. *International Journal of Social Research Methodology: Theory & Practice, 14*(1), 77–90.

Logan, E., Augustyniak, R., & Rees, A. (2002). Distance education as different education: A student-centered investigation of distance learning experience. *Journal of Education for Library and Information Science, 43*(1), 32–42.

Loyd, B.H., & Gressard, C. (1984). Reliability and factorial validity of computer attitude scales. *Educational and Psychological Measurement, 44*(2), 501–505.

McFarland, D., & Hamilton, D. (2005). Factors affecting student performance and satisfaction: Online versus traditional course delivery. *Journal of Computer Information Systems, 46*(2), 25–32.

Means, B., Toyama, Y., Murphy, R., Bakia, M., & Jones, K. (2010). *Evaluation of evidence-based practices in online learning: A meta-analysis and review of online learning studies*. Washington, DC: U.S. Department of Education, Office of Planning, Evaluation, and Policy Development.

Miltiadou, M., & Yu, C.H. (2000). Validation of the online technologies self-efficacy scale (OTSES). (Publication No. ED 445 672). Retrieved from http://www.www.creative-wisdom.com/pub/efficacy.pdf

Ni, A.Y. (2013). Comparing the effectiveness of classroom and online learning: Teaching research methods. *Journal of Public Affairs Education, 19*(2), 199–215.

Reasons, S., Valadares, K., & Slavkin, M. (2005). Questioning the hybrid model: Student outcomes in different course formats. *Journal of Asynchronous Learning, 9*(1), 83–94.

Rovai, A.P., & Jordan, H.M. (2004). Blended learning and sense of community: A comparative analysis with traditional and fully online graduate courses. *International Review of Research in Open and Distance Learning, 5*(2). Retrieved from http://www.irrodl.org/index.php/irrodl/article/view/192/274

Singh, H. (2003). Building effective blended learning programs. *Educational Technology, 43*(6), 51–54.

Summers, J.J., Waigandt A., & Whittaker, T.A. (2005). A comparison of student achievement and satisfaction in an online versus a traditional face-to-face statistics class. *Innovative Higher Education, 29*(3), 233–250.

Urtel, M.G. (2008). Assessing academic performance between traditional and distance education course formats. *Educational Technology & Society, 11*(1), 322–330.

# CHAPTER FOUR

# An Argument for the Ed.D. Project Study as an Alternative to the Dissertation

*Christina M. Dawson, Cheryl Keen, and Carol Philips*

## INTRODUCTION

In this chapter we seek to acquaint readers with the diverse student body being attracted to hybrid doctoral programs and to the ways in which applied capstone projects can meet their needs and expand their efforts to work more effectively for social justice. We present our vision of the components that should be incorporated in an applied capstone project. There are five main components: students' professional settings provide the issues that underlie their capstones; the capstones culminate in a project; the capstones relate to service and promoting social justice; theory and practice inform each other within the capstones; and deep reflection on their own learning along several dimensions is incorporated in their capstones.

Our vision is grounded in our histories as faculty members. In addition to teaching doctoral courses, we have collectively been chairing and serving on doctoral committees, both Ph.D. and Ed.D., for about 35 years and for nearly 100 students in five institutions. What differentiates our experience from that of many other researchers and doctoral faculty members is that, for the most part, our mentoring of doctoral students has taken place in hybrid programs, that is, online programs that require at least one face-to-face residency. The student population and the means of mentoring in these programs are markedly different from the brick-and-mortar institutions' education schools. Further, the number of educational doctorates offered online and the number of students pursuing them continue to rise. Based on our review of the education doctorate literature and our personal experiences on doctoral committees, we offer our suggestions about how an applied Ed.D. capstone can serve the needs of the students.

## WHO ARE THE STUDENTS IN HYBRID PROGRAMS?

Our doctoral students—who are unusually diverse, especially along the lines of race—include PK–12 and community college educators, nurse educators, and leaders in community and government agencies. Most of them have come to a doctoral program with the intention of staying in their professional settings and have goals related to addressing problems in those settings. Many are PK–12 teachers and administrators. Some of the teachers are seeking to "move up" to administration, while some of the administrators are seeking to move up within their current career track. Other students already teach at community colleges and universities that have raised their standards for faculty. Some college and university administrators seek their doctorate to meet those criteria or to climb the career ladder. We have also worked with students who are in charge of professional development at their noneducation workplaces or are employed as informal educators in many different settings.

## WHY DO SOME STUDENTS CHOOSE AN ONLINE PROGRAM?

Our experience suggests that a key feature shared by online doctoral students is the obvious one: they have chosen to undertake a hybrid doctorate rather than one at a traditional brick-and-mortar university campus. Nonetheless, the factors that motivate students to choose a hybrid doctoral program that is largely online are many and varied (Philips, 2008). Among the most common are availability, convenience, and comfort.

### Availability

Doctoral programs are not readily available everywhere. Although some of our online doctoral students live in major urban areas, others come from rural ones where the commuting distance to a program for a working professional would be burdensome, if not impossible. Others live abroad—again, some in countries where educational doctoral programs are readily available and others who have no options other than online.

## Convenience

The vast majority of students with whom we have worked are employed professionals who perceive that a hybrid program allows them to continue their work while earning a degree. These students lead very full lives, the components of which cannot be easily changed. In addition to holding a full-time job, many are members of the sandwich generation: they are raising children who are still at home while caring for their elders—including parents, siblings, and extended family members.

Since more than half of them are women and/or African American, they are likely to feel a heavy responsibility for caregiving to elders. Given these commitments, most do not even consider attending brick-and-mortar programs because they need the flexibility provided by online programs. Students never (or very rarely, as in the case of hybrid programs that require residencies) have to commit to being somewhere on someone else's schedule; they can attend class before and after work and on weekends. In addition to not having to attend classes physically, they also do not have to commute. Thus, even very busy adults can matriculate online if they are willing to add to their already substantial personal and professional workloads.

## Comfort

Many students identify a number of reasons for being more comfortable in a hybrid environment. Unlike the vast majority of brick-and-mortar doctoral students, they are often first-generation college students, as well as first-generation professionals. Some have never met a person who holds a doctorate. Related to their familial education backgrounds, about half the students whom we have taught have been students of color, whereas students of color are underenrolled in brick-and-mortar programs. In addition to class and race, another characteristic is that they tend to be deeply involved in their churches, often serving in leadership positions. Indeed, some attribute their enrollment in doctoral programs to the influence of their religious or spiritual duties and callings.

While these factors promote students' levels of comfort with each other, they also have other, more detrimental effects, including that our students very often have unrealistic expectations about the quantity and quality of work required in a doctoral program. These students often appear to be more comfortable interacting with course colleagues online than interacting in person with students who have had greater privilege. Online discussions also offer cover for those who wish not to be known by their race or disability, thus allowing their ideas—not their perceived identity—to frame their peers' interactions with them in online discussions. Many refrain from posting a photo in online discussions and might not mention race-identified life experiences until later in a semester.

## PORTRAITS OF STUDENTS

As we noted previously, regardless of the similarities among our students, there are also significant differences. To illustrate those differences, we have created composite portraits (Lawrence-Lightfoot & Davis, 2002) of two "typical" students. Since the focus of this book is on access to doctoral studies, the students we chose to describe are all African American women. However, there are demographic differences among them (e.g., class, educational history, age) as well as numerous other distinctions often related to the demographic ones. Those differences include their developmental stages, which contribute critically to learners' success or failure (Belenky, Clinchy, Goldberger, & Tarule, 1986; Kegan, 1984). Other differences involve self-confidence and role definition challenges along the doctoral journey.

### Ariadne

In many respects, Ariadne is an atypical "typical" student. In her mid-30s, she is an upper-middle-class African American who attended a small liberal arts college for her undergraduate work and an elite university for her master's degree in educational leadership. Her parents and siblings also have postgraduate degrees and are high-achieving professionals. Ariadne works in a very large urban school district as the director of professional development. By her own account, her job—to which she is dedicated and which she "loves," in large part because she believes that she contributes to social justice on a daily basis—takes up almost all of her time. She is married and has two children in elementary school.

Ariadne described two main motives for undertaking doctoral work. First, she was considering the possibility of teaching at the university level and was well aware that even as an adjunct, she would need a doctorate. Second, she wanted to learn more about how she could perform even better in her workplace. Although she had some qualms about the respect an online degree would be accorded, Ariadne decided to take the online route. For her, the primary motive was convenience. Given her 60–70-hour workweek, she was unable to imagine attending brick-and-mortar classes. She knew that an online program would demand a considerable amount of self-discipline and knew that self-discipline was one of her strengths.

### Rosemarie

Rosemarie has been a career and technical high school teacher for 27 years. Although she is proud of her professional accomplishments, she feels her work has been seen as less valuable than that of high school teachers who work with college-bound students. She has seen several reform efforts come and go and feels that her perspective has not been heard. She was attracted to the idea of getting a doctorate, thinking that if she perhaps did research that demonstrated that career and technical education teachers' perspectives were ignored in reform efforts, she might finally get some satisfaction. She has more time now that her children are grown. Last year, after her mother suffered a fall and a broken hip, Rosemarie moved into her house to serve as her primary caretaker. Although she had not clearly understood what earning a doctorate would entail, she kept hearing her late grandfather's voice: "Someone in this family needs to go all the way and get a doctorate."

## RETENTION RISKS

Now that we have told these learners' stories, we think it is very important to note that regardless of the factors that may predict that one or the other will succeed in securing a degree, they are all, in fact, skating on thin ice because of another demographic factor they share as Ed.D. students: being adult learners. As such, their academic futures depend upon the continuing good health and support of their families, keeping their jobs (both for the income and as the study site), and the absence of crises in the politics or weather of their locales.

We have worked with students who, midway through their programs, were torpedoed by all of these circumstances and more. One or both of their parents become ill, and as the closest child, they bear the responsibility of caring for the parent. A spouse who was originally supportive loses patience. A new school superintendent is not open to using the district as a research site, though his or her predecessor had been. A hurricane devastates their city; their country is the site of an epidemic or a war. On a more positive note, students in this sandwich generation are sometimes derailed by positive events such as a child's wedding, the birth of grandchildren, or a parent's 80th birthday celebration, all in a single semester.

## WHAT HYBRID ED.D. PROGRAMS OFFER TO STUDENTS

Having chosen an online learning setting for reasons such as comfort, convenience, and availability, students sometimes stumble upon rich opportunities and resources in the hybrid and largely online setting and find several benefits to hybrid Ed.D. programs. Means, Toyama, Murphy, Bakia, and Jones (2009), in a federally supported meta-analysis, demonstrated that blended learning often has better results than online or face-to-face learning. We have often found asynchronous discussions in online classrooms to be more interactive and informative than brick-and-mortar class discussions.

Because many students in online doctoral programs are often first-generation college students, they are unlikely to be in sustained dialogue with anyone who has earned a doctorate. Online pedagogies can help accelerate the socialization of these new doctoral learners. Blended learning provides several opportunities, including class discussions that enhance relationships among students' personal and professional development; face-to-face residencies, which offer community and skill building, prioritization of time and focus; peer support; and the advantage of faculty presence more often than in a brick-and-mortar classroom.

## Applied Capstone Projects Make Sense

We believe in the practical wisdom of our students, and we want to enhance their use of research in addressing problems of practice and issues of social justice. We see potential in the creation of practical capstones based on a strong understanding and interpretation of data. In our experience, we have found that the knowledge, skills, and abilities that students gain can be similar in both a Ph.D. dissertation capstone and an applied Ed.D. capstone. For instance, students do the following in both capstone experiences: examine, critique, and synthesize knowledge in a literature review; frame a problem and the related gap (in research or in practice); consider the audience for the work and significance for the field; and collaborate with a faculty mentor and committee.

However, we have found that the following knowledge, skills, and ability outcomes may be distinct to an applied Ed.D. capstone experience. Our students have a greater chance to

1. build on local knowledge (their own and that of others);
2. address limitations related to local knowledge;
3. use their knowledge of intervening variables that are place based;
4. have more dialogue partners (beyond the faculty mentor, committee, or cohort);
5. develop skills in engaging with local stakeholders and policymakers;
6. put to use in their classroom or administrative work their learning on organizational change;
7. establish and justify short-term goals related to an issue;
8. clarify ongoing implementation concerns and the need for sustainability;
9. become attuned to within-school differences and between-school differences; and
10. focus on service as they address change at the local level.

An applied capstone project may also be more in harmony with the needs of our students as adult learners. Adults prefer learning that they view as meaningful (pertinent and useful) (Merriam, Caffarella, & Baumgartner, 2007); skills are more likely to be learned in context (Lave & Wenger, 1991); contextualized learning is more likely to transfer to other situations (Perin, 2011); and students will be challenged to practice connected knowing and move beyond procedural knowing (Belenky et al., 1986).

In blended Ed.D. programs that offer applied capstone formats, students are encouraged to choose a setting that is free from a faculty member's investment and, in general, is not tied to the geographic location of a university. While they may or may not be collaborating directly with students with whom they have interacted in courses, they are sharing and studying similar issues and becoming aware of the different ways in which issues are addressed across socioculturally and geographically diverse sites.

Instead of spending extensive time in the field and then sorting through data, the student spends extensive time in project development and sorting through contending theories and research findings to apply them to the problem. Hochbein and Perry (2013) identified three skill sets needed to solve problems of practice: deciphering, debating, and designing. Students need to decipher existing literature and practice and be able to understand and comment on others' methods, findings, and conclusions. They must debate clearly and powerfully with stakeholders about the merits of existing and proposed policies and practices. Then they must be able to use the literature and the local knowledge gained from the debates to design effective approaches to local issues.

## Types of Applied Capstone Projects

We see the latter three activities outlined by Hochbein and Perry (2013) in each of the types of applied capstones we suggest or have used:

1. Curricular or program designs allow students to address local needs and to contribute to ongoing reform (e.g., first-year nursing program; integrating transfer students into a campus, district-wide offerings, support program at a community college for high-school dropouts, career exploration at a juvenile detention facility).
2. Formative or summative evaluations allow students to learn more from ongoing efforts to improve their schools or learning settings and collaborate more effectively with professional peers (e.g., of faculty development programs, community arts initiatives, charter or magnet schools).
3. Strategic plans can help students understand the nuanced effort to anticipate and plan for the future while being aware of local systemic challenges and engagement of stakeholders (e.g., school improvement plans, plans for breaking up a large school into smaller schools, plans for merging

two school districts, plans for merging colleges or programs in university settings).

4. Policy analyses and/or designs can encourage students to question their assumptions and engage in dialogue with policymakers (e.g., analysis of local policy on half-day kindergarten and proposal for full-day, analysis of college grading policy and proposal for narrative evaluations).

At the conclusion of the applied capstone project, we propose that students engage in deep reflection as an important aspect and skill. Students must reflect upon their personal and professional growth, their leadership, and on how they will continue to implement and evaluate change.

## The Value of an Applied Capstone Project Set at a Student's Worksite

It is generally preferred—and often required—that research for traditional doctoral capstones be undertaken at a site in which the student has no stake. For several reasons, we recommend that Ed.D. capstone research take place at the students' worksites and address a problem there. First, their worksites are the places about which students are concerned, often in terms of social equity issues—whether the problem they have identified is a lack of veterans' services and support or inadequate respect for diversity in elementary school classrooms. Indeed, these very concerns and passions often contributed to their reasons for pursuing a doctorate to begin with. Furthermore, the vast majority of our students plan to stay at sites and in communities that they aim to improve as a result of having doctoral authority—how much more sensible to empower them to contribute to social justice during their capstones!

Another reason for encouraging—if not requiring—local research sites is that students already have a deep practical knowledge of sites that, through the program, can be enriched with scholarly knowledge. The act of recognizing and dealing with one's own biases becomes more salient when studying one's own site. However, practitioner-learners should master this competence during their doctoral programs.

## Challenges to Hybrid Programs Offering Applied Capstone Projects

We are aware that the benefits we have reviewed of an online, applied capstone project may diminish if there are more changes in the student population of Ed.D. programs. We are familiar with the challenges of training largely part-time faculty members who have experienced only conventional capstones as students and as doctoral committee members. We are also aware that faculty members typically cannot do site visits, and hence students may lack more nuanced supervision of their capstone project. This problem could be ameliorated by adding another local instructor who could provide feedback to the faculty committee.

Student retention is a problem for all doctoral programs, and retention in hybrid programs seems to us to be more challenging. Hybrid programs should make program expectations clear so that new students can determine if their life priorities allow for the addition of at least 20 hours a week of study. They will need to manage the difficulties of the final capstone production stages, which are likely the same in hybrid and brick-and-mortar institutions. Perhaps retention would increase if an applied capstone project were introduced earlier, giving students more motivation, more engagement, and a clearer sense of the product. Courses in an applied capstone program could include exercises and assignments tailor-made to build the skills that might be used in a capstone.

## CONCLUSION

Working in hybrid programs that function largely online has provided us with an opportunity to experience a variety of doctoral pedagogies and applied capstones. We have also had a chance to work with a diverse group of students who have been traditionally underserved by higher education programs—local leaders seeking to make a deeper and richer contribution to ameliorating injustice in their own communities. Although our ideas are grounded in the hybrid Ed.D. model, we recognize that many of the features of these programs are shared with brick-and-mortar ones. Therefore, we suggest that all Ed.D. programs—online, hybrid, or brick-and-mortar—can benefit from the understandings we have presented here.

Our intention is that this chapter, in chorus with such prominent initiatives as the Carnegie Project on the Education Doctorate, will advance the dialogue about the Ed.D.'s purpose, shape, and potential. More specifically, we seek to foster change in the larger educational doctorate community's tendency to question the value of an applied capstone. We seek to strengthen the case for an applied capstone for pedagogical, practical, and theoretical reasons that demonstrate its fit with the ambitions of all Ed.D. programs. Finally, we thank the institutions in which we have taught for their role in shaping our vision, and—perhaps even more so—the students whom we have taught for leading us to that conclusion.

## REFERENCES

Belenky, M.F., Clinchy, B.M., Goldberger, N.R., & Tarule, J.M. (1986). *Women's ways of knowing: The development of self, voice, and mind.* New York: Basic Books.

Hochbein, C., & Perry, J.A. (2013). The role of research in the professional doctorate. *Planning and Changing, 44*(3/4), 181–194.

Kegan, R. (1984). *In over our heads: The mental demands of modern life.* Cambridge, MA: Harvard University Press.

Lave, J., & Wenger, E. (1991). *Situated learning: Legitimate peripheral participation.* Cambridge: Cambridge University Press.

Lawrence-Lightfoot, S., & Davis. J.H. (2002). *The art and science of portraiture.* San Francisco, CA: Jossey-Bass.

Means, B., Toyama, Y., Murphy, R., Bakia, M., & Jones, K. (2009). *Evaluation of evidence-based practices in online learning: A meta-analysis and review of online learning studies.* Washington, DC: U.S. Department of Education.

Merriam, S.B., Caffarella, R.S., & Baumgartner, L.M. (2007). *Learning in adulthood: A comprehensive guide.* Hoboken, NJ: Wiley.

Perin, D. (2011). Facilitating student learning through contextualization: A review of evidence. *Community College Review, 39*(3), 268–295. doi:10.1177/0091552111416227

Philips, C.R. (2008, April). *In students' voices: Perceptions of the first year in Utopia University's Ph.D. program.* Paper presented at the annual meeting of the American Educational Research Association, San Diego, CA.

# CHAPTER FIVE

# Reforming Practitioner- Based Ed.D. Programs

## Access, Diversity, and Impact

*Stephanie J. Jones*

## INTRODUCTION

Texas Tech University has identified an institutional priority of increasing its student enrollment to 40,000 by the year 2020 (Texas Tech University, 2010). In order to achieve this goal, the university is relying on distance learning. This case study focuses on the transition of the education doctorate (Ed.D.) in higher education administration at Texas Tech University (TTU) to a robust online Ed.D. program based on the working principles of the Carnegie Project on the Education Doctorate (CPED).

The higher education program at Texas Tech University is located in the College of Education and is a standalone program. The program currently offers an on-site master's degree in higher education, an on-site Ph.D. in higher education research, an on-site Ed.D. in higher education administration (which is being phased out), and a robust online Ed.D. in higher education administration. The majority of the program's students (60%) are enrolled in the online Ed.D. There are plans to implement an online master's degree over the next year. This chapter includes an overview of the higher education program, a discussion of the reform of the online Ed.D., the program's relationship to the CPED, and a discussion of the importance of collaborative partnerships in practice-based doctorates. It concludes with a discussion of the positive outcomes of the reformed online Ed.D. in attracting a diversified student population to the program.

## OVERVIEW OF THE HIGHER EDUCATION PROGRAM

The mission of the higher education program is to provide its students—who are predominantly employed as higher education professionals—with the skills to reform higher education organizations and to be change agents who have the skills and abilities to (1) improve student learning; (2) provide leadership that focuses on how evaluation and assessment inform practice; and (3) recognize, lead, and influence collaborative efforts among the members of the higher education community.

Prior to 2012, all doctoral degrees in the program were 66 hours beyond the master's degree. A comparison of the two doctoral degrees offered by the program— the Ed.D. and the Ph.D.—would reveal that the Ph.D. had a 12-hour research core and the Ed.D. had a 9-hour research core plus an internship. As with many programs that offer both the Ed.D. and Ph.D., there were limited curricular differences between the degrees. Prior to the implementation of the online Ed.D., the majority of students who sought a doctorate in higher education applied to the Ph.D. program, even though their career goal appeared to be higher education administration.

Conversations with these potential students seemed to indicate that their perceptions of the Ed.D. versus Ph.D. had been derived from talking to those who held the Ph.D. Potential students' perception of the Ed.D. was that it was an inferior degree that would not enable them to advance in a university or obtain a position as an executive leader in any type of higher education institution. As noted by Shulman, Golde, Conklin Bueschel, and Garabedian (2006), this is similar to the dilemma faced at many institutions in that there appears to be the perception that the Ed.D. is simply a "low-end Ph.D." (p. 25). This perception on the part of potential students and of those who were mentoring these individuals was a concern to the program faculty, two of whom held Ed.D.s and who were previously college administrators. It was apparent that the conversations occurring in the local context about the value of an Ed.D. were inaccurate, and it was important to the faculty to begin to correct these inaccuracies. The program established the goals of (1) making clear distinctions between its Ed.D. and Ph.D. degrees, (2) clearly articulating the differences to potential students and external constituents, and (3) admitting students into the doctoral program that best prepared them for their stated career aspirations.

At the time the discussion was taking place among the program faculty about establishing distinct differences between the two doctoral degrees, an online Ed.D. in higher education administration to support the needs of the State of Texas for qualified higher education administrators was in the final stages of implementation. The faculty recognized that an online-delivered Ed.D. could provide an opportunity for the program to attract a more diversified student population. In addition, it could provide greater flexibility for current higher education professionals who wanted or needed to secure their doctoral degree, thereby increasing access to advanced graduate-level education (Li & Irby, 2008) for those who could not attend on-site programs because of geographical location, employment barriers, and/or family responsibilities (Freddolino, Blaschke, & Rypkema, 2009; Saleh, 2012).

## REFORM OF THE EDUCATION DOCTORATE IN HIGHER EDUCATION ADMINISTRATION

In its original state in the spring of 2011, the curriculum for the online Ed.D. was the equivalent of that of the existing on-site Ed.D. It was recognized that an online Ed.D. could provide the program the opportunity to recruit from a wider geographical radius, but, most important, it could provide access and flexibility to those desiring to attain a terminal degree in higher education. Though the primary purpose of delivering the degree online was to serve the needs of the State of Texas, it was recognized that there were limited barriers to serving these needs across the United States, as long as TTU had the state's authorization to do so.

### Carnegie Project on the Education Doctorate (CPED)

In the fall of 2011, at the same time that the program was implementing its new online Ed.D., TTU's College of Education was invited to join the second wave of the Carnegie Project on the Education Doctorate (CPED). Perry (2012) states that CPED's goal is to help in the redesign of the Ed.D. to "make it the highest-quality degree for the advanced preparation of school practitioners and clinical faculty, academic leaders, and professional staff for the nation's schools and colleges and the organizations that support them" (p. 42). The CPED member institutions continuously engage in discourse and research about the education doctorate, specifically how to define it and reclaim its uniqueness (Aiken & Gerstl-Pepin, 2013).

The opportunity to join CPED provided a significant impetus for the program to take a second look at its relatively new online doctoral degree to see if it actually met the needs of higher education institutions, as well as to spend time determining how the Ed.D. could be further distinguished from the Ph.D. CPED describes six working principles that frame the practice-based doctorate. These principles state that the doctorate

1. is framed around questions of equity, ethics, and social justice to bring about solutions to complex problems of practice;

2. prepares leaders who can construct and apply knowledge to make a positive difference in the lives of individuals, families, organizations, and communities;

3. provides opportunities for candidates to develop and demonstrate collaboration and communication skills to work with diverse communities and to build partnerships;

4. provides field-based opportunities to analyze problems of practice and use multiple frames to develop meaningful solutions;

5. is grounded in and develops a professional knowledge base that integrates both practical and research knowledge and that links theory with systemic and systematic inquiry; and

6. emphasizes the generation, transformation, and use of professional knowledge and practice. (Carnegie Project on the Education Doctorate, n.d., para. 6)

In the fall of 2011, a representative of the program attended the CPED convening as a new second-wave member. At this time, the first cohort of online Ed.D. students was in its second semester. The CPED convening proved to be immediately beneficial to the program. We quickly saw that our efforts in delivering a practice-based online Ed.D. were not innovative enough to be competitive at the national level, based on the program's current design. Further, it was clear that there were many esteemed institutions that had redesigned their Ed.D.s to be practice oriented and had already seen success with their reformed education doctorates.

The concept that initially caught our attention was the focus of CPED member institutions on incorporating authentic problems of practice into their curriculum, which was what the higher education program had attempted to do as it worked to distinguish its Ed.D. from its Ph.D. It became immediately obvious that we had not clearly understood how to do this. The opportunity to witness examples of authentic, problem-based projects integrated into the curriculum and spread throughout course offerings became essential to our efforts to reform our Ed.D.

Having access to those involved in the first wave of CPED and to be involved in their transparent discussions of how they were leading their programs and colleges through the reform of their education doctorate provided an extensive knowledge base and wealth of resources for us. This enabled the program to establish a clear definition of the Ed.D. that could be used as a foundational basis for the development of the reformed Ed.D. The refined definition of the Ed.D. currently used by the program was developed by CPED members and is the practice-based statement that the "doctorate in education prepares educators for the application of appropriate and specific practices, the generation of new knowledge and for the stewardship of the profession" (Carnegie Project on the Education Doctorate, 2013, p. 1).

Being a part of the CPED convening and seeing how first-wave members were redesigning the Ed.D. to be delivered in an accelerated format, as well as how curriculum was focused around problems of practice within the field, accelerated our ability to reform the online Ed.D. We were able to establish credibility with TTU's College of Education and its administration by showcasing what other peer institutions were already doing and how they had redefined their education doctorates. In addition, we were able to more clearly distinguish between the purposes of the Ed.D. and the Ph.D. and articulate how they are different from one another. In addition, it was perceived that utilizing the working principles of CPED to frame the reformed online Ed.D. would help ensure a quality, rigorous online practice-based doctorate.

At the same time that the program became involved with CPED, the College of Education at TTU was also undergoing administrative transition. The incoming dean of the College of Education, Dr. Scott Ridley, arrived in the summer of 2011. Hailing from Arizona State and a wave-one member of CPED, Dean Ridley immediately began to establish and communicate his vision for the college. The message stated that Colleges of Education must reform themselves. If they are able to accomplish this, "they will establish their place in higher education and can be instrumental to the education of qualified professionals who can be change agents and influencers in many educational settings" (Dr. Scott Ridley, personal communication, August 22, 2011). The dean's message mirrors the sentiments of Shulman and colleagues (2006), who stated that the problems facing Colleges of Education are "chronic and crippling...schools of education risk becoming increasingly impotent in carrying out their primary mission—the advancement of knowledge and the preparation of quality practitioners" (p. 25), unless they face their problems and reform.

The dean is an avid supporter of the program's involvement in CPED. The college's reform initiatives align well with the CPED framework for the reform of the Ed.D. This reform agenda, in partnership with CPED members who are strong allies, was instrumental in the success that the program has had in applying the CPED working principles to an online Ed.D. Since the College's environment was already changing, the program was able to openly discuss the CPED principles with colleagues, which helped many to think differently about the future of the Ed.D. and how it could better serve the needs of education reform.

## Reformed Online Education Doctorate

As mentioned previously, the Ed.D. in higher education at TTU had been perceived as an inferior degree to the Ph.D. by many at the university and by potential students who inquired about the degrees. Comments identifying the Ed.D.

as a "Ph.D. lite" or a "low-end Ph.D." are common in the literature, as well as in and around TTU. In addition, as noted by Shulman and fellow researchers (2006), "the purposes of preparing scholars and practitioners are confused; as a result, neither is done well" (p. 26). The situation was no different in this program. Many students within the program prior to the spring 2011 semester were employees of the university. TTU is categorized as a research university (high research activity) by the Carnegie Classification of Higher Education Institutions (Carnegie Classification of Higher Education Institutions, n.d.) and has also been identified as an emerging research university within the State of Texas. The issue that this brings to light is that most students who want to pursue a Ph.D. at TTU are working full time and have no desire to be researchers or professors, but they feel that they must attain a Ph.D. to be promoted in an emerging research university.

These students state that their goal is to advance in higher education administrative careers. These motivations are in line with a replication study conducted by Storey and Richard (2013), in which enrolled students in an Ed.D. program in the United States noted their interest in pursuing a structured, part-time program that would lead to career advancement. This creates a dilemma, since potential students aspire to a practitioner-based career but perceive that they must have a Ph.D. to secure it. A challenge faced by the program was how to educate potential students on the value of the Ed.D. and the Ph.D. without undermining the value of either.

The CPED framework for the Ed.D. focuses on developing scholarly practitioners, a need that is cited throughout the research for higher education leadership (Perry, 2012; Shulman et al., 2006). Being part of a national conversation with like-minded individuals at the first convening of CPED enabled the program to redefine its discussions with potential students about the Ed.D., as well as to provide the faculty with information to help it educate potential students and others at the university that a national conversation was taking place about the value of the Ed.D.

In the fall of 2013, the reformed Ed.D. was implemented. It is competency based, and its trademark outcome is this:

> It is designed to develop scholarly practitioners that understand the importance of equity and social justice. Graduates of the program are equipped to apply theories and practical research as tools to name, frame, and solve problems of practice, using empirical evidence to evaluate impact and develop innovative solutions for colleges and universities. (*Higher Education*, n.d., p. 1)

The reformed Ed.D. is structured as a 3-year online program targeted toward the higher education professional. It is a 60-hour degree program (above the master's). The program has two foci: (1) community college administration, and (2) 4-year college/university administration. The signature pedagogy for the program is embedded fieldwork.

Students are admitted in cohorts, once a year in the fall semester. The cohort model was chosen because of its ability to bring together the experiences and expertise of students who work in multifaceted higher education roles into a collaborative doctoral learning environment (Aiken & Gerstl-Pepin, 2013, p. 172). Students complete 21 credit hours per year, 6 in the fall term, 6 in the spring term, and 9 across the summer. Students are required to attend 1 week of professional development each Summer I term for the 3 years of the program at the home campus of Texas Tech University in Lubbock. Residency is met by completing 21 hours in an academic year. In addition, students are required to pass qualifying examinations and produce individual dissertations to attain the doctorate.

The curriculum for the program is sequenced in three phases: (1) Phase 1 is knowledge level; (2) Phase 2 is guided practice; and (3) is authentic practice. All Phase 2 and Phase 3 courses utilize embedded fieldwork projects to ensure that students obtain the skills, knowledge, and competencies they need to become scholarly practitioners. Service learning is also incorporated into appropriate courses. As all students enrolled in the program work in professional positions in higher education, their institutions serve as their laboratories of practice. All coursework is designed to take advantage of students' access to authentic problems in practice at their institutions. Most courses have problems-in-practice components and require application of learning outcomes of the course in guided or authentic settings. Inquiry courses are instrumental in ensuring that students have these skills. The program requires 12 hours of inquiry courses, with a specific focus on assessment and evaluation.

What sets this program apart from others is that students are required to actually conduct an evaluation and assessment they have designed in an authentic academic setting (within their scope of influence at their institution), implement a solution based on the evaluation and assessment, and use data to measure its impact. All students are required to complete a scholarly practitioner-based dissertation, working in partnership with a higher education institution that has an identified problem-in-practice issue that needs to be resolved.

Milestones for the program are assessed in each of the three phases: knowledge level, guided practice, and authentic practice. In order to progress through the program, students must demonstrate skills and competencies throughout all phases. They are assessed at the end of each semester to determine if remediation is needed to ensure that skills and knowledge are obtained. All students are evaluated once a year through a formal program evaluation process. Students who are deemed to be in need of remediation—mainly in writing and critical thinking—are put on an academic plan designed to help them improve their skills and competencies in needed areas.

## IMPORTANCE OF COLLABORATIVE PARTNERSHIPS
## IN PRACTICE-BASED DOCTORATES

The success of the TTU online Ed.D. in higher education administration is due in part to its relationship with collaborative partners who are willing to take the time and make the effort to work with its students. CPED identifies these individuals as *critical friends*. Costa and Kallick (1993) identify *critical friends* as those who take "the time to fully understand the context of the work presented and the outcomes that the person or group is working toward" (p. 50). Others have noted that *critical friends* can help organizations make better decisions by challenging expectations and shaping outcomes (Brighouse & Woods, 1999; McDonald, 1989; Stoll & Thomas, 1996; all as cited in Swaffield, 2004). These statements describe the relationships of these critical collaborative partners to this program.

We have enjoyed many successes in collaborating with our partners. Currently, the majority of the partners are presidents of community colleges in Texas. These individuals consistently praise the higher education program for the work it is doing to make the doctoral experience meaningful and useful—at a time when doctoral programs are under scrutiny by many external constituents. These partners recognize the role that doctoral programs will play in providing a pool of qualified leaders to hire at their institutions in the future.

In addition to our partners from higher education institutions, the students enrolled in the online Ed.D. are also valuable collaborative partners. These students have been instrumental in the reform of the online Ed.D. Students who are professionals in the fields in which they study bring both a practitioner's and a student's perspective to the program. Critical dialogues and questions among the program faculty and students have enabled the program to transform the Ed.D. to a degree that is more innovative and impactful than could have been possible without the students' input.

Working with collaborative partners in the reform of the Ed.D. has been beneficial to the higher education program and has enabled it to develop an online Ed.D. that will have a direct impact on the practice of higher education. The partners who are current higher education leaders provide a practitioner perspective to the curriculum that would not have been possible if only the faculty within the program had determined what was needed. The ability to engage with a group of higher education practitioners about what skills and competencies are needed for the job has been extremely beneficial on two fronts. First, it ensures that the program faculty, in developing the curriculum for the program, is aware of the skills and competencies that are needed in today's higher education institutions. Second, the long-term benefits of the relationships that have developed among the higher education program, the College of Education, Texas Tech University, and our partners in other higher education institutions cannot be measured.

## CONCLUSION

The higher education program at TTU has successfully reformed its online Ed.D. We have seen many beneficial outcomes in the short time that the online program has been operating. It is producing scholarly practitioners who can impact higher education practice. It has developed significant relationships across the State of Texas and the United States with collaborative partners and graduates who not only invest their time and expertise in the program and its curriculum but who also have a vested interest in developing quality higher education administrators.

The reform outcome that has had the most impact on the program—indeed, one that it takes great pride in—is that offering a quality and practitioner-based online Ed.D. has enabled the program to attract a more diversified student population. As noted previously, the student population in the higher education program is largely made up of working professionals in higher education organizations, with 100% of Ed.D. students working full time and attending school part time. This is typical of many Ed.D. programs.

Prior to the spring of 2011, most of the doctoral students in the higher education program were from Lubbock, Texas, or the surrounding region, and a large number of them were employed at TTU in various administrative and faculty positions. The goal of most of the students in the program was and continues to be to complete their doctorates so that they can advance in their careers as higher education administrators. When the online Ed.D. was implemented in spring 2011, the student population quickly became diversified. It showed not only significant increases in students of color but also in areas of expertise and in the types of institutions represented through the employment of the students. This diversification has made the online Ed.D. in higher education program at Texas Tech University one that serves the needs of access and diversity in higher education and that provides a culturally rich environment in which our doctoral students can learn.

## REFERENCES

Aiken, J.A., & Gerstl-Pepin, C. (2013). Envisioning the Ed.D. and Ph.D. as a partnership for change. *Planning and Changing, 44*(3/4), 162–180.

Carnegie Classification of Higher Education Institutions. (n.d.). *Texas Tech University*. Retrieved from http://classifications.carnegiefoundation.org/lookup_listings/view_institution.php?unit_id=229115&start_page=institution.php&clq=%7B%22first_letter%22%3A%22T%22%7D

Carnegie Project on the Education Doctorate. (2013). *Design concept definitions*. Retrieved from http://cpedinitiative.org/design-concept-definitions

Carnegie Project on the Education Doctorate. (n.d.). *Education doctorate and working principles*. Retrieved from http://cpedinitiative.org/working-principles-professional-practice-doctorate-education

Costa, A.L., & Kallick, B. (1993). Through the lens of a critical friend. *Educational Leadership, 51*(2), 49–51.

Freddolino, P., Blaschke, C., & Rypkema, S. (2009). Increasing access to graduate education: A blended MSW program. *Journal of the Research Center for Educational Technology, 5*(2), 27–50.

*Higher Education.* (n.d.). College of Education, Texas Tech University. Retrieved from http://cms. educ.ttu.edu/academic-programs/psychology-and-leadership/higher-education/default

Li, C., & Irby, B. (2008). An overview of online education: Attractiveness, benefits, challenges, concerns, and recommendations. *College Student Journal, 42*(2), 449–458.

Perry, J.A. (2012, September). To Ed.D. or not to Ed.D.? *Phi Delta Kappan, 94*(1), 41–44.

Saleh, A. (2012). A closer look at online graduate degree programs in public institutions. *Review of Higher Education and Self-Learning, 5*(16), 155–163.

Shulman, L.S., Golde, C., Conklin Bueschel, A., & Garabedian, K. (2006). Reclaiming education's doctorates: A critique and a proposal. *Educational Researcher, 35*(3), 25–32.

Storey, V.A., & Richard, B.M. (2013, April). *Why do students choose a professional doctorate in education: A comparison of motivations, perceptions, and outcomes between the U.S. and the U.K.* Paper presented at the 2013 International Conference on Doctoral Education, Orlando, FL.

Swaffield, S. (2004). Critical friends: Supporting leadership, improved learning. *Improving Schools, 7*(3), 267–278.

Texas Tech University. (2010). *2010–2020 Strategic plan.* Retrieved from http://www.ttu.edu/ stratplan/docs/Making-It-Possible-Strategic-Plan-2010-Texas-Tech-9–21–10pdf.pdf

# CHAPTER SIX

# A Mixed Methods Research Project

## Combining Research, Evaluation, and Leadership Skills in Ed.D. Programs

*Thomas W. Christ*

## INTRODUCTION

Cohort-based doctoral degrees are now common, and most require one to three research courses. The New Doctoral Leadership Program (NDLP) at the University of Bridgeport in Connecticut requires seven mixed, action, qualitative, and quantitative research seminars; 18 credits of program evaluation, policy analysis, and grant writing; and 18 credits of education leadership coursework. Overarching research question: Does the NDLP meet admitted students' needs?

From a critical stance, cohort-based online Ed.D. programs are designed to save institutions money rather than improve necessary skills. An iterative mixed methods research design was used to determine whether or not the NDLP meets the needs of a highly competitive K–12 and postsecondary job market. Seminar projects, course and faculty evaluations, comprehensive examinations, and dissertations were analyzed to determine the strengths and challenges inherent in the Ed.D. Education Leadership program at the University of Bridgeport. The findings presented in this chapter include methodological strategies and lessons learned from the 17 most-offered seminars over the past 3 years. Strategies that students found to be most helpful, as well as lessons learned from faculty, will be presented along with evidence concerning the challenges associated with a program that requires 62 semester credits with few electives.

## PURPOSE, OBJECTIVES AND RESEARCH QUESTION

Cohort-based doctoral degrees in education are now common, and many are less rigorous in terms of research requirements than those previously offered. For example, the number of research courses at participating colleges in the Carnegie Project on the Education Doctorate demonstrates that a practitioner orientation rather than research and evaluation skills are emphasized, despite the applicability of those skills in the highly competitive contemporary job market.

While most cohort-based education doctorates require between one and three research and evaluation courses, the New Doctoral Leadership Program (NDLP) at the University of Bridgeport requires seven three-credit seminars specific to mixed, action, qualitative, and quantitative research; three six-credit seminars that support program evaluation, policy analysis, and grant writing; three six-credit seminars oriented toward educational leadership theories and praxis; and two six-credit seminars whose focus is on policy, law, and grant writing and procurement.

The purpose of expanding the required number of seminars in the program is the expectation of increased employability for graduates. This chapter brings to the forefront the argument that many students who enter education-oriented doctoral programs are already in administrative or leadership positions and have years of practical experience. Thus, they are well equipped to handle administrative duties but lack the policy, research, and evaluation skills that are increasingly in demand.

### (1) Overarching Research Questions

(1) What teaching strategies, activities, and curricula are deemed to be most effective in the NDLP at helping students to complete their comprehensive examination questions, their pilot research study, and their dissertation?
(2) Does the NDLP, which emphasizes research, policy, and leadership skills, meet the needs of admitted students?

### (2) Perspectives and Theoretical Framework

Cohort-based doctoral programs in education leadership are now offered and promoted by a number of institutions seeking to increase enrollment and funding (Auerbach, 2011; Young, 2006). Murphy (2007) went so far as to state that theory-oriented scholars, in contrast to practitioners, are impractical, and he views the dissertation process as a "flagrant example of privileging the university culture over the realities of practice" (p. 584). Others stipulate that professional practice dissertations prominent in Ed.D. programs use theory to solve problems, while

Ph.D. dissertations generate and test theory. The emphasis placed by the CPED on promoting a "problem of practice" dissertation may be applicable for some but not all.

The NDLP program requires that students choose a topic that is meaningful and relevant, one that demonstrates competency in research methodology. Most students choose to conduct action, quasi-experimental, or mixed methods research that is practical in application, while others conduct exploratory research using a grounded theoretical approach to analyze qualitative data or choose to conduct a program evaluation. Regardless of the topic and methodology that students choose, the dissertation is driven by the problem the students identify, the research questions they create, and the resources that they have available. In order for students to choose an applicable research design appropriate to their interests, they need a high level of competency in multiple research approaches. This was one of the reasons for requiring students in the NDLP to take numerous research and evaluation courses so they can be both "applied researchers who conduct research to inform practice" and "practitioner-scholars who utilize research to address problems of practice" (Aiken & Gerstl-Pepin, 2013, p. 163).

The debate over the amount of research preparation that is necessary in Ed.D. programs is nothing new. Freeman first published his opinion about the issue when discussing higher education degrees, and 80 years later, the debate continues in a series of articles in *Planning and Changing*, an education leadership policy journal. Hochbein and Perry (2013) emphasize the necessity of teaching multiple research approaches in professional doctorates, while Andrews and Grogen (2005) indicate that the extensive research requirements in education doctoral programs should be questioned, as most graduates only need the skills to be consumers of research. Hochbein and Perry state:

> To develop the skills for scholarly practitioners to address complex problems of practice, Ed.D. programs require mandatory research courses that extend beyond an introductory level. The field of education consists of complex problems that require sophisticated methodological and analytical solutions (Berliner, 2002). Sufficient time dedicated to research coursework provides students the opportunity to develop the sophistication necessary to decipher articles, debate challenges and design solutions. (2013, p. 190)

Aiken and Gerstl-Pepin (2013) ask the pertinent question of how to make "doctoral programs more relevant for those students seeking to become professional practitioner-scholars while supporting those who choose to serve as applied researchers" (p. 65). NDLP was designed to prepare students to become exceptional practitioners and scholars by including extensive research, evaluation, and policy-related courses in the research strand while strengthening the leadership strand by emphasizing organization theories, policy analysis, and grant-writing skills in the leadership strand of the program. Through a reduction in the number of electives, as well as a minimizing of the number of credits granted for dissertation preparation, the research and leadership strands were strengthened considerably over those of the previous program.

An examination of numerous education leadership doctoral programs created in the past decade indicates that most have minimal coursework required to prepare the researcher or the leader-practitioner well. Further threatening the strength of the leadership doctorate is the movement toward hybrid or Internet-based, 3-year cohort programs that have been added to students' options. From a critical theoretical standpoint (Christ, 2014), this format is designed to save institutions money rather than improve the skills of students. For example, California State University Ed.D. programs are considering "esummaries" of dissertations geared toward educators at the research site, while Mayer, LeChasseur, Donaldson, and Cobb (2013) speak of "individual capstone projects" based on a "portfolio of term papers written in four practica that applies major theoretical frameworks to a problem of practice" (p. 224) to take the place of the dissertation.

This chapter discusses how one of the first cohort-based Education Leadership doctoral programs in the nation was completely redesigned to include advanced research, evaluation, and administration skills that help to prepare graduates for numerous roles in today's competitive job market. The NDLP has purposely moved away from the current trend of institutions offering a fast-paced, cohort-based, practitioner-oriented degree, as it is evident that the students entering the program need a much higher level of skills to meet the demands of their administrative positions.

Results of this longitudinal study highlight how research and practitioner-based coursework can be created, evaluated, and combined to meet the needs of a diverse population of doctoral students. Empirical evidence from ten semesters of Introductory Research, Advanced Mixed Methods, and Action Research courses offered over a 3-year period were compiled, along with evidence from the 30 credits of leadership coursework, pilot projects, comprehensive examinations, and dissertations, to highlight the strengths and challenges of recreating a program designed to strengthen research, evaluation, and leadership skills for students who typically have administrative positions.

This chapter argues that the working principles related to research as specified in the Carnegie Project simply do not fit the current job market. Reviewing the research and evaluation requirements in most of the programs demonstrates that research takes a back seat to leadership and administrative skills that most of the students already possess. As of 2014, the CPED program has 87 participating schools that have agreed to frame their programs using six constructs: (1) equity, ethics, and social justice; (2) leadership knowledge; (3) collaboration and communication skills; (4) field-based opportunities; (5) practical applications of research knowledge and theory; and (6) generation, transformation, and use of professional knowledge and practice.

A review of required coursework in all of the CPED programs revealed that none required mixed methods, a few required action research, some recommended quantitative and qualitative methodologies, and many required only one formal three-credit research seminar. Arguments for practitioner-oriented degrees as promoted by the Carnegie Project were based on the premise that research-oriented programs often fail to provide the necessary skills for leaders in K–12 and higher education. Shulman, Golde, Conklin Bueschel, and Garabedian (2006) argued that it was time to reclaim the Ed.D. and redesign it for practitioners.

Although these goals were applicable for practitioner-based degrees envisioned at the turn of this century, the current competitive job market and stringent policies—including the Common Core State Standards, No Child Left Behind, and the Smarter Balance Assessment Consortium—requires that "practitioner-researchers" have much more than rudimentary practitioner-oriented skills. Expertise in multiple research methodologies, program evaluation, policy analysis, and grant writing increases the likelihood of maintaining gainful employment. Research skills are more relevant than ever to administrators, curricular experts, and program leaders due to politically driven accountability measures and policies that constrain the PK–20 public education system (Christ, 2013).

## (3) Methodology

An "iterative action oriented mixed methods research design" (Christ, 2010, p. 649) was used to create and improve the 17 new seminars that keep pace with the demands of K–12 education reforms and a highly competitive postsecondary job market. In essence, the NDLP is an intervention that follows a 4-year collaborative process of planning, acting, developing, and reflecting (Bradbury, 2007; Greenwood & Levin, 2001).

The purpose of creating 17 new seminars was to strengthen the program so that it is better matched to the students' needs. Development of the research strand in the NDLP began almost a decade ago, long before the project was implemented at the University of Bridgeport, with three courses developed to supplement traditional quantitative research. Introductory Research, Qualitative Research, and Mixed Methods Research were introduced in 2006 and have been continually refined as a result of being taught over a dozen times each. Action Research was more recently added to the sequence as a way for students to learn about the methodology and to pilot their dissertation proposals. In essence, the NDLP is an action research project with all seminars designed, implemented, evaluated, and improved following cycles of planning, acting, developing, and reflecting on curricula, strategies, and products.

Each time a course is taught, it is one action research cycle used to improve through reflection each of the 17 seminars required. Each semester the feedback from students concerning course content and curricula, faculty observations, and statistically analyzed anonymous course and faculty evaluations is used for purposeful and reflective modifications to the course content and teaching strategies. All of the research courses were designed with two goals in mind: to teach a balanced approach to research skills and to support students as they plan and write their dissertations.

## DATA SOURCES, EVIDENCE, OBJECTS, AND MATERIALS

Six steps were used to design, implement, and improve the program:

### (1) Topic Identification

An inclusive and aligned program was needed that emphasized research, evaluation, policy, and administrative skill. Faculty from the School of Education, Engineering, Business, and International Studies met in 2011 to consider applicable coursework for the education leadership doctorate.

### (2) The Research Plan

Seventeen new courses were created that included a more rigorous comprehensive examination and dissertation proposal process (requiring that the dissertation methodology be piloted) was proposed and approved by the university's deans and provost in 2012. Over the past nine semesters, all courses in the doctoral program sequence have been taught—most of them repeatedly, thus allowing for improvements to the curricula over time.

### (3) Data Collection and Analysis

Course and faculty evaluations, comprehensive examinations, dissertation proposals, pilot projects, and completed dissertations have now been analyzed to determine strengths and challenges associated with the program.

### (4) Reflection for Improvements

A review each semester of courses and projects using rubrics, analysis of student course evaluations, ratings of comprehensive examinations, and success of pilot projects, proposals, and dissertations allows for applicable changes.

## (5) Program Modifications

Improvements to course curricula, teaching strategies, and procedures are continuous. Each year, the Education Leadership Doctoral Handbook is updated, seminars are modified, and the progress of the students and their feedback to instructors is examined.

## (6) Dissemination to Stakeholders

Activities designed to share knowledge gained from the project include over a dozen conference presentations and journal articles promoting successful teaching strategies. This study demonstrates that teaching multiple mixed methods, action research, and program evaluation courses in sequence builds skills through activities.

From a longitudinal standpoint, reflecting on data to make ongoing improvements to the program, teaching pedagogy, and research, evaluation, and leadership seminars improves the program. Data from course and faculty evaluations, participant narrations, and products created by the students are continually used to make ongoing improvements to course curricula, program content, and teaching strategies. For example, data from more than two dozen introductory, qualitative, and advanced mixed methods research courses that have been taught were used to continually improve the content of the seminars. The process of using purposeful and reflective modifications to the courses based on the data from the classes each semester has resulted in improvements in the overall rigor of the research strand of the program. For a more detailed explanation of the process of creating and evaluating courses using an iterative mixed methods research design, see Christ's (2009) article in the *Journal of Mixed Methods Research* and his chapter about action research methodologies used to design research courses in the *Sage Handbook of Mixed Methods in Social & Behavioral Research* (2010).

## ED.D. PROGRAM CURRICULUM

The 17 seminars in the 62-credit doctoral program were designed with two goals in mind: (1) to teach a balanced approach of research, evaluation, and leadership skills and (2) to support students as they plan, write, and pilot their dissertations. The NDLP emphasizes that a balanced approach to learning multiple research methodologies, program evaluation and grant-writing skills, and practical application of organization leadership theories be continually developed throughout the program. The list of courses below provides an overview of how the program was redesigned to expand leadership, research, and the dissertation skills. The program requires a minimum of 4 years for completion, including 3 years of formal study and a minimum of 1 year to complete the dissertation.

During the first 2 years, students typically take one six-credit doctoral seminar and one three-credit research-evaluation course per semester. Students can take online-hybrid classes during the first year and two summers as part of the residency requirement in the program:

## (7) Education Leadership Strand

EDLD 801 Curricula Theory and Program Development (6 credits)

EDLD 804 Policy and Law (6 credits)

EDLD 805 Grant Writing and Procurement (6 credits)

EDLD 807 Organization Management (6 credits)

EDLD 808 Program Evaluation (6 credits)

## (8) Research and Evaluation Strand

EDLD 811 Intro to Research (3 credits)

EDLD 812 Quantitative Research (3 credits)

EDLD 814 Qualitative Research (3 credits)

EDLD 815 Mixed Methods (3 credits)

EDLD 816 Action Research Project (3 credits: repeatable up to 2 times)

## (9) Dissertation Preparation Strand

EDLD 813 Literature Review (3 credits: repeatable up to 2 times)

EDLD 845 Dissertation: Comprehensive Exam (3 credits)

EDLD 846 Dissertation: Proposal Defense (3 credits)

EDLD 850 Continuous Dissertation (0 credits)

## (10) Postsecondary Teaching Experience

EDLD 817 Postsecondary Teaching (3 credits: repeatable twice)

## SCHOLARLY SIGNIFICANCE/IMPLICATIONS

Students in the NDLP are introduced to several strategies specifically designed to improve how they consume and conduct research. Five are presented here to describe how they support knowledge acquisition and use.

## (1) Topic Definition

Students are taught to concurrently consider: (a) their topical interest, (b) the problem under investigation, and (c) the purpose of the research, for whom it is intended, and why it is important before formalizing a tentative overarching research question and choosing the most applicable methodology for the topic (Christ, 2007, 2009, 2010).

## (2) Worldview and Data Mixing

Discussing how research has multiple overlapping paradigms and numerous potential sources of data helps to dispel dialectic paradigmatic thinking and false conceptions that research is a linear process (Christ, 2013). Four fundamental beliefs that form the researcher's worldview are presented to help students determine how they fit into their research: (a) axiological beliefs about the nature of ethics, (b) ontological beliefs about the nature of reality, (c) epistemological beliefs about the nature of knowledge and the relationship between the knower and that which would be known, and (d) the methodological beliefs about the appropriate methods for a systematic investigation to yield warrantable assertions (Mertens, Bledsoe, Sullivan, & Wilson, 2010).

Considerable time is spent discussing, describing, and defending the researcher's worldview and his or her role in the research process, perspectives which underpin practitioner-oriented mixed and action research projects. Students formalize a table that defines their worldview and research topic in relation to how the data they propose to collect and analyze fit across a continuum of paradigms (postpositivism, pragmatism, constructivism, critical, hermeneutics, transformative) (Christ, 2013, 2014) that are placed into a matrix that helps organize the dissertation proposal process.

## (3) Methodological Maps

These are created by the students to visually display aspects of their research design. This helps students to consider how all the components of their design interact and helps to create a succinct document for potential dissertation committee members to view. Numerous methodological maps are presented from all types of research designs ranging from large-scale program evaluations to practitioner-oriented action research projects. One methodological map depicting a project involving the families of 50 firefighters who perished in the 09/11/01 tragedy (Christ & Christ, 2006) is presented as a scaffolding tool for students to view when creating their own map (see Figure 6.1).

(4)

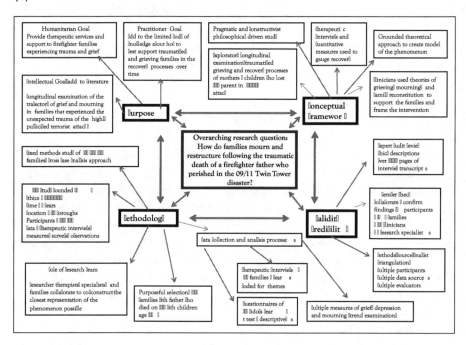

Figure 6.1. FDNY 09/11/01 family survivors: Exploratory longitudinal mixed methods analysis.

The methodological map, in combination with a heading system, is effective in helping students to see that research is reiterative and flexible, philosophy and methodology that falls upon bisecting continuums emphasized as a result of clearly defining the research problem, purpose, available resources, and whether the study is exploratory, explanatory, confirmatory, action oriented, transformative, or critical (Christ, 2013). The proposal outline first developed in 2007 continues to have merit with some modifications. Students now write their proposal using a heading system that includes the title, introduction, problem and purpose statement, background justification (literature), the role of theory, overarching and subsumed research questions, methodology statement and visual representation, procedures (role of researcher, bounding the case, qualitative and quantitative data collection, sampling, analysis, merging) and credibility/validity justification (cf. Christ, 2009).

## (5) Introduction to Research

Steps as outlined in the syllabi for introduction to research act as advanced organizers preparing students to think logically about necessary decisions when framing their final proposal. This strategy represented a major departure from the original education leadership doctoral program, which stipulated that students were not to develop a topic until the third year. Developing a researchable topic in the first year appears to help students develop the analytical skills that are necessary in a professional doctorate.

## (6) The Proposal Outline

This is designed to create personal relevance and acts as a strategy to teach students how to conceive and write each section of their research proposal. This strategy provides students with the necessary skills to understand and utilize the research components that are required for a multitude of mixed research designs. Another strategy is to thematically group students so they can share resources and at times assist each other with drafts, editing, and, in some cases, analysis and preparation of the results of their dissertations.

The heading system and questions act as a rubric for students to critique their own proposals as well as those of others in their triad. Each of the classes was treated as one cycle in the action research process, a single case study (Yin, 2009) linked to previous iterations in terms of data analysis and reflection. The researcher-teacher (Mertler, 2008) relied on multiple lenses and perspectives to view the student interactions and their work as evidence of understanding the research process.

Three-way feedback from teacher, student and peers allows for the combination of an emic and etic perspective, the researcher-teacher as an insider using interpretive validity (Maxwell, 2011, 2012). This happens while embracing a reflexive lens in which to view and understand the researcher-teacher's "place" in the courses (Christ & Elmetaher, 2012) and while interpreting various data sources that make up the iterations summarized and presented. Improvements to research, evaluation, policy and practitioner oriented seminars in the leadership doctoral program continue.

The sequence of activities is designed to improve the skill set of the new generation of researcher-practitioners. Specific strategies, course curricula, and the sequence of the program are being presented with a focus on what works well, while the researcher-teacher who is the director of the NDLP continues to work with the challenges faced in redesigning a doctoral program to meet the needs of an increasingly complex and competitive job market.

## REFERENCES

Aiken, J., & Gerstl-Pepin, C. (2013). Envisioning the Ed.D. and Ph.D. as a partnership for change. *Planning and Changing, 44*(3/4), 162–180.

Andrews, R., & Grogen, M. (2005). Form should follow function: Removing the Ed.D. from the Ph.D. straight jacket. *UCEA Review, 47*(2), 10–13.

Auerbach, S. (2011). "It's not just going to collect dust on a shelf." Faculty perceptions of the applied dissertation in the new California State University Ed.D. programs: Leadership education from within a feminist ethos. *Journal of Research on Leadership Education, 2*(6), 59–82.

Bradbury, H. (2007). Quality, consequences, and action ability: What action researchers offer the tradition of pragmatism. In R. Shanis et al. (Eds.), *Handbook of collaborative research*. Thousand Oaks, CA: Sage.

Christ, T. (2007). A recursive approach to mixed methods research in a longitudinal study of postsecondary education disability support services. *Journal of Mixed Methods Research, 1*(3), 226–241. doi:10.1177/1558689807301101

Christ, T. (2009). Designing, teaching and evaluating two complementary mixed methods research courses. *Journal of Mixed Methods Research, 3*(4), 292–325. doi:10.1177/1558689809341796

Christ, T. (2010). Teaching mixed methods and action research: Pedagogical, practical and evaluative considerations. In A. Tashakkori & C. Teddlie (Eds.), *The Sage handbook of mixed methods in social & behavioral research* (2nd ed.). Thousand Oaks, CA: Sage.

Christ, T. (2013). The worldview matrix as a tool when designing mixed methods research. *International Journal of Multiple Research Approaches, 7*(1), 86–94. doi: 10.5172/mra.2013.2458

Christ, T. (2014). Policy, scientific based research, and randomized controlled trials, the "gold" standard? Alternative paradigms and mixed methodologies. *Qualitative Inquiry, 20*(1), 72–80. doi: 10.1777/107800413508523

Christ, G., & Christ, T. (2006). Academic and behavioral reactions of children with disabilities to the loss of a firefighter parent: The world trade center attack 9/11/01. *Review of Disability Studies: An International Journal, 2*(3), 68–78.

Christ, T., & Elmetaher, H. (2012). Research teaching pedagogy: Lessons learned from an Arabic language intervention pilot study. *Research in the Schools, 19*(2), 62–74.

Greenwood D., & Levin, M. (2001). Pragmatic action research and the struggle to transform universities into learning communities. In P. Reason & H. Bradbury (Eds.), *Handbook of action research* (pp. 103–113). Thousand Oaks, CA: Sage.

Hochbein, C., & Perry, J. (2013). The role of research in the professional doctorate. *Planning and Changing, 44*(3/4), 162–180.

Maxwell, J. (2011). *A realist approach for qualitative research*. Thousand Oaks, CA: Sage.

Maxwell, J. (2012). *Qualitative research design: An interactive approach* (3rd ed.). Thousand Oaks, CA: Sage.

Mayer, A., LeChasseur, K., Donaldson, M., & Cobb, C. (2013). Organizational learning as a model for continuous transformation. *Planning and Changing, 44*(3/4), 221–236.

Mertens, D.M., Bledsoe, K.L., Sullivan, M., & Wilson, A. (2010). Utilization of mixed methods for transformative purposes. In A. Tashakkori & C. Teddlie (Eds.), *Handbook of mixed methods in social & behavioral research* (2nd ed., pp. 193–214). Thousand Oaks, CA: Sage.

Mertler, C. (2008). *Action research: Teachers as researchers in the classroom* (2nd ed.).Thousand Oaks, CA: Sage.

Murphy, J. (2007). Questioning the core of the university-based programs for preparing school leaders. *Phi Delta Kappan, 88*(8), 582–585.

Shulman, L.S., Golde, C., Conklin Bueschel, A., & Garabedian, K. (2006). Reclaiming education's doctorates: A critique and a proposal. *Educational Researcher, 35*(3), 25–32.

Yin, R. (2009). *Case study research: Design and methods* (4th ed.). Thousand Oaks, CA: Sage.

Young, M. (2006). The M.Ed., Ed.D. and Ph.D. in educational leadership. *UCEA Review, 45*(2), 6–9.

# CHAPTER SEVEN

# Supervising the Educational Doctorate Dual Award (Ed.D.D.A.)

## Juggling Truth, Relevance, and Economic Development

*Jude Chua and Yew-Jin Lee*

## INTRODUCTION

Since 2007, the National Institute of Education (NIE) of the Nanyang Technological University (NTU), Singapore, has offered, in collaboration with the Institute of Education (IOE), London, a Dual Award Doctorate in Education (Ed.D.D.A.). Students begin in either of the institutions—the "home institution"— where they complete their coursework and an Institution Focused Study (IFS) before they transfer over to the other—the "dual institution"—to complete their final dissertation. Supervisors are appointed at both institutions to oversee either the IFS or the final dissertation.

A challenge for the Ed.D.D.A. is that it is couched in environments favoring research perceived as *relevant*, and there can be a strong temptation to prescribe a narrow interpretation of *relevance* that is tightly coupled with the Singapore government's or Ministry of Education's (MOE's) goals. From this also potentially follows a somewhat dwarfed appreciation of what *good* or *quality supervision* means, with potentially unhappy faculty appraisal policy implications. Clearly the concept of *quality research* is at the very center of any eventual tussle over equitable faculty appraisal: what it means and what counts toward it. Although there is not yet any sign of a brewing struggle over this concept, there is already the beginning of some posturing interpretations that warrant preemptive interrogations of what *quality research* needs to mean, if merely to diffuse future tensions. In this chapter, by way of reflecting philosophically on what *quality supervision* for the Ed.D.D.A.

might entail, we hope to explore this and related challenges, identify some core values in supervising Ed.D.D.A. research in Singapore, and recommend some paths forward for institutions facing cultural interference in joint/international programs. So we begin with the question: What, for the Ed.D.D.A. program, might be regarded as *quality supervision?*

## WHAT IS QUALITY SUPERVISION?

Supervision that is poorly focused and thus lacks quality is marked by, for example, a failure to meet with students and to engage intellectually with their research efforts on a regular basis, indifference to their draft submissions and evolving (or not) expertise, and violations of ethical codes of conduct. Thus, if one complains about a poor supervisor by saying that he or she fails to perform some of these tasks, one is justified in asking what kind of *supervision* this is. Indeed, in the same way that a bad *argument* is not an argument, and an unjust *law* is not a law (Finnis, 1980, 1998), so also is poor *supervision* really no supervision at all, since extended, useful, or clear guidance for the learner is absent.

But *poor supervision* is still some version of supervision, and calling it *supervision that is poor* is an admission that it still belongs to the class of acts that we call supervision even though such supervision is situated at the imperfect periphery, the defective borderline, the corrupted extremity (Finnis, 1980). But of course our interest is not primarily in acts of poor supervision, but their study might offer some insight into what they contrast with and thus help somewhat to fill us in on what quality supervision might entail. For beyond meeting with students to discuss their work, paying attention to their submissions, and so forth, there may be more.

Thus we move from supervision at the periphery toward the important meaning at the center, or what has been called the focal meaning or central case (Finnis, 1980, p. 10). Supervision, as with all educational and hence professional endeavors, is centrally *designed*: it is the engineering of things or states of affairs into preferred ones (Simon, 1996, p. 111). Whatever the process might entail in its detail, it is essentially a professional/design practice. If so, then the question "What is supervision's focal meaning?" can be answered by reproducing successful methods employed in answering similar questions about other professional or design acts, as well as technologies employed in these professions and design-focused processes. These questions might include "What is teaching?" or "What is (positive) law—centrally?" or questions about design itself, such as "What is *good* design?" or "What is *design* in its focal sense?" (Chua, 2013b, 2014; Finnis, 1980).

Such methods, which are employed for discerning supervision's central case, recommend several things. To begin with, any description of the focal meaning of supervision is ultimately a choice by someone with a certain *evaluative* viewpoint, *selecting* one meaning to be significant from among a number of possible meanings (Finnis, 1980, p. 4). Because the identification of the focal meaning is an act of differentiating it from the peripheral, such differentiation is achieved only by way of normative criteria that sort out one meaning as preferred and the others as less valuable. Those normative criteria need to be sound, and theorists have to be guided by their grasp of what is good and bad, right or wrong, desirable or undesirable, all while being reflective, critical, and insightful. Only such a sound viewpoint's normative criteria are truly fit for discerning the central case (Fenstermacher & Richardson, 2005; Finnis, 1980).

But who would possess such a sound, normative viewpoint? That person would be someone we might consult in seeking his or her judgment regarding what is supervision that matters and is ideal and what is less so. Yet unless we had a sense of such a viewpoint and its set of judgments, it would be impossible for us to recognize such a person if we were to meet him/her. This means that the task of working out for ourselves that sound, practically reasonable, normative viewpoint with which to guide our judgments concerning good supervision is unavoidable.

## RELEVANCE: WHAT MATTERS IN THE SUPERVISION OF RESEARCH?

Yet not everything that has been said by experienced persons needs to be disregarded; any working out of a practically reasonable normative viewpoint could proceed by examining some of the values and ends that may have been proposed previously by persons of experience. Now, supervision primarily involves guiding or steering the research or thesis in a certain direction, so one might think of good supervision that supervises well as that which guides well, or steers well. Such steering need not be thought of as occurring only when a student is being guided formally by the supervisor; it in fact would have occurred before that—during the stages of discussion prior to acceptance of the candidate, when the interests and overarching direction of the thesis are being formulated. To steer something is to steer it in a desirable direction, toward certain values, goals, and ends. Such a desirable end has been identified as that which is "relevant" (Lee, 2013).

Of course the notion that something is or is not relevant is unintelligible without context: relevant with respect to *what*, and relevantly useful to *whom*? So although the general proposition that supervised research should be relevant is intuitive and universally welcome, the precise sense of that proposal quickly fragments and becomes subject to contestation. Rapidly asserting its dominant presence (for obvious reasons) is the MOE, with whom the NIE has a close relationship. And that relationship imposes itself strongly, impressing at least one conception of relevance—one that celebrates whatever is useful to the MOE's purposes as well as the purposes of its education officers. And such an interpretation of relevant research is surely one legitimate interpretation among others, for research and discovery can certainly inform insightfully on educational goals and practice, not least those identified as important by the planning MOE.

However, in the case of the Ed.D.D.A., this state of affairs should be cause for worry. Here are some places to start. While IOE has a tradition of critical engagement with the British government's educational policies (see, for instance, the critical postings in IOE's blogs), NIE's close and cordial relationship with the Singapore MOE means that any willingness on the part of faculty to openly criticize governmental educational policies and practices may fall prey to inertia. That inertia could translate into supervisory preferences that discourage criticality in the work of students. This is aggravated by the fact that if an Ed.D.D.A. candidate were an educational officer within the MOE, he or she would quickly grasp career implications of intellectual acquiescence rather than resistance, which translates into an incentive to work on questions that are relevantly useful to the MOE's agenda rather than topics tangential to the MOE's plans (Hayek, 2011, pp. 194–195).

Further, as with any professional doctorate, the Ed.D.D.A. risks being marketed and perceived as attractively practical, in the sense that it can usefully benefit one's practice while under MOE's employ, which then lures the unreflective interpretation that the Ed.D.D.A. student ought to focus primarily on what is instrumentally useful (that is, useful to the MOE's goals, policies, and practices) rather than to disruptively propose what is judged *uselessly* irrelevant in current discourse and policy frameworks. Thus, given the right combination, supervisor and student might mutually reinforce each other's muted criticality.

## THREE WORRIES ABOUT DOING THINGS OUR OWN WAY

Of course these tendencies are speculative projections, and the extent to which individual students or supervisors succumb to these inclinations will vary. Still, it cannot be denied that the *architecture* (if you will) or the ontological surrounding of the researcher's life-world would shape thought and behavior. For just as living in an apartment is not merely the encounter with structures but very much the interaction with the "space" (see Zevi, 1993), so also is the life of a researcher (supervisor and student) not an indifferent encounter within inert contexts but a network of intentions and deliberations afforded by the intellectual space within caving tendencies. To entertain the possibility of such tendencies, caving in is not self-evidently absurd. Indeed, the worry is that such an interpretation of "relevance" becomes *dominant* to the point of displacing other interpretations (Augier & March 2008; Ball 2003), and this worry is not always speculative paranoia.

The objection can, of course, be raised that whether or not there is in fact such a worrisome dominant interpretation is an open question. Still, any promulgation by institutional leaders of the need for research to be "relevant" will risk becoming murkily univocal with this interpretation, thus welcoming commentarial "retrieval" in order to uncover the insightfulness of the original ground if the representation of those ideas invites multiple readings, some of which are less defensible. (The meaning of "retrieval" is taken from Karl Rahner and Martin Heidegger; see Sheehan, 1985, pp. 27–38.) Case in point: the earlier-mentioned *pursuit of the relevant* was not too long ago encouraged and characterized favorably as a unique style, to be embodied by faculty so as to be in full accord with the MOE's agendas, with potential implications for setting intellectual or academic freedom aside—an implication that, it was suggested, institutional members ought never to be ashamed of, even if we were to be ridiculed by scholars internationally (Lee, 2013). Yet we feel that this prescription to do things our own way can benefit from some sharpening distinctions and argumentative steering toward the better and more defensible sense of that prescription, lest any unintended, poorer reading take hold.

The first thing to note is that the politics of education inevitably means that the purposes of education as the MOE sees it will be, among other things, economic. Now, there is no need to disparage the concern for economic goals; after all, modern catallaxies serve many important functions, not least of which is the bringing together of persons with different ends by making each of them useful to the other in their exchanges in the market, and the efficient allocation of goods through the market guided by the sources of decentralized information given in price signals avoids extreme poverty—a point we will return to later (Hayek, 1976, p. 115). Nonetheless, economic goals—especially monetary rather than multidimensional conceptions of such goals—will be a controlling concern. Thus, even if education aims at other goals besides the economic, it is likely that the economic will control the significance and also the *significations* of these other goals (Chua, 2013a).

Thus the MOE's definition of educational goods, as well as its conception of what is relevant to these goals risks being semiotically reductive; that is, the meanings of the goals and the task of education risk being constrained. If imported into our own discourse at the NIE in order to shape the axiologies we use to evaluate guided research as good or bad *qua* relevant or irrelevant, it will be unfortunate for several reasons. To give the worry some teeth, we highlight three specific concerns.

## The First Worry: Harms to Innovative Thinking

First, the obsessive instrumentalization of thinking in the service of predetermined ends may harm thinking, including thinking that is innovative. Certainly it would do no good to simply exploit known strategies and to copy and translate known means to our ends, albeit in a different context (March, 1991, 1999). Doing so would position us as followers rather than as institutional leaders in educational thinking. Yet the growth of ideas—even ideas that can be useful—is not always the product of a kind of rationalistic, Cartesian constructivism that logically unpacks insights (Hayek, 2014). Rather, the successful exploratory search for new ideas and new strategies is admixed with accidental *tumblings* into what one had not initially sought and which are unintended effects of other projects aimed at a plurality of *other* ends—that is, ends that are different from one's current goals (Hayek, 2014). For this reason, it is sometimes recommended that when designing or engineering with a goal in mind, one ought not to be obsessed with the predetermined aim but should rather be open to unforeseen consequences that may be adopted as new goals when they are preferred or welcome, in this way designing as if "without final goals" (Simon, 1996, p. 162).

In any event, the narrowing of ends by the thinning out of their conceptions entails the narrowing of a plurality of projects aimed at different ends that could have yielded mutually useful new strategies. In sum, there are consequentialist reasons to be concerned about such narrowing of minds and of research agendas by the bridling of the notion of relevance among supervisors. Such a narrowing of minds is performatively self-contradictory; it undermines what it had hoped to achieve.

## The Second Worry: Threats to Truth Seeking

Second, there are principled, deontological considerations, or considerations of appropriateness (March & Weil, 2005, p. 85) regarding any reductive notion of relevance for educational research and supervision and how it would be a betrayal of, rather than a fulfilment of, research on what is or what encircles education, something clearly unacceptable for an institute *of education*. It has also been pointed out that education derives etymologically from *educare*, which is a leading out (Ho, 2009). Taken from Plato's discussion of the cave, it represents the philosopher *qua educator* leading the beguiled masses—masses who had been caught up in their enslaved lives competing over the recognition of imitations and fighting over vain tokens for awards—out of the cave and into the world of the originals, representing the world of forms (*ideos*), the beholding of which entails the grasp of the truth. Whatever one makes of the Platonic allegory, the enduring principle is that, as an educator, one needs to seek the truth, and *educating* is therefore ordered toward that. When the philosopher educates and leads one out, s/he leads one to *the truth*. And while the truthful and the useful may overlap, at times what is expedient threatens to compromise integrity, even when expressed with diplomacy.

Again, it is often the case that the truthful may not be immediately useful and relevant. Thus the relevantly useful and the truthful need to be distinguished; one needs to be kept apart from the other if either risks being consumed or colonized by the other. For this reason, one worries about the terrors of performativity (Ball, 2003), when the usefully relevant and what works and performs consume all of our attention and thinking, so that other worthy ends are displaced. If so, then where the pressure to conform to seek the merely usefully relevant is great, that pressure needs to be tempered, and some distancing from the sources of those intellectually coercive pressures needs to be maintained. This would typically find expression in the presence and celebration of intellectual freedom, so that if the latter were absent, the ordering toward the truth would be threatened. In short, since NIE is an institute first and foremost of *education—educare*: a leading toward the truth— then intellectual freedom is a sine qua non for the fulfillment of that commitment to truth seeking derived from our identity as educators.

## The Third Worry: Complicity in Possible Injustice

Third, the driving desire to research and supervise that which is relevantly useful to someone else's ends—such as the ends that the MOE has identified—begs the question of whether those ends are good or just. If, as we have seen, conceptions of such ends can easily be thinned out or distorted, then such ends need critical reflection and, in some cases, require repudiation or correction. If so, then the pursuit of useful means for potentially suspect ends is likened to a kind of thoughtless complicity in possible injustice. If the philosopher-educator leads the masses out toward the truth, then that truth must include the truth about what is good and bad. By extension, then, we should also add that we ought to be led to and aim for not only the good of truth but also what are *truly* goods.

The broader rule in *education* is therefore to always lead persons to what is true *and truly good*. (Hereafter the "quest for the good of truth" will serve as shorthand for "the quest for the good of truth as well as the truly good.") This is at odds with any slavish instrumentalization toward ends that lack critical examination or are axiologically suspect. Whereas any willingness in principle, in the name of the truth and the good, to critique the ends proposed by the MOE or to counterpropose better ends, implies applying restraint on the desire to produce intellectually what serves those official ends, and therefore to be open to research and to supervise studies that are not useful or relevant to those official ends but are instead relevant to educational ends that scholarship itself prescribes as worth seeking. In other words, before anything else, the ordering of research and supervision toward the contribution to the self-evident good of truthful knowledge (Finnis, 1980, pp. 59–80), including knowledge about what is truly good, should be a controlling and core value, one that is supported by a commitment to intellectual freedom.

This, however, does not mean that considerations of what is relevantly useful to MOE goals are to be disregarded or that one should disregard inquiries into what might be relevantly useful to the MOE. If for the MOE and its ends, orthodoxy—the core business, so to speak—is whatever is relevantly useful to those ends, and foolish heresy is what is a deviation from the core and hence irrelevant to those ends, then for us it may be reversed: orthodoxy is whatever serves the truthful and the good, and the heretically foolish whatever is merely relevant to the MOE's ends (March, 1999).

Such talk of *orthodoxy* and *heresy* is not to be mistaken as an attempt to erect a division between the two. Rather, it highlights their intimate and mutually beneficial relationship: occasional indulgence in heresy stimulates, as a technology of foolishness (March, 1978) or a kind of searching exploratory heuristic, new perspectives that orthodoxy is typically blind to (March, 1991). The MOE is an important, ongoing interlocutor and partner, not controlling what we ought to think but nonetheless relevantly stimulating and broadening our sense of what direction to take in research and supervision. It is in this way that our unique style is our distinct advantage, as Lee (2013) has rightly emphasized, where we see the MOE's work, goals, and needs as relevantly useful to our ends, and therefore as a conversational partner in beneficial alliance rather than an object of adversarial criticism. Furthermore, the benefit is mutual, for it is also in this way that we become fully relevant and hence useful to the MOE by being a source of stimulatingly heretical exploration and hence usefully broadening the MOE's perspectives, which are always in danger of being bridled by its bias toward orthodox exploitation, as is the case for any organization.

## CONCLUSION: TRUTH SEEKING
## FOR ECONOMIC DEVELOPMENT

Let us take stock and formulate some concluding remarks about what all this means for economics. After all, the bracketing suspension of belief in the automatic veracity or normativity of research and supervision framed by or ordered toward merely economic final goals is a constant premise in our discussion, and this might invite repudiation by (policy) theorists whose starting and ending points are nothing other than the economic. Yet if our position is read as naively indifferent to economic ends, then it would have been seriously misunderstood.

We have argued that the practically reasonable commitment to the good of truth needs to be instantiated, internalized, and transmitted in research and supervision. The current trend in developmental or welfare economics is to broaden economic concepts so that truth and other non-monetary values are now considered in themselves *economic* goals rather than merely what is *usefully relevant* for a different species of goods called the *economic* (Alkire, 2006). *Economics* and its interdefining concepts, such as *poverty* and *development*, ought to be broadened into concepts that recognize the promotion and grasping of truth for its own sake and the deprivation of the same as one of the important dimensions of what constitutes a *good* or *poor* economy (Alkire, 2006; also see http://www.ophi.org.uk/).

Seen in this way, the pursuit of truth now achieves economic goals, and a fully economic argument in favor of university research and supervision ordered toward the truth is immediately apparent (Alkire, 2006; Chua, 2013a). Suffice it to say, then, that the ordering toward the truth for its own sake is not in tension with economic development *properly theorized*, but instead realizes the latter, since truth is constitutive of—rather than separate from—the *economic*. In other words, rather than find our philosophy of research and quality supervision at odds with the overarching concern with economic progress, one should instead see in this account the blueprint of a university institute fully aligned with and aimed directly at realizing a flourishing economy, precisely by not sacrificing the scholarly ordering toward the good of truth.

## REFERENCES

Alkire, S. (2006). *Valuing freedoms.* Oxford: Oxford University Press.
Augier, M., & March, J. (2008). The pursuit of relevance in management education. In J.G. March (Ed.), *Exploration in organizations* (pp. 402–408). Stanford, CA: Stanford University Press.
Ball, S.J. (2003). The teacher's soul and the terrors of performativity. *Journal of Education Policy, 18*(2), 215–228.
Chua, S.M.J. (2013a). Recent reforms in Singapore's educational landscape: What's new? *Education Today, 63*(2), 8–12.
Chua, S.M.J. (2013b). Significant designs: Translating for meanings that truly matter. *Semiotica, 196,* 353–364.
Chua, S.M.J. (2014). Inclusive design and design's moral foundations. In P. Rodgers & J. Yee (Eds.), *The Routledge companion to design research.* London: Routledge.
Fenstermacher, G.D., & Richardson, V. (2005). On making determinations of quality in teaching. *Teachers College Record, 107,* 186–213.
Finnis, J. (1980). *Natural law and natural rights.* Oxford: Clarendon Press.
Finnis, J. (1998). Natural law and the ethics of discourse. *American Journal of Jurisprudence, 43,* 53–73.
Hayek, F.A. (1976). *Law, legislation and liberty: A new statement of the liberal principles of justice and political economy.* London: Routledge and Kegan Paul.
Hayek, F.A. (2011). *The constitution of liberty.* Chicago: University of Chicago Press. (Original work published 1960)
Hayek, F.A. (2014). The result of human action but not of human design. In B. Caldwell (Ed.), *Market and other orders.* Chicago: University of Chicago Press.

Ho, P. (2009, August). *Address by director-general of education*. Address given at the Expo Hall 2, Singapore. Retrieved from http://www.moe.gov.sg/media/speeches/2009/08/26/address-by-ms-ho-peng-at-the-t.php

Lee, S.K. (2013, December). *Director's annual address 2013: Towards destination 2017*. Speech given at the National Institute of Education, Singapore.

March, J. (1978). Bounded rationality, ambiguity and the engineering of choice. *Bell Journal of Economics*, *9*(2), 587–608.

March, J. (1991). Exploration and exploitation in organizational learning. *Organization Science*, *2*(1), 71–87.

March, J. (1999). Wild ideas: The catechism of heresy. In *The Pursuit of Organizational Intelligence* (pp. 225–228). Malden, MA: Blackwell Business.

March, J., & Weil, T. (2005.) *On leadership*. Oxford: Blackwell.

Sheehan, T. (1985). Metaphysics and bivalence: On Karl Rahner's *Geist in welt*. *Modern Schoolman*, *83*, 21–43.

Simon, H.B. (1996). *The sciences of the artificial* (3rd ed.). Cambridge: MIT Press.

Zevi, B. (1993). *Architecture as space*. New York: Da Capo.

# CHAPTER EIGHT

# Ed.D. Program Dissertation Research

## Increasing the Odds of Completion

*Kelly S. Hall*

Thank you to Cheryl Keen, my colleague and editor of this chapter. This chapter would not have been possible without the collaboration of the following members of the Doctoral Program Advisory Committee at Frostburg State University (www.frostburg. edu/edd): William Aumiller, Vicki Mazer, Doris Santamaria-Makang, Beth Scarloss, Lisa Simpson, John Stodhoff, Glenn Thompson, and Gary Wakefield.

## INTRODUCTION

In 2012, 10,000 education doctoral degrees (both Ed.D. and Ph.D.) were conferred in the United States (National Center for Education Statistics, 2013). Of all Ph.D. programs, the educational doctorate takes the longest to complete: in 2012, the median elapsed time from starting graduate courses to completing an education Ph.D. was 12 years (National Science Foundation, 2014). After 10 years, 43% of all Ph.D. students who started programs have not finished and likely never will (Council of Graduate Schools, 2008). The Ed.D. is considered a professional doctorate, similar to a J.D. or M.D., though it is not tabulated through the U.S. National Survey of Earned Doctorates. Ed.D completion rates, which range from 50% to 60%, are similar to Ph.D. rates (Bair & Haworth, 1999).

Completing the dissertation is the stumbling block for most doctoral students. The writing of the dissertation is an isolating experience that results in students feeling defeated (Ali & Kohun, 2007; Lovitts, 2001). How can Ed.D. programs improve the dissertation research process and increase the odds of students completing their degree programs?

In this chapter, a "dissertation across the curriculum" or DATC approach is presented. The approach includes steps that Ed.D. programs can take to increase the odds of students completing them. These steps are informed by my experiences and studies of doctoral attrition and completion. My experience is as former director of research for a large Ed.D. program, a current member of advisory boards for two new Ed.D. programs, a developer and teacher of over one dozen graduate research courses, and a mentor for over 30 graduate students engaged in research projects. Many elements of the approach are currently being implemented at Frostburg State University (FSU) in Frostburg, Maryland, a new Ed.D. program that enrolled its first cohort in the fall 2012 term.[1]

Results of implementation of the program are promising: of the first 25-member cohort, 23 members remain. After 24 months, 40% of remaining cohort members have either already defended their dissertation proposals or have dates to do so. FSU's program is designed to be completed in 3 years. With only 5% of research doctoral students graduating in 3 years (Council of Graduate Schools, 2008), FSU has been challenged to create a program that beats these odds. Following through on its 3-year promise necessitates implementing policy and praxis toward this end.

The objective of the "dissertation across the curriculum" approach is to provide students a scaffold of learning and support for dissertation or capstone writing projects from the time they enter an Ed.D. program until they graduate. The program elements focus on programmatic and personnel issues that pose challenges for Ed.D. students and do not address admissions selection criteria or financial challenges, despite their being cited as factors affecting the likelihood of doctoral student success (Council of Graduate Schools, 2009). These elements are discussed chronologically—that is, as those implemented before, during, and after coursework, as well as throughout the program.

## RECOMMENDATIONS BEFORE COURSEWORK BEGINS

Program orientation and research topic selection are two elements of the DATC approach that take place before Ed.D. coursework begins.

### Program Orientation

I was working with early and compulsory orientation of faculty and students to dissertation-related topics is good practice, according to the Council of Graduate Schools (2010). An orientation to standards and approvals, the Institutional

Review Board, committee member roles, conducting literature searches, and campus writing and support centers will prepare faculty to help students successfully embark upon the dissertation process.

## Standards and Approval

Students who are unaware of expectations will only reach them by chance and persistence. Introducing students to dissertation standards and approval processes at the start will orient them to programmatic, institutional, and professional discipline requirements. Having an awareness of standards of rubrics and grading, templates, approval forms, and schedules will establish a foundation for student success. Students who are adequately informed of expectations of dissertation standards and approvals at the beginning of their doctoral journey will not be surprised by them at the end, nor surprised that students can fail a dissertation course during their final phase of independent work.

## Institutional Review Board

Learning about research ethics is a prerequisite to embarking upon the research process. In the orientation phase, a focus on ethical issues specifically related to education settings—such as assent of minors and teacher-principal supervisory relationships—is valuable for the Ed.D. professional. It is also helpful to take the free tutorial with certification offered by the National Institutes of Health Office of Extramural Research (2014). Early training can be followed by just-in-time training at the proposal stage so that students are not blindsided by an ethical issue during the dissertation process.

## Committee Member Roles

Creating an awareness of committee member roles will enable students to make good choices in their selection of persons who will guide and approve their dissertation research.

## Libraries and Literature Searches

Levy and Ellis (2006) explain concisely how to use a systems approach—input, processing, and output—to conduct a thorough review of literature. Libraries offer training sessions for students in how to use their databases. Using and documenting a systematic approach, students can be confident that they have performed an exhaustive search and begun to synthesize literature early.

## Writing and Support Centers

As with the propensity for conducting research (or not), some students are better writers than others. For students who need help, university writing and support centers typically offer excellent assistance.

## Topic Selection

Individual meetings with students early in the program to discuss and direct their ideas set the stage for productive integration of their topics throughout the program. I use the dissertation structure as a guide in meetings with students, which start with a discussion of a research problem. After students identify the problem, a discussion of research purpose and questions follows. With research questions posed, a discussion of potential methods for studying those questions ensues. Freeing students to select a focus early on will enable them to efficiently address that focus in course assignments throughout the program and to select committee members to guide them before their third year.

## RECOMMENDATIONS DURING COURSEWORK

One of the most critical factors in completing the doctorate is adequately preparing students for research (deValero, 2001; Malone, Nelson, & Nelson, 1999). Early sequencing, integrating, and augmenting research methods learning are three foundational elements of the DATC approach. With early, integrated, and added research learning, doctoral students will be well prepared not only to complete their degrees but also to be model scholar-practitioners.

## Early Sequencing of Research Courses

Frontloading the acquisition of research skills will equip students to consider and develop methods sections of their dissertations sooner. Dispositions and skills acquired early will support positive student outcomes if research learning is integrated throughout other course assignments.

## Integration of Dissertation Research Learning into All Coursework

Integration of research learning in every course is elemental to the "dissertation across the curriculum" approach. With it, students will gain a variety of research skills and dispositions and be better equipped to complete their dissertations.

## Style Guidelines

By the time students reach the dissertation stage, they should already be familiar with style guidelines—typically those of the American Psychological Association (APA) for Ed.D. programs. Students will be well equipped to adhere to formatting and style standards required of the dissertation if all faculty count APA correctness in grading of assignments.

## Research-Focused Texts and Assignments

Opportunities abound for Ed.D. students to acquire research acumen in every class they take. In an education history class, a formal content or meta-analysis might be conducted. In a law class, critical policy analysis could be formally taught. Planning classes offer opportunities for feasibility studies, gap analysis, and evaluation research learning. A human resource class could also be used to teach evaluation. Financial analysis can be taught in finance class. Curriculum assessment is a type of research. Integrating learning about research across the curriculum is bound to improve student graduation outcomes.

## Teach *to* the Dissertation

Rather than having students complete assignments disconnected from the dissertation process throughout the Ed.D., there is an opportunity for students to practice sections of their dissertation in all classes. Students who practice writing an introduction or a literature review, analyzing results, and drawing conclusions as they would for their dissertations will be better prepared to develop their proposals and conduct and report research findings (Hall, 2014). If students have selected general topics, and if assignments are flexible in terms of topic, they can use course assignments to develop sections of their dissertations.

## Dissertation Manuals

Manuals that address the dissertation help students to gain an understanding of what they are getting into and how to proceed. These can be listed in every syllabus. The Krathwohl and Smith (2005) guide offers checklists for proposal development. Roberts (2010) offers practical guidance and examples. Butin's (2009) guide is aimed at the education practitioner-scholar. If listed as a required or supplemental text in every class, manuals become familiar material and will assist students in the completion of their dissertations.

## Dissemination Opportunities

Dissertations lacking relevance or an audience are bound to become dust collectors. Ed.D. students often wonder how their research will matter and contribute to the wider good. Creating awareness of opportunities to present, publish, promote, and be promoted as a result of research activities stimulates aspirations, creates hope, and offers a vision beyond the dissertation goal. I have an assignment that addresses dissemination opportunities: selecting a venue, submitting, and leveraging a network.

## Assimilation of Field Experiences

Disconnecting practicum, internship, and capstone experiences from the dissertation process is inefficient. Field and service experiences offer laboratories that are ripe for gathering data and experience through a doctoral student lens (Council of Graduate Schools, 2010). An action research study is a good model for an assimilated experience (Herr & Anderson, 2005; Zambo, 2010), though it is often misunderstood and requires careful planning (Osterman, Furman, & Sernak, 2013).

## Augmentation of Research Methods Learning

The addition of research, dissertation, and special topics courses, along with research paradigms and texts, is an augmentation of research methods learning elemental to the dissertation across the curriculum approach.

## Addition of Methods Courses

Programs typically offer between two and four research courses at the end of a program sequence. Are two research courses enough to teach doctoral-level research? If research poses the most critical challenge for students, the addition of required research courses might help students meet this challenge.

## Special Topics

The Collaborative Institutional Training Initiative at the University of Miami (2012) offers virtual courses related to research. By becoming members, institutions can provide access to students and faculty.

## Dissertation Development Course

Offering a supplemental dissertation development course to a program will provide focused learning about nuances and requirements of dissertation research.

## Research Paradigm Variety

Ideological distinctions between quantitative and qualitative research paradigms are not appropriate for applied research (Trochim, 2006). "All scientific thinking is a mixture of quantitative and qualitative thinking" (Stake, 2010, p. 13). Doctoral programs tend to reflect the research paradigms of faculty members. Educational research is multifarious and is well served when both quantitative and qualitative traditions are respected and taught (Creswell, 2012; Yin, 2013). Changing the mind-set of programs involves what Andrews and Grogan (2005) described as "removing the Ed.D. dissertation from the Ph.D. straight jacket." Action research, case studies, and other applied methods are appropriate approaches for Ed.D. research, yet most are rarely used.

## Variety of Research Methods Texts

Research texts used in Ed.D. programs are typically themed based on qualitative and quantitative method types and related vocabulary and procedures. This dichotomous presentation predisposes doctoral students to believe that methods are straightforward and design choices are tied to one method. Making research decisions to conduct educational research is complex and often involves selecting methods from both traditions. For example, surveys often contain both quantitative and qualitative data yet are presented as separate methods, and random sampling is taught with quantitative methods, though it can be used to select participants for a qualitative study. More important, random sampling may not be ethical in an educational setting but is an assumption for the use of inferential statistics taught in quantitative methods. Dealing with these messy issues is not the focus of most research texts (with the possible exception of Vogt, Gardner, & Haeffele, 2012). Hence, students struggle to make appropriate research decisions that are necessary to developing their methodologies. Rather than relying on one text to teach doctoral research methods courses, I provide a long list of texts that students can reference and from which they can achieve learning objectives. Research learning objectives are framed around students' need to develop and implement a methodology, interpret results, and draw conclusions.

## RECOMMENDATIONS AFTER COURSEWORK ENDS

Most Ed.D. students who drop out do so in the post-coursework phase. Increasing the likelihood of students' graduating entails supporting them after their coursework is completed. Elements of the dissertation across the curriculum approach associated with the post-coursework phase are comprehensive examinations, restrictions, approvals and standards, and committees.

## Research Component of Comprehensive Examinations

Examining students for their knowledge and skills-applying research as a component of their comprehensive examinations ensures that they are prepared to continue independent or collaborative research work.

## Remove Restrictions on Settings and Methods

Some programs do not permit students to study the institution in which they work. Some programs require the use of mixed methods; others do not. I've heard of one program that only accepts evaluations. While restrictions on research may help programs focus their research teaching and falsely assure them of research rigor, students with research experience gained in a program adopting DATC principles should be well prepared to finish their dissertations. Doctoral students who are open to inquiry, confident about various ways to approach and undertake it, and armed with an arsenal of resources to learn about and justify their individual research choices fare better than those who never jostle with difficulties of planning and conducting educational research.

## Dissertation Standards and Approvals

Lack of dissertation structure and time management are challenges for doctoral students (West, Gokalp, Pena, Fischer, & Gupton, 2011). Providing dated checklists, rubrics, and templates provides structure and tools for time management.

## Dated Checklists

Ed.D. students are surprised at and waylaid by the number of approvals required to complete a dissertation—in effect, logistical hoops through which they must jump. It is helpful for their tracking and goal setting to supply them with checklists of milestones and approvals, with dates established by backward planning with associated offices for every term. Dated schedules supply students with a reliable means to set goals and manage their time—the most commonly articulated challenge of their doctoral studies (West et al., 2011).

## Rubrics

Though quality is ultimately reliant on committee members' judgment, adopting a rubric to clarify expectations of each section within the dissertation proposal and final product is an invaluable way to advance Ed.D. students through the dissertation process. Such rubrics may contain standards for a literature review, including a minimal number of total references, that justifies research design decisions, as well as approval categories. Clear rubric categories indicating status as either approved or not approved will inform students about which parts of their dissertation require attention. Consistent quality is also assured through the adoption and use of rubrics. With approval of a rubric by all committee members, the defense hearing can proceed with almost no risk of failure.

## Organizing Templates

What goes where? What should the document look like? Using a dissertation template, a common offering at university websites, will ease the frustration a student encounters in organizing the dissertation. Programs can modify one of these to meet a student's specific needs. A valuable addition to minimally required sections is a brief description of each section, including descriptions that match the rubric adopted by the program and any style standards required by the institution's dissertation archive.

## DISSERTATION COMMITTEES

Relationships with dissertation chairs are cited as a top challenge for doctoral completion (West et al., 2011). Effective function and structure, interaction, and accountability among dissertation committees are vital for Ed.D. candidate completion.

## Function and Structure

Function precedes structure. In this section, elements of committee function and structure are discussed.

Keep dissertation committees small. If a program admits 12 students per year and has a 3-year graduation expectation, it would need between 36 and 60 persons to serve in committee roles every year, depending on the size of the committees. If Ed.D. candidates do not graduate in 3 years (and most of them do not), the number of persons available to fill committee roles dwindles. Rarely does a department have the capacity to fill its own needs for committee members. Without the necessary human resource capacity, institutions are increasingly using two- and three-member committees. For doctoral student completion, it is better to have fewer qualified and active members than more, less active, members.

Engage committee members early. As with topic selection, early engagement of committee members is elemental to implementing the DATC approach. With early engagement of committee members, dissertation assignments completed in courses can be vetted and approved early in the Ed.D. program; thus students may be ready to defend their proposals within a couple of months of finishing their coursework.

Ensure that methodological expertise is available to candidates. Methodologists are persons who understand and can guide the research process. They are experienced with either a variety of methods and processes in general or a particular method. When leading a very large Ed.D. research program, I hired (and terminated) many adjunct research faculty. This experience taught me that good committee members might not have research course credits transcribed during their own graduate studies. Rather, I located the best committee members among faculty with a record of applied research experience and individual mentorship of students. If programs are serious about helping students get their dissertations done, they need a cadre of persons experienced with leading research.

Be selective in engaging executive administrators on campus. Administrators may be willing but not have the time to fulfill committee responsibilities. There is also the possibility of a conflict of interest from both a student and another committee member's perspective, depending on the role of the administrator. Who will make the administrative decision if there is an unresolved conflict that reaches the executive level? How will the ethical dilemma be resolved for an uncompensated committee member who serves as pro tem chair for an administrator in absentia?

## Authorship

Being a committee member is a form of authorship. In referring to Winston's (1985) tool as a means to discuss and decide who is eligible, the APA Science Student Council (2006) offers guidance about authorship determination. Committee members who are named as approvers of dissertations should meet authorship criteria.

Engage faculty throughout the institution. Good dissertation topics are occasionally outside the knowledge base of education department faculty. Expertise might be found elsewhere. Engaging persons outside the department might necessitate compensation or an incentive to engage in interdisciplinary activities. Cross-departmental engagement is encouraged by institutions but may be difficult, given that institutions of higher education are typically discipline-centric.

Clarify committee members' roles and come to a mutual agreement. Dissertation committee member roles tend to be ambiguous. Such ambiguity occurs when expectations about goals and responsibilities of a position are unclear. What are the respective roles of the chair(s) and other members? A three-member committee might include roles of advocate and institutional organizer (the chair), a topic expert, and a methodologist. To be proficient in a role, committee members "should be made aware of the responsibilities and obligations of that role, the actions necessary to fulfill the role, and the effects that the role has on various constituents" (Edmondson, 2006).

## Communication and Interaction

Communication with committee members has been mentioned as a challenge to doctoral students' completion of the program (West et al., 2011). I learned of the importance of communication and interaction among committee members in relation to students when I supervised hundreds of Ed.D. committee members. As director of Ed.D. research, it was my job to mediate issues among committee chairs and members, as well as dissertating students. I bring what I have learned to the DATC approach.

Meet regularly with candidates. Students need consistent guidance in order to move forward with the dissertation process. Reliable guidance reduces student stress and thereby increases productivity. Regular monthly 2-hour meetings between candidates and chairs serve candidates well. Dialogue could start with the list of items students were to address after the previous meeting and end with the creation of another to-do list.

Listen to and respond to students' desires and dispositions. It is disheartening when I hear, "I wanted to do interviews; but my chair thought I should do a survey. Looking back, interviews would have been a better approach to study my topic and problem." Responding to students' dispositions will stimulate their interest in the research process. Doing so requires recognition and relinquishing of personal biases and possibly repositioning committee members who are adept at a particular research method. The result will be students who are more enthused and satisfied with their research.

Explicate interaction processes among committee members. Effective communication is vital to the functioning of the dissertation committee. Leaving communication processes to chance without explicating them will result in miscommunication and misunderstandings. Do committee members communicate with the student through the chair or directly? Do they merely copy the chair? How will committee members have access to student work? How will members provide feedback? Typically, the chair sets the rules for communication processes by taking into consideration student wishes, geographic location of persons involved, availability of communication platforms, and expectations of the program. Effective communication takes the right message to the right person in the right format at the right time.

Teach students throughout the dissertation process. While the suggestion of teaching students may seem like an obvious good practice, my observation of committee members who offer little or no guidance to dissertating students is confirmed by West and colleagues' research (2011). Dissertations *are* student products, but committee members who ask more questions than they answer are nemeses to dissertating doctoral students.

## Accountability of Committee Members

Setting time limits for feedback and scheduling periodic check-ins with committee members are means of accountability. Effective communication processes among students and committee members include a time limit on when feedback is expected from committee members. Two weeks is a reasonable expectation. Without time limits, drafts will languish and possibly be forgotten among busy committee members' lists of things to do. With time limits, drafts move forward. If a particular draft does not merit a full review, it is a committee member's responsibility to return it to the student and offer guidance to make the draft reviewable.

## Periodic Check-ins

Committee members may or may not be compensated or be within the supervisory capacity of an Ed.D. department or institution. Combine these circumstances with possible conflicts between committee members (who may also have differing levels of decision-making authority) and stressed students, and conditions become unfavorable for a doctoral candidate to move forward. Establishing an effective system of accountability for committee members will not only lessen the chances for committee member–student disengagement but will also reduce the possibility of potentially litigious situations. Periodic checks with committee members are necessary to thwart disengagement and to inform the possibility of replacing committee members unable or unwilling to fulfill their roles. The institution's policy regarding the process of changing committee members can be clarified in the program handbook so that it is not used capriciously.

## THROUGHOUT THE PROGRAM

Other supports are needed to complement and implement the DATC approach. Needed are an active advisory committee, a means of support for international students and students experiencing life transitions, and external counsel.

## Appointment of an Internal Advisory Committee

Program decisions require dialogue, consensus building, and implementation. With regular advisory committee meetings, programs are positioned to respond to and monitor changes needed to implement steps of the DATC approach.

## Support for Students through Personal Life Transitions

Ed.D. students are professionals who experience life transitions. Balancing personal, work, and school responsibilities is cited as the biggest challenge for doctoral students (West et al., 2011). From my experience, major changes take place in the lives of between 10% and 20% of any given cohort of students. Programs that do not care about students' lives or fail to accommodate life changes could alienate students and increase the likelihood that they will never graduate. Programs that support doctoral students through life transitions will endear those students to the program and the university.

## Support for International Students' Unique Needs

Increasingly, Ed.D. students are international students who have unique needs. Meeting these needs will increase those students' chances of graduating and adding to the diversity of educational theory and practice in other parts of the world.

## Provision of Legal Counsel

Legal and ombudsman counsel is needed for accommodating students with special requests, needs, and complaints. An institutional signatory is sometimes needed for student use of research resources. A confidential opinion is often helpful in relation to conflict. Being acquainted with and seeking advice from an institution's general counsel or ombudsman is easier than responding to a complaint filed by a dissatisfied doctoral student.

## CONCLUDING REFLECTION

The education doctorate promises to improve professional practice and the common good. "Doing the same thing over and over again and expecting a different result" is how Albert Einstein defined insanity. Programs that implement elements of the dissertation across the curriculum not only increase the odds of doctoral students' completion of the program but also of their satisfaction with it.

## REFERENCES

Ali, A., & Kohun, F. (2007). Dealing with social isolation to minimize doctoral attrition: A four stage framework. *International Journal of Doctoral Studies, 2*, 33–49.

Andrews, R., & Grogan, M. (2005). Form should follow function: Removing the Ed.D. dissertation from the Ph.D. straight jacket. *UCEA Review, 47*(2), 10–13.

APA Science Student Council. (2006). *A graduate student's guide to determining authorship credit and authorship order.* Retrieved from http://www.apa.org/science/leadership/students/authorship-paper.pdf

Bair, C.R., & Haworth, J.G. (1999, November). *Doctoral student attrition and persistence: A meta-synthesis of research.* ASHE Annual Meeting Paper, San Antonio, TX.

Butin, D.W. (2009). *The education dissertation: A guide for practitioner scholars.* Thousand Oaks, CA: Corwin.

Council of Graduate Schools. (2008). *Ph.D. completion and attrition: Analysis of baseline demographic data from Ph.D. completion project.* Washington, DC: Author.

Council of Graduate Schools. (2009). *Ph.D. completion and attrition: Findings from exit survey of Ph.D. completers.* Washington, DC: Author.

Council of Graduate Schools. (2010). *Ph.D. completion project: Policies and practices to promote student success executive summary.* Retrieved from http://www.phdcompletion.org/information/Executive_Summary_Student_Success_Book_IV.pdf

Creswell, J. (2012). *Educational research: Planning, conducting, and evaluating quantitative and qualitative research* (4th ed.). Upper Saddle River, NJ: Pearson Education.

deValero, Y.F. (2001). Departmental factors affecting time to degree and completion rates of doctoral students at one land grant institution. *Journal of Higher Education, 72*(3), 341–367.

Edmondson, S. (2006). Role ambiguity. In F.W. English (Ed.), *Encyclopedia of educational leadership and administration* (p. 884). Thousand Oaks, CA: Sage. doi: http://dx.doi.org/10.4135/9781412939584.n492

Hall, K.S. (2014, June 6–8). *Navigating your thesis or dissertation: A map to guide your way.* Poster presented at International Research Methods Summer School, Mary Immaculate College, University of Limerick, Ireland.

Herr, K., & Anderson, G.L. (2005). *The action research dissertation: A guide for students and faculty.* Thousand Oaks, CA: Sage.

Krathwohl, D.R., & Smith, N. (2005). *How to prepare a dissertation proposal: Suggestions for students in education and the social and behavioral sciences.* Syracuse, NY: Syracuse University Press.

Levy, Y., & Ellis, T.J. (2006). A systems approach to conduct an effective literature review in support of information systems research. *Informing Science Journal, 9.* Retrieved from http://inform.nu/Articles/Vol9/V9p181–212Levy99.pdf

Lovitts, B.E. (2001). *Leaving the ivory tower: The causes and consequences of departure from doctoral study.* Lanham, MD: Rowman & Littlefield.

Malone, B.G., Nelson, J.S., & Nelson, C.V. (1999, August). *Completion and attrition rates of doctoral students in educational administration.* Paper presented at the annual meeting of the National Committee of Professors in Educational Administration, Houston, TX.

National Center for Education Statistics. (2013). Table 318.20. Bachelor's, master's, and doctor's degrees conferred by postsecondary institutions, by field of study: Selected years, 1970–71 through 2011–12. Retrieved from http://nces.ed.gov/programs/digest/d13/tables/dt13_318.20.asp

National Institutes of Health. Office of Extramural Research. (2014). *Protecting human research participants.* Retrieved from https://phrp.nihtraining.com/users/login.php

National Science Foundation, National Center for Science and Engineering Statistics (NCSES). (2014, January). *Doctorate recipients from U.S. Universities: 2012.* (NSF 14–3090). Arlington, VA: Author. Retrieved from http://www.nsf.gov/statistics/sed/digest/2012/nsf14305.pdf

Osterman, K., Furman, G., & Sernak, K. (2013, August). Action research in EdD programs in educational leadership. *Journal of Research on Leadership Education, 9*(1), 85–101.

Roberts, C.M. (2010). *The dissertation journey: A practical guide to planning, writing, and defending your dissertation* (2nd ed.). Thousand Oaks, CA: Corwin.

Stake, R. (2010). *Qualitative research: Study how things work.* New York: Guilford Press.

Trochim, W.M.K. (2006). *The qualitative-quantitative debate. Research methods knowledge base.* Retrieved from http://www.socialresearchmethods.net/kb/qualdeb.php

University of Miami. (2012, August). *Collaborative institutional training initiative.* Retrieved from https://www.citiprogram.org

Vogt, W.P., Gardner, D.C., & Haeffele, L.M. (2012). *When to use what research design.* New York: Guilford Press.

West, I.S., Gokalp, G., Pena, E.V., Fisher, L., & Gupton, J. (2011, June). Exploring effective support practices for doctoral students' degree completion. *College Student Journal, 45*(2), 310–323.

Winston, Jr., R.B. (1985). A suggested procedure for determining order of authorship in research publications. *Journal of Counseling and Development, 63*, 515–518.

Yin, R. (2013). *Case study research design and methods* (5th ed.). Thousand Oaks, CA: Sage.

Zambo, D. (2010). Action research as signature pedagogy in an education doctoral program: The reality and hope. *Innovative Higher Education, 36*, 261–271. doi:10.1007/s10755–010–9171–7

# Perspectives from Morgan State, a Historically Black University

## Rethinking Ed.D. and Ph.D. Education Programs

*Glenda M. Prime and Whitney Johnson*

## ED.D. AND PH.D. PROGRAMS IN HISTORICAL CONTEXT

The first Ed.D.s were awarded in the United States in the 1920s and early 1930s (Brown, 1990; Clifford & Guthrie, 1988) and in the UK in 1992 (Gregory, 1995). The introduction of the Ed.D. in both of these countries must be viewed in the context of the fact that the Ph.D., as the recognized terminal degree, had been established some 60 years earlier in the case of the United States and about 72 years earlier in the case of the UK (Gregory, 1995). Indeed, even in education, the Ph.D. had long preceded the Ed.D., Teachers College having awarded the first Ph.D. in education in 1893.

For the most part, however, these early Ph.D.s were awarded in the arts and sciences and represented the acme of scholastic achievement for the recipients and the ultimate evidence of credibility for the institution. By the early twentieth century, when Ed.D.s began to be offered in education, more than 50 U.S. universities were already offering the Ph.D., the raison d'être of which was the generation of new knowledge through original research. It is not surprising, then, that as institutions began to develop terminal degrees in the professional fields, many of them (medicine, law, and business are exceptions) sought to gain prestige and legitimacy in higher education by modeling themselves on established disciplines and offering the Ph.D. as the terminal degree (Toma, 2002). Even so, there was strong opposition to the offering of doctorates in these professional fields based on the argument that "practical ends and vocational aims were not appropriate for doctoral study" (Toma, 2002, p. 12).

In education, both paths to the terminal degree persisted, with some universities offering both the Ed.D. and the clearly more prestigious Ph.D. The majority of universities offering the terminal degree, however, offer one or the other, with the top-tier universities opting for the Ph.D. in most cases. The question of the distinction between the two degrees has been the focus of much discussion from as early as 1930 (Clifford & Guthrie, 1988). The recent effort by the Carnegie Project on the Education Doctorate (CPED) to reenvision the Ed.D. was fueled by the fact that there remains no clear distinction between the two.

## Blurred Lines of Distinction Between Ph.D.s and Ed.D.s

The distinction that is most often made between the Ed.D. and the Ph.D. in education is that the former is a practitioner's degree designed to prepare administrators, policymakers, and professionals for the management of the education enterprise. Its focus is on the development of practical competence. The Ph.D., on the other hand, is described as a research degree, designed for the preparation of researchers and professors who would generate new knowledge.

In spite of claims about differing emphases, there is considerable evidence that in practice, there is little difference between these two degrees. For the most part, entry requirements, curricula, comprehensive examinations, and dissertation requirements are so similar that researchers have concluded that there is, in fact, very little difference between these degrees (Baez, 2002; McNulty & Shirley, 2010; Nelson & Coorough, 1994; Osguthorpe & Wong, 1993).

However, one study of Ed.D. and Ph.D. dissertations accepted between 1950 and 1991 did find that Ed.D. dissertations employed more survey research designs and that Ph.D. dissertations employed more inferential statistics, which gave them wider generalizability (Nelson & Coorough, 1994). Where the difference between the two types of degrees is stark is in the level of prestige accorded to each.

The Ph.D. remains the degree of choice, being a mark of distinction for both the graduate and the institution. Given the similarity in the substantive aspects of the two degrees, it might seem surprising that this difference in status exists, but a look at the historical contexts of the two degrees, outlined earlier, makes it less surprising. The Ph.D., established as the pinnacle of academic achievement for over 60 years before professional degrees were introduced, had become the model for the preparation of those who would advance knowledge in their disciplines.

New programs would be measured by the extent to which they could conform to the standards and norms of the Ph.D. This prestige distinction results in and perpetuates itself through the fact that the top-tier universities, when they do offer the Ed.D., do so in addition to the Ph.D., while the comprehensive universities tend to offer only the Ed.D. Harvard University is a special case, having offered only the Ed.D. from 1920 to the present. The Harvard Ed.D. was, however, indistinguishable in form and intent from the Ph.D. We will argue later in this chapter that history and the tendency of universities to maintain the status quo in their academic programs are not the only factors that account for the lower status of the Ed.D. and, indeed, of other professional doctorates as compared to the Ph.D. We will also advance the view that deeply held assumptions about the nature of knowledge and specifically about the relationship between and relative value of theoretical and practical knowledge underlie the status difference.

## Consequences of the Blurred Distinction Between Ph.D.s and Ed.D.s

The effect of the failure to distinguish the Ed.D. from the Ph.D. in education is that we do neither well. The status difference means that students who have access to both often opt for the Ph.D., even when their prior experiences and career aspirations suggest that a practice-focused degree might better prepare them. Toma (2002) suggests that such students "underperform as Ph.D. students by arts and science standards, or they meet these standards and are more prepared for faculty or research careers than the administrative ones they desire" (p. 6). Levine (2005) also concluded that Ed.D. graduates were often well trained for neither research nor practice.

Further, a search of the literature found little evidence to suggest that administrators, system managers, and principals who have earned the Ed.D. make better leadership or policy decisions. Similarly, the prolonged time to completion of Ph.D.s in education, the high rate of failure to complete, the low publication rate of graduates, and the small number of graduates who become faculty suggest that the Ph.D. as preparation of professionals is not faring well. Levine's (2005) opinion that the lack of distinction has created a situation in which we prepare neither practitioners nor researchers adequately seems well founded.

The real losers in our failure to adequately prepare professionals either for practice or for research are our clients, from K–12 through higher education. Persistent achievement gaps and low graduation and retention rates, the underpreparation of graduates for the workforce, and the poor national standing of U.S. students compared to their international counterparts in some curriculum areas are some of the vexing problems of practice that remain unresolved. These problems require sound theorizing that is grounded in a deep understanding of practice, and we seem not to be preparing professionals who have these competencies.

## The Call for a Reinvented Ed.D.

The most common response to the ambiguity in form and purpose and the negative impact of such ambiguity has been a call from many quarters for a reinvented Ed.D. ( Guthrie, 2009; Redden, 2007) and in fewer cases for its elimination altogether (Levine, 2005). It is widely believed that a revitalized Ed.D. would address the status problem from which the degree currently suffers while better preparing practitioners. Toma (2002) suggested that "re-inventing the Ed.D. has the potential to both legitimize us, as a field, within our own institutions by setting and achieving our own standards through following our own practices, as in fields, like law, medicine and business" (p. 9). His suggested reforms are heavily premised on the need to separate the degree from the norms for doctoral education that derive largely from the arts and sciences, as well as the need to strive for the kind of autonomy enjoyed by professional degrees in medicine and law.

In addition to new delivery formats, Toma (2002) suggests a number of more substantive reforms that include increased emphasis on practical aspects of educational management, such as data-based decision making and reduced emphasis on research courses. Townsend (2002), in a similar call for a reformed Ed.D., points to the possibility of new and innovative approaches to coursework and program structure and suggests that the revised program need not be bound by "the three traditional components of the Ph.D.: courses, oral examination and dissertation" (p. 42).

Perhaps the most comprehensive effort at redesigning the Ed.D. is the Carnegie Project on the Education Doctorate (CPED). The CPED is an international consortium of 87 schools or colleges of education working collaboratively to redesign the Ed.D. The vision of the consortium is "to transform the Ed.D. into the degree of choice for preparing the next generation of practitioner experts and school (K–12) college leaders in education" (CPED, 2014). It is interesting that the view of the "practitioner expert" advanced by the CPED is one who is capable of "generating new knowledge." Indeed, the CPED defines the Ed.D. in these terms: "The professional doctorate in education prepares educators for the application of appropriate and specific practices, the generation of new knowledge and for the stewardship of the profession." These functions seem completely appropriate for the "practitioner expert," but we would argue that the last two are equally at home in a description of the purpose of the Ph.D. Perhaps this points to the view that the distinction between these two degrees might not be easily accomplished in practice and that efforts to do so might result in little more than shifts in emphasis while leaving the status difference intact.

Guthrie (2009) also makes the case for what he calls a modern doctor of education degree. He bases his case on the fact that the shift in education toward outcomes rather than inputs as the criteria for evaluation places demands for new competencies and higher levels of existing ones on practitioners and theoreticians alike. He argues that administrators and policymakers need an increased range of practitioner skills and that research scholars in education need to learn complex research methodologies and statistical analyses. He suggests that it is impossible to develop all of these competencies in a single program. In effect, he makes the case for revitalizing both the Ed.D. and the Ph.D. in education.

Calls for a distinction between the Ed.D. and the Ph.D. are, in effect, calls for a preservation of the practice/theory divide. They are based on the assumption that "knowledge how" is different from "knowledge that" and that practitioners need the former and research scholars need the latter. This distinction is nothing new, and neither is the view that *knowledge that* is of a higher status than *knowledge how*—hence, the persistent difference in the prestige afforded in the academy to one over the other.

The prevalence of the Ph.D. in education in top-tier universities and the predominance of the Ed.D. as the terminal degree in the comprehensive universities are the lingering relics of this epistemological position. This divide provides shaky ground upon which to build either the revised Ph.D. or the modern doctorate in education. The question that needs to be asked is this: What are the knowledge bases needed to prepare professionals who can accurately define and address the problems in education? Below we will explore further the relationship between theoretical and practical knowledge and the implications of that relationship for the preparation of professionals in the field.

## THEORY AND PRACTICE: SHOULD THERE BE A DIVIDE?

The history of Western thought is, to a large extent, the history of the development of our understanding about the nature of knowledge and the methods by which we come to know. The nature of theory and its relationship to practice play a prominent role in this. Our assumptions regarding this relationship profoundly influence not just what knowledge we seek to impart through education but how we seek to impart it and, indeed, how we structure the whole education enterprise. A brief exploration of the rise of scientific thinking illustrates the way in which it has been influenced by developments in philosophy and reveals that the early seventeenth century was a turning point in both (Scruton, 2002). We argue that these developments are still influential in academia.

As early as the sixteenth century, experimentation and sense data were understood to be the primary means by which scientific knowledge could be acquired. In this view, theory was to be derived from practical experimentation and observation. Theory was subordinate to practice. By the mid-seventeenth century,

Descartes, himself a physicist, totally overturned this paradigm and ascribed to the act of theorizing ultimate preeminence in the search for knowledge. He posited that everything could be accounted for through mathematical reasoning. For Descartes, everything about the world could be explained by quantifiable deduction. Theory itself was to be deduced from metaphysical propositions. Although an influential scientist (the Law of Inertia is attributed to him), he assigned a subordinate role to experimentation in the creation of knowledge. Scruton (2002) expresses the Cartesian view in the following words: "Any science that started from the mere evidence of the senses must be inferior in its conclusions to a science that began from principles so abstract that their persuasive power would be apparent to reason alone" (p. 42). Descartes proposed a mind/body dichotomy, with mind clearly superior to body. Thus Cartesian rationalism gave theory a superior status over practice.

In 1687, with the publication of his *Principia*, Newton placed theory and practice in a more balanced relationship, ascribing equal worth to each in the pursuit of scientific knowledge. However, it is commonly accepted that Newtonian physics would not have existed without the work of Descartes (Scruton, 2002), and the persuasiveness of the Cartesian view of the superiority of theorizing over practice continued to dominate. *Knowledge that* was preeminent over *knowledge how*. This, we would argue, is the genesis of the preeminence of theory over practice, which came to dominate the academy, echoes of which could be heard in the early objection from the arts and sciences to the development of the Ph.D. in the professional fields: "practical ends and vocational aims were not appropriate for doctoral study" (Toma, 2002, p 12).

Dewey, writing in the context of teacher education, placed theory and practice in a reciprocal relationship. He posited that the purpose of practice in the preparation of teachers was not merely for the development of the skills of teaching but that practice work was to be "an instrument in making real and vital theoretical instruction" (Dewey, 1904). The classroom as the field of practice was the context in which theoretical principles were acquired and understood. Dewey's prescriptions for the preparation of teachers were premised on his views that theory and practice were organically interconnected. In a similar vein, Schunk (2012) suggests that the varying situations that arise in practice are the grist for theorizing, again placing the two in an interdependent relationship.

We would argue that Dewey's view of the theory/practice relationship holds the most promise for the design of programs for the preparation of education professionals at all levels. A clear implication of this view for the doctoral degree in education is that the current divide between the Ed.D. and the Ph.D. is untenable. It is untenable because it is not true to the nature of either practice or theory.

## POSSIBILITIES FOR A REVISED DOCTORAL
## DEGREE IN EDUCATION

In this section, we advance the view that there should be a single degree for the doctoral preparation of education professionals. We base this view on the Deweyan notion that there is an existential relationship between theory and practice. Further support comes from the field of cognitive psychology, which views "knowledge development as a process of abstraction from concrete situations" (Korthagen, 2001, p. 12). In the proposed reinvented doctoral degree, course work and other learning experiences will promote integrative engagement with both theory and practice. Decisions about the specifics of content, degree requirements, and structure for the redesigned doctoral degree must be informed by answers to two fundamental questions: (1) What is the nature of the education enterprise? and (2) What are the knowledge bases needed to prepare people who can define and solve educational problems? It is certain that the answers to these questions would be drawn from both the fields of practice and theory.

We believe that the persistence of problems in education—the much-talked-about achievement gap between majority and minority students, the poor standing of U.S. K–12 students relative to international comparisons, problems of access to and affordability of higher education, poor retention and graduation rates, assessment and its impact on achievement, and declining participation of minorities in STEM fields, to name a few—derives from our failure to produce professionals who are equipped to address them. On one hand, our Ph.D.s are trained to apply research methods and analyses; on the other, they lack the deep involvement with practice that would enable them to insightfully *define* the problems of practice. So their analyses and the theorizing that results are not about the problems that really matter. The outcome is the production of esoteric publications that are seldom read by anyone but their peers.

To be fair, there is a substantial body of theory that has practical significance, but these research publications often do not impact practice, because neither researchers nor practitioners have been equipped to understand and effect the processes of change. On the other hand, our Ed.D.s have been focused on practice devoid of theoretical foundation and the research capability to interrogate their practice. The result is an emphasis on static skills that cannot respond to the changing realities of the education landscape. The issue of change management in education is germane to all of this and is perhaps the weakest area in current Ed.D. and Ph.D. programs. In a revised doctoral degree, this must be prominent.

While it is outside the scope of this chapter to attempt to prescribe the content and form of the reinvented degree, we would be guilty of empty theorizing if we did not offer some possible approaches to designing the proposed new degree. One approach might be the development of case-based or experiential modules in which participants become deeply involved in a practice-based issue or problem. Engagement with the issue would foster an understanding of both its practical and theoretical aspects. Because real-world problems are always rooted in more than one distinct discipline or field of study, each module would be facilitated by faculty from education as well as from disciplines such as sociology, psychology, politics, or economics, depending on the specific context of the module. Participants would have the benefit of theoretical insights from these areas and would be led to understand the complex nature of real-world educational issues. In this way, participants come to understand theory *in the context of real-world practice.*

We recognize, however, the need to prepare professionals for theory *generation* as well as application. The theory-generating aspect of their education would be addressed through the requirement that participants develop research questions about the context in which the module is based, which they would explore individually or collaboratively through research. In this way, both practice and theory could be addressed, with each given attention in each module.

The rich interdisciplinary interaction among faculty and between faculty and students that such an approach would spawn is reflective of the complexity of real-world issues and has the potential to transform the academy itself, where structural and organizational barriers have often limited the extent to which faculty engage in interdisciplinary work. We also believe that such approaches allow participants to experience knowledge generation as an abstraction from concrete situations. We envisage a core of such modules, as well as a range of elective ones that allow for specialization depending on interest, prior preparation, and career aspirations in administration, research, or university teaching. The core would also include modules that are specifically designed to teach research skills that could then be employed in addressing the research questions that arise out of other modules. Participants are thus learning research skills and immediately applying them in increasingly sophisticated ways to real-world issues.

We anticipate the objection that such a design would not develop the high level of research competence that the current Ph.D. provides for would-be researchers and university faculty. We respond to that objection in two ways. First, our experience with Ph.D. dissertations suggests that very few of them rise to the level of theory generation. Second, our approach could include a collaborative dissertation so as to allow for problems of larger scale to be addressed. We also envisage elective modules on more advanced research strategies, including analyses of large data sets as a basis for theory-building research or data-driven decision making. In this regard, we advocate a rethinking of the dissertation as the sine qua non for the awarding of the degree. It could be replaced by a prescribed number of publishable research papers arising out of the analyses of the issues included in the modules. For those who so choose, there could be the collaborative dissertation as just described.

Guthrie (2009), in his call for a "modern" doctor of education degree, supports his view that the Ed.D. and Ph.D. should be kept separate by the fact that education science has progressed to a point where highly sophisticated research approaches are necessary, and that a single degree could not afford the time needed to develop researcher or practitioner competencies. In our model, such competencies could be the subject of optional modules for those whose interests lead them in that direction. With regard to research competence, it has not been possible, even in current Ph.D. programs, to develop graduates such that they are highly skilled researchers at graduation. What this proposed new degree will do is give them a level of research competence that is no less than that of current Ph.D.s and, in addition, will ensure that they have the practical and theoretical insights to define significant problems for research.

It takes deep involvement with practice and a profound understanding of the contexts in which education happens to be able to insightfully define significant areas for research. This is lacking in current Ph.D. programs and results in sterile theorizing that has limited application to education in the real world. It is unrealistic to think that any program—the current Ph.D. or our proposed revision—will produce the highest levels of research competence during the course of the program of study. Skilled researchers develop new competencies and hone their skills over the course of their careers. What we aim to do is provide the competencies and the sensitivities that would be the foundation for growth throughout the life of a career.

## WHAT'S IN A NAME? PH.D. OR ED.D.?

We suggest that the degree be called a Ph.D. The question of the name of the degree is certainly a less substantive issue than the content and structure of the degree, but it is of some import. The Ph.D. will always enjoy a more elevated status within the academy for both historical and philosophical reasons. Calling the proposed redesigned degree an Ed.D. will ensure that it continues to suffer in this regard. It is true that this proposed new Ph.D. represents a departure from the accustomed Ph.D. model that currently exists in the arts and sciences, but similar calls to break out of this mold have been made in other fields as traditional ideas about the degree are being challenged. Park (2005), discussing the Ph.D. in the UK context, expressed the need for "a wholesale revision of assumptions and expectations" (p. 3) as well as the view that there is a new emphasis on skills and training. In education, we should have the courage to depart from the traditional in response to the grave problems and pressing demands of the field. In the final analysis, respect for the degree would be won or lost by the way we educate our clients.

## CONCLUDING THOUGHTS

In conclusion, the proposed new Ph.D. is a radical departure in form and intent from the current degrees, and obstacles to its widespread implementation are many. Still, we are hopeful about the possibility of change in the proposed direction. We are especially optimistic in light of the recent announcement by Harvard University that its last cohort of Ed.D. students was admitted in 2013. In the fall of 2014, Harvard admitted its first candidates to a new Ph.D. in education. The new degree has been described as "an interfaculty degree in education." It has always been true that the top-tier research universities chart the course that others follow. We hope that the Harvard initiative begins a movement toward a Ph.D. that better equips professionals to serve the dire educational needs of our society.

## REFERENCES

Baez, B. (2002, November). *Degree of distinction: The Ed.D. or the Ph.D. in education.* Paper presented at the annual meeting of the Association for the Study of Higher Education, Sacramento, CA.

Brown, L.D. (1990). *A perspective on the Ph.D.-Ed.D. discussion in schools of education.* Paper presented at the annual meeting of the American Educational Research Association.

Carnegie Project on the Education Doctorate (CPED). (2014). http://cpedinitiative.org/about

Clifford, G.J., & Guthrie, J.W. (1988). *Ed school. A brief for professional education.* Chicago: University of Chicago Press.

Dewey, J. (1904). *The relation of theory to practice in education.* Retrieved from http://people.ucsc.edu/~ktellez/dewey_relation.pdf

Gregory, M. (1995). Implications of the introduction of the doctor of education degree in British universities: Can the Ed.D. reach parts the Ph.D. cannot? *Vocational Aspect of Education, 47*(2), 177–188. doi: 10.1080/0305787950470206

Guthrie, J.W. (2009). The case for a modern doctor of education degree (Ed.D.): Multipurpose education doctorates no longer appropriate. *Peabody Journal of Education, 84*(1), 3–8. doi: 10.1080/01619560802679526

Korthagen, F.A.J. (2001). *Linking practice and theory: The pedagogy of realistic teacher education.* Mahwah, NJ: Lawrence Erlbaum.

Levine, A. (2005). *Educating school leaders.* New York: Education Schools Project.

McNulty, N., & Shirley, Z. (2010). *Battle of prestige: Ph.D. versus Ed.D.* Unpublished manuscript, University of North Texas.

Nelson, J.K., & Coorough, C. (1994). Content analysis of the Ph.D. versus Ed.D. dissertation. *Journal of Experimental Education, 62*(2), 158–168.

Osguthorpe, R.T, & Wong, M.J. (1993). The Ph.D. versus the Ed.D.: Time for a decision. *Innovative Higher Education, 18*(1), 47–63.

Park, C. (2005). New variant Ph.D.: The changing nature of the doctorate in the UK. *Journal of Higher Education Policy and Management, 27*(2), 189–207.

Redden, E. (2007, April). Envisioning a new Ed.D. *Inside Higher Ed.* Retrieved from http://m. insidehighered.com/news/2007/04/10/education#sthash.EmA40qJ4.dpbs

Schunk, D.H. (2012). *Learning theories: An educational perspective* (6th ed.). Upper Saddle River, NJ: Prentice Hall.

Scruton, R. (2002). *A short history of modern philosophy: From Descartes to Wittgenstein* (2nd ed.). London: Routledge. Retrieved from http://www.questia.com

Toma, J.D. (2002). *Legitimacy, differentiation, and the promise of the Ed.D. in higher education.* Paper presented at the annual meeting of the Association for the Study of Higher Education, Sacramento, CA. Retrieved from http://eric.ed.gov/?id=ED482308

Townsend, B. (2002, November). *Rethinking the Ed.D. or what's in a name?* Paper presented at the annual meeting of the Association for the Study of Higher Education, Sacramento, CA.

# CHAPTER TEN

# Fitness for Purpose

## Is This a Problem for Professional Ed.D. Programs?

*Marnie O'Neill*

## INTRODUCTION

Growth and proliferation of professional doctorates across a broad range of fields of knowledge since the 1990s (Bourner, Bowden, & Liang, 2001; Chiteng Kot & Hendel, 2012), to the point where they are now the dominant form of doctoral education (Miller, 2005), has prompted a debate about their purpose, their design, and their place in doctoral research education and training. The international phenomenon of professional doctorates has been attributed variously to a critique of the narrowness and the lack of multidisciplinarity, appropriate collaborative work, and skill sets preparing graduates for work attributed to the research-oriented Ph.D. (Chiteng Kot & Hendel, 2012), as well as governments' concerns about management, efficiency, and quality assurance of doctoral education, and the employability of doctoral degree holders (Bourner et al., 2001; Pearson, Cumming, Evans, Macauley, & Ryland, 2011).

Complementary explanations have attributed this to the growth of the knowledge economy, as well as increased pressure for the university (1) to reshape its role to strengthen links among education, knowledge, and the economy; (2) to diversify and create more professionally relevant programs; and (3) to develop work-based learning (Bourner et al., 2001; Chiteng Kot & Hendel, 2012; Maxwell, Hickey, & Evans, 2005) in ways that reflect government awareness that economic competitiveness can be increased through innovations in science and technology and through better education and professional preparation for the workforce (Chiteng Kot & Hendel, 2012).

A desire for doctorates that fitted the workplace promoted the development of professional doctorates that "address the career needs of practicing professionals, especially those in, or aspiring to senior positions" (Bourner et al., p. 70). Bourner and colleagues report that most professional doctorates try to integrate the professional work of candidates into their doctoral studies, with research to be undertaken on a topic that relates to a candidate's own field of professional practice in his or her working life. Thus, they conclude that professional doctorates have placed research at the service of the development of professional practice and professional practitioners. Malloch (2010) claims that changes in government policies and funding, compounded by the realities of delivery, adversely affected earlier growth and optimism, resulting in a diminished popularity and decline of professional doctorates in Australia.

Students engaged in professional doctorates are a diverse population characterized as mid-career, mid-life persons who frequently have responsibilities related to dependent children, aged parents, and their own health issues (Malloch, 2010; O'Neill, 2012; Pearson et al., 2011). They also have diverse career goals, with older students interested in career change or advancement or enhancement of professional learning (Lunt, 2011; Malloch, 2010; O'Neill, 2012). Enders (2004) cautions against striving to create formalized and unified models for doctoral training at the expense of "multiple small worlds of research training with their specific research and research training practices" (p. 427). It is possible that in Australia, professional doctorates have not been designed with sufficient flexibility and openness to recognize and accommodate these diverse needs or to maintain financial viability in small programs.

Servage's (2009) critique of human-capital explanations for the emergence of professional doctorates suggests that credentialism and positional competition theories may offer a more cogent explanation for links between education and employment. Theoretically, as the number of credentials issued increases, their value in the labor market declines; thus it is arguable that the professional doctorate is an effort on the part of institutions to meet consumer demand for doctoral-level education by broadening access and creating specialized programs for niche markets. In other words, the professional doctorate may be conceived as an effort to create "room at the top" by broadening doctoral-level offerings in ways that do not challenge the exclusivity of the conventional Ph.D. (Servage, 2009).

Levine's (2005) report on educational administration doctorates in the United States provided a salutary analysis of competitive marketization of higher degrees, where quality-control mechanisms appeared to be nonexistent and decisions were driven almost entirely by market competition. Shulman, Golde, Bueschel, and Garabedian's (2006) response, advocating curriculum revision based on best practice, assessable competencies, and greater accountability, was roundly criticized by Evans (2007). This example appears to be atypical in the professional doctorates field. Although it was assumed that most professional doctorates would be predominantly coursework degrees (and, presumably, consist of units heavily oriented to content knowledge and skills of the specific professional field) (McWilliam et al., 2002), in practice, most professional doctorates, while diverse in other ways, are commonly defined as research and coursework. The research requirement varies in the weighting accorded and in the mode of presentation, which may include (1) completion of more than one research project; (2) a portfolio allowing submission of a series of documents rather than a single dissertation; and (3) published outcomes (Bourner et al., 2001). More significantly, in Mode 1 (Maxwell, 2003), although the research requirement is smaller in scale than the research project of a Doctor of Philosophy degree, evaluation criteria are intended to be the same.

These circumstances make it more difficult to distinguish definitively between traditional Ph.D.s and professional doctorates. Bourner and fellow researchers (2001) attempt to do so on the grounds that "whereas the PhD candidate starts from what is known (that is, the literature review), professional doctorate candidates start from what is *not* known (that is, some perceived problem in professional practice)" and thus postulate that while "the 'traditional' Doctor of Philosophy degree is intended to develop *professional researchers*, the professional doctorate is designed to develop *researching professionals*" (p. 71). In practice, it has become evident that the scope of research projects and subsequent theses differ very little in the Australian context; research topics are frequently virtually interchangeable between traditional Ph.D.s and professional doctorates. For doctoral candidates in education, it seems likely that topics selected would have some connection with candidates' professional experiences and might in many instances reasonably be expected to contribute to practice. Table 10.1 offers a comparison of selected thesis topics for both forms of the doctorate in an Australian research university.

Table 10.1 Comparison of Selected Ph.D. and Ed.D. Research Topics in Education.

| Ph.D. | Ed.D. |
| --- | --- |
| Tara Tuchaai (2014): *Critical literacy practices and higher order thinking: A perspectival study of Yr11 literature students and teachers in an independent girls' school in Western Australia.* | Clayton Massey (2014): *Curriculum innovation in an independent boys' school: A case study of the social, cognitive and multimodal development of early adolescent males.* |
| Margaret McAlinden (2013): *A Qualitative study of intercultural empathy and ESL teachers.* | Paul Mercieca (2011): *Northern Soul: Social semiotics of cultural identity.* |
| Katherine Shine (2012): *Schoolteachers in the news: A historical analysis of coverage in* The West Australian *newspaper.* | Karen Marias (2007): *From finishing school to feminist academy? The social construction of gender in the case of an independent Anglican girls' school in Western Australia, 1945 to 1997.* |

| Ph.D. | Ed.D. |
| --- | --- |

Wahiza Wahi (2012): *Investigating academic literacy for employability in the language classroom in Malaysian HE.*

Suzanne Dawkins (2012): *The oral-literate continuum: Young children as story tellers.*

Shanmugam Kadakara (2012): *Status of Tamil language in Singapore: A family domain analysis.*

Patricia Kiddey (2012): *Transforming education systems: High school teachers' perspectives on large scale national literacy strategies implemented in England, the United States and Australia.*

Rozita Dass (2011): *Stakeholders' perspectives on the status of English literature in Singapore schools.*

Elaine Sharplin (2008): *Quality of worklife for rural and remote teachers: Perspectives of novice, interstate and overseas teachers.*

Mignon Shardlow (2010): *Teaching the watchdogs of democracy: The professional formation of journalists through Australian university study and early employment.*

Janina Trotman (2007): *Girls becoming teachers: An historical analysis of Western Australian women teachers, 1911–1940.*

Tess Martin (2011): *Diversity and change in the professional world of TAFE teachers: A study within the Western Australian context.*

Elaine Lopes (2009): *The Western Australian Schools of isolated and distance education: Background, issues and concerns.*

Angie Ng Kwee Sew (2009): *Professional development and its impact on delivery of quality care: Perspectives of Singapore Polyclinic's registered nurses.*

Belinda Yourn (2003): *Individual perseverance: how parents of children in the school of isolated and distance education in Western Australia manage their work as home tutors.*

Pasco Putrino (2006): *Workplace formation: How secondary school students manage structured workplace learning.*

Mi Yin Wu (2004): *Teachers' perspectives on applying the Human Dynamics Framework in their classroom: The experience of two Singapore schools.*

Karin Oerlemans (2005): *Secondary school students' engagement in educational change: Critical perspectives on policy enactment.*

Joanne Griffiths (2009): *Curriculum policy dynamics: Government and non-government education sectors in Western Australia.*

Julie-Anne Ellis (2006): *Perspectives on the "Students at Educational Risk" policy and inclusive practices in schools.*

Tan Yong Tiong Samson (2006): *Junior college curriculum reform and private tutoring in Singapore: How parents, students and tutors deal with change.*

Derek Cheung (1995): *Measurement of the degree of implementation of school-based assessment schemes for practical science.*

Jumiati Ismail (2009): *Cross-cultural business negotiation of Malaysia-Australia.*

Isabel Benjamin (2010): *"The Target of the Question": An investigation of textual features typically targeted in reading comprehension questions.*

Mitaka Yoneda (2006): *English for business purposes: Japanese professionals in Singapore.*

## THE AUSTRALIAN CONTEXT

Australian universities' ambitions to achieve high rankings in research-driven global performance tables, coupled with a rediscovered significance of Asia to Australia's financial well-being, accelerated recruitment and marketing strategies to attract higher-degree research students to Australian universities. Concomitantly, funding cuts to Australian universities increased financial imperatives to compete vigorously in the international higher education market; "all institutions (except the Australian national university) regardless of their prestige or role in research were locked into a volume building trajectory in the global market to supplement declining public funding" (Marginson, 2007, p. 22).

UNESCO Institute of Statistics data (cited in Choudaha & Chang, 2012) show an increase of 43% (from 179,619 to 257,637) in international student enrollments in Australia; the figure of 996,000 by 2025 suggested by Zeegers and Barron (2008) does not seem implausible. Less compelling is Zeegers and Barron's logical corollary that international higher-degree research students will become the means through which Australian universities build the critical mass required for dynamic, vibrant research cultures. Marginson's (2007) analysis of Australian universities' position in the global market was less optimistic, demonstrating that the proportion of foreign students enrolled in Australian doctoral programs (4.7%) was substantially lower than that of the United States (16.6%) and the UK (9.4%). He further argued that it is impossible to become a magnet for foreign research students without extensive scholarship funding.

Students find an acceptable alternative in transnational programs: in 2005, more than 100,000 students from other countries studied at Australian universities (Chapman & Pyvis, 2012). Both push and pull effects influence their decisions to enroll transnationally: a limited number of places in public institutions, ethnic quota systems, the high cost of overseas education, the desire for an international education, and openness to new ideas and experiences (Chapman & Pyvis, 2012). For older students, an additional attraction is the advantage of maintaining employment and residence in the home country, as opposed to foregoing income and incurring residential expenses in onshore programs (O'Neill, 2012).

Marginson (2007) observed that "institutions are shaped by resource dependency regimes and by regulations both prohibitive and constructive" (p. 6). Federal government "brand protection" contributes to tight regulation of Australian qualifications (Australian Qualifications Framework Council, 2013) and the requirement for courses in transnational contexts offshore (used interchangeably with transnational) to mirror onshore offerings (Australian Government, 2000, 2011). Doctoral programs are classified at level D in the Australian Qualifications Framework (AQF):

> The purpose of the Doctoral Degree is to qualify individuals who apply a substantial body of knowledge to research, investigate and develop new knowledge, in one or more

fields of investigation, scholarship or professional practice. Research is the defining characteristic of all Doctoral Degree qualifications. The research Doctoral Degree (typically referred to as a Doctor of Philosophy) makes a significant and original contribution to knowledge; the professional Doctoral Degree (typically titled Doctor of [field of study]) makes a significant and original contribution to knowledge in the context of professional practice. The emphasis in the learning outcomes and research may differ between the different forms of Doctoral Degree qualifications but all graduates will demonstrate knowledge, skills and the application of the knowledge and skills at AQF level 10. (AQF, 2013, p. 63)

Miller (2005) finds that these requirements blur the distinction between Ph.D.s and professional doctorates, claiming that as the Doctor of Business Administration (DBA) is afforded the same level of recognition as Ph.D.s by the government in Australia, these DBAs are increasingly considered to be alternatives to the Ph.D. as a doctoral and research training award. Consequently, many of the candidates enrolling in the research DBAs are practicing academics from other Australian and overseas universities (Miller, 2005).

Miller identifies another significant segment of students as private and public-sector consultants seeking either to test models developed in their practice or to enhance their personal credibility and marketability. However, like Ph.D. candidates in business and management, "the majority of applicants are typically either interested in progressing their understanding of complex management issues or have a plan to perhaps move into academia when they burn out, have achieved all they wish to in their professional role or wish to semi-retire" (Miller, 2005, p. 12).

Miller's evidence casts doubt on Servage's suggestion (2009) that professional doctorates do not "swim in the same pool" as Ph.D.s "and because the doctoral degree is the top rung on the educational ladder, the positional value of the degree in terms of its capacity to open doors to further higher education becomes moot" (p. 775). Thus the logical extension of this argument that professional doctorates are not a rival good is also open to question; their status as research degrees may be significant in the capacity of the university to sell into a competitive market (Servage, 2009). Miller (2005, p. 13) further argues that the solution to the confusion that results as Ph.D.s are outnumbered by professional doctorates and as Ph.D. testamurs are rebranded to include a speciality research is for Australian universities to consider establishing a new, advanced higher research degree that clearly differentiates university research of a very high standard from other higher research degrees. The suggestion would appear to exacerbate problems associated with credentialism, to risk further fragmentation of the pool of doctoral candidates, and to increase competition between universities for such high-prestige candidates, as well as being open to the same criticism that Evans (2007) made of Shulman and colleagues' (2006) proposal.

## THE WESTERN AUSTRALIAN CONTEXT

The preliminary estimated resident population (ERP) of Australia as of September 30, 2013, was 23,235,800 people. Western Australia continued to record the fastest growth rate of all states and territories at 3.1% (Australian Bureau of Statistics, 2013), surging to 2,517,000 as of June 2013. Of this population, an estimated 1.97 million persons were located in Greater Perth. Perth is Australia's fourth-largest (though mostly isolated) city and the world's most isolated continental capital city. Perth is closer to Jakarta, Indonesia (3007 km), than to Australia's capital city of Canberra (3,905 km by car). Adelaide (the nearest other state capital) is over 2,000 kilometers distant; Sydney is over 4,400 kilometers to the east by car (five hours' flying time). Singapore and Hong Kong are located in the same time zone as Perth and are approximately 5 and 8 hours away, respectively, by direct plane flight.

The five universities in Perth all offer undergraduate and postgraduate programs in education and thus compete for students in a relatively small, isolated population pool. In the funding squeeze described above, recruitment of students from nearby Southeast Asia offers the best opportunity to develop an increased cash flow and to enhance international visibility and reputation. Thus WA universities adopt various strategies—direct recruitment, partial and full credit for studies undertaken offshore, twinning, franchised or moderated programs, partnerships with private providers, offshore campuses, and online programs (Pyvis & Chapman, 2007)—to recruit both undergraduate and postgraduate international students. Offshore postgraduate students, like their Australian counterparts, are typically employed full time and have family commitments that make a doctoral program delivered in-country by an internationally reputable university an attractive and potentially affordable proposition (O'Neill, 2012).

## THE WESTERN AUSTRALIAN CASE STUDY

The Doctor of Education (Ed.D.) program discussed in this chapter was established by the University of Western Australia in 1993. As the university is a research-intensive institution, the major condition of approval was that the professional degree be "of the same standard, but different in kind" from the PhD. programs conforming to the AQF specifications (first introduced in 1995) that attract federal government research training scheme (RTS) funding for Australian citizens, permanent residents, and New Zealand citizens. Candidates in these categories are exempt from student contribution amounts and tuition fees for units undertaken as part of a higher degree research (HDR) course of study; the federal government provides a small portion of funding per capita "on load" in annual block grants and the balance upon successful completion of the degree.

Transnational students are not eligible for RTS funding on load but do attract completion funding for the university, which flows to the school. Although individual universities set entry requirements and fee structures, entry requirements in any one institution would be identical across the same onshore and transnational program. The university in this case study is one of the smaller Group of Eight (Go8) research-intensive universities that enrolled approximately 20,000 undergraduate and 5,500 postgraduate students in 2013.

## Design of the Doctor of Education Program

Consistent with the University Academic Council requirement for academic standards and rigor comparable with the Ph.D., admission requirements for the Ed.D. mirrored those of the Ph.D. with the additional requirement of the equivalent of 2 years of full-time professional experience. Initially, the Ed.D. was modelled on a U.S. professional doctorate and was focused on educational administration. The five coursework units (including content-driven units related to educational administration and management), the research seminar, and an oral examination across the range of content material covered in the program frequently exceeded 2 years of part-time study. Although one student completed the program within four years, one-third of the first cohort took between 8 and 10 years to complete it. The program review (1999) and revision (O'Neill, 2012) reduced taught courses to four, all focused on research training. The scaffolding explicitly sought to provide experienced practitioners returning to academic study with critical skills as research consumers, knowledge and competence in research inquiry, and skills of argument in academic writing. Candidates were expected to use each of the coursework papers to prepare their formal proposals and to develop draft material for the first chapters of their theses.

Revision of the program met AQF requirements for Level 10 research doctorates, incorporated research training to support mid-career candidates returning to study, enhanced flexibility to accommodate a wide range of research topics, and produced a program structure that could be deployed successfully in transnational settings. The effect of the changes on the local market can be seen in the improved participation and completion rates from 2005 to 2014 (Table 10.2). Even so, it is evident that the total Ph.D. completions (146) and the completions within the same period (72) continued to outweigh onshore Ed.D. completions (63).

Table 10.2. Doctoral Completions 1997–2014.

| Year | WA | Hong Kong | Singapore | Total Ed.D. Completions | Ph.D. Completions* |
|---|---|---|---|---|---|
| 1997–2004 | 24 | | | 24 | 37 |
| 2005 | 3 | 5 | | 8 | 7 |
| 2006 | 6 | 6 | 10 | 22 | 3 |
| 2007 | 4 | 6 | 6 | 16 | 9 |
| 2008 | 2 | 5 | 7 | 14 | 8 |
| 2009 | 3 | 3 | 12 | 18 | 5 |
| 2010 | 8 | 1 | 13 | 22 | 7 |
| 2011 | 3 | 1 | 6 | 10 | 7 |
| 2012 | 5 | 1 | 8 | 14 | 8 |
| 2013 | 2 | 1 | 11 | 14 | 7 |
| 22/05/2014 | 3 | | 2 | 5 | 4 |
| Total completions | 63 | 29 | 75 | 167 | 72 |
| In progress | 30 | 4 | 40 | 74 | 21 |

*Number of PhD completions 1969–1996: 74.

## Onshore Candidates

Only 24 onshore students completed the Ed.D. between 1994 (the first year of enrollment) and 2004, and the first transnational completions in Hong Kong occurred in 2005 (Table 10.2). In the 1999 program review, candidates criticized aspects of the program that led to slow progression; its insufficient focus on research training; the irrelevance of coursework content papers to final research project; and the overly narrow focus on educational administration (alternative suggestions included curriculum development and implementation, teaching and learning, professional development and career pathways, policy studies and home schooling as appropriate research topics for professional doctorates).

The career trajectories of the 27 onshore candidates who completed the program by 2005 were diverse. Ten already held principal or senior leadership positions either in government or nongovernment schools and remained in senior leadership positions; eight took up university appointments (including three who had previously held them); two international students returned home to senior leadership positions; two continued in senior leadership positions in the government education bureaucracy; two moved interstate to senior bureaucratic positions; one took up a senior technical education appointment in the Middle East; one took up a prestigious school appointment and later a university appointment in the UK; and one continued in a private consultancy.

While it could be argued that their professional doctorates contributed to their successful postdoctoral careers, it was notable that, for many candidates, neither their theses nor their postdoctoral paths were located in educational administration or in school-level education.

The diversity of post-2006 onshore postgraduate destinations (Table 10.3) suggests that the restructured degree has served the interests of the candidates. Of 21 graduates who had been in school sectors at the commencement of their candidature, 16 remained in those sectors, 1 shifted to a different area of the public service, and 4 took up university appointments (all in education-related roles). It could be argued as well that those in school sectors were already on a leadership trajectory and that the completion of a professional doctorate in education merely enhanced their career pathways rather than demonstrably enhancing their knowledge, skills, and professional attributes specific to school administration or leadership. Eleven graduates were located in the higher education sector. Of those, five already held education-related university appointments and selected the Doctor of Education as an appropriate means for consolidating their academic careers; four who were previously in the school sector achieved a career path change into the university sector; and the two overseas appointments achieved promotion on their original fields.

Table 10.3. Career Pathways of Onshore Ed.D. Graduates, 2006–2014.

| Destination | Number |
| --- | --- |
| Senior public service (1 non-education) | 5 |
| Government school sector | 7 |
| Independent school sector | 5 |
| University appointment (continuing) | 5 |
| University appointment (postgraduate) | 4 |
| Overseas appointments (TAFE and university) | 2 |
| Retired | 1 |
| Unknown | 3 |
| International returned home | 5 |
| Total | 37 |

Data for onshore international doctoral completions in the school reflect both the increased mobility of students and an increased emphasis on internationalization in university policies and marketing since 2000. Despite federal government support for visas for postgraduate research students, available scholarships for international students are fiercely contested; most international research students in the school are privately funded or supported by scholarships and sponsors from their own countries. Such funding sources favor Ph.D. rather than Ed.D. programs, as

Australian scholarships do not support students in the coursework phase of the Ed.D. In the 30-year period from 1969 to 1999, only 13 international students completed Ph.D.s (an average of 0.4 per annum), but from 2000 to 2014, 14 international students completed Ph.D.s (an average of 2 per annum).

By contrast, only eight international students completed Ed.D.s between 2004 and 2014 (an average of 0.8 per annum). These data appear to agree with Marginson's (2007) position on scholarship funding to attract international research students. Comparing international completions between onshore and transnational doctoral programs (Table 10.2), it is evident that the transnational Ed.D. contributes more substantially to the agenda of internationalization and income generation than either of the onshore doctoral programs.

## Transnational Candidates

Financial pressure made explicit by the 1994 School Review and tight competition among the five local universities provided impetus for the transnational initiative. Partnerships were established in Hong Kong and Singapore to deliver Master of Education degrees with a research training focus. Three different partnerships were formed: one with a large university in Hong Kong with a School of Continuing Education that provided a good fit; an initial partnership in Singapore with a private education and training center (Downtown) whose interest eventually moved further toward training, with the result that the partnership was dissolved by mutual consent; and a second partnership with a prestigious secondary school, which overlapped with and then replaced the first. The success of the master's programs increased demand from graduates for a doctoral program.

The transnational market in Hong Kong proved relatively volatile. Initial demand for the master's program peaked at 100+ students in one cohort. However, SARS and H1N1 virus fears, as well as economic downturns after 1997, adversely affected enrollments in this largely privately funded market. Several candidates lost their jobs, and potential candidates thus became quite reasonably risk averse. The Ed.D. program faced considerable competition for postgraduate students; cohorts tended to be small and decreased progressively across the four intakes. Candidates came predominantly from the higher education sector (nine from universities, five from polytechnic universities, and ten from various institutes of education and vocational education). The remainder were from schools (predominantly international) or were in private businesses such as language consultancies. The higher education candidates generally sought enhancement of their positions in their universities, while those in institutions such as the Hong Kong Institute of Education served both their personal interests and those of the institution as it sought to upgrade to university status.

In Singapore, three cohorts commenced Downtown, achieving the first completions in 2006. The candidates came from very diverse backgrounds, although the higher education sector was again dominant (eight students were from universities, six from the National Institute of Education [NIE], and five from polytechnic institutions). There was great variety in backgrounds among individual enrollees (National Healthcare Centre, Singapore Examination and Assessments Board, Singapore Defence Forces, Human Resources, Ear Nose and Throat Centre of Singapore General Hospital, and private education consultants). The remainder came from international schools and the Ministry of Education (MOE), either from the head office bureaucracy or from schools. Diversity of candidates was more evident in the Downtown program than in the onshore cohorts, reinforcing the importance of program flexibility.

The relationship established with the Hwa Chong Institution (HCI) was of a different type. In 2000, a memorandum of understanding was signed between the University of Western Australia (UWA) and HCI "to collaborate on a number of educational initiatives." Objectives of this Master of Education program at HCI were to:

- Upgrade and enhance the knowledge of Hwa Chong Institution staff about research and its methodologies;
- Develop the research supervision skills of Hwa Chong Institution staff;
- Bring together advanced theory and practice in education through the coursework and projects of the programme;
- Apply the knowledge developed in the courses to projects of practical and professional significance to Hwa Chong Institution; and
- Prepare participants in the programme for doctoral studies in education. (Hwa Chong Institution, n.d.)

The Ed.D. commenced in 2004. According to the HCI website, it intended to cater to the needs of professionals who wished to undertake doctoral-level study so as to expand their theoretical bases for practice, to consider current ideas and issues, and to address problems of practical implementation in education. Participants are encouraged to take up research questions that are germane to their current or projected career interests (Hwa Chong Institution, n.d.).

Four cohorts of students have since enrolled. With the agenda of capacity development within the institute, it is not surprising that the first cohort consisted almost entirely of HCI staff, with one candidate from an MOE school, one from NIE, and the principal of a prestigious Malaysian college flying in to take part. The second cohort was similarly dominated by HCI staff, with only seven private individuals—three from MOE, two polytechnic staff, and one each from the Institute of Technical Education and Nanyang Institute of

Management. The two most recent cohorts are still in progress, but HCI representation has been reduced to three in each cohort, and there is now a wider representation of others from MOE, higher education institutions, education bureaucracies such as the Department of Examination and Assessment, and private individuals.

## CONCLUSION

This chapter has argued that rather than limiting the conceptualization of professional doctorates, specifically the Doctor of Education, to constrained (and increasingly strained) definitions and hair splitting over whether professional doctoral candidates are "professional researchers" or "researching professionals" (Bourner et al., p. 71), a more productive path is to consider fitness for purpose. As an indicator of quality, fitness for purpose is inevitably a relative concept that allows institutions to define their purpose in their mission and objectives (Woodhouse, 1999). Risk of variability within larger institutions, as "purposes" become more diffuse with increased distance from the center, is enhanced in transnational programs by the greater potential divergence of views between "senders" and "receivers" (Campbell & Rozsnyai, 2002, p. 20). Marginson (2007) suggests that while internationalization in Australian universities is "unambiguously commercial... base level quality is ensured by a national system of quality assurance and periodic audit [Australian Universities Quality Agency]" (p. 20). "Quality" in the case study reported in this chapter is maintained by weighted course average requirements for progression to the thesis phase and through external thesis examinations by three independent examiners, one of whom is usually international but not necessarily "professional."

A substantial area of potential confusion emerges in conceptualizations of "the profession." O'Mullane (2005, p. 9) distinguishes between "institutionalised" professions (characterized by established codes of practice, accreditation, or registration requirements) and "non-institutionalised" professions (not specific or codified) in critiquing the lack of consensus about concepts of "significant contribution" to "professional knowledge and practice." In a broad field such as education, "the profession" cannot be regarded as a unitary concept. An analysis of the career positions, pathways, and research topics of doctoral candidates in this case study demonstrates that "the profession" extends to school sectors, educational bureaucracies, higher education institutions, and persons with roles in education in other fields of study (journalism, nursing, business training, and private consultancies). If the professional positions in which Doctor of Education candidates are located or to which they aspire are diverse, then it follows that there should not only be diversity between professional doctoral programs but also sufficient flexibility within program structures to meet the diverse needs and interests of candidates.

It may be that heavily content-driven coursework degrees that focus on knowledge, skills, and competencies of school leadership or administration in particular jurisdictions are productive practices in those contexts. However, the school partner showcased in this chapter focused on building research capacity among its staff to enhance the research agenda for its staff and students within the school. (Educational Leadership was dropped from the master's program.) Other successful candidates were not working in schools or even in educational bureaucracies where they might have been expected to provide leadership to schools. In O'Mullane's (2005) sense of "non-institutionalised" professions, it is difficult to judge "contribution to the profession" beyond candidates' own sense that their contributions were apposite to their field of work/study and contributed to their personal sense of professional membership (O'Neill, 2012).

It is argued that the Doctor of Education program foregrounded in this chapter can be judged to be successful and fit for purpose. It has successfully

(1) produced research theses judged to meet international standards of doctoral work through the independent and international examination processes;

(2) provided (and continues to do so) the diverse onshore candidature with viable pathways to personal affirmation, career enhancement or career change;

(3) met the professional and personal needs of candidature of even greater diversity in two transnational settings;

(4) created an extended revenue stream unavailable in the local context of the School of Education; and

(5) enhanced the international visibility of the school and the awareness, experience, and capacities of the academic staff involved.

On the basis of these criteria, the program resonates with the "sense of doctorateness" explored by Wellington (2013), meets Seddon's (2000, 2001) requirement of scaffolding and inducting learners into important knowledge foundations and ways of knowing characterized by intellectual rigor and discipline sustained throughout the work, and satisfies Lunt's (2002) expectation of a substantial piece of independent enquiry assessed in a way similar to that of the Ph.D. What it does not do is meet the criteria for a practitioner doctorate of the kind described by Lester (2004). Perhaps this is the point: seeking to define or constrain the concept of a doctoral program beyond the kinds of general criteria articulated by Wellington risks elimination of those doctoral forms that serve the diversity that increasingly characterizes doctoral candidates and their interests.

# REFERENCES

Australian Bureau of Statistics 3218.0. (2013). *Regional population growth, Australia, 2012–13*. Retrieved from www.abs.gov.au

Australian Government. (2000). *Education Services for Overseas Students Act 2000 (amended 2013)*. Canberra: Australian Government. Retrieved from http://www.comlaw.gov.au/Series/C2004A00757

Australian Government. (2011). *Tertiary Education Quality and Standards Agency Act 2011*. Canberra: Australian Government. Retrieved from http://www.comlaw.gov.au/Details/F2013C00169

Australian Qualifications Framework Council. (2013). *Australian qualifications framework second edition January 2013*. South Australia: Australian Qualifications Framework Council.

Bourner, T., Bowden, R., & Laing, S. (2001). The adoption of professional doctorates in English universities: Why here? Why now? In B. Green, T.W. Maxwell, & P. Shanahan (Eds.), *Doctoral education and professional practice: The next generation?* Armidale, NSW, Australia: Kardoorair Press.

Campbell, C., & Rozsnyai, C. (2002). *Quality assurance and the development of course programmes*. Papers on Higher Education Regional University Network on Governance and Management of Higher Education in South East Europe. Bucharest: UNESCO.

Chapman, A., & Pyvis, D. (2012). Enhancing quality in transnational education: Experiences of teaching and learning in Australian offshore programs. Lanham, MD: Lexington Books.

Chiteng Kot, F., & Hendel, D.D. (2012). Emergence and growth of professional doctorates in the United States, United Kingdom, Canada and Australia: A comparative analysis. *Studies in Higher Education, 37*(3), 345–364. doi: 10.1080/03075079.2010.516356

Choudaha, R., & Chang, L. (2012). *Trends in student mobility*. Research Report 01. WES Research and Advisory Services. Retrieved from http://www.wes.org/ras/

Enders, J. (2004). Research training and careers in transition: A European perspective on the many faces of the PhD. *Studies in Continuing Education, 26*(3), 419–429.

Evans, R. (2007). Existing practice is not the template. *Educational Researcher, 36*(9), 553–559. doi: 10.3102/0013189X07313149

Hwa Chong Institution (HCI). (n.d.). *The UWA-HCI collaboration*. Retrieved from http://www.hci.sg/admin/uwa/collaboration.htm

Lester, S. (2004). Conceptualising the practitioner doctorate. *Studies in Higher Education, 29*(6), 757–770.

Levine, A. (2005). *Educating school leaders*. New York: The Education Schools Project.

Lunt, I. (2002). *Professional doctorates in education*. Escalate (www.escalate.ac.uk).

Lunt, I. (2011). *Professional doctorates and their contribution to professional development and careers*. Economic and Social Research Council Grant Reference: R000223643. Retrieved from http://www.esrc.ac.uk/my-esrc/grants/R000223643/read

Malloch, M. (2010). Professional doctorates: An Australian perspective. *Work Based Learning e-Journal, 1*(1), 2010.

Marginson, S. (2007). Global position and position taking: The case of Australia. *Journal of Studies in International Education, 11*(1), 5–32. doi: 10.1177/1028315306287530

Maxwell, T. (2003). From first to second generation professional doctorate. *Studies in Higher Education, 28*(3), 279–291.

Maxwell, T., Hickey, C., & Evans, T.D. (2005). *Professional doctorates: Working toward impact*. Professional doctorates 5: Revised Papers from the Fifth Professional Doctorates Conference: Working Doctorates: The Impact of Professional Doctorates in the Workplace and Professions, Deakin University, Geelong, Australia.

McClintock, R. (2005). *Homeless in the house of intellect: Formative justice and education as an academic study*. New York: Laboratory for Liberal Learning.

McWilliam, E., Taylor, P., Thomson, B., Green, B., Maxwell, T., Wildy, H., & Simons, D. (2002). *Research training in doctoral programs: What can be learned from professional doctorates?* Evaluation and Investigations Report, Department of Education, Science and Training. Canberra: AGPS. Retrieved from http://www.dest.gov.au/archive/highered/eippubs/eip02_8/default.htm

Miller, P. (2005). Global confusion in management and business related doctorate programmes. *Review of International Comparative Management, 11*(4), 623–639

O'Mullane, M. (2005). *Demonstrating significance of contributions to professional knowledge and practice in Australian professional doctorate programs: Impacts in the workplace and professions.* Revised Papers from the Fifth Professional Doctorates Conference: Working Doctorates: The Impact of Professional Doctorates in the Workplace and Professions, Deakin University, Geelong, Australia.

O'Neill, M.H. (2012). Transnational education: A case study of one professional doctorate. *Higher Education Studies, 2*(4), 14–30.

Pearson, M., Cumming, J., Evans, T., Macauley, P., & Ryland, K. (2011). How shall we know them? Capturing the diversity of difference in Australian doctoral candidates and their experiences. *Studies in Higher Education, 36*(5), 527–542. doi: 10.1080/03075079.2011.594591

Pyvis, D., & Chapman, A. (2007). Why university students choose an international education: A case study in Malaysia. *International Journal of Development, 27*, 235–246.

Seddon, T. (2000). *What is doctoral in doctoral education?* Paper presented at the 3rd International Professional Doctorates Conference, Doctoral Education and Professional Practice: The Next Generation? Armidale, NSW, Australia.

Seddon, T. (2001) What is "doctoral" in doctoral education? In B. Green, T.W. Maxwell, & P. Shanahan (Eds.), *Doctoral education and professional practice: The next generation?* Armidale, NSW, Australia: Kardoorair Press.

Servage, L. (2009). Alternative and professional doctoral programs: What is driving the demand? *Studies in Higher Education, 34*(7), 765–779. doi: 10.1080/03075070902818761

Shulman, L.S., Golde, C.M., Bueschel, A.C., & Garabedian, K.J. (2006). Reclaiming education's doctorates: A critique and a proposal. *Educational Researcher, 35*(3), 25–32.

Wellington, J. (2013). Searching for "doctorateness." *Studies in Higher Education, 38*(10), 1490–1503. doi: 10.1080/03075079.2011.634901

Woodhouse, D. (1999). Quality and quality assurance. In Organisation for Economic Co-Operation and Development (OECD), *Quality and internationalisation in higher education* (pp. 29–44) Programme on Institutional Management in Higher Education (IMHE). Paris: OECD.

Zeegers, M., & Barron, D. (2008). Discourses of deficit in higher degree research supervisory pedagogies for international students. *Pedagogies: An International Journal, 3*, 69–84.

# ED.D. PROGRAM DIVERSITY
# AND SOCIAL JUSTICE

# CHAPTER ELEVEN

# Designing Educational Identity and Civic Courage

## Using U.S.-Israeli Cross-National Dialogue to Transform the Ed.D.

*Carol Kochhar-Bryant*

## INTRODUCTION

Educational leadership preparation programs in the United States generally address the importance of understanding and influencing the larger political, social, economic, and cultural context, but few exhibit a pedagogical focus on underlying values and personal motivation in leadership behavior. This chapter explores the concept of *educational identity* in educational leadership preparation and the instrumental value of cross-national dialogue and understanding in comprehending its potential. The chapter examines a disruptive process of reinvention of the Ed.D. leadership program, stimulated and shaped by a multi-year continuing conversation between U.S. and Israeli educators.

Visits by U.S. faculty to several academic institutions in Israel and discussions in the United States with Israeli scholars and practitioners have transformed mutual perspectives in addressing challenges and issues currently being encountered. Conversations are rooted in acknowledged commonalities between the two nations to address economic and educational inequities related to issues of race, gender, class, ethnicity, and inclusion and the challenges of preparing and retaining scholar-leaders who can create meaningful change. Drawing on connections among several ideas: (1) the "civic courage" of Freire (the educational process is never neutral), (2) Martin Buber's "dialogic existence" and the value of a common discourse, (3) Lee Shulman's "pedagogies of engagement," and (4) Mordecai Nissan's "educational identity," the chapter describes the transformative impact of cross-national scholarly exchange in integrating these constructs into the design and development of a new Ed.D. vision.

## NEW RESPONSIBILITIES OF INSTITUTIONS OF HIGHER EDUCATION IN THE INTERNATIONAL CONTEXT

The terms "international dialogue," "intercultural dialogue," and "cross-cultural communication" refer to communication that creates the conditions for dialogue among civilizations, cultures, and peoples based upon respect for commonly shared values (UNESCO, 2014). Educational leadership development programs are greatly enriched by educational and policy dialogue between countries and across a range of education stakeholders. Knowledge of global initiatives and actions can help emerging leaders to gain perspective on internationally shared educational concerns. For example, the "Education for All" movement led by UNESCO is a global commitment to provide quality basic education for all children, youth, and adults. At the World Education Forum in Dakar in 2000, 164 governments pledged to achieve education for all and identified six common goals to be met by 2015. As the leading agency, UNESCO (2014) focuses its activities on six key areas: policy dialogue, monitoring, advocacy, mobilization of funding, national education systems, and capacity development. These key areas align with educational capacity building in the United States and can lend a broader perspective to U.S. education policy-making and implementation strategies.

Educational leadership programs in the United States recognize the need for intercommunity dialogue within the nation, but few capitalize on the potential power of the cross-national experience and strategic dialogue. The strategic dialogue that many institutions of higher education (IHEs) are embarking on, including ours, is also shaped by increased public interest in the engagement of IHEs at the local and regional levels. Education is a powerful driver of development and one of the strongest instruments for reducing poverty and improving health, gender equality, peace, and stability (World Bank, 2014). This realization demands more extensive involvement of academic institutions in scaling up investment in effective educational practices, improving access and equity, ensuring the provision of quality higher education, and increasing contextually relevant research in the region.

## WHY A COLLABORATION WITH ISRAEL?

The United States and Israel share many common features in their cultures and economies. Like the United States, Israel has developed a strong economy with entrepreneurial drive and technologically driven growth, but the socioeconomic divide between population groups is growing. In some regions, such as the northern Galilee, about half of the population is Arab. A key challenge for these regions and for Israel is the disparity between Arab and Jewish populations in terms of employment and education outcomes (OECD, 2011b). Israeli society has also absorbed and integrated immigrants from 79 different countries, among whom 39 languages are spoken.

In the United States, approximately 36.3% of the population currently belongs to a racial or ethnic minority group: American Indian or Alaska Native, Asian American, Black or African American, Hispanic or Latino, and Native Hawaiian or Other Pacific Islander. Based on the 2011 Census Bureau's *American Community Survey*, which addressed populations of speakers of non-English languages, of 291.5 million people aged 5 and over, 60.6 million (21% of the population) spoke a language other than English at home, and over 300 different languages are spoken (U.S. Census Bureau, 2013).

In Israel, there is a growing social and economic divide between the center and the periphery—the Galilee in the north and the Negev region in the south—and between different population groups. The socioeconomic gap is evidenced in the rate of unemployment, the low level of salaries, the lack of absorptive capacity in traditional industries, negative migration, poverty (which is highest among the youngest population groups), and the fundamental disparity between the Arab and Jewish populations (OECD, 2011a). This uneven development poses a threat to the long-term, sustainable development of Israel.

Similarly, in the United States, the economic gap among races and other barriers to social mobility are the most compelling indicators that birth is all too often destiny. The United States faces several economic threats: stagnant growth in standard of living; a growing gap between the rich and the rest of the population; and low rates of upward mobility (Reeves, 2014). Real incomes for the top 1% of households have tripled since 1979, compared to a rise of 50% for the bottom fifth and just 36% for those in the middle (Mishel, 2011; Mishel, Schmitt, & Shierholz, 2014). The OECD found that the gap between rich and poor in 30 OECD countries has widened continuously over the three decades to 2008, reaching an all-time high, with the United States having the highest levels among them (OECD, 2011a). Furthermore, the poorest children (Black and White alike) receive the worst public education, and during the K–12 years, the achievement gap between poor and affluent children tends to widen rather than narrow (Reardon, 2011; Reeves, 2014).

Important questions that both countries are seeking to answer are these: How can governments ensure equitable investment in education for different population groups? How can universities and colleges fuel local growth by developing relevant skills and improving educational attainment levels across the multi-ethnic, multi-religious population? For example, the University of Haifa in northern Israel has been successful in broadening access to multi-ethnic populations. It is among the most pluralistic IHEs in Israel, bringing together students from older cities as well as newer development towns, kibbutzim and moshavim, new immigrants, Jews, Arabs, and Druzes.

The public expectation that economic equity and development would be driven by knowledge production, research and development, and innovation has heightened expectations that IHEs engage with the social and economic challenges facing the communities of which they are a part (Pasque, 2010; Pasque, Hendricks, & Bowman, 2006). As higher education has become central to the development of nations, it has become viewed by the public as key to achieving educational equity, access, and social mobility. In short, IHEs are being challenged to reexamine their public purposes and commitments (Chambers, 2005; Pasque et al., 2006; Pasque & Rex, 2010).

These expectations have enormous implications for educational leadership development, begging questions such as: How can we do more with our research, teaching, and service in order to strengthen the relationship between higher education and society? How can we establish exemplar pedagogy to inculcate the motivation for sustained civic participation in a complex and pluralistic society?

Higher education is uniquely positioned in both Israel and America to help future leaders understand the histories and contours of their respective challenges as diverse democracies. Both countries recognize that pluralism is a source of strength and vitality that will enrich their leadership education and help students work for the common social good (*Presidents' Declaration on the Civic Responsibility of Higher Education*, 2014). Furthermore, *engagement* of the IHE with the wider society will influence its pedagogical frameworks for leadership development (Avila, 2010; Bloom, Hartley, & Rosovsky, 2007; *National Strategy for Higher Education to 2030*, 2011). Several recommendations have been offered to IHEs to achieve a greater responsiveness to the needs of society: (1) encourage involvement of the wider community in IHE activities; (2) respond to professional development needs of the wider community; (3) focus on consequences of the work of higher education and relevance for society; (4) emphasize civic skills and leadership in the curriculum and foster a deep commitment to the public good within the professorate; (5) encourage students and faculty to target social change through their professional and applied research activities to improve particular social conditions within the community (Rex, 2006); (6) provide opportunities for international education experiences; and (7) ensure that accreditation processes include civic engagement and social responsibility criteria (Hollister et al., 2012).

During our trips to Israel, our dialogue with Israeli educational leaders allowed us to get to know each other on a much deeper level and to realize the value of mutual understanding about respective people and society. In Israel, we were directly exposed to the many complex and nuanced issues of distinct regions, including the status of Israeli minorities, the plight of migrant workers and refugees, the tensions surrounding settlements in the West Bank, and Israeli government structures. Additionally, our conversations about deeply complex issues have emphasized core relational assets: active listening, speaking considerately, openness to learning about the views of others, and deep reflection.

The U.S.-Israeli collaborative began in 2010 with a series of informal faculty exchanges and seminars, followed by visits to Israel by U.S. educators and visits to the United States by Israeli educators. The initial goal was to establish professional and personal exchanges and to identify educational issues of common interest and importance. These exchanges have also provided opportunities to enrich the leadership training of doctoral students in the United States and in Israel.

Participating faculty and students have discussed broad themes related to educational development, including: (1) international and national policies for promoting coherent sustainable educational development; (2) links between education and poverty alleviation; (3) coordinating service and human resource systems, governmental and nongovernmental organizations; (4) improving the quality of primary and secondary education; (5) developing strategies to promote educational rights, inclusive educational practices, and human service needs of children and adults; (6) educational leadership capacity building; and (7) increasing the accessibility of postsecondary education among underrepresented groups and improving vocational education opportunities. These activities for doctoral students have also driven our broad interrogation of the pedagogical assumptions and structure of our Ed.D. program.

## THE PHILOSOPHICAL GROUNDING

The work of five educational philosophers is highlighted here, as their ideas interconnect around the construct of *identity* in leadership development—Freire, Buber, Nissan and Pekarsky, and Shulman. Mordecai Nissan and Daniel Pekarsky (2009) articulated the core philosophy of the Mandel School for Educational Leadership in Jerusalem. Mandel's goal is to develop and foster influential leaders with a vision to advance education in Israel. Nissan and Pekarsky contend that "educational identity" is an essential characteristic of an educational leader and that the unique "identity view" of educational leadership emphasizes the development of a considered system of goals, values, and self-definition to which a person commits (p. 6). This view is not given adequate expression in the field of leadership training but rather is eclipsed by an opposite view—the *training view*—that focuses on the instruments and tools of management.

The *identity view* places goals and values at the focus of the development of educational leadership. A rational consideration of goals and values, along with an opportunity to actualize them through self-realization, is the basis for developing personal commitment and educational leadership.

Such leaders' commitment to their profession is built upon their self-definition as people involved in education, their view of education's goals and values, their vision of the good person and the good society, their perception of the area in which they are meant to act in this regard, and their self-perception—the beliefs, feelings, plans, and abilities connected with their work that they have developed over the course of their lives. I will call this sort of commitment "educational identity" (Nissan & Pekarsky, 2009, p. 32).

Nissan and Pekarsky contend that educational identity is facilitated by experience of and skill in dialogue not only about divisive issues but about *mutually aspirational* issues. Such leaders are expected to make and carry out decisions in keeping with their value-based educational identity rather than outside pressures or personal interests.

Paulo Freire (1921–1997), a Brazilian educator, philosopher, and leading advocate of critical pedagogy, argued that education cannot be neutral but rather demands that the educator address issues of values, beliefs, and commitments (Freire, 1998). The teacher or educational leader is by his or her presence an *intervener* in the world and is destined to choose among alternative courses of action. Freire's term "intervention" refers to the aspiration for radical changes in society in areas such as health, education, economics, employment, and others. Freire speaks to the political nature of that intervention, proposing that "education cannot be neutral or indifferent in regard to the reproduction of the dominant ideology or the interrogation of it" (Freire, 1998, p. 91). He also refers to modern business leadership development as including technical and scientific preparation but failing to address the leaders' "human and ethical presence in the world" (p. 92). The leader, therefore, needs to engage in the process of becoming a citizen, which does not occur as a consequence of "technical efficiency" but is rather the result of a political struggle to create a society that is humane and just. Freire's construct of *civic courage* connects learning and activism, which he views as the essence of human life. The educational leader takes a public stance, with integrity and at some personal risk, to challenge prevailing conditions and conventional ideas in pursuit of the common good.

Connected to the conception that educational identity is grounded in clarification of values and beliefs is Martin Buber's (1923/1958) requirement that genuine change can only come from a renewal of man's relationships. Change agents must be able to face the "other" and construct new relationships and understanding of other worldviews. They construct a world from the dual acts *of distancing* and *relating* and have two distinct ways of engaging the world. Buber (1878–1965), a prominent twentieth-century philosopher, religious thinker, political activist, and educator, spent most of his life in Germany and Israel, writing in German and Hebrew.

In contrast to the traditional philosophical answers to the question "What is man?" that fixate on reason, self-consciousness, or free will, Buber argued that man is the being who faces an "other," and a *human* home is built from relations of mutual confirmation. The "I-Thou" relation is the pure encounter of one person with another without preconditions and in such a way that the other is known without being stereotyped or classified. In contrast, the "I-It" relation is driven by categories of "same" and "different" and focuses on universal definition. An "I-It" relation *experiences* a detached thing, fixed in space and time, while an "I-Thou" relation *participates* in the dynamic, living process of an "other" (Buber, 1923/1958). Buber characterizes "I-Thou" relations as "dialogical" and "I-It" relations as "monological." Genuine change, he insists, does not occur in a top-down fashion but only from a renewal of man's relations.

Buber claims that the presence and character of the educator is more important than the content of what is actually taught. The ideal educator responds with his or her "Thou," instilling trust and enabling students to respond with their "Thou." Buber acknowledges that leaders face a tension between acting spontaneously and acting with intention. He further elaborates that in order to prepare for a life in common, educational leaders must educate in such a way that both individuation and community are advanced (Buber, 1988). This involves bringing together groups with different worldviews and educating not for tolerance but for *solidarity*—learning to live from the point of view of the other without giving up one's own view.

Finally, Lee Shulman's (2004) construct of the "pedagogies of engagement" intersects with the construct of identity. A family of problem-based pedagogies, first defined by Edgerton (1997), was expanded by Shulman to include six features or claims. These include pedagogies of engagement, understanding, performance, reflection, generativity, and commitment. These pedagogies begin with real problems that *engage* students and deepen *understanding* of research-based and practical knowledge. They lead to *performance*—knowledge of how to act—which requires decision, judgment, and action. Performance must also be interrupted or disrupted to allow for *reflection* upon performance (e.g., How did I reach this decision? What did I do that makes this performance effective?) Active performance, then, must be balanced with strategic and intentional reflection (meaning making) on one's performance.

The pedagogies create a *generativity*, or powerful desire to know more and to value engagement in order to learn. Finally, *commitment* encompasses the affective and moral component of learning and development, a commitment not just to cognitive growth but also to *new dispositions*, habits, and values (Shulman, 2005, pp. 55–56). These pedagogies assist the emerging leader in continuously forging new connections between ideas and effective practice and in performing with a sense of personal and social responsibility. The performances of practice must not only be skilled and theoretically grounded; they must be characterized by integrity and a commitment to responsible, ethical service (Shulman, 2005, p. 2). These theories and philosophies, along with the cross-national dialogue with Israeli educators, have provided intellectual grounding for our transformative process of reevaluating the assumptions upon which our leadership Ed.D. programs are predicated.

## DISRUPTING OUR TRADITIONAL ED.D. CURRICULUM

Over the past 2 years, our dialogue with Israeli educators has stimulated a reasoned analysis of our product or Ed.D. program—its intellectual content, relevance to our consumers, and, most of all, relevance for preparing our consumers to face the dominant challenges in education today in the United States and internationally. While our leadership Ed.D. program has undergone considerable change over the past 2 decades, we find ourselves in a crucible of sorts. A faculty learning community was formed in 2011 to examine literature on leadership training programs and identify core features of effective programs.

Since then, faculty have worked toward purposeful transformation through a process of "disruptive creativity" (Linker, 2014, p. 2) in rethinking the foundations of our program. Such transformation has not meant reinvention for the sake of change, but faculty recognized the need to nurture a new generation of courageous educational scholar-practitioners or *scholar-pioneers* who can harness their creativity to solve crucial social problems. Scholar-pioneers are leaders who redraw or expand the boundaries of practice and policy because they are guided by a powerful vision of the future and can translate that vision into reality regardless of the environment. The Ed.D. can serve as a powerful tool for preparing the next generation of educational leaders and for preparing committed scholar-pioneers ready for civic engagement. The U.S.-Israeli dialogue has directly stimulated a disruptive process, changing the conception and structure of our traditional Ed.D. curriculum.

## CRITIQUING TRADITIONAL LEADERSHIP PROGRAMS AND CRAFTING A NEW SET OF ASSUMPTIONS

Leadership is a complex process that is still not well understood as a construct or as a set of behaviors (Bennis, 2009; DeRue, Nahrgang, Wellman, & Humphrey, 2011). Most of what is labeled "leadership" has been considered "good management"

(Heifetz, 1994). Leadership as a field of study began with a trait-behavior model that emphasized production and efficiency and evolved to emphasize the power of the single leader, a stand-and-deliver model in which power is derived from the authority of the individual in the position of leadership (Avolio, 2007; DeRue, Ashford, & Cotton, 2009; Sithole & Mbele, 2008).

The postindustrial paradigm reflects globalization and an interconnected world (Bekker, 2010; Rost, 2007). It requires new ways of leading that are principle-centered, express collaboration and moral purposes, and can *transform followers into leaders* (transformational leadership). Leadership was redefined as a relational process of people accomplishing change together to benefit the common good (Komives, Lucas, & McMahon, 1998; Morgeson, DeRue, & Karam, 2010). Leadership now includes concepts of inclusiveness, empowerment, ethics, and purposefulness—ideas that are reflected in initiatives such as turnaround schools, community engagement, and partnerships between schools and universities.

As expressed by Nissan and Pekarsky (2009) and Freire (1998) most educational leadership programs express the "training view," which is centered on technical preparation and the provision of instruments and tools that are needed for practice. Observers agree that the training that school principals typically receive in university programs and from their own districts does not do nearly enough to prepare them for their roles as leaders of learning (Darling-Hammond, LaPointe, Meyerson, Orr, & Cohen, 2007; Morgeson, DeRue, & Karam, 2010; Rost, 2007). More than 80 percent of superintendents and 69 percent of principals think that leadership training in schools of education is out of touch with the realities of today's districts (Darling-Hammond, LaPointe, Meyerson, Orr, & Cohen, 2007).

Initial leadership preparation programs in the United States have included a collection of courses that treat management principles, school laws, and administrative requirements and procedures, with little emphasis on student learning, effective teaching, professional development, curriculum, and organizational change (AACTE, 2001; Morgeson et al., 2010; Usdan, McCloud, & Podmostko, 2000). Few have strong clinical training components that are linked to academic coursework and that pair prospective leaders with skilled veteran leaders, providing them experiences that enable them to learn the full complexity of their jobs. Many programs have been criticized as out of touch with real-world complexities, fragmented, incoherent, and lacking requirements for building communities across diverse school stakeholders (AACTE, 2001; Peterson, 2002).

## WHAT IT MEANS FOR US

We focused the interrogation of our leadership Ed.D. program on the strength of our curriculum and our field experiences to prepare leaders for a new paradigm of leadership and to make a difference in contributing to the "common good" (Komives et al., 1998; Morgeson et al., 2010). We asked: Are we incorporating the pedagogies of *engagement, understanding, performance, reflection, generativity, and commitment*? (Shulman, 2004). Are we addressing the affective and moral component of learning and development and not just cognitive growth? What strategies are we using to help students crystallize an "educational identity" (Nissan & Pekarsky, 2009), a "civic courage" (Freire, 1998), and engender an aspiration for radical changes in society and an ability to challenge prevailing conditions and conventional ideas in pursuit of the common good (Freire, 1998)? This self-interrogation led to another set of questions related to the assumptions, content, and processes of our curriculum and pedagogy:

1. How can an Ed.D. program cultivate a sense of "identity" for social commitment to the community and help students clarify values associated with their identity?
2. What is the developmental and transformative process for crystallizing a leadership identity, and how does it deepen over time?
3. What are the pedagogical strategies and instructional environments for creating committed leaders?

It is our goal over the coming 2 years to work as a faculty community, in dialogue with our Israeli partners, to continue to integrate the concepts and processes related to educational identity and civic courage as central to the development of the effective educational leader. These include the following:

1. Design the curriculum to build fluency in research-based and experiential knowledge.
2. Combine experiential and critical analytic learning to address actions and choices in educational leadership. Since the leader's value-commitments deeply affect and guide his or her actions and choices in the education policy arena, the program challenges leaders to reflect on the use of power and position to influence the quality of education in their domain of authority.
3. Prepare leaders to identify and explore ethical complexities in policy formation and important values that underlie policy choices and the manner of their implementation.
4. Create "laboratories of practice" as authentic field-based settings in which theory and practice inform and enrich each other and allow students to address complex problems of policy and practice (Shulman, 2005).
5. Ensure that students exit the program with greatly enhanced capacity and interest in the design of innovative solutions to address the problems of policy and practice.

6. Deepen students' skills in using data to understand the effects of innovation and prepare them to gather, organize, judge, and analyze situations, literature, and data through a critical lens (Shulman, 2005).
7. Prepare students to target social change through their professional and applied research activities to improve social conditions within the community, particularly for vulnerable populations.

Faculty participants in this continuing U.S.-Israeli dialogue, together with the reinvention team at GW, recognize the potential power and benefits of the cross-national experience. This cross-national conversation has implications beyond the boundaries of the Ed.D. program reinvention. It will advance our commitment to actively engage with the social and economic challenges facing the communities of which we are a part and with the global community.

## REFERENCES

American Association of Colleges for Teacher Education. (2001, March). *PK–12 educational leadership and administration*. Washington, DC: Author.

Avila, M. (2010). Community organizing practices in academia: A model, and stories of partnerships. *Journal of Higher Education Outreach and Engagement, 14*(2), 37–63.

Avolio, B.J. (2007). Promoting more integrative strategies for leadership theory-building. *American Psychologist, 62*, 25–33.

Bekker, C.J. (2010). Prophet and servant: Locating Robert K. Greenleaf's counter-spirituality of servant leadership. *Journal of Virtues & Leadership, 1*(1), 3–14.

Bennis, W. (2009). *On becoming a leader* (3rd ed.). Jackson, TN: Perseus Books.

Bloom, D.E., Hartley, M., & Rosovsky, H. (2007). Beyond private gain: The public benefits of higher education. In J.J. Forest & P.G. Altbach (Eds.), *International handbook of higher education* (pp. 293–308). Dordrecht, Netherlands: Springer.

Buber, M. (1958). *I and thou* (2nd ed.; R.G. Smith, Trans.) New York: Scribner's, 1958. (Original work published 1923)

Buber, M. (1988). *Education and world view*. In M. Friedman (Ed. & Trans.), *Pointing the way: Collected essays*. Atlantic Highlands, NJ: Humanities Press.

Chambers, T. (2005). The special role of higher education in society: As a public good for the public good. In A.J. Kezar, T.C. Chambers, & J. Burkhardt (Eds.), *Higher education for the public good: Emerging voices from a national movement* (pp. 3–22). San Francisco, CA: Jossey-Bass.

Darling-Hammond, L., LaPointe, M., Meyerson, D., Orr, M.T., & Cohen, C. (2007). *Preparing school leaders for a changing world: Lessons from exemplary leadership development programs*. Stanford, CA: Stanford Educational Leadership Institute.

DeRue, D., Ashford, S.J., & Cotton, N. (2009). Assuming the mantle: Unpacking the process by which individuals internalize a leader identity. In L.M. Roberts & J.E. Dutton (Eds.), *Exploring positive identities and organizations: Building a theoretical and research foundation* (pp. 213–232). New York: Taylor & Francis.

DeRue, D., Nahrgang, J., Wellman, N., & Humphrey, S. (2011). Trait and behavioral theories of leadership: An integration and meta-analytic test of their relative validity. *Personnel Psychology*, *64*(1), 7–52.

Edgerton, R. (1997). *Higher education*. Unpublished paper. Philadelphia: Pew Charitable Trusts Education Program.

Freire, P. (1985). *The politics of education*. Westport, CT: Bergin & Garvey.

Freire, P. (1998). *Pedagogy of freedom: Ethics, democracy and civic courage*. Lanham, MD: Rowman & Littlefield.

Heifetz, R.A. (1994). *Leadership without easy answers*. Cambridge, MA: Belknap Press.

Hollister, R.H., Pollock, J.P., Gearan, M., Reid, J., Stroud, S., & Babcock, E. (2012). The Talloires Network: A global coalition of engaged universities. *Journal of Higher Education Outreach and Engagement*, *16*(4), 81–101.

Komives, S.R., Lucas, N., & McMahon, T. (1998). *Exploring leadership for college students who want to make a difference*. San Francisco, CA: Jossey-Bass.

Linker, J. (2014). *The road to reinvention: How to drive disruption and accelerate transformation*. San Francisco, CA: Jossey-Bass.

Mishel, L. (2011). *We're not broke nor will we be: Policy choices will determine whether rising national income leads to a prosperous middle class*. Economic Policy Institute Briefing Paper #310. Washington, DC. Retrieved from http://www.epi.org/publication/were_not_broke_nor_will_we_be/

Mishel, L., Schmitt, J., & Shierholz, H. (2014). Wage inequality: A story of policy choices. *New Labor Forum*, *1*(6), 1–6. Retrieved from http://nlf.sagepub.com/content/early/2014/08/04/109 5796014544325

Morgeson F.P., DeRue, D.S., & Karam, E.P. (2010). Leadership in teams: A functional approach to understanding leadership structures and processes. *Journal of Management*, *36*, 5–39.

*National strategy for higher education to 2030*. (2011). Dublin: Department of Education and Skills.

Nissan, M., & Pekarsky, D. (2009). *Educational identity as a major factor in the development of educational leadership*. Jerusalem, Israel: Hebrew University.

OECD. (2011a). *Divided we stand: Why inequality keeps rising*. Paris: OECD.

OECD. (2011b). *Higher education in regional and city development: The Galilee, Israel*. Paris: OECD.

Pasque, P.A. (2010). *American higher education, leadership, and policy: Critical issues and the public good*. New York: Palgrave Macmillan.

Pasque, P.A., Hendricks, L.A., & Bowman, N.A. (Eds.). (2006). *Taking responsibility: A call for higher education's engagement in a society of complex global challenges*. National Forum on Higher Education for the Public Good, University of Michigan, Ann Arbor.

Pasque, P.A., & Rex, L.A. (2010). Complicating "just do it": Leaders' frameworks for analyzing higher education for the public good. *Higher Education in Review*, *7*, 47–79.

Peterson, K.D. (2002). The professional development of principals: Innovations and opportunities. *Educational Administration Quarterly*, *38*(2), 213–232.

*Presidents' declaration on the civic responsibility of higher education*. (2014). Boston, MA: Campus Compact.

Reardon, S.F. (2011). The widening socioeconomic status achievement gap: New evidence and possible explanations. In R.J. Murnane & G.J. Duncan (Eds.), *Whither opportunity? Rising inequality, schools, and children's life chances*. New York: Russell Sage Foundation.

Reeves, R.V. (2014). *Saving Horatio Alger: Equality, opportunity and the American dream*. Washington, DC: Brookings Institution.

Rex, L.A. (2006). Higher education has done well, we can do more: A Report from the Wingspread Access, Equity and Social Justice Committee. In P.A. Pasque, L.A. Hendricks, & N.A. Bowman (Eds.), *Taking responsibility: A call for higher education's engagement in a society of complex global challenges*. Ann Arbor: National Forum on Higher Education for the Public Good, University of Michigan.

Rost, J. (2007). Moving from individual to relationship: A postindustrial paradigm of leadership. *Journal of Leadership & Organizational Studies, 4*(4), 3–16.

Shulman, L. (2004). *Teaching as community property: Essays on higher education*. San Francisco, CA: Jossey-Bass.

Shulman, L. (2005, Spring). Pedagogies of uncertainty. *Liberal Education*. Washington, DC: Association of American Colleges and Universities.

Sithole, P., & Mbele, T. (2008). *Fifteen year review on traditional leadership: A research paper*. Human Sciences Research Council, Democracy and Governance, South Africa.

UNESCO. (2014). *Introducing UNESCO: What we are*. Paris, France. Retrieved from http://www. unesco.org/new/en/unesco/about-us/who-we-are/introducing-unesco/

U.S. Census Bureau. (2013). *American community survey*. Washington, DC: U.S. Department of Commerce, Economics and Statistics Administration.

Usdan, M., McCloud, B., & Podmostko, M. (2000). *Leadership for student learning: Reinventing the principalship*. A Report of the Task Force on the Principalship School Leadership for the 21st Century Initiative Institute for Educational Leadership. Washington, DC: Institute for Educational Leadership.

World Bank (2014). *Education overview*. Retrieved from http://web.worldbank.org/WBSITE/ EXTERNAL/TOPICS/EXTEDUCATION/0,,contentMDK:20575742~menuPK:282393~ pagePK:210058~piPK:210062~th,eSitePK:282386,00.html.

# CHAPTER TWELVE

# Activating Graduate Teaching Experience to Challenge Microaggression in Evaluations of Minority Faculty

*Lerona Dana Lewis*

*The university values your thoughtful feedback, however comments about a teacher's accent, age, disability, gender, race, religious beliefs, and sexual orientation are inappropriate and will render your evaluation invalid.*
—ANONYMOUS STATEMENT FOR INCLUSION ON STUDENT EVALUATIONS

## INTRODUCTION

There is growing concern over the validity of student evaluations of teachers (SETs) in assessing teaching ability (Canadian Association of University Professors, 2006; Dua & Lawrence, 2000; Finch, 2003). For instance, Lindahl and Unger (2010) describe students as being cruel and malicious toward teachers in their comments on SETs. Research by Evans Winters and Twyman Hoff (2011) has highlighted the possibility that students collaborate and conspire to put negative comments on Black teachers' SETs, a phenomenon that they describe as "electronic lynching." Despite this concern, decision makers often consider student ratings on SETs to be a convenient way—and often the only way—of assessing teaching (Berk, 2005; Harris, 2007; Kember & Wong, 2000; Lazos, 2012). The use of SETs seems to be firmly entrenched in most universities in North America. However, from the perspective of faculty of color, SETs can often be sites of institutional discrimination, rife with microaggressions and stereotypes that negatively affect promotion or tenure and course funding (Griffin, Pifer, Humphrey, & Hazelwood, 2011; Turner, González, & Wood, 2008).

At universities that do not guarantee funding for education doctoral students, low SET results can affect the livelihoods of students of color who may rely on part-time teaching positions to support themselves, and "negative" evaluations may lower the possibility of being rehired. The effect of negative SETs may be further compounded for graduate students of color. Teaching appointments obtained when one is a graduate student may serve as a stepping-stone to permanent university positions. I argue that universities must protect faculty of color at predominantly White institutions (PWIs) from racial microaggressions that occur in SETs.

In this chapter, I draw from my experiences as a graduate student pursuing a Ph.D. in education at a research-intensive university in Eastern Canada. This university may be characterized as a PWI. After describing my experiences with SETs, I discuss the relevance of critical race theory (CRT) and microaggressions in analysing SETs. CRT provides the analytic framework to expose the injustices associated with SETs and the ways in which they disenfranchise faculty of color teaching at PWIs. Critical race theorists are known as "Crits" (Delgado & Stefancic, 2012). I use ATLAS.ti to conduct a thematic analysis of student comments on SETs. The analysis reveals that SETs can be a site of racial microaggressions (Sue et al., 2007).

The microaggressions described on SETs fit the Ontario Human Rights Commission's (OHRC) description of discrimination that may occur in workplaces—forms of discrimination the OHRC advocates that employees should be protected against (see http://www.chrc-ccdp.gc.ca/eng/content/what-discrimination; http://www.ohrc.on.ca/en/iii-principles-and-concepts/3-grounds-discrimination-definitions-and-scope-protection; and http://www.ohrc.on.ca/en/policy-and-guide lines-racism-and-racial-discrimination/part-1-%E2%80%93-setting-context-understanding-race-racism-and-racial-discrimination).

I describe the ways in which I approached my department to recommend changes to departmental SETs. I suggested that the statement provided at the beginning of this chapter could be included on SETs to indicate that comments that are deemed microaggressive will invalidate the SETs. I was unaware—as perhaps were personnel in my department with whom I shared my concern—that the Canadian Association of University Teachers had already recognized the problem and issued a policy titled *Use of Anonymous Student Questionnaires in the Evaluation of Teaching* (CAUT, 2006). Perhaps this lack of awareness has led some to perceive my concerns as an individual problem.

I argue that the failure to locate negative racialized comments on SETs within an antiracist framework may not reflect individual culpability but is rather the culmination of factors associated with institutional racism. I refer to the argument that universities were traditionally designed as White spaces primarily for White males and founded on principles and values that situate Whites as the norm in universities. Everyone else is positioned as a guest. Consequently, the difficulties that faculty of color encounter with SETs often remain unaddressed.

## GRADUATE STUDENT EXPERIENCES WITH SETS

As a graduate student I taught the course Multicultural Education, a compulsory course in the baccalaureate education program. Student evaluations are conducted online and anonymously at the end of each semester. I was surprised, confused, and hurt when I read the vitriol and racialized comments that students made about me on the SETs. I experienced heightened awareness of my "Blackness" in a predominantly White institution where I had heretofore felt welcomed. This awareness of perceived difference left me feeling vulnerable. When one is a rarity in his or her workplace, one feels vulnerable in a way that may (and sometimes may not) be justified (Stewart, 2009, p. 32).

As far as I was aware at the time of writing this chapter, there were no Black female tenured professors in my department in the Faculty of Education. I found the explanation of my desire to reach out to a professor who was a Black woman in this quote from Audre Lorde (1984/2007):

> As a Black woman, I find it necessary to withdraw into all Black groups at times.... Frequently when speaking with men and White women, I am reminded of how difficult and time consuming it is to have to reinvent the pencil every time you want to send a message. (p. 72)

I believed that another Black woman would empathize with my experience, understand my concerns about SETs, and perhaps even inform me that other Black professors have similar stories.

In the absence of a Black female professor to confide in, I turned to the literature to understand the experiences of Black women teaching at universities in North America. As chance would have it, the first text that I found contained a chapter by Wilson Cooper and Gause (2007) that gave me my first insight into the centrality of race in defining the experiences of university faculty. I took four main ideas from this chapter. First, Black and White faculty have different classroom teaching experiences because of different expectations that students have from them. Second, most White students at PWIs have little or no prior experience with faculty of color, so their expectations of faculty are often shaped by stereotypes. Third, students tend to resist concepts related to oppression, privilege, and racism.

These three points are all related to faculty of color receiving negative comments and poor ratings on SETs. The final point that I took away from the article was that the impact of race and racism on SETs was important for administrators and all faculty, not just faculty of color, to understand and that this experience was not unique to me. Other researchers (Atwater, Butler, Freeman, & Carlton Parsons, 2013; Evans-Winters & Twyman Hoff, 2011; Henry & Tator, 2009; Lazos, 2012; Patton & Catching, 2009; Schick, 2002; Stanley, 2006) corroborated the ideas related to different experiences for Black and White faculty—the relatively hostile nature of PWI for faculty of color and higher chances of negative evaluations for faculty of color compared to White faculty. The work of these scholars provided the impetus for me to speak publicly in department meetings, for which I was a student representative, about my experiences with SETs.

Certainly, not all persons of color teaching at a PWI may be subjected to racist comments on their SETs. However, there is consistent evidence in the literature that faculty of color are very likely to receive negative, racialized comments, implying that poor ratings given to faculty of color on SETs are neither coincidental nor individual but rather institutional. I applied to teach again but was not rehired. Believing that my SETs contributed to the decision not to rehire me, I met with several administrators in my department. At one such meeting, I was told that if I were a professor going up for tenure I would have to get my evaluation numbers up. The racialized comments on my SETs were largely elided despite the call by the CAUT for increased awareness of SETs in transmitting prejudices.

While I received encouragement from most of the faculty with whom I shared my concern about SETs, I must reiterate López's (2003) "marginalize and/or trivialize race and racism in education" because they are responsible for shaping future educational leaders. Critical race theory provides the analytic framework for exposing the injustices associated with SETs and the way they disenfranchise faculty of color teaching at PWIs.

## RELEVANCE OF CRITICAL RACE THEORY

Earlier I used the terms "Black" and "person (or faculty) of color." While Black may be included in the expression "person of color," I make the distinction because I identify as a Black woman. The term "person of color" may include other groups such as Asians, Latina/Latinos, and Aboriginal peoples. I use "person of color" and recognize its limits in accounting for the range of histories, cultures, and experiences among different groups and within different groups. By using the term "person of color". I also intend to convey that I share Stewart's concern for broader conceptualizations of the people that students think of as having authority, expertise, and influence in universities.

I understand race to be "a vast group of people loosely bound together by historically contingent, socially significant elements of morphology or ancestry" (López, 1993, p. 7). Race mediates the lives of all people in modern societies, including Whites. This definition rejects the notion of a biological basis of racial categorization and highlights the social, historical, and contemporary conditions that produce race categories. Hall (1997) explained that humans have the propensity to classify people into groups, and race is one of the primary forms of human classification used today. He added that classifications could be generative in nature, leading to the attribution of qualities to members of groups based on the classifications themselves. Race classification becomes a commonsense code, and even those oppressed by the classification accept the hegemonic ideologies embedded in it (Hall, 1997).

CRT may be defined as a radical legal movement that seeks to transform the relationships among race, racism, and power (Delgado & Stefancic, 2012). CRT emerged out of a desire to move beyond the critical legal studies' inability to articulate the central role of race classification and its inherent racism in law in the United States (Aylward, 1999). CRT is a useful framework because of the basic tenets on which the theory is founded. Crits believe that racism is a normal part of everyday experiences—it is insidious, permanently embedded in social relations, structures, and thought. Crits argue that race and racism play central roles in perpetuating and maintaining institutionalized discrimination against people of color. Crits reject color-blind ideologies that advocate equal treatment of everyone regardless of race. Refusing to see color negates the persistent effects of legacies such as slavery and colonialism that contribute to social disparities in everyday life today (Delgado & Stefancic, 2012). In the field of education, Ladson-Billings (1998) used CRT to reveal how color-blindness and purported "neutrality" operate through the hidden curriculum in schools. She also discussed the ways in which racism affected pedagogy and financing of schools, contributing to inequity and a lessening of chances for school success.

Race consciousness, the antithesis of color-blindness, centers on race, calling for deliberate identification of the invisible workings of Whiteness and White privilege in ordinary life (Delgado & Stefancic, 2012). Crits advocate the use of counter-stories that legitimize the experiential knowledge of subordinated groups who use their experiences to question commonly accepted ideologies that perpetuate discrimination (Ladson-Billings, 1998). The power of counter-stories lies in the ability to reveal knowledges that have been silenced in traditional scholarship (Crenshaw, Gotando, Peller, & Thomas, 1995).

Crits also believe that the mutual benefits of White privilege accrued to both poor and elite Whites often means that there is no incentive for them to work to change existing social structures (Delgado & Stefancic, 2012). While Crits emphasize race, other possible sites of oppression such as gender, class, disability, and nationality operate together to subordinate people of color. These interlocked yet mutable sites of oppression may be theorized using the intersectionality theory (Crenshaw, 1991). For example, Black women in academia may experience the effects of intersecting forces of marginalization because of, for example, gender, class, race, or ability. These basic tenets are relevant to this inquiry because I seek to deliberately identify the workings of race and privilege on the SETs that contribute to racial microaggression.

## STILL SURPRISED TO HEAR THAT SLAVERY EXISTED IN CANADA

Slavery refers to the enslavement of African people in the Americas and the Caribbean during the trans-Atlantic slave trade from the 16th to the 19th centuries. Canadian CRT has been heavily influenced by the work of Crits in the United States. Yet in Canada, adopting the CRT lens has been difficult because of the collective denial of the existence of slavery there (Aylward, 1999). In the Canadian context, this denial means that naming racism can become problematic, because systematic racism tends to go unrecognized.

Racism can easily be ascribed to a few "bad people." Individuals from minority groups who claim to experience racism can be framed as being oversensitive (Aylward, 1999). However, quoting James Walker, Aylward underscores that "African Canadians experienced exclusion and separation from mainstream institutions amounting to a Canadian version of 'Jim Crow'" (p. 125). In a more recent manifestation of this phenomenon, racist immigration laws restricting Blacks from entering Canada because of "climate unsuitability" were removed only in 1953 (Williams, 1997). It has been argued more generally that Canada has historically used racialized immigration policy to supply immigrant labor. Today, in Canadian and U.S. universities, racism continues in a form described by Sue and colleagues (2007) as "ambiguous and nebulous" racial microaggressions.

## RACIAL MICROAGGRESSIONS: ARE THEY REAL?

One of the ways that racism can manifest is through racial microaggressions. Psychologist Chester Pierce described microaggressions in the 1970s. He theorized microaggressions as the major vehicle of racism in America. Describing them as "gratuitous and never ending" (Pierce, 1974, p. 515), he signaled the repeated uninhibited nature of oppression by a dominant group over a subordinate group (see also Romero, 2006), who outlines the ways that Critical Race Theorists used the concept of microaggression to describe the interaction of African Americans and Mexicans with the American criminal justice system).

Microaggressions are "brief and commonplace daily verbal, behavioral, or environmental indignities, whether intentional or unintentional, that communicate hostile, derogatory, or negative racial slights and insults towards People of Color" (Sue et al., 2007, p. 271). Racial microaggressions can be directed at people of color automatically and unconsciously. When interacting with racial or ethnic minorities, people committing acts of microaggression are unaware that they have done so. The existence of racial microaggression was contested and described as "macrononsense"

(Jahangiri & Mucciolo, 2008; Schacht, 2008). However, several scholars offer ample evidence to validate that they have been experienced by racialized peoples (Clark, Kleiman, Spanierman, Isaac, & Poolokasingham, 2014; Estacio & Saidy-Khan, 2014; Solorzáno, 1998; Sue, Lin, Torino, Capodilupo, & Rivera, 2009).

## DESCRIPTION OF RESEARCH

Situating this qualitative inquiry within the social constructivism paradigm, I use a methodology grounded in CRT, which emphasizes the significance of race in analyzing data. The data consist of anonymous, online comments on SETs of two faculty of color in two different universities in the United States and Canada. My SETs are from the course Multicultural Education, and the other SETs cover a 6-year period for courses in science education taught by a male professor in the United States. I use the qualitative data analysis software ATLAS.ti to organize and conduct a thematic analysis of the data. The use of qualitative software such as ATLAS.ti is still the subject of controversy. It may appear contradictory to use software based on grounded theory, which is situated within the positivist paradigm, with the research located in the social constructivism paradigm. However, I adhere to the assertion by Patti Lather (2006) that hybrid approaches "within, against and across traditions" that layer complexity and foreground problems are useful in conceptualizing research (p. 53).

As a sociological theory of knowledge, social constructivism explains how individuals construct and use knowledge in socially mediated contexts. It may also refer to how a society or group constructs a discipline. Working across traditions presents opportunities for knowledge expansion. Blismas and Dainty (2003) contend that CAQDAS (computer-assisted qualitative data analysis) is a tool of data management rather than an analytic tool and argue that it inhibits "the multiplicity of approaches that can be used to induce meaning from complex data sets" (p. 463). Welsh (2002) explains that opposition to CAQDAS stems from the belief that the software distances researchers from their actual data. I agree with her when she says that CAQDAS can be used without taking a grounded theory approach. When used appropriately, software can enhance the "quality, rigor and trustworthiness of research" (Welsh, 2002).

However, established theoretical insights could be used with CAQDAS in designing the conceptual framework. Themes from the data can be linked directly to known concepts (Rambaree, 2013). Following Friese (2012), I posit that, given the advances in CAQDAS, it can be used for much more than organizing data, and fears about loss of researcher creativity are largely unfounded because the researcher is responsible for analyzing and interpreting the data.

I uploaded the comments into ATLAS.ti and followed the steps of thematic analysis described by Rambaree (2013). I engaged in open coding of the data and categorized comments as positive or negative. I focused on the negative comments because they are thought to have detrimental effects on the advancement of faculty of color (Griffin, Bennett, & Harrris, 2013; Lazos, 2012). I reviewed the evaluations while considering four guiding questions:

(1) How do students describe the teachers?
(2) How do students perceive their interactions with the teachers?
(3) What types of comments do students make about teachers with respect to race?
(4) How do students describe teacher competence to teach the course?

I compared these codes created with the definition of microaggression as provided by Sue and fellow researchers (2007). I put the codes into larger categories and then collapsed them into the following for tropes:

(1) hostile descriptions of faculty of color,
(2) accusations that faculty of color are racist,
(3) accusations that faculty of color play the "victim/race card," and
(4) descriptions of faculty of color using racial slights or insults that attempt to associate teacher incompetence with race.

## ANALYSIS OF MICROAGGRESSIONS IN STUDENT EVALUATIONS

Several authors have written about the ways in which students retaliate against professors who present counterhegemonic ideas on race, racism, privilege, and merit, all of which are ideas that make students uncomfortable (Boatright-Horowitz & Soeung, 2009; Dua & Lawrence, 2000). The experiences of the professors could thus be similarly analyzed; however, this analysis focuses on exploration of instances of racial microaggression in SETs. The relationship between student resistance to teaching and the presence of microaggression became evident after I used the network view in the ATLAS.ti to connect the codes to the quotations visually. Below I discuss each of the tropes in an attempt to clarify how the students' comments might be viewed through the lens of microaggression.

### (1) Hostile Descriptions of Faculty of Color

Students used hostile language in the evaluations to describe faculty of color. Some examples found on the SETS are "attitude," "disagreeable man," "angry and confrontational," or "unapproachable." When examined under the lens of racial microaggression, it can be argued that these comments communicate hostility and degradation of the professors, whether intentionally or not. These comments can therefore be situated within the framework of microaggression as defined by Sue and colleagues (2007, 2008).

## (2) Accusations That Faculty of Color Are Racist

This trope underscores the ways in which the students engage in name calling. Students refer to faculty of color as racist or biased. The exemplar "Racist teacher. I learnt nothing in the class" can be understood as the student claiming that his or her academic advancement was hindered because he or she perceived the teacher as racist. This is an example of reverse racism wherein the power associated with racism and race appears misunderstood by the student. In the context of a PWI where Black faculty are underrepresented, the student frames racism from the perspective of an individual, not the systemic, entrenched practices of racialized oppression that a Black person is likely to encounter.

An exemplar from the student SETs states that "speaking with members of my group which was all white we used to leave the class feeling guilty and felt as though fingers were pointed at [us] regarding what black people went through it was all about black people." By speaking on behalf of other students on their evaluation, this student seems to be emphasizing that other White students in the class shared their opinion, thereby attempting to increase the credibility of their statement accusing them of racism—in other words, that there was more than one person who held the same opinion that the teacher was racist and was pointing fingers at them—Dlamini (2002) referred to the practice of White students expressing solidarity against what they perceive to be a racist teacher of color as "cliqu-ing." I endorse her explanation of the underlying message of cliqu-ing as an attempt to say to the teacher: "This is not just my opinion. A number of us (insiders) think the same way about you." The microaggressive nature of these two comments is found in their direct assault on the teacher's credibility, encompassing what Sue and fellow researchers describe as "put-downs or a pattern of disrespect" (Sue et al., 2007, p. 183).

## (3) Accusations That Faculty of Color Play the "Victim/Race Card"

A student wrote: "He needs to stop playing the victim card and realize we don't hate him because he is black. This is not a race class." The comment suggests that the student seems to perceive the professor to be "overly sensitive" about issues relating to race. By suggesting that the teacher is "playing the victim card" and following up with the statement "we don't hate him," the student at

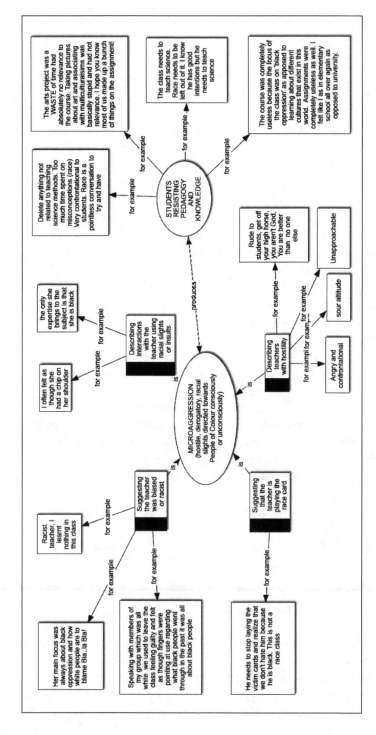

Figure 12.1. Analysis of Microaggression in Student Evaluations.

this PWI seems to saying "we" are not oppressing you. This student is responding individually in his or her review, yet he or she uses the collective pronoun "we." Using "we" suggests an attempt to signal that the majority of the people in the classroom at the PWI perceive the Black professor to be overly sensitive at best, or, at worst, trying to be manipulative (See the Ontario Human Rights Commission for an explanation of the common myths related to racism: http://www.ohrc.on.ca/en/policy-and-guidelines-racism-and-racial-discrimination/part-1-%E2%80%93-setting-context-understanding-race-racism-and-racial-discrimination). As Sue and his team of researchers (2007, 2008) discuss, negating or denying the experiences of oppression due to racism is a form of racial microaggression.

## (4) Descriptions of Faculty of Color with Racial Slights or Insults That Attempt to Associate Teacher Incompetence with Race

One student used the proverbial "chip on her shoulder" descriptor to describe the Black female teacher. Although it is difficult to know what message the student hoped to convey, this comment can be interpreted to mean that the teacher is perpetually angry. Again, this statement—together with statements that attempt to link the teacher's race to teaching competence—are forms of microaggression because they embody "implicit racial snubs" (Sue et al., 2008). Generally, I argue that these negative comments written about faculty of color on SETs constitute forms of microaggression. Many of these comments have the effect of conveying rudeness, insensitivity, and thoughtlessness to/about the teacher, embodying microaggression.

## THE DIALECTS OF MICROAGGRESSION AND STUDENT RESISTANCE TO PEDAGOGY

This review of the SETs suggests that teacher candidates in university education programs appear not to appreciate the relevance of oppression and race in teaching. These students may be unwilling to consider these factors in their future teaching practice. "To accept the racial realities of POC [persons of color] means confronting one's own unintentional complicity in the perpetuation of racism" (Sue et al., 2008, p. 277). It seems that students are unprepared to confront racism; instead they appear to disengage from the teacher and to perpetuate acts of microaggression on their SETs. Researchers (e.g., Sue et al., 2009) explain that when racism is discussed with "White brothers and sisters," powerful embedded emotional reactions such as "anger, guilt and defensiveness" surface. Thus a major concern for education programs is that there seems to be a dialectic relationship between microaggression and student resistance to knowledge and pedagogical strategies that faculty of color present in the classroom. Students discredit the intellect and competence of faculty of color and, as a result, many students claim not to learn anything.

For instance, the analysis reveals that in the multicultural course, students desired to learn about "other cultures" as shown in the following quote: "The course was completely useless because the focus of the class was on 'black oppression' as opposed to learning about *different cultures that exist in this world* [my emphasis]." Students seemed to expect the teacher to present them with content information on the "Other." They seemed unprepared to understand the impact of systemic oppression that can be imposed on one group of people by another, interpreting course content as "black oppression." Here the ideas presented by bell hooks seem relevant. Students seemed to expect encounters with the imagined Other that would not challenge but instead "reinscribe and maintain the status quo" (hooks, 1992, p. 22). In the science education course, students seemed to believe that race was inconsequential in the teaching of science, as expressed in the comments "we need to learn science" and "forget the race and racism piece." Students learning to teach science did not seem to want to explore the ways in which science education might reproduce oppression in student populations that are marginalized.

## WHERE DO WE GO FROM HERE?

The emergence of a possible link between faculty of color and student resistance to knowledge and pedagogy and workplace microaggression may lead university administrators to attempt to dissuade faculty of color from teaching subjects about race and racism. In the current neoliberal context, where university students are increasingly positioned as customers or clients instead of learners seeking to develop critical skills (Lindahl & Unger, 2010), university decision makers at PWIs might consider this option to be the best way of keeping students comfortable in the classroom. However, this approach would be unfortunate, because it would deny faculty of color the chance to contribute to education praxis that can be enriched by our unique standpoint and experiential knowledge (Solomon, Portelli, Daniel, & Campbell, 2005). Not least, it would be a form of discrimination.

As suggested by Lazos (2012), another approach might be to encourage faculty of color to adopt middle-class behaviors so that they seem less "militant" (intimidating) to their students and leave out contentious issues of race and racism in order to improve their scores on SETs. Again, this approach would be problematic because it suggests that race and class can be separated. It may also lead to the reification of the belief that faculty of color have to be groomed to "fit" into traditionally White university spaces where they do not belong.

The better alternative is for university personnel to begin to embrace the idea that SETs are sites of workplace microaggression. Universities might then educate students on acceptable ways of completing SETs so that they can be critical but not hostile. Universities can try to help students understand why accusing a Black teacher of being racist or "playing the race/victim card" is a form of racial microaggression. Examples of inappropriate comments might also be included on evaluation forms or course syllabi.

University decision makers who review course evaluations should understand the controversies surrounding SETs and the ways in which SETs can transmit stereotypes about people of color and lead to racial microaggressions. Administrators should review SETs together with the disturbing comments about race, gender, and age, be encouraged to talk about their own experiences, and their colleagues should be prepared to offer them meaningful support.

Unfortunately, well-meaning White colleagues and administrators may also unconsciously contribute to the injurious effects of microaggression for faculty of color. For example, a White colleague may say to a Black professor that he or she had received negative reviews earlier in his or her teaching career, trying to explain away the microaggressive comments as growing pains of university teaching. This is a form of microaggression—specifically, microinvalidation (Sue et al., 2007). The comment trivializes the negative psychological effect that Black professors may experience as a result of the racialized comments on their SETs. The point is that there is a need to educate students, faculty, and administrators about microaggression on SETs. Microaggression is harmful because the cumulative negative effects of microaggressions can hinder performance and drain the recipients' energy (Solórzano, Ceja, & Yosso, 2000). Obviously this review is based on SETs from two faculty of color, so generalizations are not possible. Future study that specifically assesses SETS for the presence of microaggression is recommended.

Sarah Ahmed, referring to colleges and universities, warns that there are risks associated with speaking about racism. By speaking out against racism, you can "become the problem you bring" and get in the way of "institutional happiness." She explains that claims of racism can be seen as an attack on the organization, hurting the organization and those who identify with it (Ahmed, 2012). Using a CRT lens, which centers on race in the analysis, I am arguing that SETs as they currently operate foster workplace racial microaggression, which in itself is a subtle form of racism. Course evaluations must be reassessed in order to prevent students from engaging in active resistance to knowledge and pedagogy of faculty of color but also to curb this insidious and often invisible form of racism against faculty of color.

In Canada, unlike in the United States where there are popular discourses that have led to collective denial, slavery and racism may be among the factors preventing universities from changing the way in which SETs are conducted and utilized. The Canadian Human Rights Commission and the Ontario Human Rights

Commission offer specific recommendations that employers might consider to reduce the occurrence of discrimination related to racism in the workplace. Can universities continue to ignore the existing research on the experience of faculty of color with SETs? If these concerns are ignored, what might be the implications for harassment and discrimination against faculty of color at PWIs?

## CONCLUSION

I concur with Ahmad (2012) when she says that members of institutions like universities who suggest that it is the organization that is damaged when claims of institutional racism are made create "a space for Whiteness to be reasserted," thereby keeping racism intact. If, as a society, we accept the category of race in our schools and university workplaces, we might do well to consider bell hooks's challenge that "mutual recognition of racism, its impact both on those who are dominated and those who dominate, is the only standpoint that makes possible an encounter between races that is not based on denial and fantasy" (hooks, 1992, p. 28).

## REFERENCES

Ahmed, S. (2012). *On being included: Racism and diversity in institutional life*. London: Duke University Press.

Atwater, M., Butler, M., Freeman, T., & Carlton Parsons, E. (2013). An examination of black science teacher educators' experiences with multicultural education, equity, and social justice. *Journal of Science Teacher Education, 24*(8), 1293–1313. doi: 10.1007/s10972–013–9358–8

Aylward, C. (1999). *Canadian critical race theory: Racism and the law*. Winnipeg: Fernwood Publishing.

Berk, R. (2005). Survey of 12 strategies to measure teaching effectiveness. *International Journal of Teaching and Learning in Higher Education, 17*(1), 48–62.

Blismas, N. G., & Dainty, A. R. J. (2003). Computer-aided qualitative data analysis: Panacea or paradox? *Building Research & Information, 31*(6), 455–463. doi: 10.1080/0961321031000108816

Boatright-Horowitz, S. L., & Soeung, S. (Producer). (2009). Teaching White privilege to White students can mean saying good-bye to positive student evaluations. [doi:10.1037/a0016593]

Canadian Association of University Professors (CAUT). (2006). *Use of anonymous student questionnaires in evaluation of teaching*. Retrieved from http://www.caut.ca/about-us/caut-policy/lists/caut-policy-statements/policy-on-the-use-of-anonymous-student-questionnaires-in-the-evaluation-of-teaching

Clark, D. A., Kleiman, S., Spanierman, L. B., Isaac, P., & Poolokasingham, G. (2014). "Do you live in a teepee?" Aboriginal students' experiences with racial microaggressions in Canada. *Journal of Diversity in Higher Education, 7*(2), 112–125. doi: 10.1037/a0036573

Crenshaw, K. (1991). Mapping the margins: Intersectionality, identity politics, and violence against women of color. *Stanford Law Review, 43*(6), 1241–1299. doi: 10.2307/1229039

Crenshaw, K., Gotando, N. T., Peller, G., & Thomas, K. (Eds.). (1995). *Critical race theory: The key writings that formed the movement*. New York: The New Press.

Delgado, R., & Stefancic, J. (2012). *Critical race theory: An introduction* (2nd ed.). New York: New York University Press.

Dlamini, N. S. (2002). From the other side of the desk: Notes on teaching about race when racialized. *Race Ethnicity and Education, 5*(1), 51–66.

Dua, E., & Lawrence, B. (2000). Challenging White hegemony in university classrooms. *Whose Canada is it?* Special issue of *Atlantis, 24*(2), 105–122.

Estacio, E. V., & Saidy-Khan, S. (2014). Experiences of racial microaggression among migrant nurses in the United Kingdom. *Global Qualitative Nursing Research, 1.* doi: 10.1177/2333393614532618

Evans-Winters, V.E., & Twyman Hoff, P. (2011). The aesthetics of White racism in preservice teacher education: A critical race theory perspective. *Race Ethnicity and Education, 14*(4), 461–479. doi: 10.1080/13613324.2010.548376

Finch, F.E. (2003). Are student evaluations of teaching fair? *Computing Research News, 15*(2), 2.

Friese, S. (2012). *Qualitative data analysis with Atlasti.* Los Angeles: Sage.

Griffin, K.A., Bennett, J., & Harrris, J. (2013). Marginalizing merit? Gender differences in Black faculty discourses on tenure, advancement, and profesional success. *Review of Higher Education, 36*(4), 489–512.

Griffin, K.A., Pifer, M., Humphrey, J., & Hazelwood, A. (2011). (Re)defining departure: Exploring Black professors' experiences with and responses to racism and racial climate. *American Journal of Education, 117*(4), 495–526.

Hall, S. (1997). Race, The floating signifier featuring Stuart Hall. http://www.mediaed.org Retrieved August 24, 2014, from Media Education Foundation http://www.mediaed.org/assets/products/407/transcript_407.pdf

Harris, T.M. (2007). Black feminist thought and cultural contracts: Understanding the intersection and negotiation of racial, gendered, and professional identities in the academy. *New Directions for Teaching and Learning, 2007*(110), 55–64. doi: 10.1002/tl.274

Henry, F., & Tator, C. (2009). Theoretical perspectives and manifestations of racism in the academy. In F. Henry & C. Tator (Eds.), *Racism in the Canadian university: Demanding social justice, inclusion and equity* (pp. 22–59). Toronto: University of Toronto Press.

hooks, b. (1992). *Black looks: Race and represenation* Toronto: Between the lines.

Jahangiri, L., & Mucciolo, T. W. (2008). Characteristics of effective classroom teachers as identified by students and professionals: A qualitative study. *Journal of Dental Education, 72*(4), 484–493.

Kember, D., & Wong, A. (2000). Implications for evaluation from a study of students' perceptions of good and poor teaching. *Higher Education, 40*(1), 69–97.

Ladson-Billings, G. (1998). Just what is critical race theory and what's it doing in a nice field like education? *International Journal of Qualitative Studies in Education, 11*(1), 7–24. doi: 10.1080/095183998236863

Lather, P. (2006). Paradigm proflieration as a good thing to think with: Teaching reseach in educaton a a wild profusion. *International Journal of Qualitative Studies in Education, 19*(1), 35–57.

Lazos, S. (2012). Are student teaching evaluations holding back women and minorities? In G. Muhs y Gutiérrez (Ed.), *Presumed incompetent: The intersections of race and class for women in academia* (pp. 164–185). Boulder: University Press of Colorado.

Lindahl, M.W., & Unger, M.L. (2010). Cruelty in student teaching evaluations. *College Teaching, 58*(3), 71–76. doi: 10.1080/87567550903253643

López, G.R. (2003). The (racially neutral) politics of education: A critical race theory perspective. *Educational Administration Quarterly, 39*(1), 68–94.

Lopez, I.H. (1993).The social construction of race: Some observations on illusion, fabrication, and choice. *Harvard Civil Rights-Civil Liberties Law Review, 29*, 1–62.

Lorde, A. (2007). *Man child: A Black lesbian feminist response.* New York: Crown Publishing. (Original work published 1984)

Patton, L.D., & Catching, C. (2009). "Teaching while Black": Narratives of African American student affairs faculty. *International Journal of Qualitative Studies in Education, 22*(6), 713–728. doi: 10.1080/09518390903333897

Pierce, C. (1974). Psychiatric problems of the Black minority. In S. Arieti (Ed.), *American handbook of psychiatry* (pp. 512–523). New York: Basic Books.

Rambaree, K. (2013). *Three methods of qualitative data analysis using ATLAS.ti: 'A posse ad esse'.* Paper presented at the ATLAS.ti User Conference 2013: Fostering Dialog on Qualitative Methods, Berlin.

Romero, M. (2006). Racial profiling and immigration law enforcement: Rounding up of usual suspects in the Latino community. *Critical Sociology, 32*(2-3), 447–473.

Schacht, T. E. (2008). A broader view of racial microaggression in psychotherapy. *American Psychologist, 63*(4), 273.

Schick, C. (2002). Keeping the ivory tower white: Discourses of racial domination. In S. Razack (Ed.), *Race space and the law: Unmapping a White settler society* (pp. 99–119). Toronto: Between the Lines.

Solomon, P., Portelli, J., Daniel, B., & Campbell, A. (2005). The discourse of denial: how white teacher candidates construct race, racism and "white priviilege". *Race Ethnicity and Education, 8*(2), 147–169.

Solórzano, D. G. (1998). Critical race theory, race and gender microaggressions, and the experience of Chicana and Chicano scholars. *International Journal of Qualitative Studies in Education, 11*(1), 121–136. doi: 10.1080/095183998236926

Solórzano, D., Ceja, M., & Yosso, T. (2000). Critical race theory, racial microaggressions, and campus racial climate: The experiences of African American college students. *The Journal of Negro Education, 69*(1/2), 60–73. doi: 10.2307/269626

Stanley, C.A. (2006). Coloring the academic landscape: Faculty of color breaking the silence in predominantly White colleges and universities. *American Educational Research Journal, 43*(4), 701–736. doi: 10.3102/00028312043004701

Stewart, A. (2009). *You must be a basketball player.* Nova Scotia: Fernwood Publishing.

Sue, D. W., Capodilupo, C. M., Nadal, K. L., & Torino, G. C. (2008). Racial microaggressions and the power to define reality. *American Psychologist, 63*(4), 277–279. doi: 10.1037/0003–066X.63.4.277

Sue, D., Capodilupo, C. M., Torino, G. C., Bucceri, J. M., Holder, A. M., Nadal, K. L., & Esquilin, M. (2007). Racial microaggressions in everyday life: Implications for clinical practice. *American Pyschology, 62*(4), 271–286.

Sue, D. W., Lin, A. I., Torino, G. C., Capodilupo, C. M., & Rivera, D. P. (2009). Racial microaggressions and difficult dialogues on race in the classroom. *Cultural Diversity and Ethnic Minority Psychology, 15*(2), 183–190. doi: 10.1037/a0014191

Turner, C.S.V, González, J.C., & Wood, J.L. (2008). Faculty of color in academe: What 20 years of literature tells us. *Journal of Diversity in Higher Education, 1*(3), 139–168.

Welsh, E. (2002). Dealing with data: Using NVivo in qualitative data analysis process. *Forum: Qualitative Social Research, 3*(2).

Williams, D. (1997). *The road to now: A history of Blacks in Montreal.* Ontario: Véhicule Press.

Wilson Cooper, C., & Gause, C.P. (2007). "Who's afraid of the big bad wolf?" Facing identity politics and resistance when teaching social justice. In D. Carlson & C.P. Gause (Eds.), *Keeping the promise: Essays on leadership, democracy, and education.* New York: Peter Lang.

# CHAPTER THIRTEEN

# Ed.D. Socialization Contexts

## Origins, Evolving Purpose, Demographic Trends, and Institutional Practices

*Zarrina Talan Azizova*

## INTRODUCTION AND RATIONALE

Today's Doctor of Education (Ed.D.) programs battle to resolve widespread confusion and uncertainty about their identity under the research university roof and their purpose within and outside academia. Such conditions create a perplexing academic and professional socialization context for doctoral students. According to scholars, socialization is an important and inevitable process in doctoral training (Austin, 2002; Gardner, 2008, 2009; Gardner & Barnes, 2007; Golde & Dore, 2001; Mendoza, 2007; Mendoza & Gardner, 2010; Weidman & Stein, 2003; Weidman, Twale, & Stein, 2001). Tierney (2008) further proposes a postmodern view of academic and professional socialization in order to understand it as a meaning-making act on the part of doctoral students who make sense of their degrees and academic/professional experience through their own unique backgrounds and current contexts in which their programs/institutions reside.

However, research examining academic and professional socialization as a meaning-making act of students in education doctorate programs is scarce. Yet students' perceptions and interpretations of what this degree means to them academically and professionally—and whether these two are separate terms—can broaden perspectives of education scholars and practitioners and offer some clarifications regarding the evolving and highly debated purpose of the Ed.D. degree.

Mills (1959) once asserted that the exercise of *sociological imagination* might promise a deeper understanding of a problem/phenomenon when three elements are connected: history, society, and an individual meaning-making act. Gubrium and Holstein (1997) further acknowledge the specific roles of history, society, and institutional structures in one's meaning making. Therefore, this chapter serves to fulfill a conceptual prerequisite for future research on Ed.D. students' meaning making of the purpose and utility of the Ed.D. degree and their academic/ professional socialization during the course of study. I will configure a broader context for the education doctorate by examining its historical origins, evolving purposes, demographic trends, and issues related to the projections of the Ed.D. degree by schools, colleges, and departments of education (SCDE). I will conclude with a discussion of implications and provide recommendations for future research on Ed.D. programs and students.


## CONTEXT


The first Ed.D. degree was conferred by Harvard University in 1921. Ninety years later, Harvard ended its Ed.D. program and replaced it with the traditional Ph.D. with certain areas of specialization in education in an effort to end confusion between the two doctoral degrees (Basu, 2012). Indeed, debates over the feasibility of offering Ed.D. degrees in colleges, schools, and departments of education that also award Ph.D. degrees have been proliferating (Evans, 2007; Levine, 2005; Olson & Clark, 2009; Shulman, 2007; Shulman, Golde, Bueschel, & Garabedian, 2006). The debates stem from a number of biases, including: (1) a perception of the Ed.D. as a "low-end Ph.D.," which contributes to the inferiority complex, (2) convoluted purposes and requirements of the Ed.D. that attempt to differentiate between the preparation of scholars and the preparation of leading practitioners, and (3) limitations that restrict dissertations to "soft," applied research for degree completion (Lin, Wang, Spalding, Klecka, & Odell, 2011; Shulman et al., 2006). An important observation here is that the primary stakeholders—Ed.D. students themselves—are absent from those debates.

Yet those students should be involved as the ones who explain their choice and the academic/professional utility of this degree. Neither research studies nor public media address voices of Ed.D. recipients. Instead, these debates illustrate a top-down approach to decision making on the part of university-based academicians— usually Ph.D. holders—who decide which degree, and why, deserves to remain in school catalogues, why it should remain, and whether to offer reforming strategies. The roots of such decision making in education are historic and therefore warrant a deeper examination so as to strengthen our understanding of forces that have been shaping the Ed.D. degree in its longstanding struggle between the two prescribed professional identities: the pure academic or the strictly professional.

## HISTORY AND EVOLVING PURPOSE OF THE ED.D.

From the mid-nineteenth century on, American higher education began to undergo two parallel developments: the integration of normal schools to prepare qualified teachers for secondary education, and the creation of a robust research system within institutions of higher learning. These two developments had competing interests (Oakes & Rogers, 2001), a circumstance that eventually affected doctoral degrees in education.

Specifically, in the second half of the twenty-first century, secondary school enrollment grew substantially and thus created a greater need for qualified teachers (Borrowman, 1965). In 1859, Illinois Normal University led the transformation of normal schools from secondary-level institutions to institutions of higher learning (Borrowman, 1965). For the first time, an academic discourse took shape around the need to recognize education as a field of study within university curricula. Charles Kendall Adams's (1888/1965) famous address to the New England Association of Colleges and Preparatory Schools serves as one of the few examples of this discourse. He called for the teaching of pedagogy in colleges and universities and proposed a specific curriculum for courses such as history of education, philosophy of education, methods in school reform, and teachers' seminars. Some prominent university presidents and reformers of the time—including Charles Eliot and Stanley Hall, to name a few—actively participated in these academic discussions, raising the question of whether education could be seen as a science and thus become a university discipline (Borrowman, 1965).

The publication of Josiah Royce's essay "Is There a Science of Education?" (1981/1965) signified university scholars' growing attention to pedagogical studies and a move toward collaboration with public school practitioners and normal school teachers. Yet despite the presence of nascent schools and departments of education on university campuses, the skepticism about the academic nature of education remained strong among university-based academicians (Brubacher & Rudy, 1997). Thus the conflicting ideas about whether education was an academic, university-level discipline or merely a professional preparation, became central in the establishment and development of colleges, schools, and departments of education.

Around the turn of the twentieth century, John Dewey (1904/1965), together with a few others, called for the implementation of a laboratory-school concept in the universities' schools of education to connect teacher preparation with practice. James Earl Russell, the dean of Columbia University's Teachers College from

1897 to 1927, followed this sentiment in an essay (1924/1965) addressing the dichotomy between academic and professional purposes of degrees in education. Russell attempted to clarify that "The academically-minded teacher asks what the subject will do for the student; the professionally-minded teacher asks what the student will do with the subject" (p. 210). Furthermore, he called for a resolution of the conflict, suggesting that "academic training is the foundation upon which all professional training rests" (p. 212). Research universities met such a vision of practice-based academic preparation with resistance. However, beginning in the mid-1950s, the connection between teachers' academic preparation and practice became institutionalized in various forms. For example, in 1962, Stanford professor Robert Bush used the term "clinical professor in education" for the first time (Hearn & Anderson, 2001).

Concurrent with those developments in the nineteenth and early twentieth centuries, American universities began to be profoundly influenced by the German model of a research university and began the rapid development of graduate programs domestically. A doctoral degree was conferred by Yale University in 1869–1870 (Geiger, 2005), marking the beginning of the path toward today's highly specialized doctoral programs. The Yale degree was the first of a total of 163,765 terminal degrees awarded to students thus far, according to the most recent records (Snyder & Dillow, 2013).

As scholarship gained prestige on American campuses in the early twentieth century, professional schools, colleges, and departments of education began launching graduate-level programs as well (Brubacher & Rudy, 1997). The first doctoral degree in education was the Doctor of Philosophy, awarded by Teachers College, Columbia University, in 1893 (Shulman et al., 2006). Years later, Harvard established the Ed.D. degree, based on the rationale that education should have its own separate title from the arts and sciences (Dill & Morrison, 1985).

By the year 1931, the Ed.D. (as a substitute for the Ph.D. in education) became available at six research-oriented institutions: Boston University, Harvard, Johns Hopkins, the University of Southern California, and Stanford (Freeman, 1931). Other universities offered both degrees in education. The requirements of the Ed.D. were different from those of traditional Ph.D. degrees and were designed to address the professional rather than the pure academic nature of the studies. At all those institutions, the Ed.D.s did not include two foreign language requirements but required professional experience and "a thesis which organizes existing knowledge instead of discovering new truth" (Freeman, 1931, p. 1). In its official report of 1931, Johns Hopkins University stated specifically that Ed.D. dissertations should be problem-driven and solution-oriented and emphasize, for example, "new techniques for evaluating pupil-growth, or teacher-growth" or "prediction of success in the selection of electives in high schools" (p. 131).

Stanford University (1931) articulated the difference between two degrees, stating that "the Ph.D. stands for ability in pure science, the Ed.D. for ability in applied science" (Freeman, 1931, p. 145). Moreover, as far as the requirement of professional experience was concerned, Stanford clarified that "it [the Ed.D] is a little more difficult to obtain than the Ph.D." (p. 144). In addition, in some institutions the distinction between the two degrees stemmed from each degree's affiliation with either schools of education or graduate colleges. Schools of education tended to oversee Ed.D. degrees, while graduate colleges governed the Ph.D. degrees in education (for example, Indiana University).

Common perceptions of career tracks of Ed.D. and Ph.D. holders were different as well. For example, Harvard's report about its graduate degrees in education stated:

> It is true that most candidates for the Doctor's degree in education at Harvard, as at other institutions, eventually become college teachers of education. Very likely something ought to be done to develop their competence to teach in colleges and universities or to enter into college or university administration. This has seemed to the Harvard faculty, however, a distinct and separate task. The Doctor's degree is granted at Harvard solely as a reward for work that has as its final concrete result, a thesis that expands our knowledge or adds to our understanding of education. (Freeman, 1931, p. 118)

In addition, Johns Hopkins University outlined more specifically the difference in career expectations. While Ph.D. students were prepared for the kind of education research that is necessary for university-based careers, Ed.D. students received cultural and professional training that is important to school settings.

Overall, this historical sketch illustrates that the Ed.D. emerged as a "modified version" of the Ph.D., subsequently contributing to a widespread belief among the opponents of Ed.D.s that this degree was a less-demanding alternative to the Ph.D. degree. They argued that the Ed.D. required fewer academic credits and offered only professional rather than academic career trajectories. Today, however, whatever distinctions still exist between the two degrees have become blurred. Studies undertaken at various times (Anderson, 1983; Deering, 1998; Osguthorpe & Wong, 1993) have found that the differences in research and credit requirements have been disappearing for the last 4 decades. In addition, there has been an increase in faculty career options that are equally accessible to Ed.D. and Ph.D. holders. Moreover, the emphasis on applied research addressing and solving critical issues in public schools has extended to Ph.D. programs as well.

In the wake of a growing scrutiny of Ed.D. degrees (Levine, 2005; Shulman et al., 2006), the Carnegie Foundation has launched an initiative to provide helpful clarifications about the purpose of the Ed.D., the "professional doctoral in education [that] prepares educators for the application of appropriate and specific practices, the generation of new knowledge, and for the stewardship of the profession"

(Carnegie Project on the Education Doctorate, 2014). As is evident in this definition, the generation of new knowledge becomes the indispensable element of academic and professional training in Ed.D. programs.

This very likely takes place as a result of the impact of a knowledge-based economy on higher education, as well as changing assumptions of what constitutes knowledge. Within the knowledge-based economy context, research in education is expected to generate pragmatic knowledge such as solutions to public school problems, predictions of pupil success in an increasingly diverse and complex learning environment, and tested pedagogies and school practices. Kennedy (2001) takes a philosophical approach, asserting that "Education is a public good and consequently education ideas must be evaluated against all of society's regulative ideals, not just against a criterion of truth" that is a single regulative ideal of higher education institutions (p. 46). She further states that because education is a public good, education researchers face a constant need to address shifting social norms and other political and demographic trends. Therefore, education research demands the generation of new knowledge derived from problem-based research that will build the state's capacity to provide solutions and improvements to social and economic problems in public education in a timely manner.

Such focus on the creation of useful and practical knowledge exemplifies the need for a purposeful engagement between university research and the socioeconomic fabric of K–12 public education. To illustrate this, Oakes and Rogers (2001) provide a contemporary case study of the University of California's engagement in building the capacity of the state's K–12 system by reconfiguring education programs' activities and integration of education theory, research, graduate studies, and professional practice. The university places equal emphasis on both the purely academic aspects of education research and the professional practice in education, perhaps signifying that the historical dichotomy between research and professional practice can finally be reconciled. The need for problem-based research is a result of the growing complexity of K–12 settings, a situation that warrants some discussion in this chapter.

## DEMOGRAPHIC LANDSCAPE

Demographics are important indicators of who articulates education problems, who seeks research-driven solutions, and who is affected by education research. I will begin this section by exploring the K–12 demographic context as a preamble to the demographic context of Ed.D. programs. It is important to address current and projected changes in elementary and secondary settings, as these changes shape public policy as well as the research and practice of education researchers— education faculty and doctoral students alike. Issues that require research- and evaluation-driven answers, decisions, and practice are increasingly complex, as they are linked to demographic shifts, poverty, lack of academic preparedness, inadequate public funding, shifting public opinion, standards-based teacher performance, and accountability, to name a few.

## K–12 Trends

Overall, the National Center for Education Statistics (NCES) projects an annual increase of 7% in total enrollment in public elementary schools and 5% in public secondary schools from the fall of 2012 to the fall of 2021 (Snyder & Dillow, 2013). Spending per pupil in public elementary and secondary schools in constant 2011–2012 dollars increased from about $5,000 to $11,000 from 1971 to 2010. The expenditure of gross domestic product on elementary and secondary education grew from $110 billion to about $550 billion over the last 40 years, or 4.5% of GDP in 2011. An increase in the number of public schools to approximately 15,600 took place between 1989 and 2007 (Snyder & Dillow, 2013). These changes simply reinforce the axiom that when the expenditure of public dollars grows, calls for public accountability get louder as well.

At the same time, public schools operate within a more complex sociodemographic fabric. Under the Disability Education Act, today's schools open the doors of traditional classrooms to pupils with disabilities. This group constitutes about 13% of total enrollment, which is a significant increase from the 8.3% reported in 1977. According to the data of 2010, 60.5% of pupils with disabilities spend more than 80% of their educational time inside mainstream classrooms, which is a significant change from the corresponding figure of 31.7% in 1989 (Snyder & Dillow, 2013). Such a finding suggests that today's teachers are required to have more formal preparation in teaching pupils with special needs.

Other demographic categories have been growing rapidly in public education. Public K–12 schools receive more pupils from Hispanic and Asian/Pacific Islander populations and non-English-speaking communities. The percentage of Hispanic pupils grew from 13.6% to 23.1% between 1995 and 2010 and is projected to increase to 26.7% by the year 2021 (Snyder & Dillow, 2013). Asian/Pacific Islander attendance also shows a change from 3.7% to a projected 5.9% by the year 2021 (Snyder & Dillow, 2013). An increase in enrollment of racial/ethnic minority pupils is evidenced in public schools by a higher percentage of students receiving free or reduced-rate lunches, while the enrollment of White pupils is significantly lower in such schools. To illustrate, schools with a 75% or higher eligibility rate for free or reduced-price lunches exhibit the following pattern of racial/ethnic enrollment: 6.2% White, 41.4% Black, 38% Hispanic, 14.5% Asian, 19.2% Pacific Islander, and 31.4% American Indian/Alaskan Native (Snyder & Dillow, 2013). These enrollment figures do not add to 100% because some students identified with more than one racial/ethnic enrollment category.

Furthermore, pupils eligible for free or reduced-price lunches have lower writing achievement levels than noneligible pupils. A closer look reveals that only 54% of Black pupils eligible for free or reduced-price lunches, as compared to 71% of noneligible Black pupils, achieve proficiency in writing. Similar trends are evident in other racial/ethnic groups: 59% of eligible Hispanic pupils as compared to 74% of noneligible Hispanic pupils; 66% of eligible American Indian/Alaskan Native pupils as compared to 86% of noneligible American Indian/Alaskan Native pupils; and 76% of eligible White pupils as compared to 88% of noneligible White pupils. Academic performance is significantly lower for Black and Hispanic students in mathematics as well. Performance in the highest-level mathematics courses by 17-year-olds indicates that only 1% of Black pupils and 1% of Hispanic pupils achieve a score of 350 or above, as compared to 8% of White pupils, where a score of 350 or higher indicates proficiency in solving multistep problems with the use of algebra (National Science Foundation, 1996).

In addition to the problems of higher poverty and lower academic preparedness, dropout rates remain higher for Black and Hispanic pupils: 7.3% and 13.6%, respectively, compared to 5.1% of their White counterparts. Such a situation demands teachers' attention and immediate intervention, especially given the fact that education policy mandates that schools and teachers close achievement gaps between minority and non-minority pupils and between socioeconomically disadvantaged and more advantaged children (No Child Left Behind, 2002). The education policy places a major focus on teacher quality and qualifications, which are believed to be essential to pupil achievement and school improvement. Public school students, parents, and community organizations challenge the implementation of "highly qualified" teacher provisions, noting the large proportion of alternatively certified teachers in schools located in low-income and minority districts (*Renee v. Duncan*, 2010; *Renee v. Duncan*, 2012; *Renee v. Spellings*, 2008).

Not surprisingly, the number of teachers seeking advanced degrees in education is trending upward. The increasing percentage of master's and specialist degree holders—from 23.1% in 1961 to 60.4% in 2006 (Snyder & Dillow, 2013)—indicates teachers' investment in specialized training and preparation for teaching occupations. However, only a very few teachers hold doctoral degrees: 0.8% of White teachers, 2% of Black teachers, and 1.1% of Hispanic teachers (Snyder & Dillow, 2013). Income incentives for teachers to attain doctoral degrees are quite weak: those teachers with a doctorate earn an average annual salary of $59,200 compared to $58,400 for those with education specialist qualifications and $54,800 for master's degree holders. However, the difference in income is more significant between teachers with bachelor's degrees ($43,600) and master's or specialist degrees. Despite a growing Hispanic pupil population and a need for qualified Hispanic teachers to serve as role models, Hispanic teachers lag in master's-level qualifications—34.1% as compared to their White (45.7%) and Black (41.4%) colleagues (Snyder & Dillow, 2013).

The teacher's profile in public schools has been changing in other respects as well. Teachers become more vocal, articulating their perceptions of problems that occur in their schools. Pupils' unpreparedness to learn, poverty, and lack of parental involvement are among the most frequently reported problems (Snyder & Dillow, 2013). While the economic incentives for teachers to attain the doctoral degree are weak, can their personal experience and desire to resolve educational problems be powerful enough to cause them to explore solutions through the pursuit of a doctoral degree in education? As Labaree (2003) observes, most teachers state that their goal of pursuing doctoral studies is to improve schools. This warrants an examination of the profile of a typical doctoral student in education.

## Ed.D. Students

Projections of overall higher education enrollment from 2008 to 2019 anticipate an increase in minority representation (Hussar & Bailey, 2011). Demographic shifts in all doctoral programs are already apparent (Bell, 2011; Hussar & Bailey, 2011; Snyder & Dillow, 2013). According to available data, 57,047 doctoral students were enrolled in graduate programs in education in the fall of 2010, and they comprised 17% of total graduate enrollment across all graduate programs in higher education. Total graduate enrollment in education breaks down as follows: Whites 63.4%, Black/African American 12.4%, Hispanic 8.2%, Asian 2.7%, American Indian/Alaskan Native 0.6%, Native Hawaiian/Other Pacific Islanders 0.4%, persons of two or more races 1.4%, and unknown ethnicities/races 10.4%. The annual average increase for total graduate enrollment in education is evident in figures for 2000 to 2010: Asian/Pacific Islanders 5.6%, Hispanic/Latino 4.5%, Black/African American 3.8%, White 0.9%, and American Indian/Alaskan Native 0.3%.

Overall, education as a field awards about 13.3% of doctoral degrees (Bell, 2011). Women receive a higher percentage of doctorates than men—68% compared to 32% (Bell, 2011), which has been a growing trend since the mid-1980s. The academic year 2010–2011 produced 3,064 male and 6,559 female graduates of doctoral programs in education (Snyder & Dillow, 2013). In comparison, 797 men and only 156 women received doctoral degrees in education during the 1949–1950 academic year (Snyder & Dillow, 2013). During the academic year 2010–2011, doctoral programs in education awarded 71% of their degrees to White graduates, 14.4% to Blacks, 6.2% to Hispanics, 4.5% to Asian/Pacific Islanders, 0.5% to American Indians/Alaskan Natives, 1.8% to persons of two or more races, and 1.6% to students of unknown ethnicities/races (Snyder & Dillow, 2013).

According to available data, between 2008 and 2010, the typical doctoral student profile in education was a White woman (68.6%) returning to doctoral education 12.5 years after starting graduate education and 16.2 years after the completion of a bachelor's degree. The typical doctoral student in education was about 40 years old, which is older in comparison to other fields. Most students were enrolled part time while maintaining jobs outside of academia. The profile of a doctoral student in education is unique in other respects as well. For example, the choice of a primary work activity after completion of the degree differs somewhat from other fields. Education doctorates tend to choose teaching (42.9%) as a primary activity, followed by management and administration (37.7%). Education doctorates allocate only 9.9% of their activity to research as a graduate assistant work option, yet 35.1% of doctoral graduates choose employment in a postsecondary educational institution (Snyder & Dillow, 2013). This post-graduation professional trend can be explained by work norms generally held by faculty in colleges, schools, and departments of education.

## Faculty of Education Profile

As Tierney (2001) observes, education faculty usually rank last in hours spent on research and publish fewer refereed articles than faculty in any other academic/professional field. Education faculty, however, rank high in time spent on administrative duties (Tierney, 2001). Indeed, compared to other professional fields and schools, education faculty tend to have somewhat unique employment trends. First, tenure distribution in education indicates that there are fewer tenured faculty as compared to their counterparts in other fields, except in health sciences (National Study of Postsecondary Faculty, 2004). Specifically, in institutions with a tenure system, tenured faculty constitute about 36.1% of total faculty; those not on tenure track make up 32.6%; and those on tenure track make up 24.7%. About 6.6% of education faculty are employed by institutions without a tenure system. The field of education has joined the growing trend of hiring more part-time faculty, which decreases the number of full-time, tenure-track positions across the board (Tierney, 2001).

Second, education faculty are more likely to be females than males, with the largest difference observed in part-time modes of employment: 41.7% of full-time faculty are males, and 58.3% of full-time faculty are females. In contrast, 34.2% of part-time faculty are males, and 65.8% of part-time faculty are females (NSOFP, 2004).

Third, figures for full-time faculty in education show a slightly higher percentage of Black faculty compared to the overall demographic of faculty in higher education. Race/ethnicity of education faculty is distributed as follows: White 80.5%, Black 7.8%, Hispanic 4.7%, Asian/Pacific Islander 4.8%, and American Indian/Alaskan Native 2.2% (Snyder & Dillow, 2013). In teacher education programs specifically, White males and females make up 22.2% and 63.9% of faculty respectively, Black males and females make up 0.9% and 6.4% respectively, Hispanic males and females make up 1.3% and 2.2% respectively, and American Indian/Alaskan Native females make up 1.6% of faculty (Snyder & Dillow, 2013).

Overall, the composite faculty profile reveals some uniqueness. Collectively, education faculty are more practice-oriented than research-oriented, and about one quarter of them do not have to perform traditional tenure-track duties.

## INSTITUTIONAL PRACTICES

Generally held values regarding education programs have historically revolved around the dichotomy of understanding education as a field of practice and as a field of study, a situation that is likely to create ambiguous academic and professional socialization cultures for students. Some scholars (Labaree, 2003; Neumann, Pallas, & Peterson, 1999) suggest that doctoral students in education experience a conflict between their professional identities as teachers and the respective research cultures of their doctoral programs, which warrants a more nuanced understanding of students' meanings. Kennedy (2001) comments on this contemporary conflict, stating that "education programs have tried valiantly to conform to university norms, but because of the tension between knowledge warranted through formal research methods and knowledge warranted through personal experience," education programs still find it difficult to fit comfortably into higher education institutions (p. 29). However, as Arthur Levine (2001) predicts, the research agenda in colleges, schools, and departments of education will be increasingly field- or practice-oriented, and, as a consequence, doctoral research training in education should also go in that direction.

Yet in the wake of a growing scrutiny of doctoral education, various colleges, schools, and departments of education are attempting to restructure and reform their doctoral programs to distinguish the scientific nature of the Ph.D. from the professional nature of the Ed.D. (Shulman et al., 2006). Some CSDEs differentiate their degrees to address students' enrollment patterns: while Ph.D. students tend toward a full-time residency mode of study, Ed.D. students are simply deprived of such an opportunity because of their commitment to outside employment (Lin et al., 2011). Such differentiation in student enrollment contributes to an intentional conceptualization of the purposes of the two degrees as distinct: the Ph.D. is for the preparation of "researchers," and the Ed.D. is for "the preparation of advanced school practitioners" (Lin et al., 2011, p. 23). Consequently, the "pedagogy of the leader-scholar community," "program design and evaluation of effectiveness," and "scholar-practitioner" are a few examples of new terms evident in the reform discourse geared toward the Ed.D. degree (Golde, 2007; Lin et al., 2011; Olson & Clark, 2009; Shulman, 2007; Shulman et al., 2006).

A troubling aspect of these conversations is the fact that these reforms and discussions are predominantly academic, zooming biases and concerns over the preservation of prestige and legacy of Ph.D. degrees. Decisions on restructuring Ed.D. degrees continue to originate in the idea of what the Ed.D. should *not* be, as compared to the Ph.D. in education. This approach cannot yield useful outcomes for Ed.D. programs, nor can it help students navigate cultural nuances for a meaningful academic and professional socialization experience and a distinct professional identity development.

## IMPLICATIONS

In attempting to distinguish graduate-level provisions for academic preparation and for professional preparation, colleges, schools, and departments of education have made the usual error of comparing the Ed.D. degree with the Doctor of Philosophy, and such a failure to create a distinct identity for Ed.D. programs may send conflicting messages to doctoral students in these programs. As Guthrie (2009) asserts, the Ed.D. degree "deserves a distinct purpose, program standing, and pride" (p. 8). Evans (2007) clarifies that continuing to conceptualize practitioner and scholar activities as dichotomous does not help either degree in education articulate clearly its identity. He proposes that "we would do better to think in terms of a unitary scholar-educator class or set of activities to which people make differential contributions according to time, talents, interests, and abilities" (p. 555).

Indeed, the reforms of the Ed.D. might need to merge the macro and micro social dimensions of the issue at stake. That is, the conversations need to begin with the acknowledgment of history, shedding light on the origins and evolution of the confusion of purposes and intentions of Ed.D. degrees. Then the focus needs to be placed solely on the complex socioeconomic context in which contemporary programs reside and on the constituencies who are rightfully demanding research-driven solutions for public school improvements. Finally, the conversation needs to engage one of the primary stakeholders of learning and research processes—the Ed.D. doctoral students themselves. As Pallas (2001) contends, education programs should stop viewing doctoral students "as passive recipients" (p. 7). Instead, programs need to recognize students' personal epistemology, specialized knowledge, experience, expertise, skills, and abilities (Labaree, 2003; Pallas, 2001).

Weaving all three elements into reforming decisions may help the Ed.D. degree achieve a distinct and unique academic/professional identity. To accomplish these tasks, more research on students themselves is essential. Future research on the education doctorate should probe Ed.D. students' perceptions and meanings concerning their choice of the degree, their academic experiences in their programs, and the potential utilization of attained as well as generated knowledge in their professional settings.

## REFERENCES

Adams, C. (1965). The teaching of pedagogy in colleges and universities: New England Association of Colleges and Preparatory Schools, Addresses and Proceedings. In M. Borrowman (Ed.), *Teacher education in America: A documentary history* (pp. 86–92). New York: Teachers College Press. (Original work published 1888)

Anderson, D. (1983). Differentiation of the Ed.D. and Ph.D. in education. *Journal of Teacher Education, 34*(3), 55–58.

Austin, A. (2002). Preparing the next generation of faculty: Graduate school as socialization to academic career. *Journal of Higher Education, 73*(1), 94–122.

Basu, K. (2012). Ending the first Ed.D. program. *Inside Higher Education.* Retrieved from https://www.insidehighered.com/news/2012/03/29/country%E2%80%99s-oldest-edd-program-will-close-down

Bell, N. (2011). *Graduate enrollment and degrees: 2000 to 2010.* Washington, DC: Council of Graduate Schools and Graduate Record Examination Board.

Borrowman, M. (Ed.). (1965). *Teacher education in America: A documentary history.* New York: Teachers College Press.

Brubacher, J., & Rudy, W. (1997). Professional education. In L. Goodchild & H. Wechsler (Eds.), *ASHE reader series: The history of higher education* (2nd ed., pp. 379–393). Boston: Pearson Custom Publishing.

Carnegie Project on the Education Doctorate (CPED). (2014). About CPED. Retrieved from http://cpedinitiative.org/about

Deering, T. (1998) Eliminating the Ed.D. Degree: It's the right thing to do. *Educational Forum, 62*(3), 243–248.

Dewey, J. (1965). The relation of theory to practice in education. In M. Borrowman (Ed.), *Teacher education in America: A documentary history* (pp. 140–171). New York: Teachers College Press. (Original work published 1904)

Dill, D., & Morrison, J. (1985). Ed.D. and Ph.D. research training in the field of higher education: A survey and proposal. *Review of Higher Education, 8*(2), 169–186.

Evans, R. (2007). Comments on Shulman, Golde, Bueschel, and Garabedian: Existing practice is not the template. *Educational Researcher, 36,* 553.

Freeman, F. (1931). Practices of American universities in granting higher degrees in education: A series of official statements collected and edited with the authorization of the executive committee of the society. *Yearbook XIX of the National Society of College Teachers of Education.* Chicago: University of Chicago Press.

Gardner, S. (2008). What's too much and what's too little: The process of becoming an independent researcher in doctoral education. *Journal of Higher Education, 79*(3), 327–349.

Gardner, S. (2009). The development of doctoral students: Phases of challenge and support. *ASHE-ERIC Higher Education Report, 34*(6), 1–14.

Gardner, S.K., & Barnes, B.J. (2007). Graduate student involvement: Socialization for the professional role. *Journal of College Student Development, 48,* 369–387.

Geiger, R. (2005). The ten generations of American higher education. In P. Altbach, R. Berdahl, & P. Gumport (Eds.), *American higher education in the twenty-first century: Social, political, and economic challenges* (2nd ed., pp. 38–70). Baltimore, MD: The Johns Hopkins University Press.

Golde, C. (2007). Signature pedagogies in doctoral education: Are they adaptable for the preparation of education researchers? *Educational Researcher, 36*(6), 344–351.

Golde, C., & Dore, T. (2001). *At cross purposes: What the experiences of doctoral students reveal about doctoral education.* Philadelphia: Pew Charitable Trust.

Gubrium, J.F., & Holstein, J.A. (1997). *The new language of qualitative method.* New York: Oxford University Press.

Guthrie, J. (2009). The case for a modern Ed.D. degree (Ed.D.): Multipurpose education doctorates no longer appropriate. *Peabody Journal of Education, 84*(1), 3–8.

Hearn, J., & Anderson, M. (2001). Clinical faculty in schools of education: Using staff differentiation to address desperate goals. In W. Tierney (Ed.), *Faculty work in schools of education: Rethinking roles and rewards for the twenty-first century* (pp. 125–150). Albany: State University of New York Press.

Hussar, W.J., & Bailey, T.M. (2011). *Projections of educational statistics to 2019* (NCES 2011–017). Washington, DC: National Center for Education Statistics, Institute of Education Sciences, U.S. Department of Education.

Kennedy, M. (2001). Incentives for scholarship in education programs. In W. Tierney (Ed.), *Faculty work in schools of education: Rethinking roles and rewards for the twenty-first century* (pp. 29–58). Albany: State University of New York Press.

Labaree, D. (2003). The peculiar problems of preparing educational researchers. *Educational Researcher, 32*(4), 13–22.

Levine, A. (2001). So what now? The future of education schools in America. In W. Tierney (Ed.), *Faculty work in schools of education: Rethinking roles and rewards for the twenty-first century* (pp. 211–218). Albany: State University of New York Press.

Levine, A. (2005). *Educating school leaders.* New York: Education Schools Project.

Lin, E., Wang, J., Spalding, E., Klecka, C., & Odell, S. (2011). Toward strengthening the preparation of teacher educator-researchers in doctoral programs and beyond. *Journal of Teacher Education, 62,* 239.

Mendoza, P. (2007). Academic capitalism and doctoral student socialization: A case study. *Journal of Higher Education, 78*(1), 71–96.

Mendoza, P., & Gardner, S. (Eds.). (2010). *On becoming a scholar: Socialization and development in doctoral education.* Sterling, VA: Stylus Publishing.

Mills, C.W. (1959). *The sociological imagination.* New York: Oxford University Press.

National Science Foundation. (1996). Elementary and secondary indicators and science education. In National Science Foundation, *Science & engineering indicators* (pp. 1–36). Washington, DC: National Science Foundation.

National Study of Postsecondary Faculty. (2005). *Report on faculty and instructional staff in Fall 2003.* Washington, DC: National Center for Education Statistics, U.S. Department of Education.

Neumann, A., Pallas, A., & Peterson, P. (1999). Preparing education practitioners to practice education research. In E.C. Lagemann & L.S. Shulman (Eds.), *Issues in education research: Problems and possibilities* (pp. 247–288). San Francisco, CA: Jossey-Bass.

No Child Left Behind (NCLB) Act of 2001. (2002). Pub. L. No. 107–110, 115, Stat. 1425.

Oakes, J., & Rogers, J. (2001). The public responsibility of public schools of education. In W. Tierney (Ed.), *Faculty work in schools of education: Rethinking roles and rewards for the twenty-first century* (pp. 9–28). Albany: State University of New York Press.

Olson, K., & Clark, C. (2009). A signature pedagogy in doctoral education: The leader-scholar community. *Educational Researcher, 38*, 216.

Osguthorpe, R.T., & Wong, M.J. (1993). The Ph. D. versus the Ed. D.: Time for a decision. *Innovative Higher Education, 18*(1), 47–63.

Pallas, A. (2001). Preparing education doctoral students for epistemological diversity. *Educational Researcher, 30*(5), 6–11.

*Renee v. Duncan*, 623 F.3d 787, 2010 U.S. App. LEXIS 19933 (9th Cir. Cal. 2010).

*Renee v. Duncan*, 2012 U.S. App. LEXIS 9504 (9th Cir. Cal. 2012).

*Renee v. Spellings*, 2008 U.S. Dist. LEXIS 49369 (9th Cir. Cal. 2008).

Royce, J. (1965). Is there a science of education? In M. Borrowman (Ed.), *Teacher education in America: A documentary history* (pp. 100–127). New York: Teachers College Press. (Original work published 1891)

Russell, J. (1965). A summary of some of the difficulties connected with the making of a teachers college. In M. Borrowman (Ed.), *Teacher education in America: A documentary history* (pp. 208–217). New York: Teachers College Press. (Original work published 1924)

Shulman, L. (2007). Practical wisdom in the service of professional practice. *Educational Researcher, 36*(9), 560–563.

Shulman, L., Golde, C., Bueschel, A., & Garabedian, K. (2006). Reclaiming education's doctorates: A critique and a proposal. *Educational Researcher, 35*, 25.

Snyder, T., & Dillow, S. (2013). *Digest of education statistics 2012*. (NCES 2005–172). Washington, DC: National Center for Education Statistics, Institute of Education Sciences, U.S. Department of Education.

Tierney, W. (2001). *Faculty work in schools of education: Rethinking roles and rewards for the twenty-first century*. Albany: State University of New York Press.

Tierney, W. (2008). *The impact of culture on organizational decision making: Theory and practice in higher education*. Sterling, VA: Stylus Publishing.

Weidman, J.C., & Stein, E. (2003). Socialization of doctoral students to academic norms. *Research in Higher Education, 44*(6), 641–656.

Weidman, J.C., Twale, D.J., & Stein, E.L. (2001). *Socialization of graduate and professional students in higher education: A perilous passage?* San Francisco, CA: Jossey-Bass.

# CHAPTER FOURTEEN

# Promoting Social Justice Through the Indian Leadership Education and Development (I LEAD) Ed.D. Program

*Jioanna Carjuzaa, William G. Ruff, and David Henderson*

*Authors' Note:* In this chapter, the terms Indigenous, American Indian, Native, and Indian are used interchangeably in our context and do not imply any sort of definite nomenclature.

## INTRODUCTION

The Indian Leadership Education and Development (I LEAD) program, a collaborative endeavor of Montana State University in Bozeman (MSU), the state's land grant institution, and Little Big Horn College, the Crow tribal college, was initially designed to recruit, educate, certify, and place American Indian educators in administrative positions in schools on or near reservations with high Indian student enrollments. In the process, it has developed into a culturally responsive project to mitigate oppression.

I LEAD was originally designed primarily to support American Indian school leaders pursuing an M.Ed. in educational leadership and principal certification. As it has evolved, it has come to include students pursuing their doctorates. Currently in its third iteration, I LEAD boasts 70+ graduates who have joined the ranks of American Indian K–12 school leaders since 2009. When I LEAD began, there were approximately 13 American Indian administrators in Montana; today there are over 100 American Indian school leaders, including the graduates and those in the current I LEAD cohort serving in schools. Of these I LEAD participants, 20 are currently pursuing Doctor of Education (Ed.D.) degrees.

Three interconnected subsystems drive the preparation and support of I LEAD participants before and after graduation—Indigenous identity, culturally responsive pedagogy, and field-based praxis (Henderson, Ruff, & Carjuzaa, in press). With a combination of face-to-face and online coursework and an in-school induction program overseen by qualified mentors, participants can earn an Ed.D. in educational leadership as well as superintendent certification. The curriculum focuses instruction on local school improvement initiatives through problem-based learning assignments. In addition to leadership coursework, summer sessions include a series of seminars focusing on Indian education and Indigenous cultural activities. Upon completion of the program, all participants are expected to serve as administrators in schools serving American Indian children for a period of time equal to the length of their education and training.

## Our Montana Context

Montana is geographically the fourth-largest state in the United States, but it was not until 2010 that the population reached the 1 million mark. The first inhabitants were American Indians, and today 12 tribal nations call Montana home. Montana has seven Indian reservations, each of which is a sovereign nation and supports a tribal college. According to the 2010 Census, the percentage of American Indians in Montana was 6.5%, and for the 2012–2013 academic year, the American Indian K–12 student population in Montana was reported to be 13.5%, a rate 10 times the national average (Montana Office of Public Instruction, 2013).

Approximately 92% of all American Indian and Alaska Native K–12 students across the United States and in Montana attend regular public schools (U.S. Census Bureau, 2011). In Montana, American Indian youth attend regular public schools on or near reservations with high concentrations of other American Indian students. But many American Indian students are unsuccessful in their respective learning communities, and a staggering 50% of American Indian students in Montana—as is the case nationally—do not graduate from high school. To address these inequities, the I LEAD program was designed to slow the revolving door of school leaders, especially in Indian country, so that school improvement efforts could be implemented. In this chapter, we will discuss how I LEAD doctoral students have impacted both MSU's educational leadership program and faculty, as well as how their voices influence education in Montana as a whole.

## Decolonizing the Ed.D. Program

One of the key contributions of I LEAD has been its impact on the MSU faculty and their perceptions of the doctoral program, the curriculum in general, and specifically the capstone project, the dissertation. A distinguishing feature of a doctoral program lies in the ability of its graduates to articulate the theories, applications, and contexts of a specific discipline of study—simply put, a doctoral graduate should be able to articulate the current structure of a given field of study. The dissertation is a demonstration of that ability to articulate and thus provides the cornerstone for the attainment of the doctorate.

However, not all dissertation topics are valued equally. For example, Joseph Murphy, the former dean of Vanderbilt University's School of Education, noted: "The Ed.D. is a degree that produces research that shouldn't be researched by people who shouldn't be researching" (Murphy, 2014). At the other end of the spectrum, there are dissertation topics treating important voices, viewpoints, and frameworks that are too seldom articulated in mainstream academic deliberations and debates and that are still being marginalized within discussions of social justice and educational equity.

Whose voices are important, seldom articulated, and still marginalized? The I LEAD approach to the doctoral program has encouraged American Indian students to engage the nexus of American Indian identity, the struggle for self-determination, and its misfit place in the social justice movement of the early twenty-first century. We have found that American Indian identity must run counter to the current trend of democratic social justice. How can a doctoral program at a land grant university take on culturally responsive pedagogy to facilitate a space for the authentic voices of American Indian educators to articulate their views and embrace cultural diversity in schools serving American Indian communities?

We see culturally responsive pedagogy as a way of reconciling issues of power in the natural tension between Westernized academic standards and a more contextualized perspective of knowing, assessing, and valuing. Carjuzaa and Ruff (2010) examined issues of culturally sensitive assessment, specifically within the context of preparing a female American Indian I LEAD doctoral candidate. As instructors with a Westernized worldview, they had to shift their traditional approach in order to fairly evaluate a research topic proposal written from an Indigenous perspective. When any instructor and student approach a topic from different worldviews, there can be a disconnect between their assumptions. Because disconnected assumptions can arise in a variety of ways, there is an increased need for communication and a renegotiation of the criteria for evaluation to ensure that both individuals are using a common set of assumptions.

In a broader way, Grande (2009) wrote about the tension between American Indian sovereignty and democratic social justice. This tension is the result of a misalignment of assumptions. On the one hand, democratic social justice is a rights-based idea and aligns with the colonizing notions of Westernized academics. On the other hand, sovereignty is a land-based idea. Specifically, there is a chasm between mindsets. In Western thought and politics, the idea of land is related to rights such as the right to own land, to convey title to land, and other powers. Therefore, when we discuss sovereignty as a land-based idea, the assumption of a rights-based mindset follows closely. Yet this is not the case for American Indian scholars. Land-based implies a network of relationships—a relationality with the land and everything associated with the geographic location, including animals, people, plants, and history.

These sorts of fundamental identity frameworks have to be considered when American Indian doctoral students dissertate. American Indian sovereignty is threatened by general societal pressure for identity appropriation such as co-opting Indigenous values (ecological sustainment) and corporate pressure for the commodification of Indianness (corporate branding of mascots, and totems). On the other hand, the democratic social justice model fueled by a growing diversity of articulations of critical theory is drawn more toward the notion of cultural ambiguity and less toward issues of self-determination and tribal sovereignty.

## THE 4RS AND RELATIONALITY IN I LEAD

The visionary Crow Chief Plenty Coups knew the importance of being educated. As he once famously said to his people, "Education is your most powerful weapon. With education, you are the white man's equal; without education, you are his victim, and so shall remain all your lives" (Little Big Horn College, 2009). Although Indians have always valued education, what they have encountered in Westernized educational systems is the colonization of their minds and identity.

As Indian sovereignty has evolved and grown, so too has Indian education, resulting in programs throughout Indian country that have been developed with an increasing deference to Indian tribal leader design and implementation. Kirkness and Barnhardt (1991) described four "Rs" as critical components for academic success by Indigenous students in higher education; also, Wilson (2008) highlighted the need for relationships in all aspects of Indigenous interaction. I LEAD has embraced these approaches and has exercised due diligence in honoring Indian cultures and tribal leadership, which has played a key role in the design and implementation. After all, I LEAD was collaboratively designed to prepare and support American Indian school leaders and leaders of school systems working in high-population American Indian communities with the knowledge, skills, and understanding to improve educational equity and college/workforce readiness for the children of those communities.

Relying on the recommendations of Kirkness and Barnhardt's (1991) seminal research, I LEAD faculty adopted a willingness to learn *from* rather than *about* Indigenous peoples. This has created opportunities for a reconceptualization of the education process that recognizes issues of sovereignty, identity, culture, and place (Lincoln & Cannella, 2009; Mihesuah, 1998). As educators in I LEAD, we are also responsible for the ethical use of knowledge that has been entrusted to us. This provides a venue for Indigenous voices as well as a critical examination of the systems and discourses that continue to promote colonization.

The four requirements, or 4Rs, for promoting more equitable relationships and interactions between Indian and non-Indian faculty and students in higher education that Kirkness and Barnhardt (1991) described include: *respect, relevance, reciprocity,* and *responsibility*. These four values are intricately intertwined in the I LEAD program design, but another key factor, *relationality*, is the cornerstone of the program's success (Wilson, 2008). The I LEAD faculty have used the 4Rs and relationality as the template for negotiating inequities within the education system and transforming the relationship between I LEAD doctoral students and I LEAD faculty, staff, administrators, and other students in educational leadership (Carjuzaa & Ruff, 2010).

## Respect

In I LEAD, respect for Indigenous knowledge is valued; learning from Indigenous perspectives and listening is important. Historically, within the context of Western academia, these practices were seldom recognized. Indigenous knowledge has been relegated to a lower, more provincial status—an alternative knowledge that is marginalized within general society and certainly within the academy. Additionally, the study of Indigenous knowledge has often resulted in romanticizing traditions and customs (Carjuzaa & Fenimore-Smith, 2010).

## Relevance

From the beginning, I LEAD faculty recognized that the program demonstrated relevance beyond traditional graduate theory and practice because schooling in Indigenous communities faced unique challenges due to isolation, cultural colonization, and reservation poverty. This context required I LEAD faculty to listen and experience reservation schooling as doctoral students shared what would be a relevant curriculum to meet the needs of their schools and communities.

## Reciprocity

Reciprocity within I LEAD implies a give and take within the education process that has largely been absent in Western pedagogy. It is an issue of power. The power differential is determined by whose knowledge is valued, who determines the importance of ideas, and who determines the rules for procedures for examining knowledge. Dismantling or interrogating this power differential requires an examination of the purposes—who initiates and who benefits—and clarification of institutional policies and procedures that inform protocols (Carjuzaa & Fenimore-Smith, 2010). Reciprocity within an educational context demands collaboration, the interchange of ideas, power sharing, and learning *from* the other.

## Responsibility

The practice of responsibility in I LEAD rests with both Indigenous communities and program participants. Indigenous communities have realized that the school system often does not protect their cultural traditions, values, and knowledge. The school system values Western perceptions of the world and conceptions of knowledge as frames for educating youth and maintaining the status quo (Smith, 1999). I LEAD prepares school leaders to "control their own knowledge and retain a custodial ownership that prescribes from the customs, rules, and practices of each group" (Battiste, 2000, p. 136).

## Relationality

These 4Rs provide entry into the relationship-building process among I LEAD faculty and doctoral students and Indigenous communities and nurture collaboration within Indigenous schools to create policy change. It is relationality that has allowed us to create intimate, ongoing relationships and build trust and understanding while embracing Indigenous ways of knowing. Relationality is key in Indian country; negotiating relationality is not easy. As Wilson (2008) has observed, "The relational way of being was at the heart of what it means to be Indigenous" (p. 80). The most important lesson learned by the faculty and university staff was that relationality lay at the heart of I LEAD's success.

"We Lead Who We Are"—the MSU Educational Leadership Ed.D. program—has always been guided by the Interstate School Leaders Licensure Consortium (ISLLC) standards for exemplary school leadership. Standard Five of the six standards states: "An education leader promotes the success of every student by acting with integrity, fairness, and in an ethical manner" (Council of Chief State School Officers, 2008). With the advent of I LEAD, these standards have been complemented with the 4Rs and relationality in order to provide a more culturally responsive program. Additionally, I LEAD has embraced the work of Parker Palmer and such ideas as "we lead who we are"—at the same time a simple and complex concept. Palmer (1998, 2004) has suggested that as professionals tap into and deepen their identity and then choose to live and lead from that identity with integrity, these professionals become increasingly authentic in their leadership practice.

The I LEAD faculty fully embrace the ISLLC standards, the 4Rs and relationality, and the importance of identity and integrity in preparing these Indigenous doctoral students to be authentic in their practice as well as in their academic activities. Palmer (2004) has suggested that identity or *beingness* (ontology) informs awareness of how we know and understand (epistemology), which ultimately informs our behavior and its innate value-laden nature (axiology). I LEAD doctoral students have responded positively to faculty member encouragement that the students embrace, articulate, and lead from their Indigenous identities. Willingness to be congruent— to bring who they are to what they do—is the essence of integrity and has resulted in an uncommon capacity to be authentic in their scholarship and their practice.

In a recent phenomenological study of some of our I LEAD doctoral students who have been leading schools in high-population Indian communities, we investigated how they have used their Indigenous identity and integrity to create an authentic leadership that has helped them navigate a Westernized public school framework that can create cultural disconnects with the Indian communities they serve (Henderson, Carjuzaa, & Ruff, under review). Using the *leadership triad model* (Henderson, 2007) as a theoretical lens to examine their leadership practices, these doctoral students and school leaders were clear that their Indigenous identity not only enhanced their leadership but also helped them build relational bridges between their schools and often-skeptical communities.

But arriving at a place where their identity and integrity guided their study as doctoral students was not a given. As one doctoral student stated in the study regarding their identity and their experience at MSU in the doctoral program:

> There were some who really tried to prove who's more *Indian*, and I think that was a result of their own identity being challenged. Because their ideas of what's acceptable as a Native were being challenged by others and by the program.... I went to tribal college, and we had to verbalize what our community and culture believe, and just that was powerful. (Personal communication with Crow doctoral student, May 23, 2014)

For some of these students, resolving these cultural clashes within MSU's Westernized Ed.D. program initiated a pilgrimage into deeper appreciation for who they were as people and as American Indian school leaders. This identity and integrity congruence has also made its way from their doctoral courses into their everyday school leadership. Another participant in the study stated:

> I'm Blackfeet first, and a principal next. So a lot of things I do relate back to my Blackfeet culture and traditions, and character in general. I try to bring those practices as much as I can into the school. I smudge if I can, way before everybody gets here, because talk is really a bad thing sometimes, on your spirit—on your soul. (Personal communication with Blackfeet doctoral student, May 28, 2014)

Guarding their identity from diminishment within Westernized institutions was a real and critical struggle not just to be authentic but also to maintain their identity at the most basic of levels. The I LEAD doctoral program has been enhanced by the integrity of these Indigenous students; as faculty and as facilitators in these Indian students' doctoral education, we have come to be more honest about our own identity disconnects, something that has resulted in a better program and a scholarship within our ranks that has made us more intentional in both integrity and authenticity.

## CONCLUSIONS AND IMPLICATIONS

I LEAD has provided an excellent foundation for the ongoing development and honoring of Indigenous identity as well as the articulation of American Indian sovereignty. However, the evolution of the program has been accompanied by significant challenges. The faculty does not feel the program has arrived—constant reassessment must be engaged in, as it is so easy to return to Westernized institutional colonization when that has been what the non-Native faculty has primarily known. The complex realities of privilege and ego are always at the door of any institution that does not continually question its tacit assumptions. Most of us almost always find it easier to avoid the courageous self-examinations and conversations demanded by a culturally responsive pedagogy.

When identity and integrity are viewed as central to helping doctoral students become authentic leaders, then what those students' identities are become central, and how they bring that identity with integrity demands a learning space where our most vulnerable and heartfelt selves can show up, both faculty and students. This means that curriculum and pedagogy can never be viewed as "sacred cows" but must always be open to scrutiny to determine if they are, in fact, remaining relevant to those who best know their communities. To honor who someone is at her/his core and to listen deeply to her/his understanding of her/his community's culture and needs is one of the greatest gifts we can offer as educators. But this requires a fundamental cultural humility that too often can be viewed as weakness among people known for their mastery of a discipline and who have been recognized and rewarded for their ability to know and not necessarily for taking the risk in saying, "I didn't know that; thank you for teaching me."

But there are great rewards for a doctoral program that embraces a willingness to be co-created with students. Not only have our Native students deepened their commitment to becoming leaders who lead for social justice; our non-Native students have also become increasingly aware of their own privilege and how social inequity pervades all aspects of our society. Our program and those of us who are part of it have come to realize how complex and nuanced inequity is and how difficult being committed to democratic ideals can be. But I LEAD has become, in a sense, a medieval pilgrimage for all involved—a sacred journey to a holy place, where the journey is more important than the destination. As a result, the struggles and challenges along the way to become a culturally responsive Ed.D. program have been as great a reward as any destination at which we might hope to arrive.

Another major impact of the I LEAD program and its American Indian doctoral students has been a significant influence in Indian country and Montana's P–20 education system. Since relationality was a cornerstone of these students' doctoral education, this ability to build relationships has become increasingly realized in their communities with improved communication between tribal institutions and public schools, fostering an overall improved sense of community. Also, because program faculty discovered early on that the input of tribal elders in the development of the program was critical and because Wilson's (2008) relationality was implemented as well, I LEAD has helped these American Indian doctoral students cultivate relationships across Indian country.

One specific outcome has been the proposal by I LEAD doctoral students and acceptance by the board of the School Administrators of Montana (SAM) professional association for an Indian School Leaders caucus within SAM so that school leaders who have a significant Indian student population in their schools (in other words, many of Montana's schools) can come together to help each other implement culturally responsive pedagogy for historically underserved students that will, in turn, improve schooling for all students, Native and non-Native. In the end, these efforts will help Indian communities realize their own sovereignty while creating schools that honor Indigenous culture across Indian country.

I LEAD doctoral students are practicing in uncommon and powerfully authentic ways in their Indigenous communities—their voices speak to social justice with great hope. As one doctoral student stated:

> I don't think you guys at the university will ever understand the road that you are paving for schools and administration and leaders that are Indians…seeing the progress that's being made…. But I think we've never really had a voice, and you're giving reservation schools a voice. We just used to be a black eye for the state—that's how we felt. And this is giving us more of a voice. It's still years to come, but I think it's showing we are trying as hard as everybody else. We have administrators who are not only as qualified as everybody else, but who've been able to work on reservation schools for some time now. I think it goes to show that you can get a lot more trust. (Personal communication with Dakota Sioux doctoral student, May 27, 2014)

And this trust is reshaping schools and communities across Indian country, as well as these doctoral students, within a Westernized educational institution that has become less colonizing and more committed to cultural humility and culturally responsive pedagogy.

# REFERENCES

Battiste, M. (2000). Maintaining Aboriginal identity, language, and culture in modern society. In M. Battiste (Ed.), *Reclaiming Indigenous voice and vision* (pp. 192–208). Vancouver, BC: University of British Columbia Press.

Carjuzaa, J., & Fenimore-Smith, K. (2010). The give away spirit: Reaching a shared vision of ethical Indigenous research relationships. *Journal of Educational Controversy, 5*(2).

Carjuzaa, J., & Ruff, W.G. (2010). When Western epistemology and an Indigenous worldview meet: Culturally responsive assessment in practice. *Journal of the Scholarship of Teaching and Learning, 10*(1), 68–79.

Council of Chief State School Officers. (2008). *Interstate School Leaders Licensure Consortium (ISLLC) standards.* Retrieved from http://www.wallacefoundation.org/knowledge-center/school-leader ship/principal-evaluation/Pages/Educational-Leadership-Policy-Standards-ISLLC-2008.aspx

Grande, S.M. (2009). American Indian geographies of identity and power: At the crossroads of Indigena and Mestizaje. In A. Darder, M.P. Baltodano, & R.D. Torres (Eds.), *The critical pedagogy reader* (2nd ed.). New York: Routledge.

Henderson, D. (2007). *The leadership triad: Identity, integrity, and authenticity.* Unpublished doctoral dissertation, University of Montana, Missoula.

Henderson, D., Carjuzaa, J., & Ruff, W.G. (Under review). Reconciling leadership paradigms: Authenticity as practiced by American Indian school leaders. *International Journal of Multicultural Education.*

Henderson, D., Ruff, W.G., & Carjuzaa, J. (In press). Social justice leadership for American Indian sovereignty: A model for principal preparation. *Journal of Education and Social Justice.*

Kirkness, V.J., & Barnhardt, R. (1991). First nations and higher education: The four Rs—Respect, relevance, reciprocity, responsibility. *Journal of American Indian Education, 30*(3), 1–8.

Lincoln, Y.S., & Cannella, G.S. (2009). Ethics and the broader rethinking/reconceptualization of research as construct. *Cultural Studies: Critical Methodologies, 9*(2), 273–285.

Little Big Horn College. (2009). *Apsáalooke writing tribal histories project: Apsáalooke Crow Indians of Montana tribal histories.* Retrieved from http://lib.lbhc.cc.mt.us/history/3.09.php

Mihesuah, D.A. (1998). *Natives and academics: Researching and writing about American Indians.* Lincoln: University of Nebraska Press.

Montana Office of Public Instruction. (2013). *Montana American Indian student achievement data report.* Retrieved from http://opi.mt.gov/pdf/IndianEd/Data/13INEDStudentDataRpt.pdf

Murphy, J. (2014, June 1). *Productive professional doctoral programs.* Keynote address at Carnegie Project on the Education Doctorate Conference, Denver, CO.

Palmer, P. (1998). *The courage to teach.* San Francisco, CA: Jossey-Bass.

Palmer, P. (2004). *A hidden wholeness: The journey toward an undivided life.* San Francisco, CA: Jossey-Bass.

Smith, L.T. (1999). *Decolonizing methodologies: Research and Indigenous peoples.* New York: St. Martin's.

United States Census Bureau (2011). *State and county quick facts: Montana.* Retrieved from http://quickfacts.census.gov/qfd/states/30000.html

Wilson, S. (2008). *Research is ceremony: Indigenous research methods.* Black Point, Nova Scotia, Canada: Fernwood Publishing.

# CHAPTER FIFTEEN

# The Authentic Ed.D. Program

## Project-Based and Counter-Hegemonic

*Four Arrows, aka Don Trent Jacobs*

## INTRODUCTION

A number of challenges and controversies related to credibility, respect, access, goals, instruction, and curricula continue to plague the professional education doctorate (Ed.D.) in the United States. I contend that educational hegemony is significantly responsible for this situation, as it has resulted in a stifling of the degree's most logical manifestation as the highest level of preparation for developing educational leaders and practitioners who want to *make the world a better place.* The degree is positioned to be a serious threat to the hegemons because of two ideas that are inherently part of the original intentions for it. The first is that motivated working adult professionals are to be relatively self-directed. The second is that programs would emphasize authentic, critical, real-life, praxis-oriented study, that is, project-based learning (PBL). They might produce graduates who know about the effects of neoliberalism on schools or would influence curriculum so that Helen Keller's critique of capitalism and structural inequalities would at long last be studied. I suspect that such Ed.D. graduates would also be committed to education that promotes social/ecological justice and sustainability as part of their transformational objectives.

Hegemony is a slippery concept to grasp. Although the Italian researcher and political economist Antonio Gramsci (1971) is most associated with the term, I define it as "the process by which we learn to embrace enthusiastically a system of beliefs and practices that end up harming us and working to support the interests of others who have power over us" (Brookfield, 2005, p. 93). In the context of my argument, those who have such power are the ruling elite who significantly influence laws, policies, curricula, standards, texts, instructional approaches, media, and dispositions. Their goal is to make sure that education does not disrupt their economic, ideological, or political interests. Those who come to believe that they know best become complicit in the production of harm without fully realizing it. We are all susceptible to the dangers of hegemony without awareness and training. I disagree with Adorno, Frenkel-Brunswik, Levinson, and Sanford (1950), who blame susceptibility on an authoritarian personality. Furthermore, those who realize that they have bought into something that is harmful to the greater good, yet lack the will to protest, often become masters of denial and rationalization.

Unfortunately, the hegemons are probably not worried because, for the most part, Ed.D. programs have never fully actualized these two ideas, and their job security is not threatened. Student access to self-directed, self-paced orientations is absent or weak, in spite of supportive rhetoric. Full-term, syllabus-driven coursework is widespread and, where PBL is used, students are often set loose without sufficient direction and support. Although there are a few universities that implement PBL programs successfully, they tend to keep it relatively quiet in their marketing.

An effective, self-paced, and PBL-centered Ed.D. program requires innovative thinking and committed action. It calls for intensive, collaborative work toward determining student research agendas so that they fulfill the needs and desires of the students, reflect the university vision, and assure high-quality and original contributions to the body of academic knowledge. Coursework must be designed to provide each student with multidimensional lenses through which to view their project while cultivating skills and dispositions that will continue to serve beyond it. Self-paced completion of such courses, plus evidence of impactful work toward improving some significant social, organizational, or ecological problem, would culminate with the final oral defense and graduation.

Presentation of project work might take a variety of forms, such as a standard academic thesis, alternative or arts-based dissertations (Four Arrows, 2008), or transcripts and/or logs that record action research data and other notes. All of this outside-the-box effort is too often thwarted by habits cultivated in K–16 schools that serve hegemonic ideas about competition, authoritarian expertise, hierarchy, letter grading, privilege, structural inequality, suppression of critical thinking and creativity, and other harmful praxes.

Indeed, most educators participate in the maintenance of educational and cultural hegemony to some degree because of their own education. Ed.D.s typically produce leaders who continue the hegemonic cycle begun in elementary school. In an *Inside Higher Ed* blog responding to an article about the closing of Harvard's Ed.D. program, the first and oldest one in the United States, Basu (2012) writes that educational researchers and doctoral candidates too often develop knowledge that has little use in the real world, regardless of whether they are pursuing a Ph.D. or an Ed.D., implying that the entire controversy is more about university profits than the greater good. Yoshikawa, the academic dean at the Harvard Graduate School of Education, ironically and unwittingly endorsed this allegation when he said, "Increasingly, the Ed.D. is seen as a practice degree, but at Harvard it has always been a research degree" (Basu, 2012). By "practice degree," he surely means real-world applications, the kind that are best informed with PBL. He declared that the Ed.D. program that will continue at Harvard will focus only on preparing educators for administrative positions. In other words, it will become an even better way to assure that hegemonic education is passed on by Harvard's prestigious graduates.

In this chapter, I introduce four topics that might lend credibility to the contention that hegemonic barriers haunt the Ed.D., namely:

1. the greater good as the ultimate Ed.D. goal and which makes it especially vulnerable to educational hegemony;
2. a long history of scholarship regarding educational hegemony that can be used to support my argument;
3. the rhetoric, opposition, and realities relating to PBL; and
4. the connections among educational hegemony, worldview, and hypnosis.

## THE ED.D. AND THE GREATER GOOD

Since there is general agreement among practitioners that the Ed.D. is about applying knowledge and research in educational settings, the ultimate goals in these settings must be considered when determining student research agendas. This would help students select projects that align at a deep level with their most significant and passionate interests, even if their desired outcomes do not occur until long after graduation. Without this process in mind, hegemony can flourish by inserting its own goals, which compromises the ability of educators to use the Ed.D. in its highest service. But are there such *ultimate* goals?

I think there are such far-reaching goals and that they are widely embraced in the hearts of most educators. They relate to making the world a better, more peaceful, happy, egalitarian, and healthy place. Indeed, this seems to be how the father of educational philosophy, John Dewey, envisioned teaching and learning, as indicated in the following excerpts from his famous declaration (Dewey, 1897):

1. I believe that all education proceeds by the participation of the individual in the social consciousness of the race. [A student should] emerge from his original narrowness of action and feeling, and to conceive of himself from the standpoint of the welfare of the group to which he belongs.

2. I believe that knowledge of social conditions, of the present state of civilization, is necessary.
3. I believe that the individual who is to be educated is a social individual and that society is an organic union of individuals.
4. I believe that education, therefore, is a process of living and not a preparation for future living.
5. I believe that education is the fundamental method of social progress and reform.
6. I believe that much of present education fails because it neglects this fundamental principle of the school as a form of community life. It conceives the school as a place where certain information is to be given.
7. The most formal and technical education in the world cannot safely depart from this general process. (pp. 77–79)

If these precepts were arguably true when Dewey wrote them more than 100 years ago, it can hardly be reasonably argued that they are not applicable today in an era when so many life systems are at a tipping point or beyond and when social systems are drastically off balance. If education is conceived as that which can save us, and the education doctorate as the highest level for preparing educational leaders, can there be any more important counter-hegemonic action for the long haul than to create an effective Ed.D.?

## RELATED EDUCATIONAL HEGEMONY SCHOLARSHIP

As Dewey is the paramount philosopher for progressive education from a century ago, Noam Chomsky may be his counterpart today. Chomsky concurs with Dewey on many points, but he does not think that the failure of education is merely a problem with pedagogy. He argues prolifically that educational hegemony is to blame. Hegemons, he says, have intentionally used education to replace concepts such as equality, autonomy, critical thinking, experiential learning, and social justice with concepts such as accumulation and domination. In his presentation before a large group of educators at the University of Arizona titled "Education: For Whom and for What?" (Chomsky, 2012), Chomsky explains how higher education, throughout American history, was established by those in power as a tool to assure continuation of their power.

Chomsky is not alone in his ideas about educational hegemony, and although there is little to nothing in the literature that connects it directly to the Ed.D. debate, there is sufficient ancillary scholarship to support the assertion that the Ed.D. is a target of hegemony.

Although I make no attempt to describe it here in depth, it may be worthwhile to briefly mention the literature. For example, there are thousands of publications about critical pedagogy theory that refer to educational hegemony. Although some believe that this discourse is merely "the history of white men engaged in conversations with themselves" (Yancy, 1998, p. 3), the true power of the material remains relevant to our topic. Besides, minority groups also see educational hegemony as a fundamental challenge, especially American Indian educators. For instance, in my recent book *Teaching Truly: A Curriculum to Indigenize Mainstream Education* (2014), I expose specific examples of corporate hegemony and its damaging influence on eight subject areas in K–12 schools.

Another source of relevant scholarship is the anti-neoliberalism movement. Numerous publications have surfaced in recent years about the role of schools in challenging neoliberal hegemony, works such as Abendroth and Porfilio's 2014 edited volume titled *School Against Neoliberal Rule: Educational Fronts for Local and Global Justice: A Reader*, or Henry Giroux's 2010 text, "Bare Pedagogy and the Scourge of Neoliberalism: Rethinking Higher Education as Democratic Public Sphere."

Hegemony in teacher training has also been a hot topic over the years in work such as "Student as Consumer: A Critical Narrative of the Commercialization of Teacher Education" (Porfilio & Yu, 2006). I chose this particular text because it was published in the same year that the National Council of Accreditation of Teacher Education (NCATE) removed the phrase "social justice" from its Glossary of Terms for program accreditation, an important indicator of educational hegemony in itself. As well, David Horowitz's Orwellian-named organization, the Center for Academic Freedom, used "hegemony" to describe those wanting to keep social justice in the Glossary. There is even literature about hegemonic implications for service learning programs in and out of teacher preparation schools, such as "Disrupting the Hegemony of Choice: Community Service Learning in Activist Placements" (Chovanec, Kajner, Mian, & Underwood, 2011).

The scholarly literature about adult education provides the most relevant application of educational hegemony to the Ed.D. Sissel, Hansman, and Kasworm (2001) describe how universities look down on adult, self-directed learners, seeing them as unable to "devote sufficient time, energy and resources to intellectual engagement" because their "environment of valuing family, work and engagement in the community is not central to collegiate relationships" (p. 25). Yet, in both his 1999 and 2008 works, Peter Mayo refers to the writings of Freire and Gramsci to reveal how adult education is a high-stakes opportunity for personal and social transformation because it has the potential to step away from state policy and corporate influence, and why this makes it so vulnerable to hegemony. As well, Mayo and English (2012) argue that corporate and neoliberal hegemony has reached dangerous levels in adult education. Kasl and Yorks (2010) make a similar argument about the suppression of choices in adult learning. These and other works make it clear that adult professional Ed.D. students constitute a real threat to the educational hegemons.

In spite of such publications, I could find only one source that significantly relates educational hegemony to the Ed.D. debates: a paper by Miles Bryant, Melissa Byington, and Richard Torraco titled "The Hijacked Ed.D.," presented on October 8, 2007, at the 21st Annual Women in Educational Leadership Conference in Lincoln, Nebraska. It stated:

> Quite simply, because the Ed.D. had to be fashioned out of the same cloth as the Ph.D., it has never fully realized its potential as a professional degree for professional educators. That is, the Ed.D. was stopped *in transit* and subjected to the hegemony of an academy dominated by Arts and Science disciplines. (p. 2)

Not even the Carnegie Project on the Educational Doctorate (CPED), a prestigious research project begun in 2007, has produced significant literature about educational hegemony's possible influence on the problems it has supposedly been addressing. I checked amazon.com to see if any books had come out from the project. In 2006, the Carnegie Corporation published a book on how to structure doctoral programs in a variety of fields, but I could find none emerging from the Project. On the current CPED website, there is a page titled "Definition of and Working Principles of the EdD Program Design" that was apparently written by the CPED Consortium in October 2009, during the third year of the CPED Project. It lists six relatively neutral goals for the professional doctorate in education, goals such as being framed around social justice and ethics and integrating both practical and research knowledge. These outcomes, albeit benign, are relatively common objectives listed in many Ed.D. program descriptions, and they do not specifically address self-paced or PB-based work.

The good news is that, despite this policy absence, one of CPED's consortium schools did post a progress report that made it onto Google. I refer to the 2008 Progress Report from the Neag School of Education's Ed.D. program at the University of Connecticut. Dated October 2008, it listed some recommendations that came out of the school's four semesters of committee work with the CPED project (Neag School of Education, 2008). A chart lists three lessons learned along with implications for those lessons. The implications are:

1. Core courses, inquiry courses, and laboratories of practice work best when they are integrated into a unified process.
2. The capstone project can be developed through a student's coursework. It does not have to be a separate entity that is undertaken once coursework is completed.
3. One way to enhance student learning and track student progress is to ask students to compose concept maps that integrate new ideas from their inquiry projects.

The school, one of the top-ranked graduate schools in the country, seems to have had the courage to implement the lessons learned, starting at the beginning of the program. On their 2014 website, they refer to their CPED membership in this way:

> As a participant in this select group, the Neag School redesigned its Ed.D. in Educational Leadership as a doctorate of practice. In the revised format, the program engages students in applied inquiry about a problem inherent in leadership, teaching or school reform. Students are encouraged to examine topics that inform equity of educational opportunity.

## PROJECT-BASED LEARNING (PBL) RHETORIC AND REALITY

There is a large body of research as well as anecdotal data to support project-based learning (PBL), which includes related approaches such as practice-based, place-based, and competency-based learning (BIE, n.d.). The research supporting competency-based learning, with its emphasis on self-pacing, also indirectly supports the efficacy of PBL (Sturgis, Rath, Weisstein, & Patrick, 2010). However, the fact that these approaches are seldom a mainstay in American doctorates hints at hegemonic implications, especially in the absence of contradictory data to rationalize such omissions.

When scholars do challenge PBL, their arguments seem weak, such as the one offered by Hye-Jung and Cheolil (2012), who discredit PBL by claiming that teachers tend to "grade the finished product only" (p. 215). Kirschner, Sweller, and Clark (2006) argue that constructivist-, discovery-, and problem-based methods of instruction simply do not work (pp. 75–86). They further state that PBL is likely to be ineffective, especially with novice learners, because the learners' cognitive memories will be overwhelmed (p. 77). A rebuttal by Bryant (2011) in the *Journal of Research in Education* challenges their conclusions, saying, "When a more accurate and descriptive definition of PBL is applied to these sources, they no longer support Kirschner et al.'s argument. In fact, my analysis revealed that a few of these sources even refute their claim" (p. 159). A common feature of some forms of hegemonic rebuttal concerns program requirements for limiting concept definitions or inappropriate demands for objectivity. Nonetheless, defining characteristics are important, and my reference to PBL uses the definition from the Glossary for Educational Reform: "Project-based learning refers to any programmatic or instructional approach that utilizes multifaceted projects as a central organizing strategy for educating students."

Yet not all research that is critical of PBL is necessarily bad scholarship. Rather, it matters only that there be reasons other than disparaging scholarly arguments for any lack of PBL implementation. In a personal example, while I was recruiting international contributors for my book *The Authentic Dissertation* (2008), many doctoral students told me how difficult it was to get authentic PBL projects past their dissertation committee members and that the need to complete unrelated coursework nearly caused them to drop out of their programs.

Granted, it is difficult to know when dissertation committee or syllabi decisions are influenced by legitimate reasoning and when they simply result from habit or hegemony, but these factors must be considered. For instance, if we teachers are told to give letter grades, do we oblige in the belief that they do no harm, are ultimately beneficial, and also are better for us? If so, this is hegemony. Do we merely grade from our long habitual exposure to how it's done throughout our own schooling? Or do we do so reluctantly, owing to fear of reprisal? These are the kinds of questions we must ask ourselves about the Ed.D.

I encounter opposition to implementing the form of Ed.D. that I propose from progressive educators who believe in the importance of a credible, action research-oriented program and who are even savvy about educational hegemony. I have heard some comments over the years as arguments for continuing more traditional approaches to doctoral education. I offer these quotes as an opportunity to reflect about the Ed.D., as well as an opportunity to determine which are grounded in research and experiential wisdom and which in hegemony.

> It is best for students to learn from coursework about various subjects so they can better explore interests for a dissertation topic because they are not ready to start considering one when they come into the program.

> I think the coursework is what the doctoral program is about, not just the dissertation project. It is not about just getting a degree but learning.

> We have always focused students on their dissertation project indirectly by teaching them to research and write better.

> Students cannot use what they do in coursework for their dissertation, as this is against the "double-dipping" policy.

> A doctorate is about learning about the field in general and this is as important, or even more important than the dissertation project. I don't want to water down my courses with individual students who want to design their own ways to learn what I think they should know.

> Academic freedom is compromised with a dissertation focus (PBL) requirement for all students and for all faculty.

> Faculty are not trained or prepared to integrate coursework and doctoral work on the dissertation...we're not there yet.

> Faculty do not have the skills or the time to work with students in ways to help them land a solid PBL project or dissertation that will sustain them through the program and their careers.

Students don't really know what they want to do and prefer taking directed courses until they do.

Students come to the Ed.D. without sufficient critical thinking skills.

The last point may well be a legitimate concern. There is research showing that education majors are significantly less likely to have a critical thinking disposition than other college majors (Eigenberger, Sealander, Jacobs, & Shellady, 2001), though this is an insufficient reason for not doing PBL, the very process in which such critical thinking can at long last be properly taught! Overall, one asks whether these comments are grounded in habitual practice or if they reflect serious research interpretations and honest reflection on lived experience. Are they fear-based? Do they underestimate faculty and student potential? Do they reflect legitimate concerns that a PBL-based doctorate would not have credibility? Only by critically and courageously reflecting on our beliefs and decisions can we answer such questions.

Another indication that hegemony is partially responsible for on-the-ground opposition to PBL manifests in how few American doctorates use it compared to how many European ones do. According to Osguthorpe and Wong's (1993) survey of doctoral-granting colleges and schools of education, 98% of the institutions that have an Ed.D. program require the dissertation, and most engage it in the third stage of the program, after students have completed required and elective coursework. Over the years, I have found few Ed.D. programs in the United States that emphasize a from-Day-One, self-paced, PBL focus on a dissertation or project. I have acknowledged the Ed.D. approach at Connecticut's Neag School of Education; also, Vanderbilt's Peabody College website states that students engage in research projects that examine pressing questions right from the beginning of their Ed.D. program.

A third program, at the College of Educational Leadership for Change at Fielding Graduate University, offers a distributed-learning model that is beginning to give students the option of a self-paced PBL or the option of a more traditional approach. Another PBL-friendly program is the University of Pennsylvania's Ed.D., which was begun 7 years ago. An insider told me confidentially that they are just recently promoting it on their website and that, like other Ed.D. program administrators with similar ideas in mind, they are still hesitating, owing to the stigma of breaking with the more traditional approach.

Nonetheless, by word of mouth, this school of education has doubled its student enrollment since the introduction of a PBL option. In a traditional or typical Ed.D. program, students ground the preparation of their final project in their coursework and rely on their workplaces for data collection and opportunities for applied study that culminate in a dissertation. From the first day of the program, students spend a significant amount of time planning for their dissertations in

206 | FOUR ARROWS, AKA DON TRENT JACOBS

structured and supervised settings. By the end of the planning sequence, students have completed a substantial segment of their dissertations. This systematic approach to the dissertation allows students to defend in their last semester of the program and within 36 months.

At Fielding Graduate University's College of Educational Leadership for Change, our distinctive focus on inquiry-based leadership cuts across the program. The website reads:

> Since students develop their dissertation questions early in the program, they ground the preparation of their dissertations in the coursework and at their places of employment. Working closely with faculty, students develop a project designed to identity, analyze, report and make recommendations about an actual problem (http://www.gse.upenn.edu/degrees_programs/midcareer/program).

As I have suggested, similar programs are commonplace in many parts of Europe, especially in Great Britain, where PBL- or dissertation-based work starts on Day One and becomes the main focus for all coursework. As well, the following announcement from Maastricht University of the Netherlands, one of the top 100 universities in the world, unapologetically promotes its PBL approach:

> Problem-Based Learning (PBL) clearly illustrates the university's innovative character. This educational model has been at the core of Maastricht University ever since it was founded. UM is the only university that applies this effective and successful system in all its programmes. An increasing number of universities in the Netherlands and abroad have adopted PBL.... PBL is a student-centered approach to learning. Your teachers are there to help you along, but you are in charge of the learning process. This increases your motivation and gets you thoroughly interested in the subject matter. (Maastricht University, 2012).

## HEGEMONY, WORLDVIEW, AND HYPNOSIS

If you agree by now with my position that the concept of educational hegemony is slippery, hold on to your proverbial hat as I introduce two of its bedfellows, worldview and hypnosis. Equally mysterious and controversial, these concepts are vitally important and intricately interwoven with hegemony. Like hegemony, they are seldom afforded attention in higher education, though there are exceptions within the fields of anthropology, psychology, and medicine. To fully comprehend educational hegemony and its potential influence on the Ed.D., having a sense of how worldview and hypnosis theories play out is essential. (For more, see my forthcoming text, *Point of Departure.*)

Edward T. Hall (1983) defines worldview as "the underlying, hidden level of culture...a set of unspoken, implicit rules of behavior and thought that controls everything we do" (p. 47). Some theorists believe there are as many worldviews as there are cultures, values, philosophies, ideologies, and religions. Others believe that these perspectives water down the importance of the deeper meaning that Hall offers. For example, a worldview question, rather than a cultural one, is whether one believes that humans are the centerpiece or highest rung of creation. According to how we answer this and other questions, we fall into one of two historically observable worldviews: a dominant, Western-derived one and an Indigenous one.

In the 1950s, Robert Redfield, a distinguished professor at the University of Chicago, led a team of notable anthropologists who agreed with his premise that there are essentially only these two worldviews. He valorized—but did not romanticize—the Indigenous perspective and believed that civilization's radical departure from it resulted in "the loss of a unified, sacred and moral cosmos and its replacement by a thoroughly fragmented, disenchanted and amoral one" (Naugle, 2002, p. 248). Furthermore, Redfield (1953) saw this original human worldview as a constructive basis for a critique of dominant culture, explaining that the latter is always trying to destroy the former.

Hypnosis can be instrumental in creating a worldview, as well as in buying uncritically into hegemony. Hypnotic learning during alternative states of consciousness and alternative brainwave experiences is a part of nature's survival repertoire for a number of animals. As well, the use of intentional trance for learning is common within the Indigenous worldview. In contemporary civilization, hegemonic forces have pushed it into the fringes of society as something to be used only by licensed physicians or stage performers. As a result, we have lost our own *intentional* hypnotic skills and have yielded control of the phenomenon to our preachers, peddlers, and politicians—or any other persons we allow to have some authority over us, including our teachers.

In medicine, the powerful attributes of the placebo effect, which is essentially hypnosis, are similarly suppressed so that hegemony and its subsequent profits in fields of medicine are unfettered by its influence. For example, two Harvard scholars, Herbert Benson and Ted Kaptchuk, have stood firm despite years of ridicule and dismissal of their facts, which show that from 30% to 90% of successful results from actual drugs or surgery occur with placebo comparisons, even when the patient knows he or she is in the placebo group. Benson's history of this unfortunate process up until 1995 can be found in his text *Timeless Healing: The Power and Biology of Belief* (1996) and in his coauthored article in the *Journal of the American Medical Association* (Benson & Epstein, 1975) titled "The Placebo Effect: A Neglected Asset in the Care of Patients." Kaptchuk's journal article of 1998, "Intentional Ignorance," is another good history of this controversy, the other side of which is reflected in a 1994 article in the *New England Journal of Medicine* that states that placebo controls themselves are unethical and have little or no efficacy in medical practice (Rothman & Michels, 1994, pp. 394–398).

I offer this as another example of how hegemony suppresses autonomy and self-paced, experiential learning.

In an article about hunter-gatherers published in the *American Anthropologist*, Lee writes:

> We live in an era in which the line between real and non-real has become dangerously blurred. What is real has become a scarce commodity and the pursuit of the "real" sometimes becomes a desperate search.... We don't have to search far for evidence of this proposition. The Disney Corporation produces and distributes in a single fiscal year, perhaps in a single week, more fantasy material to more people than entire archaic civilizations could produce in a century. States of the Left, Right, and Center and their bureaucracies also produce prodigious volumes of fantasy. (1992, p. 32).

Perhaps what we believe about education *has* become dangerously blurred, as Lee says. Worldview, hypnosis, and hegemony all start with words, so the impact of curriculum and instruction cannot be overstated. In his text *A Time Before Deception*, Thomas Cooper (1998) offers a scholarly study of how words were seen as sacred to American Indians. They understood words as being about descriptions of reality, and they thought that people who lied had a mental illness whereby they could not distinguish truth from falsity. I submit that an alien looking down on the earth today might suspect that humanity is indeed acting as if it is mentally ill. Perhaps seeing our education system in this light is too strong an allegation, and it is unfair or extreme of me to suggest that suppression of a self-paced, self-directed, PBL-based Ed.D. program contains hegemonic factors, worldview, and hypnosis to degrees that rise to the seriousness with which Lee and Cooper address our contemporary situation. I leave it to the reader to decide.

## REFERENCES

Abendroth, M., & Porfilio, B. (Eds.). (2014). *School against neoliberal rule: Educational fronts for local and global justice: A reader*. Charlotte, NC: Information Age.

Adorno, T., Frenkel-Brunswik, E., Levinson, D., & Sanford, R.N. (1950). *The authoritarian personality*. New York: Harper & Brothers.

Basu, K. (2012, March 29). Ending the first EdD program. *Inside Higher Ed*. Retrieved from http://www.insidehighered.com/news/2012/03/29/country%E2%80%99s-oldest-edd-program-will-close-down#ixzz39Qj2JubR

Benson, H. (1996). *Timeless healing: The power and biology of belief*. New York: Scribner.

Benson, H., & Epstein, M. (1975). The placebo effect: A neglected asset in the care of patients. *Journal of the American Medical Association, 232*(12), 1225–1227.

BIE. (n.d.). *Research*. Retrieved from http://bie.org/objects/cat/research

Brookfield, S.D. (2005). *The power of critical theory: Liberating adult learning and teaching*. San Francisco, CA: Jossey-Bass.

Bryant, L.H. (2011). A re-examination of the argument against problem-based learning in the class-room. *Journal of Research in Education, 21*(2), 157–166.

Bryant, M., Byington, M., & Torraco, R. (2007, October 8). *The hi-jacked EdD.* Paper presented in conjunction with a panel discussion at the 21st Annual Women in Educational Leadership Conference, Lincoln, NE. Retrieved from cpedinitiative.org/files/The%20HiJacked%20EdD.doc

Carnegie Project on the Education Doctorate (CPED). (2014). *Definition of and working principles for EdD program design.* Retrieved from http://cpedinitiative.org/working-principles-professional-practice-doctorate-education

Chomsky, N. (2012). *Education: For whom and for what?* [Video file]. Retrieved from www.youtube.com/watch?v=80OLJTVnFeo

Chovanec, D.M., Kajner, T., Mian, A., & Underwood, M. (2011). Disrupting the hegemony of choice: Community service learning in activist placements. *Proceedings of the Canadian Association for the Study of Adult Education.* Toronto, Canada: Ontario Institute for Studies in Education of the University of Toronto. Retrieved from http://www.adulterc.org/proceedings/2011/papers/chovanec_etal.pdf

Cooper, T. (1998). *A time before deception: Truth in communication, culture, and ethics.* Santa Fe, NM: Clear Light.

Dewey, J. (1897, January 16). My pedagogic creed. *School Journal, 4*(3), 77–80. Retrieved from http://www.infed.org/archives/e-texts/e-dew-pc.htm

Eigenberger, M.E., Sealander, K.A., Jacobs, J.A., & Shellady, S.M. (2001, April). Disposition toward thinking critically: A comparison of pre-service teachers and other university students. *North American Journal of Psychology, 3*(1), 109–122.

Four Arrows [Don Trent Jacobs]. (2008). *The authentic dissertation: Alternative ways of knowing, research and representation.* London: Routledge.

Four Arrows [Don Trent Jacobs]. (2014). *Teaching truly: A curriculum to indigenize mainstream education.* New York: Peter Lang.

Giroux, H.A. (2010). Bare pedagogy and the scourge of neoliberalism: Rethinking higher education as a democratic public sphere. *Educational Forum, 74*(3), 184–196.

Gramsci, A. (1971). *Selections from the prison notebooks* (Q. Hoare & G.N. Smith, Trans. & Eds.). London: Lawrence & Wishart.

Hall, E.T. (1983). *The dance of life: The other dimensions of time.* New York: Doubleday.

Hye-Jung, L., & Cheolil, L. (2012). Peer evaluation in blended team project-based learning: What do students find important? *Journal of Educational Technology & Society, 15*(4), 214–224.

Kaptchuk, T.J. (1998). Intentional ignorance: A history of blind assessment and placebo controls in medicine. *Bulletin of the History of Medicine, 72*(3), 389–433.

Kasl, E., & Yorks, L. (2010, January). Whose inquiry is this anyway? Money, power, reports, and collaborative inquiry. *Adult Education Quarterly, 60*(4), 315–338.

Kirschner, P., Sweller, J., & Clark, R. (2006). Why minimal guidance during instruction does not work: An analysis of the failure of constructivist, discovery, problem-based, experiential, and inquiry-based teaching. *Educational Psychologist, 41*(2), 75–86.

Lee, R.B. (1992, March). Art, science, or politics? The crisis in hunter-gatherer studies. *American Anthropologist, 94*(1), 31–54.

Maastricht University. (2012). *Inspired by quality: Strategic programme 2012–2016.* Retrieved from http://www.maastrichtuniversity.nl/web/Main/AboutUM/OurOrganisation/UMOrganisation/MissionStrategy/StrategicProgramme20122016.htm

Mayo, P. (1999). *Gramsci, Freire and adult education: Possibilities for transformative action.* New York: Routledge

Mayo, P. (2008). Antonio Gramsci and his relevance for the education of adults. *Educational Philosophy and Theory, 40*(3), 418–435.

Mayo, P., & English, L.M. (2012). *Learning with adults: A critical pedagogical introduction.* Rotterdam, The Netherlands: Sense.

Naugle, D.K. (2002). *Worldview: The history of a concept.* Grand Rapids, MI: William Eerdmans.

Neag School of Education. (2008, October). *CPED progress report.* Retrieved from http://www.cadrei. org/wp-content/uploads/2011/08/CPED-Progress-report.pdf

Neag School of Education. (2012). [Website]. Retrieved from http://edlr.education.uconn.edu/ linkservid/A416CFC6-EAB8-12A9-725526F6EE7E2F85/showMeta/0/

Osguthorpe, R.T., & Wong, M.J. (1993). The PhD versus the EdD: Time for a decision. *Innovative Higher Education, 18*(1), 47–63.

Porfilio, B., & Yu, T. (2006). "Student as consumer": A critical narrative of the commercialization of teacher education. *Journal for Critical Education Policy Studies, 4*(1). Retrieved from http://www. jceps.com/index.php?pageID=article&articleID=

Redfield, R. (1953). *The primitive world and its transformations.* Ithaca, NY: Cornell University Press.

Rothman, K.J., & Michels, K.B. (1994). The continuing unethical use of placebo controls. *New England Journal of Medicine, 331*, 394–398.

Sissel, P.A., Hansman, C.A., & Kasworm, C.E. (2001). The politics of neglect: Adult learners in higher education. In C.A. Hansman & P.A. Sissel (Eds.), *Understanding and negotiating the political landscape in adult education* (pp. 17–27). San Francisco, CA: Jossey-Bass.

Sturgis, C., Rath, B., Weisstein, E., & Patrick, S. (2010). *Clearing the path: Creating innovation space for serving over-age, under-credited students in competency-based pathways.* Retrieved from http:// www.evolllution.com/program_planning/the-growth-of-competency-based-programs/

Yancy, G. (1998). *African-American philosophers: 17 conversations.* New York: Routledge.

# CHAPTER SIXTEEN

# Leveraging Multiplicity in the Ed.D. Cohort toward Transformation of Practice

*Paris T. Priore-Kim*

## INTRODUCTION

The warp and weft of our nation's educational framework, layered and taut, leave little room for significant changes in pattern. Educational practice and policy, mired in complexity, avoid reform. Limited by our own personal and professional epistemologies, we tend toward confirmation of the themes that guide our quotidian practice. We rely on notions of "mastery" and "expertise" to guide us when we should be looking toward inquiry and development. Rarely are we able to challenge our own practice and pedagogy at a foundational and paradigmatic level by unravelling our routines and habits of mind.

The Ed.D. program has the capacity to disrupt the stasis of praxis often directed by a continuum of action and reaction without reflection. By convening practitioners from different spheres of personal and professional experience, the Ed.D. is capable of fostering encounters with divergence that, in turn, expose our assumptions and unlock our inclination to investigate them. Through discourse that leverages diversity and multiplicity toward a critical examination of practice, the Ed.D. can move us from routine response or reaction to transformative reflection.

Through pedagogy rooted in reflective practice, the Ed.D. is able to draw on diversity (e.g., ethnic, cultural, and professional), navigate divergence, and orchestrate convergence to ignite reflective practice and foster a "scholarship of integration" (Schön, 1987, p. 31). This pedagogy, aimed at the interrogation of assumptions, along with a curriculum that surfaces tensions between the familiar and the unknown, generates a complexity that elevates reflection and compels metacognition in a way that disturbs the regularity and the routine of practice. This disruptiveness not only works against the stubbornness of our own habits but ultimately constitutes the potential of the Ed.D. to work against the intractability of the current system.

## A DISRUPTIVE PEDAGOGY

Reflective practice and commitments to social justice constitute focal points of many Ed.D. programs (Wergin, 2011). These aims demand a pedagogy that calls for disruption of habit and the development of a critical consciousness "in which we examine the values, assumptions, ideals and ideologies which constrain the way we think, feel and act" (Mezirow, as cited in Newman, 2006, p. 65). This pedagogy should displace us from familiar vantage points such that we see more deeply inward and more broadly outward. The deeper awareness that derives from a close examination of one's assumptions and beliefs, particularly when plumbed in dialogue with others, lies at the root of paradigmatic change. This requires working beyond superficial levels of communication and delving into discourse grounded in intrapersonal and interpersonal understanding, which shakes us from habitual patterns of thinking. Engaging practitioners in this kind of discourse is a vital function of the Ed.D. pedagogy. It is what distinguishes it from traditional templates and, ultimately, what offers us the traction for improvement and reform.

### A Developmental Approach to Practice

The capacity of the Ed.D. to initiate transformation hinges on its ability to impart a charged consciousness that triggers our engagement in "intelligent action, and [compels us] to inquire into the effects of that action" (Wergin, 2011, p. 131). This cycle of critical reflection, evaluation, and scrutiny should reprise continually. In any context, this approach is valid, but in a rapidly changing world it is absolutely necessary. The shifting global and economic landscapes and the complex challenges borne out by them spur us toward a developmental and evaluative approach to practice that privileges critical reflection and inquiry over the traditional and static aims of expertise and infallibility.

### Agility Versus Infallibility

The dynamism of a developmental approach is increasingly necessitated by the current nature of knowledge (particularly since it has been ignited by technological capability), requiring increased flexibility and reflexivity from educators. Jarvis (1999) notes the shift in the very concept of knowledge, due to technology, from something that remains fixed and certain to something more fluid and mutable. Due to this mutability, teaching and learning require not only agility but also elements of risk-taking and experimentation. The ability to adjust, to deviate, and to venture is supported by practice that views unexpected information as valuable data for improvement of practice.

## Implementing Reflective Practice

Schön (1987) hails these breaks from spontaneous routine as moments of "reflection-in-action" that allow practitioners to conceive of and implement new actions intended to explore the newly observed phenomena and to test their understandings of them (p. 28). This type of on-the-spot reflection often results from surprise or the unexpected, calling into question the assumptions of "knowing-in-action" (Schön, 1987, p. 28). Schön (1983) cautions practitioners against relying on "knowing-in-action," which describes the tacit and spontaneous knowledge that directs actions, making practice more repetitive and routine and obscuring opportunities for reflection (p. 61). On the one hand, professional practice depends on many of these actions that are carried out without thinking and that derive from deeply internalized understandings. On the other, opportunities for improvement and reform are made apparent when practitioners are committed to repeated examination of our expectations and outcomes, leaving themselves completely open to the unexpected.

Plaiting together reflection and knowledge is the task of the Ed.D. such that practitioners reflexively draw on it both for renewal and improvement of practice. Juxtaposing practice with theory such that each is offset and examined by the other is another exercise of the Ed.D. curriculum. In these ways, the Ed.D. cultivates "scholarship into professional practice" (Wergin, 2011, p. 121). This scholarship relies on inquiry, open-mindedness, flexibility, and imagination in order to cultivate emergence and development.

## TRANSFORMING PROFESSIONAL PRACTICE: THE CPED MODEL

Committed to the transformation of practice through redefinition and redesign of the education doctorate since its inception in 2007, the Carnegie Project on the Education Doctorate (CPED) currently convenes a consortium of 56 member schools of education around the examination and development of a meaningful and relevant degree for practitioners. The CPED (2009) model centers specifically on transformation of professional practice and couples the aim of knowledge generation with "stewardship of the profession" (CPED, 2009, "Definition and Working Principles," para. 3). Scaffolded on principles that include social action and justice, generation and use of professional knowledge, and synthesis of practical and research knowledge, the CPED template is aimed at preparing practitioners "for accomplished and responsible practice in the service of others" (Shulman, as cited by Perry, 2013, p. 117).

Formation within the CPED model constitutes engagement with theory and research such that practitioner experiences, assumptions, and options can be explored and dissected. The pedagogy initiates questions of justice and calls candidates to a close examination of their ethical and philosophical stances on educational policy and practice. Candidates grapple with complex and authentic problems of practice and work collaboratively toward developing plans of action in response to those problems. Inquiry characterizes teacher and learner mindset as much as it does elements of the curriculum, fueling discourse as well as discovery. These aspects of the experience can be enhanced in the community of a cohort. As relationships are forged, as shared purposes emerge, and as multiple strengths are acknowledged and leveraged, the cohort has the potential to generate cohesion and cogency around action.

## A CASE STUDY IN MULTIPLICITY: THE ED.D. COHORT AT THE UNIVERSITY OF HAWAI'I

The inaugural Ed.D. cohort at the University of Hawai'i, established in July 2011 and composed of 28 practitioners from K–12 and postsecondary institutions, illustrates the development of a CPED model. A continual interplay of research knowledge, theory, and practical experience spawned complex dialogue regarding improvement of practice. The rich diversity of the cohort distinctly enriched the dialogue, extending it in uncharted directions due to the fission and fusion of multiple knowledge bases and ways of knowing.

### A Broad Range of Professional Experience

Cohort participants represented 21 institutions from across the island chain, spanning kindergarten through postsecondary levels. The scope of experience was spread across different spheres of practice. Both public and private institutions were represented, including the country's largest independent school for Indigenous children. Teachers and administrators came to the cohort from practice across a range of grade levels and a range of specialties, including special education, gifted and talented populations, twice-exceptional populations, and Hawaiian-focused education. They came from schools with economically advantaged populations, as well as those with indigent populations. Their pedagogies ranged from "Western" or "colonial" to culture-based and Indigenous. The cohort also included specialists in curriculum and information technology.

## A Broad Range of Cultural Perspectives

The cohort was racially and ethnically diverse, which is a common trait of almost any group in Hawai'i. Individuals in the group identified as Caucasian, Chinese, Chamorro, Filipino, Japanese, Native Hawaiian, and Portuguese. Although Hawai'i is a tiny state in terms of both population and geography, the range in its ethnic and cultural diversity is vast. Individual ethnic cultures are recognized, and some blend to form an "island" culture. It is important to note that a dichotomy exists between the pleasant coexistence of multiple cultures in Hawai'i and the mostly quiet—but occasionally significant—tensions that ultimately arise from the differences among them. This dichotomy remains subtle as a result of the prevailing attitude of good will within the island culture. Nonetheless, critical concerns that center around justice, access, and opportunity for indigenous islanders fuel a charged political argument.

## LEVERAGING DIVERSITY TOWARD REFLECTIVE PRACTICE

These aspects of diversity augmented the cohort's exploratory and evaluative functions. As a member of the cohort, I credit the expansion of my thinking on matters of educational practice and policy as much to this diversity as to the curriculum. Diversity constitutes not only a structure through which we engage in discourse but also an active agent in shaping a reflective mind-set that seeks to distill action from discourse. When leveraged toward critical and ethical examination of practice, diversity (and the divergences that accompany it) challenges minds and hearts to higher levels of understanding. This exercise, over time, develops habits of mind and heart that embed themselves deeply in our responses to problems of practice and inquiry into praxis. We become accustomed to the notion that our experience, our vantage point, our epistemology are limited informants. We also realize an energy and an empowerment that derive from communal understanding and commitment.

The pedagogy in the University of Hawai'i program called for disruption of habit and the development of a critical consciousness. It compelled convergence between disparate personal and professional narratives, moving us from familiar vantage points and urging us toward unexplored perspectives. The dialectics that structured much of the discourse offered insight into that which Dewey (1938/1997) termed "intelligent action," informed by the deconstruction and re-construction of experience. The dialogue forced our thinking away from habitual pathways and offered new vistas on renewal and reform.

These processes imparted an awareness of multiple perspectives that was implicit and that cultivated plasticity in our thinking. The experience seems to fit Mezirow's notion of "transformational learning," which he describes as:

> The process by which we transform our taken-for-granted frames of reference (meaning perspectives, habits of mind, mind-sets) to make them more inclusive, discriminating, open, emotionally capable of change, and reflective so that they may generate beliefs and opinions that will prove more true or justified to guide action. Transformative learning involves participation in constructive discourse to use the experience of others to assess reasons justifying these assumptions, and making an action decision based on the resulting insight. (Mezirow & Associates, 2000, p. 7)

The deeper awareness produced by a close examination of our own assumptions and beliefs, particularly in juxtaposition to those of others, fostered an acuity that continued to extend our vision for and understanding of practice.

## FLEXING THE COHORT

The training of practitioners in this discourse was accomplished in several ways. The cohort structure offered varied opportunities for developing critical discourse and for establishing trust. With regard to the latter, the continuity of the cohort over a 3-year period was significant and will be discussed in the next section. The large group was often divided into smaller heterogeneous groups whose composition could be altered easily and frequently without compromising diversity. Activity in these small groups frequently demanded that we aggregate and analyze theory and data around practice and policy. In terms of skills, these exercises involved active listening, sensitive questioning, and group facilitation. Beyond that, they also required empathy, open-mindedness, and, at times, self-restraint as differences in perspective, experiences, and philosophy surfaced. These differences, in fact, fuelled the most transformative conversations.

These conversations occasionally engendered discomfort and disquiet, something that often accompanies critical reflection and meaningful growth, but they also offered lenses through which practice could be examined and evaluated with clarity and honesty. They prompted the kind of critical reflection described by McDougall and Davis (2011) that allows us to stand "outside of our practice to see what we do from a wider perspective" and to "disclose the...unquestioned assumptions that structure our teaching practices, particularly those that we may not have been aware of previously" (p. 438). The breadth of experience and the range of realities brought to bear on the conversations forced close scrutiny of our individual and collective values and objectives.

## Disparity and Convergence

By leveraging diversity and compelling convergences between our different realms of experience, we repeatedly engaged in the "hunting of assumptions" (Brookfield, 1995), which structures a platform for evaluation and renewal. By convening multiple voices, perspectives, and philosophies, our constructs of praxis were stretched to new dimensions. The intentional orchestration of discourse that not only validated a range of epistemologies but also depended on them generated a panoramic view of praxis by moving us to places of uncertainty, curiosity and imagination.

Wackerhausen (personal communication, January 25, 2014) asserts that creating convergences between disparate epistemologies leads to transformative reflection. He submits that we tend to reflect on those things that "our kind typically thinks about," which are related thematically to our everyday practice (Wackerhausen, 2009, p. 465). He calls this "first order reflection," whereby we reflect from "certain interests and perspectives embodied in our profession." He contends that our capacity for high-level reflection is limited by "the insufficient (ontological and) epistemic reach of our own profession" (Wackerhausen, 2009, p. 458). Stretching the range of epistemologies to which learners are exposed allows them to grapple with surprising and challenging information—information that exposes deficiencies and uncertainties and that elevates healthy discomfort about practice. The impetus to realign, to renew, to reform comes out of this discomfort.

## Establishing Norms of Respect and Trust

Critical reflection in and of itself can prove unsettling. Mezirow and associates (2000) mention that "an intensely threatening emotional experience" can manifest when a subjective reframing of our ideas or beliefs occurs (p. 6). Group discourse propelled by multiple epistemologies and divergent experiences brought a potential fragility to our cohort. The flow from orientation to disorientation and then to reorientation generated everything from epiphany to unrest. The resulting current of energy was frequently an impetus for constructive action and conveyed the power of the pedagogy.

However, the broad scope of experiences and beliefs ushered some dissonance into the discourse. Underlying the powerful potential of the collective narrative was the tension born of vastly divergent personal and professional experiences and the well of preconceived notions that accompanied them. In light of this potential threat, a solid structure of respect and safety that militated against schism needed to be cultivated. We needed to embrace divergence and dissonance without fearing debilitating discord.

## An Appropriate Timeline

An operational element in this regard was simply time. There was time for the group to develop collectively; time for operating principles to evolve from shared values; and time for mutually respectful relationships to grow (Mezirow, 2000). The cohort's capacity to sustain dialogue depended on successful norming around interpersonal communication, collaboration, and—most important—the development of trust.

These norms evolved gradually by means of the curriculum over the first 2 years of the program. Early on, small-group brainstorming provided a safe environment in which to articulate and test ideas. Low-stakes team assignments allowed us to discover and rely on one another's strengths. Rigor and complexity also galvanized teams and partnerships as they grappled with challenges and setbacks. These processes allowed us to assess our priorities and to identify common goals. Basically, these smaller groupings that flexed the diversity of the whole allowed us to come to know one another and, ultimately, to value one another.

## Faculty Mindset

It is vital to note that attentive listening, open-mindedness, sensitivity to multiple cultures, and respect for multiple epistemologies were all modelled by the faculty over the entire course of study. The value of their actions and attitudes cannot be understated with regard to the cultivation of trust and respect in a community of learners. Furthermore, open conversations between the cohort and the faculty concerning curriculum and program design exemplified reflective practice and furthered the ethical imperatives of the Ed.D.

## BUILDING COHESION AND A COLLECTIVE NARRATIVE

The tone set by the faculty, coupled with the early incremental steps taken to foster communication and collaboration, created a platform for deeper reflection and more meaningful exchange in the second year. The curriculum employed the personal narrative in a variety of ways to probe our core values by way of our personal histories and philosophies. We found ourselves sharing these narratives with one another quite openly and candidly, recognizing that we had incrementally forged the trust that allowed us to do so. My sense is that the relationships, as well as the trust that bolstered them, were stronger because they were built in spite of differences. It follows that productively navigating diversity and divergence in a cohort breeds resilience and even cohesion. The understanding that emerged from the "storytelling" in these exercises eroded barriers that might otherwise have existed and expanded our views of reality. Assumptions were exposed and stereotypes were dislodged. Commonalities and shared aims were also unveiled. From these individual narratives, a collective narrative was being spun. While trust leverages diversity toward reflection, this collective narrative leverages diversity toward shared plans of transformative action.

## STRADDLING SAMENESS AND DIFFERENCE IN THE CONSULTANCY PROJECT

Generating plans for transformative action was also the aim of the Consultancy Project in the second year. This exercise designated small teams from the cohort as "consultants" charged with researching and analyzing problems of practice in educational institutions other than their own. In this regard, the differences and convergences between multiple spheres of practice were exploited to spark inquiry, to offset assumptions, and to define and reframe problems.

While problem solving typically focuses conversations on educational practice, Schön (1983) asserts that "problem-setting" is a critical function of professional practice (p. 18). He describes a kind of dialogue that we might establish with challenging situations. In the best cases, we conduct what Schön (1987) calls a "reflective conversation with the materials of a situation" that liberates us from assumptions that might obscure our view of new avenues to effectiveness (p. 158). Problem-setting and conversations "with the materials of the situation" were the tasks of each consultant team, aided by the varied set of their lenses.

These assignments placed us in situations that were at once familiar and foreign. The work took place in stages, beginning with a period in which the team spent time in the field learning about the institution to be studied. It was critical to enter this period with a completely open mind, with assumptions suspended and preconceived notions erased. Only now do I fully understand the impact of our first year's work on this project and on the development of an "inquiry" mindset. We went on to gather data with no agenda other than to bring clarity to the problem and to reflect on what we observed as authentically as possible.

## THE INSIDER/OUTSIDER DUALITY

Throughout the project, my team could not help but maneuver between subjectivity and objectivity, experiencing the play between divergence and convergence with regard to our experiences and those of the practitioners at the institution under study. Our distant perspective as "outsiders" made the relationships between aims and outcomes more apparent. Our shared perspective as fellow practitioners brought understanding and empathy to the challenges in praxis. Our objectivity allowed us to bring theory to bear on practice, and our subjectivity allowed us to understand the disjunctions between theory and practice.

Ultimately, what we offered the institution under study were reports that described our "conversation with the materials of the situation." Our "outsider" perspectives revealed unseen obstacles as well as new pathways. The perspectives we shared as practitioners identified plans of action that were feasible and practical. The process of holding competing values and managing tensions between the familiar and the unknown that led to this result constructed a platform for the dissertation in practice in the third year.

## NAVIGATING COMPLEXITY WITH METACOGNITION

The mindset that values multiplicity and navigates ambiguity supports the process of the action research dissertation. Although the work was conducted in our own institutions, the "insider"/"outsider" positionality of the Consultancy Project echoed oddly in this culminating exercise. We were simultaneously "in" the research and hovering above it. In many cases, analysis was less about coding and sorting and more about articulating impressions and describing understandings.

What feels like fogginess at times actually fuels and facilitates another way of seeing. I liken this fogginess to Schön's (1987) "indeterminate zones of practice—uncertainty, complexity, uniqueness, conflict," which, he submits, are vital elements in the epistemology of the modern research university (p. 27). Schön (1987) speaks of the "scholarship of integration—the synthesis of findings into larger, more comprehensive understandings" that characterizes much of the work of the Ed.D. (p. 31). This kind of scholarship, Schön suggests, is about designing. Herein lies the potential for transformation and improvement.

In the action research dissertation, I was led to a scholarship of integration through metacognition. Metacognition was the only manner in which I could navigate the complexity generated by the duality of my positionality, by the multiplicity of the data, and by the many resulting ambiguities. It constituted the necessary control of my own cognitive process in order to recognize and honor competing values, to form an impression instead of an opinion, and to reflect rather than respond. It created a flux against the flow of my own practice, discharging me from tacit knowing and propelling me toward examination, evaluation, and synthesis, from which a design for improvement emerged.

## CONCLUSION

A pedagogy that embraces multiplicity and invites a scholarship of integration creates an environment for discourse that leads to transformative learning and action. It leverages diversity toward reflection and seeks benefits from the insights that derive from multiple narratives. It welcomes divergence, which sparks dialectic and offsets routine patterns. It summons dialogue that not only honors but also relies upon every voice.

When dialogue involving multiple contexts and epistemologies is systematically convened, a healthy disorientation persists. Similarly, a momentary fogginess manifests when we approach inquiry with aims of inclusion and synthesis. Clarity surrounding our philosophies, our praxis, and our aims might blur. Questions might supplant previously assumed answers. Problems might sprawl and subsequently redefine themselves. In this process, we are compelled to explore previously unconsidered planes of thought. Discourse becomes complex and propels our thinking down new pathways and into new dimensions.

Complexity trains our capacity to hold and consider competing values in the interest of right and ethical action. It urges us toward abstract thinking that allows us to integrate multiple contexts and strands of disparate information in order to attain an authentic view of the whole. It should not stand as an obstacle but rather as an opportunity to foster vision and stimulate design. The inequities, the conflicts, and the uncertainties that render improvements in educational practice challenging are housed in complexity. Navigating it capably is a social imperative.

Wergin (2011) asserts that "reflection on experience, in dialogue with others, is the key to authentic education and social change" (p. 123). The pedagogy and curriculum that leverage multiplicity and generate complexity reject uniform aims and outcomes and seek understanding with a broad view toward the good in common. They anticipate tension while promoting cohesion, and they temper divergence through convergence. The artfulness of this approach is in navigating the seam that ties the value of the individual to the value of the group. Consistent with the aims of the Ed.D., the pedagogy and curriculum that honor multiplicity and invite synthesis directly address issues of justice and gird practitioners for social action.

## REFERENCES

Brookfield, S. (1995). *Becoming a critically reflective teacher*. San Francisco, CA: John Wiley & Sons.

Carnegie Project on the Education Doctorate (CPED). (2009). *Working principles for the professional practice doctorate in education*. Retrieved from http://cpedinitiative.org/resource-library/

Dewey, J. (1997). *Experience and education*. New York: Touchstone. (Original work published 1938)

Jarvis, P. (1999). *The practitioner-researcher.* San Francisco, CA: Jossey-Bass.

McDougall, J., & Davis, W. (2011). Role reversal: Educators in an enabling program embark on a journey of critical self-reflection. *Australian Journal of Adult Learning, 51*(3), 433–455.

Mezirow, J., & Associates. (2000). *Learning as transformation: Critical perspectives on a theory in progress.* San Francisco, CA: Jossey-Bass.

Newman, M. (2006). *Teaching defiance: Stories and strategies for activist educators.* San Francisco, CA: Jossey-Bass.

Perry, J.A. (2013). Carnegie Project on the Education Doctorate: The education doctorate—a degree for our time. *Planning and Changing, 44*(3/4), 113–126.

Schön, D. (1983). *The reflective practitioner.* New York: Basic Books.

Schön, D. (1987). *Educating the reflective practitioner.* San Francisco, CA: Jossey-Bass.

Wackerhausen, S. (2009). Collaboration, professional, identity and reflection across boundaries. *Journal of Interpersonal Care, 23*(5), 455–473.

Wergin, J. (2011). Rebooting the Ed.D. *Harvard Educational Review, 81*(1), 119–139.

# CHAPTER SEVENTEEN

# Critical Discourse Analysis of Ed.D. Program Narratives

## Engagement with Academic Conferences and Publications

*Mariam Orkodashvili*

## INTRODUCTION: AIMS AND GOALS OF THE RESEARCH

This chapter examines the attitudes and views of Ed.D. students concerning opportunities to participate in international and national conferences, annual meetings, seminars, webinars, and workshops in regard to the quality of their academic as well as practical work. In addition, the importance of publications for young, emerging scholars and education practitioners is discussed and considered. The research is conducted through critical discourse analysis. The discourses that doctoral students engage in produce a wealth of material for critical analysis to examine their attitudes and feelings about their career goals and opportunities for academic enhancement. Matters of learning are often closely related to discourse and identity. In other words, critical discourse analysis contributes to an understanding of learning—a primary issue in educational research.

The chapter provides an overview of the perspectives of Ed.D. students on conferences, annual meetings, seminars, and webinars held on a regular basis and in which they have an opportunity to participate. The importance of online participation is particularly underscored, since a number of students are unable to attend these conferences or meetings in person because of financial constraints. Hence, modern technological advances open up various opportunities for academic enhancement and engagement to socioeconomically disadvantaged students and to students from remote parts of the world.

Blind peer-reviewed papers in various international scholarly journals and online publications provide a further opportunity for doctoral students to become engaged in global scholarly communities and debates on current educational issues. This chapter analyzes the narratives extracted from the interview and survey results of Ed.D. students regarding the opportunities that are available to them to become engaged in scholarly activities taking place in different parts of the world. Finally, the chapter summarizes the strategies of critical discourse analysis that can be implemented to extract recommendations and suggestions that doctoral students can use to pursue their academic goals and to make their career paths smoother.

By way of discourse analysis, educational research explores which views of learning are important, what counts as real knowledge, what methodologies are most useful, what the relationship is between the researcher and the researched, and what the position of education is among other disciplines. In addition, it investigates the ideas of power and empowerment through education policymaking, an important step toward effective social transformation and the achievement of social justice. Critical discourse analysis is an effective way to investigate all of these issues and to draw meaningful inferences.

## THEORETICAL FRAMEWORK: CRITICAL DISCOURSE ANALYSIS

In linguistics, the representatives of *critical discourse analysis* talk about social interactions that take linguistic forms (Fairclough, 1995, 1996; Fowler, 1993; Hastings, 1998; Titscher, Meyer, Wodak, & Vetter, 2000; Van Dijk, 1977, 1985; Van Dijk & Kintsch, 1978; Wodak, 1989). Fairclough (1996) points to the three-dimensional character of any discourse: a piece of text, an instance of discursive practice, and an instance of social practice. Social practices can be thought of as ways to control the selection of certain structural possibilities and the exclusion of others, as well as the retention of these selections over time in particular areas of social life (Fairclough, 2004, p. 226). Educational linguistics makes use of the methods of critical discourse analysis to draw meaningful conclusions from the data, to conduct concept-based research, and to help design empirically informed policies and evaluation strategies (Paulston, 1998; Peters, 2013; Rogers, 2004).

Further, the representatives of cognitive sciences (Dancygier & Sweetser, 2005; Fauconnier & Turner, 2002; Goody, 1995; Hart, 2007) discuss the instances of conceptual mapping and cognitive modelling in order to understand the workings of the human mind and its perceptions of reality. These methods enable researchers to extract, through linguistic, conceptual, and metaphorical means, important information from respondent narratives that the respondents use in order to delve deeper into the true attitudes and motives of the social actions of individuals affected by the researched issue.

In addition, Woodside-Jiron (2004) talks about the language and power of critical discourse analysis to make sense of public policy, a further significant point to be made in regard to critical discourse analysis for Ed.D. narratives. The concepts of power, empowering, and ideology are conveyed in the discourses through the use of modality.

The respondents refer to these concepts in order to make sense of public policy as related to education. Because the Ed.D. students are mainly practice-oriented professionals, most of them see the purpose of their papers or dissertations to be the development of practical strategies for the empowerment of communities to participate in education and to achieve social justice. They are aspiring experts who wish to build communities of practice, and especially of practical leadership, around them. Hence, the concepts of power and empowerment, as expressed through linguistic means, make an important contribution to the overall picture of Ed.D. student attitudes toward their studies and prospects, as well as their visualizations of themselves in their societies and the roles that they intend to play in the process of wider social transformation.

## METHOD OF INQUIRY

The main method of implementation for the present research is critical discourse analysis of the narratives and interviews of the Ed.D. students. This method involves linguistic, sociolinguistic, pragmatic, and extralinguistic analysis of the discourses produced during interviews, surveys, and narratives. A sociocognitive and linguistic analysis of the narratives enables the researcher to understand the attitudes and opinions of the students regarding the issue of academic engagement and to identify the major challenges and obstacles that the students encounter in their attempts to actively engage in scholarly work.

The cognitive, semantic, lexical, semiotic, morpho-syntactic structures that the students produce during interviews, as well as the pragmatic and extralinguistic frames in which the narratives are produced, create the conceptual and linguistic framework of the critical discourse analysis that is often implemented in education research in order to get to the core of the problem, understand the real challenges facing the communities involved, and construct the conceptual model through the cognitive map derived from the discourse analysis. Individuals are involved in meaning making when they interact with the texts of social practices (Lofland & Lofland, 1995; Rubin & Rubin, 1995; Silverman, 1993). To be more precise, the present research puts critical discourse analysis to work in interpretive research in education.

The data have been gathered through interviews and surveys conducted with Ed.D. students most of whom were affiliated with various U.S. universities. U.S. students made up about 75% of the interviewees. The rest of the respondents were either international students residing in the U.S. and attending classes (and thus participating in conferences more often) or online students doing long-distance Ed.D. courses while residing in their hometowns.

The most interesting feature of critical discourse analysis is that the data occur naturally—that is, in their natural environment—rather than being extracted from laboratory experiments or secondary sources. In the majority of cases, the interviewer has the opportunity to observe the reactions and emotions of the respondent and to make more meaningful inferences about the interviewee's response. The present research analyzes the data to draw conclusions about the social practices that are revealed through linguistic means. This process sheds light on the practices of social change, transformation, and learning.

## BACKGROUND INFORMATION ON ED.D.
## COURSES AND GRADUATE CAREER PATHS

Doctor of Education (Ed.D.) programs at most U.S. and European universities offer courses oriented mainly to developing and mastering practical skills for educational leadership, management, or policy analysis. Oftentimes they are aimed at qualification enhancement for working professionals and educational practitioners who specialize in evidence-based practices for school or college improvement and in transformational leadership. They usually aim to develop practice-oriented experts in educational policy and leadership. The applicants are often mid-career professionals who aspire to improve their career opportunities. Therefore, the courses offered in Ed.D. programs are mainly practice-oriented—unlike Ph.D. programs, which focus on research-oriented theoretical courses. Even the dissertation for the Ed.D. course is usually called Applied Dissertation and is required to focus on the problem of practice.

Most Ed.D. programs continuously involve students in producing research-based papers that are often presented at international conferences and annual meetings or published in scholarly journals. The upshot of this is that more and more Ed.D. students participate in international scholarly conferences and annual meetings and thus have more opportunities to publish their work.

The conferences or annual meetings that doctoral students participate in are most often organized by the Comparative and International Education Society (CIES),the American Educational Research Association (AERA), the Association for the Study of Higher Education (ASHE), the British Educational Research Association (BERA), the European Educational Research Association (EERA), the American Association for the Advancement of Curriculum Studies (AAACS), and the University Council for Educational Administration (UCEA), among others. Almost all of these organizations make special arrangements for graduate students to participate in their annual meetings. For example, UCEA runs a Graduate Student Summit Orientation at its annual meetings; CIES organizes dissertation and publication workshops for graduate students and young scholars; AERA organizes graduate student seminars in which students can discuss their dissertation topics with peers and professors and receive valuable feedback from them. In addition to annual meetings, each of the educational associations runs a number of online webinars and discussions throughout the year with the help of special-interest groups in which the members actively participate.

The scholarly journals in the field of education are numerous—*The International Journal of Educational Development, Compare, European Education,* and *Comparative Education Review* are just a few. Of course, neither the list of conferences nor the list of journals is exhaustive. They are merely indicative of the vast possibilities doctoral students have to engage in academic work.

Regarding career paths, graduates of Ed.D. programs usually serve as college presidents, academic deans, student affairs deans, directors of institutional development, registrars, directors of admissions, directors of residence life, and vice presidents of higher education institutions. In addition to careers in educational administration, some Ed.D. graduates also pursue teaching careers at teaching-centered colleges and universities or sometimes at research universities—much like Ph.D. students, who usually teach at research-oriented universities. Some Ed.D. graduates work at policy research centers, resource management departments, education planning institutions, or education data processing centers.

Many students from transitional and developing countries work in ministries of education, enter into senior management positions in international development agencies, or serve as senior administrators and faculty members in local universities. Sometimes they also engage in public- or government-sector work and conduct policy analyses in the field of education planning and management.

## EMPIRICAL ANALYSIS: CRITICAL DISCOURSE ANALYSIS OF THE ED.D. STUDENT NARRATIVES

The surveys and interviews with Ed.D. students made it possible to extract important information about their attitudes, aspirations, challenges, disappointments, or achievements during their studies and after graduation. The questions regarding their expectations of the program and their aspirations for the future were included in the interviews, since it was assumed that those indicators would be related to the degree of student engagement in academic conferences and publications. The students who were happy with their studies would be also interested in participating in academic and scholarly activities of their respective professional and academic communities. They would be more willing to share their findings, ideas, and opinions with their colleagues and international scholars and to publish their papers. Therefore, questions that were related to the academic and scholarly engagement of the Ed.D. students were included in the interviews and surveys.

The respondents were initially divided into two major groups: those Ed.D. students who felt that they had been practice oriented from the beginning of their studies and were, consequently, content with the career path that they had been pursuing for the last several years and those who had chosen the Ed.D. program of studies without being sufficiently informed of the practical workload and intensity of the courses offered in the program. These respondents were often stressed by the amount of study required and felt disappointed and overwhelmed. The percentage distribution of satisfied and dissatisfied students was about 85% satisfied and 15% dissatisfied or stressed out.

The first question of the interview was whether the students' expectations regarding their particular Ed.D. program had been met and to what extent. The most frequently used expressions, epithets, and metaphors by the satisfied Ed.D. students were: *quite happy with what I am doing; I am really in-line with my aspirations; I am content with my studies; I am doing what I am interested in; I would not bear the theoretical focus of the Ph.D. course, now that I am looking at my Ph.D. friends; I really need to advance my chances of getting a well-paid position at a governmental/public institution.*

On the other hand, the most frequently used lexical units by dissatisfied respondents were: *a bit disappointed; not quite what I had expected; well, you know, I thought it would be different; well, in the beginning it was OK, but later.... I don't know, I sort of lost the track; sometimes I feel I don't know where I'm moving; I'm stuck on my dissertation right now, it isn't moving anywhere; I'm stressed out with the workload that I have to do; sometimes I feel really exhausted.*

The syntactic structures used by the satisfied Ed.D. students in their speeches and narratives were long, often complex, and well organized: *considering the fact that I'm planning to implement my dissertation ideas in my workplace, I decided to present some of the major statements and findings at the conference to get the feedback from the folks there; The claim I'm trying to make seems original and interesting, I want to challenge the audience, maybe later, I'll hit one of the top journals.* In addition, the syntactic structures of satisfied Ed.D. students often used participial phrases that emphasized the cohesive links between the ideas: *having said that, I do believe I have good chances of receiving a good job offer after the defense of my dissertation; realizing the necessity of practical application of my hypothesis, I intend to apply to several policy analysis centers or public offices.*

It is interesting to note that the syntactic structures used by the Ed.D. students who were disappointed with their choice were mostly elliptical and included a number of omissions and hesitations or conversational gap fillers. A few examples will illustrate the point: *Well..., I feel, you know, out of place...there; well..., sort of, not the right thing; could've done better...; didn't hit the right button; hmmm, feel diverted from...well, don't know, my goals, I guess.*

The interesting finding, then, is that the satisfied Ed.D. students used longer syntactic structures and engaged in longer discourses and conversations while discussing their career paths and aspirations than did the Ed.D. students who felt disappointed and perhaps diverted from their primary goals. The latter used short, elliptical sentences and used a lot of gap fillers to compensate for their conversational pauses because they were looking for the appropriate words and phrases that matched their judgments and criticisms. This might reflect the fact that they did not wish to blame anyone but themselves for a wrong choice. Therefore, they hesitated while putting the ideas into proper words and phrases to express themselves.

It is also important to note that, in a number of cases, the real feelings and attitudes of the disappointed respondents were implied rather than explicitly stated; many times, the real aspirations and feelings of disappointment needed to be inferred from what they were saying because they were not expressing their feelings openly. Perhaps this occurs not because they are afraid to reveal their true feelings and attitudes but because they are contemplating or making judgments regarding their career paths and academic lives and are, therefore, not quite sure what lies ahead: *yeah, I'm trying to find the right way; I will discuss and reconsider the issues with the right people.*

The next part of the interview concerned the goals and aspirations of the Ed.D. students and how the doctoral program would help them to attain their goals. Again, the replies were diverse and varied from student to student. The disappointed Ed.D. students would reply in a slow, hesitant manner: *well, I don't know what the future holds for me; I don't really want to go on like this; I might change the course, I'm not sure;* while the content students knew exactly what they wanted to do in the future: *I've already sent out a number of applications to different organizations, hope I'll hit the top notch stuff eventually; if you don't try, nothing will come out; tough in the beginning but I'll make it, I know.*

The third part of the interview concerned the opportunities that the respondents had to participate in conferences and annual meetings of scholarly educational associations and how helpful and encouraging their university academic and administrative staff were regarding their engagement in scholarly communities. The students from wealthy universities clearly had a better chance of obtaining funding to participate in the conferences and annual meetings, and they were naturally quite happy regarding the support that their universities offered them: *I'm happy my department offered the travel support to the conference; they usually support Ed.D. students to participate in a couple of conferences per year. Thanks to my academic advisor, I made it here, he was so much encouraging.*

On the other hand, there were some Ed.D. students who, although they had quite supportive supervisors, could not participate in scholarly events owing to financial issues at their universities or departments: *well, it is not about my professor not supporting me, no, on the contrary, he wants me to engage in such stuff a lot, but the department does not offer any funds. This is annoying. It seems we are not moving anywhere with such an approach.*

The next question concerned the possibilities of the Ed.D. students publishing their papers in international journals of high academic standing. The natural consequence of participating in conferences and annual meetings is meeting people, getting feedback, and obtaining information about publications and potential journals to which participants can submit their papers. In fact, some of the active and satisfied students did manage to get their papers published: *I published one piece last year. I hope to submit a longer one this year.* However, certain students who couldn't participate in conferences still managed to submit pieces of work online. The explanation was that they could at least try to submit a paper *somewhere* to enhance their job-hunting efforts: *Well, I'll try submitting a piece of my dissertation somewhere, will look better on my CV and may help get a decent job.*

It is noteworthy that while happy and satisfied students used lexical units such as *top notch*, or *hit the top class journal*, the disappointed students used expressions such as *at least decent job; might look better.* Interestingly, most of the latter-type expressions were delivered with an ironic or sarcastic tone of voice.

The use of pronouns as referents appeared to be one more indicator of Ed.D. students' attitudes toward their academic prospects and engagement. The use of the pronouns *we, our [department], the organization gave us the grant* suggested a feeling of inclusion and integration into a student's academic community. The students who were content with their career prospects generally used these pronouns and displayed an attitude of belonging to the teacher and student body at their universities: *we often organize seminars on current education issues; the state approved our education project; they offered us to get engaged in the discussion of the new education policy.* These phrases clearly show that the students consider themselves to be integral parts of their university and department, to have common interests, and to pursue common goals.

On the other hand, the Ed.D. students who were disappointed in their study programs or career prospects mainly used third-person pronouns—*they, their, them*—thus indicating that they did not belong to the university community where they studied: *they decided to change the courses; their program is not sufficient for further career promotion; I told them several times to have a new attitude.* The students clearly indicated that they did not belong to the academic circles in their departments and criticized them in the third person, thus suggesting that they had nothing to do with the problem. This way, they created a mental space that distanced them from the mainstream academic community of their university.

Modality is one more important tool that was used by the respondents in constructing their discourses. The ideas of power, empowering, and certainty/uncertainty are most effectively conveyed through modal verbs such as *must, have to, can, could, may, might, should, need to,* and so on. The students produced the constructs with multiple modalities to talk about their attitudes about their studies, their academic engagement, and their views on career prospects: *I have to engage in conferences and publish to make my ideas known to peers, colleagues, professors who might provide insightful remarks; I must keep track of news and developments to be in-line with academic communities and trends that impact communities; we should empower disadvantaged communities to engage in education and mainstream societies; my research can appear helpful for contributing to building social justice.* In this way, Ed.D. students expressed their attitudes about their goals and aspirations.

## METAPHORICAL CONCEPTUALIZATIONS OF ED.D. STUDENTS: EDUCATION FOR SOCIAL JUSTICE

Metaphor pervades the conceptual system of human beings (Lakoff & Johnson, 1981). Spatial orientations, objects, temporal indices, referencing—all these categories help to get to the true meaning of a metaphor. One of the core strategies of critical discourse analysis is to recognize and identify the metaphors used in written or spoken pieces in order to understand communicants' attitudes, feelings, emotions, and opinions regarding different issues through their conceptual maps, which oftentimes use metaphors as building blocks.

Individuals use words, phrases, and metaphors in order to make sense of their experiences. Metaphors highlight the features that are unique or highly characteristic of a certain object, state, process, condition, or abstract concept. In the discourses that the Ed.D. students produced, the concept of practical leadership appeared to be the dominant one. Because the majority of Ed.D. programs offer enhancement skills to practicing professionals, concepts and metaphors such as *attaining leadership position, making an impact on communities, innovating academe,* and *leading the communities towards the right goal* appeared to predominate. Nearly 98% of the respondents used leadership-related metaphors in their speeches.

The second-most-frequently uttered or implied concept appeared to be one related to *social justice.* Attaining *social justice* through *leadership* and *innovations* was the pervasive topic that Ed.D. students reiterated in their interviews. Since *social justice* is a complex philosophical concept that has been debated but never agreed upon over the centuries, the purpose of the present chapter is not to attempt to reexamine the idea. The general point that can be made here is that Ed.D. students cling to this concept as a way of envisioning their goals in terms of achieving social justice in their respective communities. The main idea that they try to convey while talking about this issue is their interest in designing and implementing policies that would enable disadvantaged communities to gain access to education and participate in the workforces of mainstream societies.

Thus they intrinsically connect the idea of *social justice* to an opening up of educational opportunities to wider communities and to giving them equal chances for development and self-realization. One of the respondents even mentioned the topic of his paper to be presented at a conference: *implementing educational leadership with reference to human appreciation systems.* He clearly connected his leadership skills in education with the social impact that he wanted to make on the community.

Another interesting point is that being practice-oriented individuals, the Ed.D. students clearly underlined the fact that the main purpose of participating in conferences and publishing their papers was to gain easy access to *fellow co-thinkers* globally with whom they could cooperate, exchange ideas, or even initiate new projects. Therefore, the practical application of academic involvement in conferences or publications turned out to be one more goal of the Ed.D. students.

In summary, the most interesting finding in terms of the metaphorical conceptualization of the Ed.D. programs and courses was the frequent visualization among Ed.D. students of building educational leadership for social justice and of using the opportunity to participate in conferences and to publish to attain their goals.

The metaphors most often used by the respondents were connected to the concept of educational leadership and its implications for social justice.

Since the Ed.D. programs in most universities are practice oriented, the highest attainable goal as perceived by Ed.D. students is achieving educational leadership and making an impact through policymaking on the communities involved. The most commonly used metaphors by Ed.D. students, therefore, were: *promising leader, innate leadership abilities, making a social impact, achieving social inclusion for ethnic and racial minorities, conducting and evaluating policies for effective educational reforms, leading the group of policymakers in achieving the desired goals, including as many communities as possible, opening up educational opportunities for socioeconomically disadvantaged communities, widening the scope of activity, participating in global outreach programs, attaining a top/leading position in education policymaking field, I participate in the conferences to build up meaningful relationships with other educationalists from different universities; I might strike up some handy conversations with people there [i.e., at the conference] who can give me helpful tips on how to develop my project further; if I manage to publish in international journals I will get the feedback on what I am doing now, participating in the conference will help me meet the people and hear some views on further practical applications of my hypothesis.* Hence, Ed.D. students constantly try to find the practical connection between their academic involvement and their prospects for implementing their ideas on education for leadership and social justice in the future.

In summary, it can be inferred from the noted metaphors that Ed.D. students are very much leadership-oriented, aspiring individuals. This feature may be considered to be the single characteristic that most distinguishes Ed.D. students from other degree students or academic communities. It can thus be assumed that if

Ed.D. students are satisfied with their study programs, they are much more ambitious than any other degree students—even more ambitious than Ph.D. students, who might be concentrating solely on the theory aspect of educational issues.

## REFLECTIONS

Now we can build a conceptual model for Ed.D. students based on the discourse analysis and conceptual mapping developed with the information extracted from the discourses of the surveys and interviews.

As we can see from the model, the students see the realization of their goals through active participation in academic events. The interesting point is the referential deixis that usually consists of spatial-temporal units. In the case of the present model, the students who feel happy with the course usually use the referents *we, here, our department* in order to emphasize the condition of belonging to the academic community of their university. In addition, regarding the modality, the respondents usually use modal verbs to express their attitudes toward certain conditions, actions, states, or future intentions.

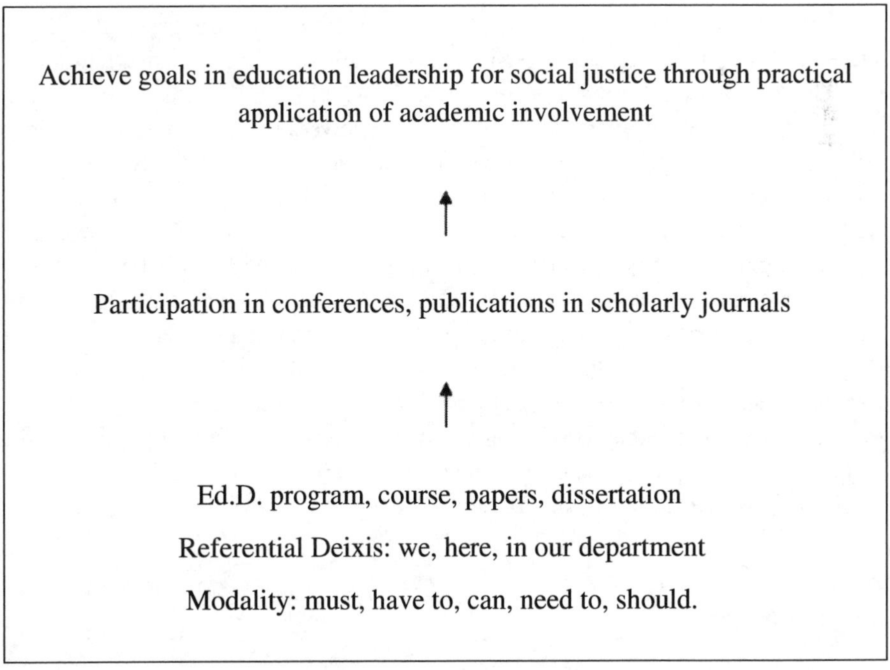

Achieve goals in education leadership for social justice through practical application of academic involvement

↑

Participation in conferences, publications in scholarly journals

↑

Ed.D. program, course, papers, dissertation

Referential Deixis: we, here, in our department

Modality: must, have to, can, need to, should.

Figure 17.1. Conceptual mapping of Ed.D. student academic involvement through a conceptual model built with the help of critical discourse analysis.

## CONCLUSIONS

Satisfied students use long syntactic structures, enter into long conversations, and eagerly offer recommendations on how to use the degree and the knowledge. Therefore, critical discourse analysis can engender valuable information for prospective or beginning Ed.D. students to help them make informed decisions about their futures and to avoid the disappointments that a small percentage of students in the present study revealed. On the other hand, in expressing their attitudes, disappointed students use short syntactic structures, ellipses, interjections as gap fillers, and an ironic tone, all of which provide implications rather than openly expressed statements and positions.

It is noteworthy that the Ed.D. students can be perceived as unique individuals who are in a position to empower themselves and the communities around them to make meaningful transformations in society through public policy analysis, implementation, and evaluation. Power, language, and participation are the dominating repertoires reiterated throughout the discourses that the Ed.D. students engender. One of the most effective ways to trace this fact is through the analysis of modality that is usually implemented in these discourses.

Critical discourse analysis gives insight into the mental images of the Ed.D. students through the lexical expressions, syntactic structures, and metaphors they use. Unlike the quantitative method of analysis, which calculates numbers and percentages of the populations and samples involved, critical discourse analysis attempts to present the mental and cognitive images that the individuals create in relation to different issues, and it identifies pragmatic and semantic frameworks that the individuals employ when discussing those issues. Therefore, orders of discourse are perceived as the social organization and control of linguistic variation.

Texts can bring changes in individuals' knowledge, beliefs, attitudes, values, experience, and perceptions of future prospects. It might even be claimed that there could be a causal relationship between texts and social practices. Together, the two make up discourses that are critically analyzed and provide invaluable material for linguistics, social psychology, and education research and policymaking. Therefore, learning that is seen as social transformation can be combined with the framework of critical discourse analysis.

## REFERENCES

Dancygier, B., & Sweetser, E. (2005). *Mental spaces in grammar: Conditional constructions*. New York: Cambridge University Press.

Fairclough, N. (1993). *Discourse and social change*. Cambridge, MA: Polity Press.

Fairclough, N. (1995). *Media discourse*. London: Edward Arnold.

Fairclough, N. (1996). Critical discourse analysis in the 1990s: Challenges and responses. In E. Pedro (Ed.), *First international conference on discourse analysis* (pp. 289–302). Lisbon: Portuguese Linguistics Association.

Fairclough, N. (2004). Semiotic aspects of social transformation and learning. In R. Rogers (Ed.), *An introduction to critical discourse analysis in education* (pp. 225–235). Mahwah, NJ: Lawrence Erlbaum.

Fauconnier, G., & Turner, M. (2002). *The way we think: Conceptual blending and the mind's hidden complexities*. New York: Basic Books.

Fowler, R. (1993). *Language in the news: Discourse and ideology in the press*. London and New York: Routledge.

Goody, E.N. (Ed.). (1995). *Social intelligence and interaction: Expressions and implications of the social bias in human intelligence*. New York: Cambridge University Press.

Hart, C. (2007). Critical discourse analysis and conceptualization: Mental spaces, blended spaces and discourse spaces. In C. Hart & D. Luke (Eds.), *Cognitive linguistics in critical discourse analysis: Application and theory* (pp. 107–132). Newcastle, UK: Cambridge Scholars Publishing.

Hastings, A. (1998). Connecting linguistic structures and social practices: A discursive approach to social policy analysis. *Journal of Social Policy, 2*, 191–211.

Lakoff, G., & Johnson, M. (1981). *Metaphors we live by*. Chicago and London: University of Chicago Press.

Lofland, J., & Lofland, L.H. (1995). *Analyzing social settings: A guide to qualitative observation and analysis* (3rd ed.). Belmont, CA: Wadsworth.

Paulston, R.G. (1998). *Mapping the postmodernity debate in comparative education discourse*. Pittsburgh, PA: University of Pittsburgh School of Education.

Peters, M.A. (2013). *Education, science and knowledge capitalism: Creativity and the promise of openness*. New York: Peter Lang.

Rogers, R. (Ed.). (2004). *An introduction to critical discourse analysis in education*. Mahwah, NJ: Lawrence Erlbaum.

Rubin, H.J., & Rubin, I.S. (1995). *Qualitative interviewing: The art of hearing data*. Thousand Oaks, CA: Sage.

Silverman, D. (1993). *Interpreting qualitative data: Methods for analyzing text, talk and interaction*. Thousand Oaks, CA: Sage.

Titscher, S., Meyer, M., Wodak, R., & Vetter, E. (Eds.). (2000). *Methods of text and discourse analysis*. Thousand Oaks, CA: Sage.

Van Dijk, T.A. (1977). *Text and context: Explorations in the semantics and pragmatics of discourse*. London and New York: Longman.

Van Dijk, T.A. (1985). *Strategic discourse comprehension: Linguistic dynamics*. Berlin and New York: de Gruyter.

Van Dijk, T.A., & Kintsch, W. (1978). *Cognitive psychology and discourse: Current trends in text linguistics*. Berlin and New York: de Gruyter.

Wodak, R. (Ed.). (1989). *Language, power and ideology: Studies in political discourse*. Amsterdam and Philadelphia: John Benjamins.

Woodside-Jiron, H. (2004). Language, power, and participation: Using critical discourse analysis to make sense of public policy. In R. Rogers (Ed.), *An introduction to critical discourse analysis in education* (pp. 173–205). Mahwah, NJ: Lawrence Erlbaum.

# CHAPTER EIGHTEEN

# Giving Voice Through the Practitioner-Based Ed.D. Program

*Jocelyn Romero Demirbag*

## INTRODUCTION

The University of Hawai'i (UH) Ed.D. program in Professional Practice resulted from Phase II of the Carnegie Project on the Education Doctorate (CPED). The colloquium hoped to work collaboratively to bring about change and transformation to American education. Invited to join the project in 2011, UH aligned with 48 schools to strengthen the Ed.D. program as a degree that focused on leadership careers in professional practice. In particular, UH sought "to produce graduates who are reflective practitioners equipped with essential understandings of research" (CPED, 2011).

UH Cohort I began in July 2011 with 30 diverse participants from the University of Hawai'i system, the Department of Education, Hawai'i's independent schools, and the country's largest system for indigenous children, the Kamehameha Schools. The students included both administrators and teachers representing a wide range of ethnic diversity, as well as a number of frequently marginalized communities. Eighty percent of the students identified themselves as primarily Native Hawaiian, Japanese, Filipino, Chinese, Chamoru, Portuguese, or mixed; the rest were Caucasian. Eighty percent of the cohort was female, and the average student age was in the early-to-mid-40s. Approximately one-third of the cohort conducted projects focused on teaching Native Hawaiian students.

Over my 3-year journey to an Ed.D. program, what began as a numerical study of the financial sustainability of Maui's small independent schools developed into stories of both the schools' struggle for financial sustainability and my own for the understanding of practitioner-based research. Giving voice to Maui's schools and practitioners allowed their experiences to be heard by their local accrediting association. It also transformed my sense of self and assisted in advancing the nature of an Ed.D. program in professional educational practice.

## THE ED.D. DISSERTATION AS A VEHICLE
## FOR VALUES-BASED RESEARCH

The UH program charged us as existing practitioners with conducting action research that would result in a dissertation. We were expected to engage in questions and problems from our daily practice. With this expectation, the program launched us into a realm that McNiff and Whitehead (2010) described as inherently political. Because action research is practice-based, it presupposes that "When you identify your research issue and formulate your research question, you imply that you intend to do something about it" (p. 41). As action research is conducted from the practitioner's point of view, the researcher and her values stand at the center of the project.

The values I brought to my research derived from my socialization in the 1960s and 1970s by Asian descendants of Hawai'i's plantations who were shaped by the Great Depression. A small-town quality dominated Maui—one of neighborliness, collaboration, and extending a hand when needed. My role models taught me that "hard work always pays off" and that "giving back" when you can is the natural and right thing to do. I also learned early on that Hawai'i was Honolulu-centric and that residents of neighboring islands must work harder to be heard, seen, or understood if they wanted to have a voice. It remains the case that neighboring islands are not sought out as part of the complete picture for the state; instead, they must ask to be included.

As a school administrator, I served the local, state, and national educational community by conducting school licensing and accreditation visits and by leading administrators within a national educational organization. The schools we licensed tended to be very small, frequently ranging from 50 to 100 students. By visiting these, schools I learned that schools with fewer than 100 students had been operating for many years. I saw that teachers and administrators worked willingly for very low salaries. I noticed that many independent schools around our state charged incredibly low tuitions. Most important, I observed that these schools functioned and offered a beneficial service to their communities—they provided educational options desired by parents as well as educational environments tailored to individual students' needs.

Many of these small schools appeared to be "scraping by" and going into the new school year with budget deficits. The demographics and budgets from these small schools did not look like those from the significantly larger and wealthier schools that comprised the National Association of Independent Schools (NAIS) membership. I respected the fact that, despite their limited resources, these small schools continued to exist, serve, and make a difference in the world for many students and their families.

In conducting action research, I felt personally called to represent Maui's small independent schools. Specifically, I wanted to relay the schools' voices to the local accrediting organization in order to help it understand the financial sustainability of these schools; such an understanding held implications for the schools' accreditation status. If the association understood the nature of Maui's small independent schools, it might more effectively serve these schools through the accreditation process. What might look numerically like a financially weak situation might not be the definitive explanation for a school's success or failure. Could these schools' strategies for financial sustainability be articulated, measured, and evaluated? If so, who could be better suited to provide this articulation than the schools themselves?

## Values-Based Research 1: Values and Culture

Dr. Sanjeev Sridharan (2013) challenged the cohort to explicitly identify the cultural values that guided our projects and that "bring the community into our work." In the summer of 2012, we identified numerous methods for incorporating culture and community into one's research. These methods served to recognize a values-based lens within research, and the tenets included: "Understand that the solution is not imposed; you co-create the solution with the community and it needs to fit the context"; "Create opportunities for participants to sit and share their stories"; "How would we allow the group we are studying to frame the questions of research? Explicitly identify who is asking the questions for what purpose[s]"; "Establish clarity about what each party needs from the other. Be clear about intentions. For example, establish early whose voice will be represented."

My cohort colleagues inspired me during these cultural conversations. A couple of them wanted to write their dissertations in the Hawaiian language. Others wanted to use research methodology that aligned with Hawaiian or Chomoran cultural protocol. Many of them intended to collect oral histories or to solicit storytelling. The act of explicitly acknowledging cultural values within my research served to define my methodology and changed my research plan.

## Values-Based Research 2: Values in Action

I originally planned a project that would focus on the IRS Tax Form 990s of Maui's small, independent schools. But after considering the role of cultural values, I wanted to honor the communities of each school and incorporate their stories into the research instead of relying solely on numeric documents to express financial sustainability. As discussed by Berliner (2006), in order to provide useful research and not just relevant research, I needed to include "the emic view—the insiders' view of what is happening in a learning environment" (p. 274). Berliner noted that "the subjects' feelings, beliefs, understandings, critiques, and suggestions for improvement of the research" were most often missing from research (p. 274).

I redesigned the project to include the IRS Tax Form 990 data as a numerical reality for a 3-year time period, but I also decided to conduct interviews at the schools and allow school officials to speak for themselves about what their financial sustainability meant. As stated by Patton (2002), "The key questions are about what counts as knowledge, who counts as a knower, and who says so" (p. 224). The project became an opportunity for Maui's small schools to self-define their existence. If my own values and experiences defined my practice, I believed that would hold true for other school leaders on the island as well.

I conducted research in three phases according to the following questions: What do the Hawai'i experts say about small-school financial sustainability? What do the numbers say about small-school financial sustainability on Maui? What do the small Maui schools say about their own financial sustainability? The identified themes and benchmarks were then compared to quantitative guidelines and benchmarks offered by other experts such as GuideStar, Nonprofit Finance Fund, NAIS, and the National Business Officers Association. How did the qualitative data described by Hawai'i experts correspond with the quantitative benchmarks and guidelines set by other experts? How did the expert data compare to what the numbers said and to what the schools said?

## THE ED.D. DISSERTATION AS PRACTITIONER-BASED RESEARCH

Seven key strategies emerged from Hawai'i's experts in relation to small-school financial sustainability, and each had been cited by three of the five experts. Were I not a practitioner in the field, I would have concluded my findings from the experts at this point and moved on to the numerical findings. However, because I *am* a practitioner in the field, a particular strategy mentioned by just two experts (whom I'll identify as P.H. and D.A.) began to haunt me: *personal sacrifice*. When I asked P.H. a question about how he knew whether or not a school was financially viable, he began to speak about cash flow. That much I had expected. It is what he did to manage cash flow that led me to the strategy I call "personal sacrifice." His story caused me (J.R.D.) to shift my thinking about financial sustainability within a small school. Below are some excerpts.

## Stories That Resonate

*P.H.:* I don't think I ever had in all 8 years I was there more than 3 months' payroll in the bank. And so it was quite often a struggle. Often I had to go ask people who I knew could afford it not to cash their check, to hold on to their check until something happened and more money came in.

*J.R.D.:* Do you mean their paychecks?

*P.H.:* Paychecks, yeah. And I mortgaged my house on two different occasions to get working capital to make it through down periods. And so it was a small [school] and a family; the faculty and staff were really close.... I knew who really needed to cash their check and who had a working spouse who could tide them over without their checks. We never missed payroll but some people had to hold their check for a couple of months sometimes even.

P.H.'s story took me aback. Not only had he asked his staff not to cash their paychecks for 2 months, and not only did his staff agree, but he mortgaged his house for the school's benefit. Twice! P.H. also shared that his efforts had been very successful but came at a huge personal price: "So I lasted 8 years as president and the [school] grew to about 600 or 700 students. And that pretty much killed me. I ended up getting divorced from all the travel and fundraising and everything. So I left."

Why would anyone go to such personal extremes on behalf of a school? The answer that resonated with me as a practitioner was "because they love the school and what it is doing that much." They wanted the school to succeed and would do what it took to ensure that success. This is the reason I gave up vacations, and why my own daughter told me when she was growing up that she knew the school came first and that our family came second. This is the reason that teachers paid for their own supplies and worked extreme hours for low pay. On April 8, 2013, I wrote in my journal:

When P.H. told me about mortgaging his house to keep the school going, that was a moment when the project changed for me. It became more personal. About people and what they do because they care. It made me remember all the people doing "crazy" things—like buying land for the school on their credit card—to keep a school going. It reminded me of the aspect of faith and commitment—the values necessary to keep a small school going.

The notion of P.H. personally sacrificing in order for his school to succeed resonated so much with my own experience that I decided to add a question about its role within the interview questions for the school heads and business officers (i.e., "Have you or your staff made personal sacrifices to keep the school going?"). When the research from all three phases was concluded, personal sacrifice emerged as the central strategy for the financial sustainability of Maui's small independent schools. But had I not been a practitioner with experiences that resonated with a small piece of the data, the core findings of my study might have been different.

## Knowing the Field

I also looked at data from phase two differently because of my experience as a practitioner. While the Form 990s offered a breakdown of schools' financial data, benchmarks for school expenditures, strategies for sustainability, and additional data about the financial sustainability of Maui's schools, practitioners in the field knew that there were individual school circumstances and stories at play within each school's very complex environment. "Every indicator has a 'situation' or story attached to it as to how it got there."

"People create the institution, not numbers" (J.R.D. Memo, July 19, 2013). Some of these stories were not identifiable through the Form 990 information but were known to those of us who lived and worked in the community. These stories included whether or not a school head was experienced or inexperienced, whether or not there were capital campaigns under way, and how many volunteers a community event required.

## Recognizing the Data

There were also remarkable stories of human beings "defying" what one might expect. "School 2" charged the lowest level of tuition, yet despite an extensive capital campaign to rebuild its campus, it held a debt ratio of only 5%. Practitioners on the island knew that this was because School 2 had a financial "angel" committed to the school; the angel raised enough money for the projects to completely pay for them. The abilities, resources, and commitment of an individual within a small school community had a significant impact that went against expected outcomes. As a result, schools "defied all odds" in the quality of the education offered.

In phase three, I observed that, in general, the excerpts coded from the schools' interviews were significantly longer than those from the interviews with the experts. I also noted while reading the transcripts, the participants exhibited a different kind of "excitement" or "energy." The school representatives enthusiastically told stories about their own institutions and their experiences at these institutions, rather than speaking from the viewpoint of accumulated knowledge. I realized that the expert from phase one who had brought to life the concept of "personal sacrifice" had also been telling stories. This led me to wonder what other data might have been collected had I asked the experts specifically to share stories from their experience.

What I again recognized as a practitioner is that I resonated strongly when we discussed the schools' strategy of "passion and heart" for the mission. I wrote in my journal that "passion and heart for the mission is the heart of what I want to talk about in my project. Quite literally. In reading what people do for their schools, there is an energy. *This* is what makes a school and fuels it" (January 24, 2014). At the same time, during a finance committee meeting with my own school in which we were reviewing a dashboard for accreditation, what really hit me is that in addition to what they express numerically, the dashboard markers are *advancement* markers.

Advancement is what keeps the school going. The job of advancement is to "fuel passion and heart for the mission" (J.R.D., Memo, January 22, 2014). In an independent school, the advancement team reaches out into the greater community, as well as within the school community, with the clear and relevant mission of the school. If an advancement team succeeded in promoting passion and heart for the mission, then the school also supported the strategies of donor assistance and "good enrollment." In a smaller school, where a designated advancement team was less likely to exist, to the extent that all the staff encountered by the community reflected passion and heart for the mission, that spirit was contagious if backed up by good teaching. As in phases one and two, results from phase three would likely have been different if I were not a practitioner.

## IMPLICIT CHALLENGES IN DEVELOPING AN ED.D. PROGRAM

Schön (1983) validated the practitioner's experiences as a source of knowledge and recognized that when professionals work as reflective practitioners, "we can claim with confidence that practice and practical knowledge are *individual, personal, subjective,* and *dynamic*" (p. 133). He described theory itself as "individual and subjective, since it is the individual practitioner who has innovated in a uniquely changing practice situation and learned from the experiences" (Schön, 1983, p. 132). However, the reality of the reflective practitioner's experience may clash with the technical rationality that has directly or indirectly shaped academic thinking and teaching. This potential clash is natural when moving into a new paradigm.

Despite the intention of developing practice-based signature pedagogy, the technical rational ideal of "basic science yield[ing] applied science" has deep roots within academia (Schön, 1983, p. 24). Shulman (2005) reminded us that we research and teach as we have been taught. Signature pedagogies "form habits of the mind, habits of the heart, and habits of the hand" (p. 59). The concept of professional practice as a valid source of knowledge must evolve into a consistent habit of mind for both the faculty and the students.

Professors participating in the program agreed to help develop and implement a practice-based program, but their own academic experience may need to catch up with that reality. Students in the program stretched to discover the unique approach most suited to their action research rather than act on their own unconscious influence of technical rationality. The interaction between striving faculty and student practitioners encouraged the habit of recognizing the knowledge available through reflective professional practice.

As the student practitioners reflected on their practice, faculty members sought to expand their thinking and actively form new habits of thought. Over their 3 years together, the faculty and students grew to accept that a unique, creative approach to a problem of practice might not fit well into the five-chapter dissertation that a faculty member might have written in the past. Using third-person language when describing the story behind research conclusions might lead to passive writing that edited out the human beings within the research.

"We have become increasingly cognizant of the many tensions that surround professional preparation, from the competing demands of academy and profession to the essential contradictions inherent in the multiple roles and expectations for professional practitioners themselves" (Shulman, 2005, p. 53). Just as a practitioner-based Ed.D. required students to analyze their professional experience, it asked faculty to transcend their experience before they could successfully impart a new signature pedagogy that made sense of uncertainty, performed artistically, and solved problems (Schön, 1983). What coaching and training might be necessary to support faculty and students whose own experience of signature pedagogy was shaped by technical rationality?

In addition, the concept of Ed.D. "training" and professional "preparation" as a basis for signature pedagogy may need to be rephrased. After all, the professionals within UH Cohort I had already worked within their fields as leaders in some capacity. The students might have sharpened and improved their practice or might have moved into another professional aspect of it, but was the Ed.D. really "training" these veteran leaders for a career and position that they might already hold? Perhaps the single most important benefit the Ed.D. student received through the program was the confidence she now placed in her own experience. Further, it may be more accurate to state that the Ed.D. boosted access to positions of community leadership or social justice through the increased credibility that the practitioner gained after receiving the degree.

## GIVING VOICE TO A COMMUNITY

Through my process of conducting action research within an Ed.D. in professional educational practice, the leadership practitioners within Maui's small independent school community came together in the spirit of collaboration. These heads and business officers put their individual voices on the table and allowed me to gather them up and represent our island's experience. What does giving voice to a community look like?

A small group of small schools on a small island came together to share their strategies for financial survival. This is a collaborative gesture rather than a competitive one. The school leaders contributed to an adjusted ideal of financial sustainability for small independent schools on Maui. They asked their local accreditation association to explicitly state the measures used to set accreditation terms. They asked their association for help rather than scrutiny. They asked their association to include perspectives on the accreditation commission that look like their own—small schools run by women from neighboring islands. And they asked their association to look at the communal impact their schools have when determining the schools' validity.

Ultimately, my Ed.D. journey into professional educational practice led me to a destination that I did not anticipate. It led to a recognition—and then to an acceptance—that the knowledge I had gained over the past 20 years through work experience was valid in and of itself. My own professional experience was a basis for reflection and theory that "leaves us at a loss to explain, or even to describe" the practitioner's artful competence as a source of credibility (Schön, 1983, p. 20). This kind of inner destination is transformative in its potential for social justice. Acknowledging our own voices liberates us and allows us to "do something" about the problems we face (McNiff & Whitehead, 2010).

One need not pass the supreme test of technical rationality in order to be considered knowledgeable; as practitioners, we may reflect upon our own experiences, trust in the conclusions we have arrived at after years of experience, and share them with others. In reflecting on and sharing our experiences with the community around us, the stage is set for the emergence of a collaborative, communal voice. My journey included experiential resonance with my participants' interviews and intuitive perception of the energy behind the numbers. Had I approached the project as an academic without practical experience, my findings would have been very different. With support from practitioner colleagues as well as faculty advisors striving to develop a practical approach to research, practitioner-based knowledge within the UH Ed.D. program led to students' personal growth, the advisors' expanded vision of what practical action research might look like, 28 new, diverse, and reflective practitioners with increased access to community leadership, and the articulated voices of their communities.

## REFERENCES

Berliner, D.C. (2006). Toward a future as rich as our past. In C.M. Golde & G.E. Waldor (Eds.), *Envisioning the future of doctoral education: Preparing stewards of the discipline—Carnegie essays on the doctorate.* San Francisco, CA: Jossey-Bass.

Carnegie Project on the Education Doctorate (CPED). (2011, October 5–7). *Phase II—New member programs descriptions.* Proceedings of the University of Vermont Convening, Burlington, VT.

McNiff, J., & Whitehead, J. (2010). *You and your action research project* (3rd ed.). New York: Routledge.

Patton, M.Q. (2002). *Qualitative research and evaluative methods.* (3rd ed.). Thousand Oaks, CA: Sage.

Schön, D.A. (1983). *The practitioner-researcher: How professionals think in action.* New York: Basic Books.

Shulman, L.S. (2005). Signature pedagogies in the professions. *Daedalus, 134*(3), 52–59.

Sridharan, S. (2013, July 8). *Qualitative data analysis: Research design and sampling.* Lecture 8, University of Hawai'i EDCS 732.

# CHAPTER NINETEEN

# The 100 Dinners Project

## An Ed.D. Capstone Project Grounded in Conceptual Change Theory

*Audrey Hovannesian*

All change, even very large and powerful change, begins when a few people start talking with one another about something they care about. Simple conversations held at kitchen tables, seated on the ground, or leaning against doorways are powerful means to start influencing and changing our world.
—WHEATLEY & KELLNER-ROGERS, 1996, P. 67

## INTRODUCTION

Throughout history, areas across the United States have undergone demographic upheavals that have caused periods of change, confusion, and conflict. Our country's uniqueness derives from diverse populations able to merge to create an eclectic society drawing from the attributes of its parts. Often the intersection of these parts is located within schools, where children learn to navigate their way through new environments and create unique cultures of their own. As students try to embrace new cultures, they may encounter preexisting teacher and staff perceptions of their culture, race, ethnicity, gender, socioeconomic status, and so forth that may or may not be accurate. A focus on teacher perception of students is of great importance because of the key role it plays in how "connected" a student feels within the classroom. How connected a student feels has been shown to affect motivation and engagement and result in a reduction of substance abuse, engagement in violence, or initiation of sexual activity (McNeeley, Nonnemaker, & Blum, 2002).

Teachers who are unfamiliar with changing student demographics may rely on perceptions of students formed by outside sources such as the media (Solórzano & Yosso, 2001), teacher preparation courses (Raths, 2000), or other teachers. Perceptions formed by such constructs often do not align with actual student attributes. Though teachers design lessons to best fit their students, their perceptions of students may alter lesson directions and result in a lack of student-teacher connection or "school connectedness" (Furlong & O'Brennan, 2010).

The *100 Dinners Project*, a participatory action research study, was designed to align teacher perceptions of students with actual student attributes. The Conceptual Change Theory Protocol (CCTP) was the vehicle employed to identify current teacher perceptions of students, how perceptions were formed, and how to reshape perceptions found to be misaligned to actual student attributes. CCTP has previously been used to reshape student perceptions of math and science concepts (Posner, Strike, Hewson, & Gertzog, 1982). Because of the similar underlying structure of conceptual formation, this study used CCTP to reshape perceptions teachers held regarding their students to increase school connectedness. This involved learners' (i.e., six participating teachers identified as team members) identification of current perceptions of students through facilitator-led discussions (team meetings). Team members experienced a critical situation (a dinner/home visit) that exposed them to new information regarding their students, followed by encouragement and guidance to restructure perceptions (team meetings).

Key to CCTP is the catalyst of perceptual reformation—the critical situation. Dinner/home visits served as the critical situation to assist in the reshaping of teacher perceptions by placing teachers in an unfamiliar social environment. The dinner/home visit provided for social interaction among teachers, students, and parents—something not often experienced—to increase communication and provide educators with valuable information about students and their families (Ginsberg, 2007). During the fall of 2010, this researcher was employed at a junior high school located in the "high desert" region of Southern California. Originally a desert getaway for celebrities in the 1950s, the area has increasingly become home to populations from a variety of ethnic backgrounds moving from urban regions across California. Though the community demographic has shifted from 84% White, 10% Hispanic, 3% Asian, and 3% other races in 1980 (Myers & Park, 2001) to 31% White, 43% Hispanic, 20% Black, and 6% other races in 2009 (City-Data.com, 2012), teacher demographics at the participating junior high school site remained relatively static: at the turn of the new century, 87.5% of teachers identified as White, while in 2011, 77% identified as White. This shift in student demographics contributed to a disconnect between staff and students that led to discipline issues and low staff morale, culminating in low school connectedness.

In 2010, the school's student population consisted of 881 7th- and 8th-grade students. Of all students, 89.80% received free or reduced lunch. Further, 57% of students were identified as Hispanic/Latino, 28% as African American, and 11% as White. The remaining 4% claimed various other ethnic backgrounds. In contrast, teachers identified as 77% White, 17% Hispanic/Latino, and 6% Asian and African American.

CCTP has demonstrated effectiveness in changing subject-content concepts in students. To address issues of low school connectedness, this study was driven by two questions: (1) How can this protocol change teacher perceptions? and (2) How have dinner/home visits served as a critical situation and acted as a catalyst for perceptual change among team members?

Study participants included a *100 Dinners Project* team composed of six volunteer junior high classroom teachers ("team members"). Included on the team was a teacher-researcher facilitator (the author). The six team members represented 20% of the credentialed teaching staff. The number of participating team members was purposely limited to maintain a small, tightly knit action research group. The selection process ensured representation from each grade level (7th and 8th grade), CORE subject area (English and math), and representatives from other departments (science, electives, and special education). Team members received a $1,000 stipend as compensation for time taken to complete the dinner/home visits, write narrative reflections after each dinner/home visit, attend team meetings, and complete an individual interview. In addition to the *100 Dinners Project* team, participants included parents of students from each team member's classroom who partook in dinner/home visits. No compensation was provided to parents.

## STEP 1: IDENTIFICATION OF CURRENT STUDENT PERCEPTIONS

To identify teacher perceptions of students, team members completed the Teacher School Climate Survey to assess School Climate. The survey was created from the 2008–2009 California School Climate Survey (CSCS) (WestEd, 2004) and researcher-created items. The CSCS is used statewide to guide school improvement and foster positive teaching and learning environments. The CSCS has been used since 2004 by California school districts as part of No Child Left Behind (NCLB, 2002) compliance and is used nationally by schools participating in the Safe Schools Healthy Students program.

The CSCS is a unidimensional measure with acceptable reliability ($\alpha = .82$ to .88) and concurrent validity ($r = .44$ to .55) across 18 sociocultural groups (Furlong & O'Brennan, 2010). Cronbach's alpha was not calculated due to only six responses. Five survey responses were complete. Survey results were not shared with team members during the study. Survey results are presented as a data visualization spectrum (see Figure 19.1).

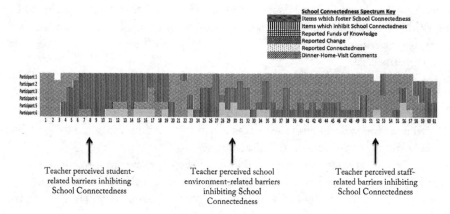

Teacher perceived student-
related barriers inhibiting
School Connectedness

Teacher perceived school
environment-related barriers
inhibiting School
Connectedness

Teacher perceived staff-
related barriers inhibiting
School Connectedness

Figure 19.1. Teacher School Climate Survey Spectrum.

Responses indicated a concentration of student-related items that inhibited or acted as barriers to school connectedness related to extrinsic student traits. Although team members identified nearly all students as being healthy, physically fit, alert, and rested when they arrived at school, they also identified some students as being unwilling or unable to turn in homework assignments and lacking pride in their work. Team members also overwhelmingly identified their student perceptions as based on other extrinsic traits such as being disruptive or lacking respect for staff. Team members reported that students occasionally engaged in physical altercations with other students. Team members also reported perceiving students as moderately or mildly dealing with alcohol- or drug-related issues. Harassment and bullying were perceived as moderate to severe problems among students. Other barriers reported were vandalism and theft.

Team members' perceptions of students supported prior findings on school connectedness. Based on team members' perceptions, students demonstrated extrinsic behaviors that acted as barriers to school connectedness related to school protocols and staff relationships. Students were perceived as having few intrinsic issues related to school connectedness, including overall health and mental capacity. Although students were perceived as demonstrating extrinsic behaviors related to barriers to school connectedness such as missing assignments or being disruptive, they were also perceived to harbor intrinsic elements (healthy, alert, rested) that foster school connectedness.

As Figure 19.1 reveals, team members perceived fewer barriers to school connectedness related to school environment than student-related barriers. When asked about their own teaching and behaviors, team members indicated that their actions fostered school connectedness. Results not only uncovered current perceptions that team members held regarding students but also indicated that actions taken to resolve school connectedness should focus on the teacher-student relationship. With team member perceptions identified, the study moved to Step 2 of CCTP.

## STEP 2: DISCUSSION OF CURRENT STUDENT PERCEPTIONS

At the first team meeting, dinner/home visit protocols, safety protocols, and current perceptions of students were discussed. Team members engaged in a discussion led by the researcher-facilitator regarding perceptions of junior high school students in general, and then specific students. Responses were recorded on a poster-sized sheet of paper for team members to view.

Team members identified junior high school students in general as "squirrely, sweet, hormonal, inquisitive, having pride, doing well, being monsters, caring what their peers think, and having high, unrealistic expectations." Perceptions of their specific students included "coming from broken homes, affected by deaths, having baggage, multicultural, rural, transient, having a gang mentality, as well as having a pack mentality." These perceptions were similar to findings on the Teacher School Climate Survey.

After the initial perceptions discussion, the dinner/home visit protocol was shared with team members. The protocol included how to solicit dinner/home visits from students' families, how to conduct a dinner/home visit, and how to stay safe when entering the homes of strangers. After the meeting, team members read a script to their class describing the *100 Dinners Project* and distributed parent information packets containing a parent/guardian letter describing the program and voluntary sign-up information. Ten families were randomly selected from the volunteers for each team member.

## STEP 3: CONCEPTUAL CONFLICT WITH CURRENT CONCEPTIONS: DINNER/HOME VISITS

The conceptual conflict or critical situation proposed by this study was a new version of the traditional home visit. Home visits involve teachers visiting students' homes. Home visits provide interactions among teachers, parents, and students that increase communication and may provide information about the students and their families (Ginsberg, 2007). The dinner/home visit concept adds the sharing of a family meal, in addition to the traditional semistructured parent-teacher conferences home visit. The addition of a meal increases opportunities for unstructured social interaction to discover family funds of knowledge. This increase in family information, in addition to the team member being in an unfamiliar setting, allows the dinner/home visit to be a vehicle for reshaping teacher perceptions of students. In addition to the 10 dinner/home visits that each team member participated in, they completed a written narrative reflection after each dinner/home visit. The reflections had no formal structure; team members were instructed to record the dinner/home visit, their thoughts, and their feelings.

The written reflections were collected throughout the study and analyzed using Ryan and Bernard's (2003) four-category approach when inducting themes from qualitative data. These categories include word analysis, scrutiny of large text blocs, analysis of linguistic features, and physical text manipulation. Emergent key themes identified were similar to themes from the *Teacher School Climate Survey*. Themes related to items that either fostered or inhibited school connectedness emerged from the reflections. Other identified themes included discovery of funds of knowledge, evidence of change in perceptions, evidence of emerging connectedness, and descriptions of dinner/home visits.

To ensure reliability of identified themes and codes, an external coder marked a random 20% sample of the written reflections. The external coder was selected based on his or her educational expertise and educational practitioner experience. The researcher and the external coder met for approximately 2 hours to discuss the study and task. The external coder and researcher achieved an 81% agreement in identified codes. The 19% discrepancy was attributed to codes with low frequencies.

Team member reflections supported findings from the Teacher School Climate Survey and revealed similar descriptions of student-related barriers affecting school connectedness, as well as descriptions that fostered school connectedness. Figure 19.2 identifies the reported barriers and items that foster school connectedness, as well as a focus on discussions of funds of knowledge, an emergence of change in teacher perceptions, increased connectedness, and identification of dinner/home visits as a critical situation.

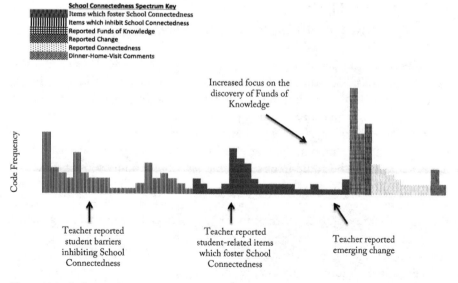

Figure 19.2. Reflection Spectrum.

Reflections indicated that intrinsic student-related behaviors fostering school connectedness included students being bright, smart, amazing, excellent, role models, hardworking, and helpful. Student-related barriers to school connectedness were similar to those identified in the survey and were related to extrinsic student behaviors. Team members attributed poor grades to a lack of organization and focus, resulting in missing assignments.

Reflections also uncovered similar extrinsic peer issues as identified in the survey such as bullying, fighting, and being disruptive. Team members also discovered difficulties with peers and the local community. A difficult issue described by all team members was separation from family members. In addition to family separations, team members described loss of family members. One team member reported that a student's "father had died of a drug over dose and his mother was also a drug addict and a manic depressant/bipolar. [Student name omitted] was also little when his father died but he was present when his mother over-dosed accidentally on her medication." Team members also discussed health issues affecting students.

Team members' style of recording family and student difficulties was matter-of-fact and included parallels between these difficulties and student behaviors identified as barriers to school connectedness. Reflections offered insights and reasons for the previous survey responses and indicated that team members were beginning to uncover reasons for barriers previously identified as disruptive, defiant, or lacking focus. Team members' reporting demonstrated their continuous gathering of information as they began to reshape and form new perceptions.

Though team members shared stories of student difficulties and family hardship, they also included details of how families had overcome and persevered. This demonstrated that team members were involved in the third step of CCTP, in which conceptual conflict created an environment for challenging earlier perceptions and becoming cognizant of the actual issues affecting their students' lives, as well as family strengths and resources termed funds of knowledge.

Reflections revealed a focus on discovery of funds of knowledge or new information about family backgrounds, talents, and resources. (In fact, this was the most frequently mentioned code, discussed by all team members a total of 135 times.) Discovery of funds of knowledge was referenced more frequently than barriers, fostering, or change. Team members wrote about discovery of funds of knowledge through references to family traditions, culture, ethnicity, hopes, dreams, occupations, and food. A large number of funds of knowledge (See Figure 19.2) were shared during the dinner portion of the dinner/home visit.

In addition to acquiring funds of knowledge from students and their families, team members felt inclined to share their own funds of knowledge, which created connections to their personal backgrounds and the backgrounds of their students. One team member stated: "We ate pozole; a personal favorite of mine, and Mom made it just like my mom makes it without the pig's feet." The meal also helped the participants to relax and provided an opportunity for social interaction, allowing for numerous topics to be shared. Team members reported gaining new knowledge about topics of interest from funds of knowledge. Reflections also included descriptions of discovering funds of knowledge through student and family pride in sharing special interests or prized possessions. Descriptions of funds of knowledge permeated each reflection. Not only did team members report information they learned; they did so with intricacies that indicated funds of knowledge's deep impact. To have such recall of specific events is attributed to team members' newfound interest in their students and families and the transition from Step 3 in CCTP (conceptual conflict) to Step 4, when team members begin to restructure or change their perceptions, something that results in greater connectedness with students and their families.

Each team member self-reported instances of change throughout his or her 10 reflections. Change among team members included changes in perceptions of students, families, and funds of knowledge. The change translated into new behaviors among team members. Reflections of change regarding how they perceived their students were mentioned by all team members. Team members also noted changes in perceptions they held regarding their students' families.

Because of their dinner/home visit experiences, team members began to view students as individuals rather than as a mass of students. Team members also attributed their change in perception directly to the dinner/home visits instead of other information sources such as assignments or current communication methods.

Reflection formats themselves also demonstrated the change process. Though no reflection format was provided, each followed a similar pattern of first describing extrinsic and intrinsic behaviors and attributes of parents and students, followed by descriptions of the meal, which often included acquiring funds of knowledge. The final section of the reflections summarized learning about their students and families and how their own perceptions had changed or altered. This pattern mirrors CCTP and assisted in demonstrating the applicability of CCTP in reshaping teacher perceptions of students.

As demonstrated by the reflections, team members actively entered the final step (restructuring and building new perceptions) of CCTP. Reflections demonstrated their ability to recognize and verbalize the changes in their perceptions of students, as well as changes in their own behavior. Reflections also revealed increased connectedness. Team member responses revealed that they, as well as students and parents, were exhibiting behaviors that increase school connectedness. This was indicated by students' sharing personal belongings and information with the team member, bonding with the family, wanting another family visit, sharing concern for the student, and reporting that now they "knew" the student. Team members demonstrated increased connectedness with the family through discussions of similar heritages.

Team members also formed a connection based on similar religious backgrounds. Signs of increased connectedness consisted of team member descriptions of changes in their behaviors or teaching styles based on their new knowledge. Reflections demonstrated that team members were actively engaged in the process of reshaping their perceptions of students. During the conceptual conflict period of CCTP, team members underwent a process of moving from focusing on extrinsic student and family factors (missing assignments, limited finances) to a focus on intrinsic student and parent-related factors (funds of knowledge and actual student and family attributes) that foster school connectedness. These changes in perception and increases in school connectedness were attributed to team member reflection data regarding dinner/home visits.

The change catalyst, dinner-home visits, was discussed throughout the reflections. Dinner/home visits are a new form of home-school communication. Reflections demonstrated the meal's role in increasing connectedness between team members and families. Introduction of dinner/home visits as a new form of home-school communication provided team members with the opportunity to witness often-unseen customs and traditions that foster school connectedness. The meal introduced an element of reciprocation of goodwill and sharing to form new perceptions of students and families through an experience perceived as culturally bonding throughout the world: eating. As meals are infinitely customizable based on culture, tradition, and experiences, meals send deep messages while satisfying the basic human need for nourishment.

During the period when team members participated in dinner/home visits, a second team meeting occurred one month after the first team meeting. Meeting time was spent describing dinner/home visits already completed. Transcriptions revealed team members' use of the words "amazing" and "interesting" to describe their dinner/home visit experiences. The researcher-facilitator did not structure the discussion. However, evidence of changes to teachers' perceptions of students began to emerge.

## STEP 4: ENCOURAGE AND GUIDE CONCEPTUAL RESTRUCTURING TO BUILD NEW CONCEPTIONS: FINAL TEAM MEETING AND INDIVIDUAL INTERVIEWS

The final team member meeting took place approximately 3 months after the first team meeting, at which time the majority of team members had completed their dinner/home visits. The researcher-facilitator led a discussion regarding any changes in the initial perceptions of team members regarding their students that took place as a result of dinner/home visits.

When asked to describe their students after the completion of the dinner/home visits, team members reported, "charming, brats, family-oriented, really cute, followers, polite and respectful, quicker to respond to discipline, and not as defiant." Also discussed were possible changes to curriculum, pedagogy, or forms of communication to align with the student population. Team members were very receptive to integrating funds of knowledge and newly acquired student attributes into instruction. These descriptions indicated a change in perception that was further explored in individual interviews.

Individual interviews were coded using a grounded theory approach. Key themes and codes identified earlier through analysis of the reflections were used to code the individual interview transcriptions. Figure 19.3 shows individual interview code distribution.

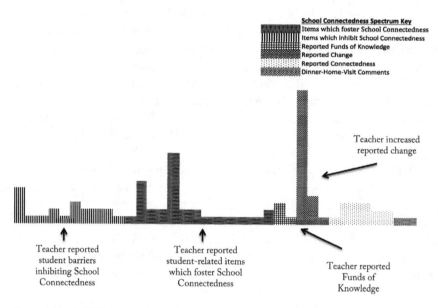

Figure 19.3. Individual Interview Spectrum.

As demonstrated in Figure 19.3, individual interviews reported a substantial drop in barriers inhibiting school connectedness in areas related to students, parents, and teacher behaviors. Completion of CCTP yielded a change in team member perceptions of students away from student-related barriers toward their actual attributes. Interview responses focused on issues of change and items fostering school connectedness. This shift in team member focus demonstrated successful completion of the change protocol.

A reported change that was supported by the reflections' findings was an emphasis on intrinsic student attributes versus a focus on extrinsic student behaviors.

Interviews revealed that increases in school connectedness paralleled the reflections. Responses revealed that team members or their students and parents were now exhibiting behaviors related to being connected because of their dinner/home visit interaction.

## REFLECTIONS

Opportunities such as the *100 Dinners Project* allowed teachers to gain insight into students' lives. Team members directly attributed study participation to increased knowledge of actual student attributes and the reshaping of their perceptions toward their students. "I learned a lot about my student and his family, things I couldn't have learned only through my class interactions with my student." The *100 Dinners Project* allowed for enough interaction to reshape teachers' perceptions of their students via CCTP.

Although the *100 Dinners Project* did not uncover the role that teacher socialization played in the formation of student perceptions, teacher socialization may incorporate similar change catalysts to increase school connectedness and to shape accurate perceptions of students. New teacher candidates, identified as being driven to belong to the group providing new information (Solomon, 1997), may be driven by these new perceptions. Just as teacher candidates may assimilate into accepting a school climate driven by low levels of school connectedness, they, too, can assimilate to a school climate with high levels of school connectedness. Contrary to previous findings, support was not found for the influence of the media (Solórzano & Yosso, 2001) as a source of information to form teachers' perceptions of students. Team members did not indicate that newspapers, social media, or television news had influenced their perceptions.

## RECOMMENDATIONS

Future research may include CCTP in situations related to reshaping teachers' perceptions of students, as well as in educational situations where change is required. CCTP's ability to reshape team members' perceptions may carry over to reshaping their perceptions related to educational issues, such as a new curriculum or administration. To address budget concerns of implementing a change project, not all staff may need to participate in order to create change at a school site. Use of CCTP may be successful if a group of change agents influences other staff members.

It is recommended that educational leaders use student and parent surveys to measure perceptions of school climate to identify inconsistencies between perceptions of these groups and teachers' perceptions. The California School Climate Survey (CSCS) has two accompanying surveys—the California Healthy Kids Survey and the California Parent Survey—to measure student and parent perceptions of similar constructs. Knowledge of the perceptions of these three groups will provide a comprehensive assessment of school climate and identify actual or perceived barriers to school connectedness.

Educational leaders should create an accountability protocol that addresses school climate so as to hold school sites accountable for maintaining adequate levels of school connectedness. Accountability protocols may be aligned with a school district's strategic plan. Under the strategic plan, an action committee may be created to monitor and report on school connectedness. Protocols should be put in place to identify activities that increase school connectedness. Such activities must be customized to each school site, even among school districts with similar student and community demographics. Many factors must be included in the customization of school connectedness activities. These factors include staff comfort level with community outreach activities, grade level, safety concerns, immediate need, and available resources.

In addition to dinner/home visits, other forms of critical situations may be employed. Options include hosting a school-site potluck dinner and inviting multiple families to attend and visit with teachers. Other suggestions include fundraisers or endorsing a certain restaurant and receiving a percentage of sales on a designated night. Teachers may be present at these functions and thus interact socially with students and families. School sites might consider identifying parents willing to serve as school ambassadors and willing to open their homes to host staff meetings and allow teachers who are perhaps uncomfortable with the individual dinner setting to interact with students and families outside of the classroom. Finally, educators might increase interaction with students and families by collecting information regarding community, sporting, or other outside school events that students are a part of. Educators might coordinate visits to these events in order to capture student interests and increase interaction with students and families outside of school.

In designing critical change situations, districts and schools should allocate funds to cover activity costs. Many team members discussed the limited finances of families and wanted to contribute to the meal themselves. Additionally, legislation such as the Nell Soto Parent Involvement Program (1999), designed to assist schools with these types of activities, should be funded.

## LIMITATIONS

The greatest limitation in the study was teacher-participant sample size. While six team members allowed for close contact with the researcher throughout the study, generalizability of results are limited. Another possible limitation is a self-selection bias for teacher and family participants. Team members received a stipend for participating and may have been interested in school connectedness. It is possible that parents who were willing to participate had higher-performing children. Though it was a concern that families of students with poor grades might not participate, this was not the case, as students showed a variety of academic achievement and behavior. Family volunteers may have been limited due to the financial burden of preparing a meal for a teacher.

A final limitation involved the dinner/home visits that occurred close to the end of the school year. Team members frequently mentioned wishing they had more time to implement changes to instructional practices they were motivated to enact as a result of their participation. "It is too bad we could not have done this sooner so we could try to prevent students from slipping through the cracks." Findings may have indicated higher levels of change if team members had enough time to introduce their new knowledge into the curriculum.

## CONCLUSION

The *100 Dinners Project* contributed to increased school connectedness and aligned school connectedness to the concept of "it takes a village to raise a child." A comprehensive education requires a bond among schools, parents, and community. Team members discussed the bonds created with their students and students' families. One team member indicated a continuing new bond: "When I walked out of the house, the family left the door open. I think it was a gesture to show that I'm welcomed at their home anytime." Another team member wrote: "The one thing that should be valued the most is a good education alongside with good people that support one another."

The concept of a village requires those within the village to venture out and discover their surroundings and other inhabitants. This venturing out was described as becoming "more human" to students. One team member summarized the dinner/home visit experience as "an opportunity to see the student in their home environment with their families and expectations."

It is time to make a change in our academic structure to reflect a "village" concept in education that celebrates students' whole life, beyond what is found in the classroom. One team member described the importance of individuals working together with the need to "figure out the balance" of communication and interaction between home and school. Parents, the community, and teachers are ready to come together. As one team member stated, "I learned from this visit that our parents want the schools to be more open," and he appreciates the fact that there are caring people who want to make these visits to connect with the community.

There was another topic that came up that really meant a lot to him: the lack of community in our schools and neighborhoods. He recalled his youth, when you knew your neighbors and kids played together. He wishes things could be more like that again.

The *100 Dinners Project* demonstrated that it is possible to increase school connectedness, which results in open and connected schools. Joining home-school resources to create the "village" can, as one team member stated, create "a map, like a road to success." Along this road to success, one team member summarized the effect of this study best by explaining that parents, students, and teachers now "know each other as friends, as well as educational partners."

## REFERENCES

City-Data.com. (2012). Victorville, California. Retrieved from http://www.city-data.com/city/Victorville-California.html

Furlong, M., & O'Brennan, L. (2010). Relations between students' perceptions of school connectedness and peer victimization. *Journal of School Violence, 9*, 375–391.

Ginsberg, M.B. (2007). Lessons at the kitchen table. *Educational Leadership, 64*(6), 56–61.

McNeeley, C.A., Nonnemaker, J.M., & Blum, R.W. (2002). Promoting school connectedness: Evidence from the national longitudinal study of adolescent health. *Journal of School Health, 72*(4), 138–146.

Myers, D., & Park, J. (2001). *Racially-balanced cities in California, 1980–2000.* Public Research Report No. 5. Race Contours Project, University of Southern California.

Nell Soto Parent Teacher Involvement Grant, Senate Bill 33. (1999).

No Child Left Behind (NCLB) Act of 2001. (2002). Pub. L. No. 107–110, 115, Stat. 1425.

Posner, G.J., Strike, K.A., Hewson, P.W., & Gertzog, W.A. (1982). Accommodation of a scientific conception: Toward a theory of conceptual change. *Science Education, 66*, 211–227.

Raths, J. (2000). Teachers' beliefs and teaching beliefs. *Early Childhood Research and Practice, 13*(1), 385–391.

Ryan, G.W., & Bernard, H.R. (2003). Data management and analysis methods. In N. Denzin & Y. Lincoln (Eds.), *Handbook of qualitative research* (2nd ed., pp. 769–802). Thousand Oaks, CA: Sage.

Solomon, R.P. (1997). Race, role modeling, and representation in teacher education and teaching. *Canadian Journal of Education, 22*(4), 395–410.

Solórzano, D.G., & Yosso, T.J. (2001). From racial stereotyping and deficit discourse. *Multicultural Education, 9*(1), 2–8.

WestEd. (2004). *California school climate survey.* Retrieved from http://www.wested.org/project/california-school-climate-survey-cscs/

Wheatley, M.J., & Kellner-Rogers, M. (1996). *A simpler way.* San Francisco, CA: Berrett-Koehler.

# CHAPTER TWENTY

# An Examination of the Intersecting Identities of Female Ed.D. Students and Their Journeys of Persistence

*Amanda J. Rockinson-Szapkiw*
*and Lucinda S. Spaulding*

## INTRODUCTION

The purpose of this chapter is to discuss challenges specific to female Ed.D. students, given their intersecting roles and identities as females and scholars within the sociocultural context of academia. This chapter is motivated by research suggesting that a vital reason many women choose not to begin or persist in Ed.D. programs is that they experience conflict between their identities as females and emerging scholars—a conflict between "the enduring sense of who they are and who they want to become" (Cobb, 2004, p. 336). The stress of maintaining separate identities as scholars and females and their corresponding roles and responsibilities can cause motivational problems that lead to attrition (Lynch, 2008). The consequences of stress may also include choosing to deny aspects of the female identity. After presenting an overview of the nature of the Ed.D. degree and a theoretical foundation for identity, we examine tensions that females experience in the various stages of the Ed.D. as they negotiate their potentially conflicting identities as females and scholars within their social and academic contexts. Strategies for successfully negotiating multiple roles and identities leading to persistence as a candidate within an Ed.D. program are provided.

## THE EDUCATIONAL DOCTORATE

Women are accessing higher education at increasing rates and represent approximately 60% of the Ed.D. population (National Science Foundation, 2009). This trend is positive, but when compared to other disciplines, the outcomes for Ed.D. programs and the women pursuing doctorates are not as positive. While the average doctoral attrition rate across disciplines has hovered around 50% for decades (Bowen & Rudenstine, 1992), attrition in education programs can reach as high as 70% (Ivankova & Stick, 2007; Nettles & Millett, 2006). For students who persist, time to degree completion is likely to be higher than students from other disciplines (Wao & Onwuegbuzie, 2011). This elevated rate may be explained by the finding that Ed.D. programs also have the highest rates of *stop-out*, where students withdraw for a period because of factors related to health, finances, professional obligations, or family commitments (Nettles & Millett, 2006). Most Ed.D. students maintain full-time employment in professions that are incredibly demanding and time consuming (e.g., teachers or administrators), which is another reason a large percentage of Ed.D. students stop-out or fail to complete their degrees (Wao & Onwuegbuzie, 2011).

Attrition rates are further compounded by the proliferation of distance Ed.D. programs, which women often take advantage of. In past decades, many women did not pursue doctorates because of their desire or financial need to remain in their profession. Many did not have the ability to uproot their families to enroll in doctoral programs requiring residence near or on campus. However, the expansion and growing acceptance of the distance Ed.D. (that is, blended and online) program has opened doors and removed barriers that once prevented women from pursuing doctorates. While distance Ed.D. programs offer greater access and opportunity to women, selection of an online Ed.D. also increases the likelihood of attrition, since attrition in distance doctoral programs can be 10% to 20% higher than residential programs (Leeds et al., 2013; Terrell, 2005). Students in distance programs report higher levels of loneliness and isolation; they feel less socially integrated into the university and program, a situation that leaves them more likely to withdraw (Lovitts & Nelson, 2000). Furthermore, compared to other disciplines, education ranked lowest in doctoral student publications (15% versus 30%) and presentations (30% versus 37%) (Nettles & Millett, 2006).

While many of these statistics are general to men and women, according to the National Science Foundation (2009), women are more likely than men to be late completers and less likely to complete their doctorate. Given the multiple dimensions of their identity, many female Ed.D. students struggle to effectively balance their familial, professional, and academic demands (West, Gokalp, Peña, Fischer, & Gupton, 2011) and to negotiate the intersection of their identities, increasing their likelihood to stop-out or withdraw altogether.

## FEMALE IDENTITY

A discussion about female identity, especially within the context of academia, requires a conceptualization of identity that is dynamic, multidimensional, complex, and contextual (Moradi, 2005; Ricoeur, 1988). Jones and McEwen's (2000) conceptual model of multiple dimensions of identity suggests that individuals have multiple dimensions of identity (e.g., gender, race, religion) that intersect and are influenced by one another and contextual factors. Within this model, identity dimensions are illustrated as intersecting circles around the core sense of self, defined as an individual's values and most valued "personal attributes and characteristics" (Jones, 1997, p. 383).

The circles signify that "no one dimension may be understood singularly; it can be understood only in relation to other dimensions" (Jones & McEwen, 2000, p. 410). The development and salience of each identity dimension is dynamic and influenced by personal context and experience (e.g., family, sociocultural conditions, academic disciplines). Through engagement in the doctoral process, female doctoral students need to intersect their developing identities as scholars with other dimensions of their identities, including mothers, wives, daughters, grandmothers, women of color, or professionals. These identities and associated roles are not discrete and are rarely isolated; thus, female Ed.D. students often experience tension and conflict between their dimensions of identity and the corresponding roles and responsibilities.

## INTERNAL CONFLICT

Female doctoral students report numerous internal struggles as they develop who they want to become in relation to who they are. One participant in a recent study noted that as a female Ed.D. candidate, she engages in a lot of "internal battles" as she seeks to be true to herself as a mother, daughter, wife, student, and scholar. She explained that she desired to do research and to be an excellent teacher and a nurturing mother. Sometimes these desires clashed, and internal turmoil ensued (Rockinson-Szpakiw, Spaulding, Swezey, & Wicks, in press). Female doctoral students often report difficulty in juggling their multiple identity dimensions and the corresponding roles and responsibilities of students, teachers, researchers, wives, daughters, and mothers (Hyun, 2009; Spaulding & Rockinson-Szapkiw, 2012). Smith, Maroney, Nelson, Abel, and Abel (2006) noted that being a graduate student in the twenty-first century is much more complicated than it was 30 years ago, as the primary concern of a student—especially a female student—is not limited to academics.

Females need to balance financial, maternal, community, spouse, and family-of-origin responsibilities in addition to academic ones. This is a source of stress—or, more precisely, *distress*—which, if left unmanaged, can result in mental health problems (Johnson, Greaves, & Repta, 2007). The "stress of trying to be successful as both a mother and a student contributed to dissatisfaction in both roles" (Haynes, Bulosan, Citty, & Grant-Harris, 2012, p. 3) and even dissatisfaction with life. Guilt and shame over not being able to balance time for family, time for self, time for exercise, and time to meet expectations ensues (Brown & Watson, 2010).

Internal conflict is also experienced as the identities of scholar and student develop and become salient, at which time women begin to differentiate (see Bowen & Rudenstine, 1992 for definition) from or within their family units or professions. In returning to school—perhaps after identifying as the nurturing educator or mother who always takes care of the family or schoolchildren—female Ed.D. students may need to evaluate personal values and beliefs about what it means to be a mother, wife, or professional teacher. Cognitive dissonance is often experienced, as long-held beliefs about the self as wife, mother, or professional teacher are at variance with the behaviors required to be a successful student and scholar. For example, a woman's identity prior to beginning her degree may be wrapped up in nurturing her family. She may believe that "A good wife and mother cooks dinner and has it on the table at 5 o'clock every evening." However, working on the doctorate requires her to spend evenings away from her family, causing her to experience cognitive dissonance. Further, she may find it necessary to spend a significant amount of time studying with her colleagues, and she begins consulting them in regard to future career decisions. Thus disruption is caused in the familial and, especially, the marital relationship, since the husband is used to her seeking his counsel. Wellington and Sikes (2006) explain that "family and personal relationships are sometimes strained and can even break down as a result of a student's involvement in their studies" (p. 731).

On the other hand, disruption in relationships can negatively affect persistence in doctoral studies (Carter, Blumenstein, & Cook, 2013). When unable to manage the clash of roles and negotiate the seemingly conflicting identity dimensions of female and scholar and to successfully differentiate them, sense of self can be lost. The failure to balance work, school, and personal life and the inability to intersect multiple identity dimensions has even led some students to change their aspirations, to withdraw from the Ed.D., to postpone or forsake the goals of marriage or motherhood, or to divorce.

## SOCIAL CONTEXTS

Unfortunately, the expectations of others—in social and academic contexts—may intensify internal tensions. Perpetuating the belief that women cannot successfully embrace the multiplicity of who they are, external influences increase the lack of satisfaction and the likelihood of withdrawing from the doctoral program. Signals within their everyday lives communicate to women that their identity as scholars does not fit the mold of the female, or, conversely, that their sense of who they are as females does not fit the model of academia.

Within some social circles, persistence in a doctoral program is considered unwomanly. Family and friends may advise women to quit when the program of study begins to interfere with their female roles and responsibilities—advice that contrasts significantly with advice offered to male students from their social networks (Carter et al., 2013). In interviewing doctoral students who were teaching assistants, Lynch (2008) found that many of them believed that *academic invisibility* was necessary when they were with their families and in social situations. When a mother increases her maternal visibility during the day (by, for example, attending field trips or staying home with children), she downplays her academic identity to "preserve...[her] status as a 'good mother'" (Lynch, 2008, p. 597). Lynch (2008) described the similarities between the cultural roles of a "good mother" and a "good student" as follows: "Graduate students are judged on their devotion to their career path as much as their grades or output. In a similar vein, culturally appropriate mothering demands an intense commitment of time, energy, and devotion to one's children" (p. 596). Some feel they need to deny part of themselves in order to be successful; in social contexts, they become *scholarless* in order to be viewed as good mothers or good wives. Conversely, in academic contexts, they feel the need to become *genderless* in order to succeed in their program and discipline.

## ACADEMIC CONTEXTS

*Maternal invisibility* has been documented as essential to survival in the academic environment (Carter et al., 2013). Mothers may choose not to display photos or artifacts of their children in their offices because they "believe that their status as a mother will detract from the perception that she is a 'serious student'" (Lynch, 2008, p. 596). Displaying female identifiers may cause them to be dismissed by peers or even discriminated against. The stereotypical notion that a female who is concerned with maternal and familial issues cannot be a serious scholar serves to marginalize or call into question a female's identity as a scholar. Judgments and stereotypes in academic settings can result in undue pressure that leads to underperformance and isolation (Steele, 1997).

Years of isolation and underperforming can negatively affect women's ability to develop a full sense of self. The underrepresentation of females among faculty due to the unfriendliness of the academic culture and the resulting lack of female mentors for Ed.D. students (Moyer, Salovey, & Casey-Cannon, 1999) also contribute to this. Lack of female mentors may make it difficult for mothers think-ing about pursuing a doctorate to envision how they might add the role of student, and eventually the identity of scholar, to their already existing identity dimensions and roles and responsibilities. Conversely, women without children might feel that adding the dimension of "mother" is incompatible with higher education, and they may postpone or forsake having children altogether. Lack of female role models who have experienced and negotiated these tensions influences attrition, as re-search demonstrates an association between female persistence and connections with female role models in higher education programs (Seymour & Hewitt, 1997).

## IDENTITY AND AGENCY

Female Ed.D. students' success in negotiating their identity tensions within their sociocultural contexts is highly associated with agency (Nasir & Saxe, 2003). In other words, how female doctoral students manage and negotiate these internal identity tensions and also the external forces that confound them are influential in their persistence in a doctoral program and their experiencing a full sense of self. For women to persist in the doctoral journey, they must successfully intersect all of these dimensions. Failure to successfully intersect these dimensions leads to disequilibrium and a negative sense of self, factors that increase the likelihood of withdrawal or dissociating an identity dimension as one identity is chosen over the other (Stimpson & Filer, 2011).

Alternatively, highly educated women with careers are less likely to have chil-dren than their male counterparts and to "give up" the desire to be a mother (Baker, 2012). Others may divorce or lack marital satisfaction because of lack of time, poor communication, and change in role and lifestyle that may arise during doctoral studies (Bergen & Bergen, 1978; Cao, 2001; Giles, 1983; Middleton, 2001).

## STRATEGIES FOR MANAGING INTERSECTING IDENTITIES

While external and internal struggles exist, and some women believe that they need to become genderless in order to succeed in an Ed.D. program, others demonstrate that it is possible to successfully integrate multiple identities into multiple contexts (Rockinson-Szapkiw et al., in press). Women can exhibit strong identities as females while also taking pride in their professional, academic, and scholarly practices. There are creative strategies to successfully negotiate multiple dimensions of identity, thereby leading to Ed.D. completion. These strategies in-clude (a) integrating the family; (b) honoring and balancing identity dimensions; and (c) developing a strong support system.

## FAMILY INTEGRATION

The decision to pursue a doctorate should not be made without having candid conversations with family members. This conversation needs to include a discussion about the nature of the doctoral process, the sacrifices that will be required from *all* along the way, the differentiation that will occur, and the need to renegotiate personal and familial beliefs and values, especially those concerning the female identity and the roles of mom, wife, and daughter. Before choosing to begin the doctorate, the family needs to ensure that earning the degree aligns with the family's shared values and beliefs (e.g., "education is valuable"; West, 2014), and women need to ensure that earning the degree aligns with their values and belief systems.

The conversations that begin prior to entry need to continue throughout the entire process, because familial understanding and support are essential to doctoral student persistence (Rockinson-Szapkiw et al., in press) and the maintenance of positive familial relationships (Wellington & Sikes, 2006). Female Ed.D. students do not need to maintain academic invisibility in their familial contexts; on the contrary, they need to communicate their varying needs during each distinct phase of the doctoral journey (entry, coursework, comprehensive exam, dissertation), as each requires a different type and level of commitment. In turn, they need to encourage their families to do the same.

While identity transformation causes inward reflection on personal growth and future aspirations, female Ed.D. students need to intentionally look outward and recognize the needs of those around them. Quite simply, there are times when trying to be a good mother *and* a good doctoral student are incompatible, and the "stress of trying to be successful as both a mother and a student contribute[s] to dissatisfaction in both roles" (Haynes, Bulosan, Citty, & Grant-Harris, 2012, p. 3). When it comes to this, students need to consider the core sense of self (i.e., values and attributes) in making decisions related to the salience of an identity dimension and its corresponding roles and responsibilities, keeping in mind that attainment of a doctoral degree is inherently a long-term process that requires sacrifice and stamina but yields significant rewards when achieved.

This is not a decision that should be made in isolation, since family input, needs, and values also need to be considered. Rather than allowing the input to compound internal tensions and conflicts, it needs to be thought of as additional insight that can be used to critically evaluate and reflect upon identity dimensions in a new way and, consequently, to develop a greater understanding of the dimensions and their intersections while maintaining positive family relations. The more family members feel included and understand the doctoral process, the more likely they are to discourage academic invisibility and encourage their wives, mothers, or daughters to embrace the multiplicity of who they are.

## HONORING AND BALANCING MULTIPLE
## DIMENSIONS OF IDENTITY

Negotiating multiple dimensions of identities along with the corresponding roles and responsibilities throughout the inherently challenging doctoral process can produce stress. Sometimes this stress should be welcomed.

> Stress can be beneficial as it awakens in the doctoral student increased attentiveness to tasks, scholarship, excellence, and progress. It serves as a portent to press on to the prize and toward the academic finish line. Stress compels students to keep their commitment to advancing in their program and finishing well. (Sosin & Thomas, 2014, p. 56)

However, distress—that is, "when pressures to perform exceed the capacity, or perceived capacity, to produce" (Sosin & Thomas, 2014, p. 56)—should not be welcomed, as it makes the female Ed.D. student susceptible to burnout, departure from the doctoral program, and dissociation and denial of self (Haynes et al., 2012; Johnson et al., 2007).

Distress and its consequences are avoided by recognizing that there is a time to honor each dimension of self, allowing one or a combination of a few identity dimensions to take center stage or to be salient at the same time. Time can be defined as stages in lives or as segments of the day. While one woman may choose to wait until later in life (e.g., after her children are grown) to pursue her doctorate, another may creatively schedule completing her responsibilities as a student at 3 a.m. before her husband and children awake at 7 a.m. This strategy is congruent with Jones and McEwen's (2000) model of multiple identity dimensions, which highlights the dynamic nature of identity and its development and the salience of particular elements of identity across time. Practical strategies that female Ed.D. doctoral students can use to help them honor their identity dimensions during the doctoral process include both time and organization management and boundary setting.

Time is perhaps the most precious commodity for women with multiple identity dimensions and corresponding—and sometimes conflicting—roles. Time must be managed well, and to do so, women need to assess their time commitments before adding the doctorate and accurately account for the additional time needed to devote to the degree requirements, which vary depending on the stage and the skill level and aptitude of the student. With time being finite, schedules may need to be modified and responsibilities and roles adjusted to make time available. Establishing a schedule is not enough; students need to set short- and long-term goals (e.g., daily, weekly, monthly) and list the actions and resources needed to reach each goal, being mindful that "setting small increments toward goal completion affects motivation as there are consistent accomplishments occurring on a weekly basis" (Hardy, 2014, p. 35).

In addition to allotting time to work on the doctorate, women need to allocate a designated space free of distraction so they can focus on nurturing their academic identity. This physical space is especially important for women enrolled in distance Ed.D.s, which typically involve asynchronous learning—meaning that the student is free to work where and when it is most convenient. While this flexibility is often the very factor that motivates enrollment in such a program, it is sometimes difficult for family members and friends to recognize the need for the student to study or "go to class" when there is no brick-and-mortar classroom or library to frequent. It is important to include essential family members and friends in the establishment of a schedule and designation of space to ensure that each member's needs are communicated and considered and that everyone is in agreement and respects the study plan. This plan may need to be revisited each semester, during each phase of the degree, and as schedules and needs change over the course of time.

Establishing boundaries during the doctoral process, specifically during the dissertation phase, is also essential. Individuals with the intrinsic motivation and the prerequisite skills and knowledge needed to enter and persist in doctoral studies are naturally recognized by those in their personal and professional communities as people who can be depended upon to perform a task and to perform it well. Thus, they are frequently looked to and leaned upon. Women need to communicate their needs to those around them and politely decline requests to take on additional roles and responsibilities, being careful to differentiate between optional and essential tasks (Sosin & Thomas, 2014) not related to the identity dimensions taking center stage.

## DEVELOPMENT OF A STRONG SUPPORT SYSTEM

As women with female role models are more likely to persist (Seymour & Hewitt, 1997), and because there is a positive relationship between academic integration and persistence (Tinto, 1993), women should seek to integrate socially and academically into their program of study. During program selection, they should consider programs that use a cohort model (Spaulding & Rockinson-Szapkiw, 2012); if such a model is not employed, they can use various technologies (e.g., a Facebook group) to develop a supportive community with peers in their courses (Rockinson-Szapkiw, Spaulding, & Heuvelman-Hutchinson, 2014). These relationships are helpful for academic support and functional assistance but also provide a sense of connectedness and a source of emotional support during challenging times.

Building professional relationships with faculty and identifying a mentor early in the coursework phase is also essential to persistence and to helping women envision how they may intersect their identity dimensions and roles that often seem to be in conflict. Female Ed.D. students can identify faculty with research agendas that reflect their own interests and volunteer to assist. With publishing and presenting being the primary outcomes of mentor relationships in doctoral programs, this collaboration assists the student in her transformation from student to scholar—from a *consumer* of research to a *producer* of research. Assuming the identity of *scholar* is essential as students transition into the final phase of the degree and are required to produce a dissertation by "competently address[ing] a research question via self-directed study, research, analysis, and interpretation; that is, perform the work of an independent scholar" (Ponton, 2014, p. 100).

## CONCLUSION

Understanding identity from a multidimensional framework provides a lens for understanding how female Ed.D. students' multiple dimensions of identity relate and how each inherently affords or limits perspectives and opportunities as well as agency and follow-through. Managing the intersection of multiple identity dimensions in academic and social contexts, though complex, is possible.

## REFERENCES

Baker, M. (2012). Fertility, childrearing & the academic gender gap. *Women's Health & Urban Life*, *11*(2), 9–25.

Bergen, G., & Bergen, M. B. (1978). Quality of marriage of university students in relation to sources of financial support and demographic characteristics. *The Family Coordinator*, 27(3), 245–250.

Bowen, W. & Rudenstine, N. (1992). *In pursuit of the Ph.D.* Princeton, NJ: Princeton University Press.

Brown, L., & Watson, P. (2010). Understanding the experiences of female doctoral students. *Journal of Further and Higher Education*, *34*(3), 385–404.

Cao, W. (2001). How male and female doctoral students experience their doctoral programs similarly and differently. Paper presented at the annual meeting of the American Educational Research Association, Seattle, WA.

Carter, S., Blumenstein, M., & Cook, C. (2013). Different for women? The challenges of doctoral studies. *Teaching in Higher Education*, *18*(4), 339–351.

Cobb, P. (2004). Mathematics, literacies, and identity. *Reading Research Quarterly*, *39*(3), 333–337.

Giles, F. (1998). The effects of doctoral study on marriage and family: An ethnographic study. Paper presented at Annual Meeting of the American College Personnel Association, Houston, TX.

Hardy, V. (2014). Assessing and allotting resources. In A.J. Rockinson-Szapkiw & L.S. Spaulding (Eds.), *Navigating the doctoral journey: A handbook of strategies for success*. Lanham, MD: Rowman & Littlefield.

Haynes, C., Bulosan, M., Citty, J., & Grant-Harris, M. (2012). My world is not my doctoral program...or is it? Female students' perceptions of well-being. *International Journal of Doctoral Studies*, *7*(1), 1–17.

Hyun, J.H. (2009). *An exploration of the coping strategies in female counseling doctoral students' marriages.* Unpublished doctoral dissertation, Department of Counseling and Psychological Services, Georgia State University. Retrieved from http://digitalarchive.gsu.edu/cps_diss/37

Ivankova, N.V., & Stick, S.L. (2007). Students' persistence in a distributed doctoral program in educational leadership in higher education: A mixed methods study. *Research in Higher Education, 48*(1), 93–135. doi:10.1007/s11162–006–9025–4

Johnson, J.L., Greaves, L., & Repta, R. (2007). *Better science with sex and gender: A primer for health research.* Vancouver, BC, Canada: Women's Health Research Network.

Jones, S.R. (1997). Voices of identity and difference: A qualitative exploration of the multiple dimensions of identity development in women college students. *Journal of College Student Development, 38*(4), 376–386.

Jones, S.R., & McEwen, M.K. (2000). A conceptual model of multiple dimensions of identity. *Journal of College Student Development, 41*(4), 405–414.

Leeds, E., Campbell, S., Baker, H., Ali, R., Brawley, D., & Crisp, J. (2013). The impact of student retention strategies: An empirical study. *International Journal of Management in Education, 7*(1), 22–43.

Lovitts, B.E., & Nelson, C. (2000). The hidden crisis in graduate education: Attrition from Ph.D. programs. *Academe, 86*(6), 44–50.

Lynch, K.D. (2008). Gender roles and the American academe: A case study of graduate student mothers. *Gender and Education, 20*(6), 585–605.

Middleton, S. (2001). Making room: The place of academic study. Paper presented at the annual meeting of the American Educational Research Association, Seattle, WA.

Moradi, B. (2005). Advancing womanist identity development: Where we are and where we need to go. *Counseling Psychologist, 33*(1), 225–253.

Moyer, A., Salovey, P., & Casey-Cannon, S. (1999). Challenges facing female doctoral students and recent graduates. *Psychology of Women Quarterly, 23*(3), 607–630.

Nasir, N.S., & Saxe, J.B. (2003). Ethnic and academic identities: A cultural practice perspective on emerging tensions and their management in the lives of minority students. *Educational Researcher, 32*(5), 14–18.

National Science Foundation (NSF). (2009). *Doctorate recipients from U.S. universities: Summary report 2007–08.* Chicago: National Opinion Research Center.

Nettles, M.T., & Millett, C.M. (2006). *Three magic letters: Getting to Ph.D.* Baltimore, MD: The John Hopkins University Press.

Ponton, M. (2014). The transition from autonomous to self-directed learning. In A.J. Rockinson-Szapkiw & L.S. Spaulding (Eds.), *Navigating the doctoral journey: A handbook of strategies for success.* Lanham, MD: Rowman & Littlefield.

Ricoeur, P. (1988). *Time and narrative* (vol. 3). Chicago: University of Chicago Press.

Rockinson-Szapkiw, A.J., & Spaulding, L.S. (2014). *Navigating the doctoral journey: A handbook of strategies for success.* Lanham, MD: Rowman & Littlefield.

Rockinson-Szapkiw, A.J., Spaulding, L.S., & Heuvelman-Hutchinson, L. (2014). Connecting at a distance: The relationship between Facebook use and doctoral connectedness. *Journal of University Teaching & Learning Practice, 11*(3).

Rockinson-Szapkiw, A.J., Spaulding, L.S., Swezey, J.A., & Wicks, C. (in press). Poverty and persistence: A model for understanding individuals' pursuit and persistence in a doctor of education program. *International Journal of Doctoral Studies.*

Seymour, E., & Hewitt, N.C. (1997). *Talking about leaving: Why undergraduates leave the sciences.* Boulder, CO: Westview Press.

Smith, R.L., Maroney, K., Nelson, K.W., Abel, A.L., & Abel, H.S. (2006). Doctoral programs: Changing high rates of attrition. *Humanistic Counseling, Education, and Development, 45,* 17–31.

Sosin, L., & Thomas, J. (2014). Managing stress and burnout. In A.J. Rockinson-Szapkiw & L.S. Spaulding (Eds.), *Navigating the doctoral journey: A handbook of strategies for success.* Lanham, MD: Rowman & Littlefield.

Spaulding, L.S., & Rockinson-Szapkiw, A.J. (2012). Hearing their voices: Factors doctoral candidates attribute to their persistence. *International Journal of Doctoral Studies, 7,* 199–219. Retrieved from http://ijds.org/Volume7/IJDSv7p199–219Spaulding334.pdf

Steele, C.M. (1997). A threat in the air: How stereotypes shape the intellectual identities and performance of women and African-Americans. *American Psychologist, 52,* 613–629.

Stimpson, R.L., & Filer, K.L. (2011). Female graduate students' work-life balance and the student affairs professional. In P.A. Pasque & S.E. Nicholson (Eds.), *Empowering women in higher education and student affairs: Theory, research, narratives, and practice from feminist perspectives* (pp. 69–84). Sterling, VA: Stylus.

Terrell, S. (2005). A longitudinal investigation of the effect of information perception and focus on attrition in online learning environments. *Internet and Higher Education, 8*(3), 213–219.

Tinto, V. (1993). *Leaving college: Rethinking the causes and cures of student attrition* (2nd ed.). Chicago, IL: University of Chicago Press.

Wao, H.O., & Onwuegbuzie, A.J. (2011). A mixed research investigation of factors related to time to the doctorate in education. *International Journal of Doctoral Studies, 6,* 115–134.

Wellington, J., & Sikes, P. (2006). A doctorate in a tight compartment: Why students choose to do a professional doctorate and its impact on their personal & professional lives. *Studies in Higher Education, 31*(6), 723–734.

West, J., Gokalp, G., Peña, E.V., Fischer, L., & Gupton, J. (2011). Exploring effective support practices for doctoral students' degree completion. *College Student Journal, 45*(2), 310–323.

West, L. (2014). Communicating needs and nurturing familial relationships. In A.J. Rockinson-Szapkiw & L.S. Spaulding (Eds.), *Navigating the doctoral journey: A handbook of strategies for success.* Lanham, MD: Rowman & Littlefield.

# ED.D. PROGRAM POWER
# TO CREATE SOCIAL JUSTICE
# AND EQUITABLE
# COMMUNITY LEADERSHIP

# CHAPTER TWENTY-ONE

# Transforming the Ed.D. Program into a Force for Culturally Relevant Leadership

*Michael L. Washington*

## INTRODUCTION

In her 2006 presidential address to the American Educational Research Conference Annual Meeting, Gloria Ladson-Billings (2006) cited Kenneth B. Clark (1965) as she referenced the national dilemma of growing achievement gaps among different races and cultures within education.

> There is at present nothing in the vast literature of social science treatises and textbooks and nothing in the practical and field training of graduate students in social science to prepare them for the realities and complexities of this type of involvement in a real, dynamic, turbulent, and at times seemingly chaotic community. And what is more, nothing anywhere in the training of social scientists, teachers or social workers now prepares them to understand, to cope with, or to change the normal chaos of ghetto communities. These are grave lacks which must be remedied soon if these disciplines are to become relevant to the stability and survival of our society. (p. xxix)

Though Ladson-Billings is known for her work in K–12 environments, her message is equally vital to postsecondary educational institutions. American society is becoming more culturally diverse with each passing decade. This chapter focuses on the process of creating an "Ed.D. in Intercultural Leadership" that broadens the vision of the Ed.D. (Usher, 2002; Wergin, 2011) to address more than just empirical research, organizational leadership, and community collaboration. It suggests that doctoral educators and administrators shift from offering a few culturally relevant courses to developing an all-encompassing transformative curriculum into Ed.D.

programs that focus on multicultural and intercultural engagement and leadership. This new paradigm shift includes several key elements such as a focus on building reciprocal relationships, guided self-reflection among educational leaders, a constructivist approach to leadership (Lambert, 1995), and critical inquiry into race-related policies and practices. Additionally, the Ed.D. in Intercultural Leadership would be student centered rather than administrator centered.

## CONTRIBUTING THEORETICAL FRAMEWORKS

There are numerous U.S. government agencies that constantly maintain quantitative data on ethnic demographic patterns; this phenomenon is also evident in our daily public interactions. We have come a long way from the traditional "nuclear family." Even today, countless Americans still believe in the "rags to riches" concept that everyone has an equal opportunity and that there are no glass ceilings (Harro, 2000). These myths only perpetuate "social-blindness" through the intentional and unintentional applications of meritocratic principles (Villegas & Lucas, 2002).

Nowhere is this more prevalent than in our schools. From K–12 to graduate school, diversity and disparity are a constant reality. John Dewey recognized this disconnect among educators as far back as 1938 (Dewey, 1938). In the 1980s, we read the works of James Banks (1981, 1999) as he laid the foundation for multicultural education. Later on, Gloria Ladson-Billings (1995) and Geneva Gay (2000) clarified our need for culturally relevant pedagogy. However, these were established as approaches to teaching, not as urgent social requirements for administration or leadership.

Within the past 10 years, a growing number of scholars, including Floyd Beachum at Lehigh University, have explored the application of cultural relevance toward educational leadership. Unlike most of these studies, Beachum's (2009) focuses on K–12 at-risk and urban educational environments. Even community college leadership programs do not focus enough on cultural diversity, despite recent increases in both community college enrollment and racial diversity (Fry, 2009). So how might a redeveloped Ed.D. program address the diverse needs of a pluralistic society at predominantly White institutions of higher education?

In order to reinvent the Ed.D. for the purpose of addressing the needs and challenges of a culturally pluralistic society, multiple theoretical frameworks were deemed appropriate by a committee of educational Ed.D. program experts from five different California public universities. Since the California State University system currently offers 14 different Ed.D. programs, these program experts, with over 65 years of combined leadership experience, were well suited to the task. Ultimately, three frameworks were selected that guided the research for the development of this chapter.

## Culturally Relevant Pedagogy

As a practice, culturally relevant pedagogy (CRP) was popularized by Gloria Ladson-Billings (1995) and also by Geneva Gay (2000), with her work in the development of culturally responsive teaching. Despite the fact that there are several Ph.D. programs that are already practicing the principles of CRP, this has not been the case regarding Ed.D. programs in general. The Ed.D. panel of experts utilized for this research recommended CRP as its preferred framework for the development of a more culturally relevant Ed.D. in higher education because of three propositions that comprise the foundation of CRP:

1. Students must experience academic success (Ladson-Billings, 1995).
2. Students must develop and/or maintain cultural competence (Gay, 2000).
3. Students must develop a critical consciousness (Freire, 1970) through which they challenge the status quo of the social order.

## Critical Race Theory

The late Derrick Bell (1973) is widely considered to be the "father" of critical race theory (CRT), which gained popularity in the mid-1980s. CRT was established from a growing body of legal scholarship that challenged the dynamics of race, power, and the American legal system (Crenshaw, Gotanda, Peller, & Thomas, 1995).

According to Delgado and Stefancic (2001), the following themes are ever present in CRT:

1. Racism is ordinary instead of aberrational and deeply ingrained within American society.
2. CRT scholars claim that concepts of meritocracy, caste systems, color-blindness, and neutrality must be confronted and questioned (Delgado & Stefancic, 2001; Ladson-Billings & Tate, 1995).

Utilizing CRT as a framework in the reformation of a culturally relevant Ed.D. allows educators, researchers, and administrators to better critique policies that lack social consciousness and practice discrimination—issues that are just as prevalent in higher education as they are in society in general (Delgado et al., 2001).

## Critical Pedagogy

Paulo Freire was instrumental in the formulation of critical pedagogy as we know it today. His *Pedagogy of the Oppressed* (1970) describes this philosophy as more than a "pedagogy of practice." Indeed, it is also a social movement and a call for a "praxis-oriented" approach to education. Since critical pedagogy is an approach that supports advocacy, it is often the framework of choice among participatory action researchers, who value its emphasis on active engagement. A more culturally relevant Ed.D. would be congruent with a participatory action research approach because of its emphasis on practice over theory.

## COLLEGE ENROLLMENT AND GRADUATION RATES

Part of what fuels the need for a more culturally relevant Ed.D. is the changing ethnic and cultural landscape of the nation. Minority populations are growing, especially in Asian and Latino communities throughout the nation (Casas & Ryan, 2010; Perez & Hirschman, 2009). Yet there remains a disparity when comparing college enrollment rates of high school graduates from different ethnic groups. Nationally, 72% of White high school graduates went on to college in 2010 compared to 50% of Latino high school graduates and 44% of African American high school graduates (Aud et al., 2011).

Though racial disparities occur in the initial transition between high school graduation and college enrollment, the dilemma persists when significant percentages of students of color fail to complete college. Though all ethnicities have essentially increased their graduation rates over the years, the disproportion between specific ethnicities remains consistent, with White and Asian students graduating at significantly higher rates than Blacks and Hispanics (Ginder, Kelly-Reid, & Mann, 2014).

### Social Mobility

These enrollment rates eventually take their toll on the social mobility of ethnically diverse populations. The median annual family income for a White family of four between 1990 and 2009 was $62,545—almost twice the median annual income of Latino families ($39,730) and African American families ($38,409) (U.S. Census Bureau, 2011).

Though these financial disparities are influenced by several factors, educational attainment is among the most prevalent, as illustrated by these recent peak unemployment rates from the U.S. Bureau of Labor Statistics (2012):

Unemployment peaked at 9.3% for Whites in October 2009;

Unemployment peaked at 13.1% for Latinos in November 2010;

Unemployment peaked at 16.7% for African Americans in August 2011.

Education is often considered to be the "great equalizer," especially by marginalized populations that utilize a privilege that previous generations had no access to. Though the country is no longer in a tailspin from the Great Recession, recovery is slow and least evident among the marginalized. Poverty has reached levels not seen since the Reagan administration of the 1980s, as the middle class shrinks and poverty rates increase.

According to the U.S. Census (2011), as much as 15.1% of the U.S. population lives in poverty, with Whites comprising 9.9%, Asians comprising 12.1%, Hispanics comprising 26.6%, and Blacks comprising 28.4% of this group. What makes this particularly alarming is that the poverty levels for these ethnicities far exceed their respective population percentages, with the exception of the White population, which experiences an inverse outcome.

These statistics continue to influence college enrollment and graduation rates for disenfranchised populations. The development of a more culturally relevant Ed.D. would take these and other social, financial, and political factors into consideration and integrate them into the doctoral curriculum as a mainstay instead of a side note.

## Culturally Biased Assessments

Standardized tests that are racially and culturally biased contribute to the ongoing stratification of our society (Grodsky, Warren, & Felts, 2008). Some examples of these tests are the SAT (Scholastic Aptitude Test or Scholastic Assessment Test); IQ (intelligence quotient); the ACT (American College Testing); the GRE (Graduate Record Examination); the MCAT (Medical College Admission Test); and the LSAT (Law School Admission Test). As well, high school exit examinations are required in many states throughout the nation.

These tests are designed to establish academic standards of excellence in their respective fields, yet racial, cultural, religious, gender, and language biases are commonplace (Green, 2008; Toldson, 2012), resulting in the widening of achievement, academic, and opportunity gaps nationally (Lynch & Engle, 2010a, 2010b). A culturally relevant dialectic approach to addressing educational inequities includes the elimination of didactic teaching methods typically associated with less effective banking system pedagogical practices (Freire, 1970; Gay, 2000; Ladson-Billings, 1995).

## The Changing Landscape of Education

The Ed.D. was established nearly a century ago when higher education was generally viewed as a privilege or right among financially affluent and political elites.

This was before the Servicemen's Readjustment Act of 1944 (P.L. 78–346), also known as the G.I. Bill (Adams, 2000), which provided educational opportunities for the less affluent. Not only did the G.I. Bill provide educational resources for veterans; it also provided options for low-interest loans to purchase homes and start businesses. Most of these veterans were not part of the financially affluent or political elite but were comprised mostly of culturally diverse lower- or middle-class citizens and blue-collar workers looking for better opportunities in the growing economy of the postwar baby boom (Adams, 2000).

The post-World War II era would bring about unprecedented social and cultural transitions that would have a significant impact on educational opportunities—including, for instance, Executive Order 9981 (1948), which ended segregation in the military (Taylor, 2012). This legislation preceded *Brown vs. Board of Education* (1954), in which the question of "separate but equal" was put to rest through a reversal of the U.S. Supreme Court's *Plessy vs. Fergusson* decision (1896) (Groves, 1951).

The principles of today's Ed.D. are still grounded in an era that predates the 1957 "Little Rock Nine" incident (Bartley, 2007); the Civil Rights Act of 1964 (Aiken, Salmon, & Hanges, 2013), the Higher Education Act of 1965 (U.S. Congress, 2008), and the 1965 Voting Rights Act (Hillstrom, 2009). Though the Ed.D. is often referred to as a "practitioner's" doctorate, the history, implications, and practice of education since the inception of the Ed.D. have changed profoundly.

## Marginalized Populations

Considering the growth rate of minority populations across the United States, the term "minority" is gradually becoming nonsensical as the terms "people of color" or "students of color" become more politically apt and commonly used terms. One of the contributing factors to this change is the growing Latino population. Latinos are the largest minority group at 4-year institutions of higher education, representing 16.5% of all 18- to 24-year-old college students (Lopez & Fry, 2013). According to a recent report from the Pew Research Center (Lopez & Fry, 2013), 49% of Latino high school graduates were enrolled in college, compared to 47% of White high school graduates, making Latinos the largest ethnic group matriculating from high school to college. Despite this increase, Latinos, along with other marginalized, at-risk college students, continue to face a number of environmental and psychological challenges.

"White privilege" is a term that has gained popularity while simultaneously polarizing mixed student populations because of the controversy and history of racism. Current scholars in the field refer to White privilege as a condition of generational advantage that exists in American society for the benefit of the

White population (Alexander, 2012 ; Rothenburg, 2005; Wise, 2011). According to Tim Wise (2011), it is a condition that cannot be shed because the advantages have been created over 400 years of oppressive practices that have become traditional and a part of the values and beliefs taught and handed down generationally. Though multitudes of White Americans are culturally sensitive or aware and do not actively or intentionally exercise prejudice or discrimination, the policies and social advantages of White privilege are still available to them, ingrained in law and the justice system, and are often unavoidably reproduced by White Americans (Alexander, 2012; Wise, 2011).

Michelle Alexander's 2012 publication *The New Jim Crow: Mass Incarceration in the Age of Colorblindness* states that there is a resurgence of government policies and legal actions that erode the gains of the Civil Rights Movement and are the equivalent of the racist and discriminatory Jim Crow laws of the nineteenth and twentieth centuries. The "War on Drugs" is used as an example of government policy and practice to justify racial profiling, inequitable jail and prison sentencing, and the mass incarceration of Black and Brown men. As of 2013, 47.2% of the inmate population at local jails was White, compared to 35.8% Black, 14.8% Latino, and 1.4% Native American (Carson & Golinelli, 2013). It should be noted that while Whites comprise 72.4% of the national population, and Blacks make up only 12.6% of the population, the prison incarceration rate for Blacks is more than twice their national population percentage at 35.8%.

Other issues of marginalization and discrimination also exist within the lesbian, gay, bisexual, and transgender (LGBT) community, as well as with women. Because of the controversy surrounding state legislation, federal legislation, and school policies, college students of the LGBT community are often denied federal funds for tuition, fees, and other living expenses that domestic partners and married couples in heterosexual relationships are granted without question or delay (Burns, 2011). While state and federal courts debate the issue, students from the LGBT community go without funding, a situation that often delays or halts their educational progress (Burns, 2011).

The only exception to group marginalization appears to be among women. As a result of this gender gap (Hawkins, 1996), enrollment and graduation rates of women of all races have been on the rise for several years, as compared to men. A Pew Research Center report of the U.S. Census Bureau data indicates that women have outpaced men in college enrollment and graduation rates since at least 1994 (Hawkins, 1996; Lopez & Gonzalez-Barrera, 2014). This gap is widest among Blacks and Hispanics (Lopez & Gonzalez-Barrera, 2014). Despite this trend, upon entering the employment market, men continue to outpace women in terms of pay and advancement (Patten, 2014). This may suggest that the phenomenon is more correlated with socioeconomics than race or gender (Wilson, 2007).

## Psychosocial Factors

The use of sociological and psychological applications within the context of education plays a vital role in understanding and addressing the needs of underserved populations. In his seminal publication *The Souls of Black Folk*, W.E.B. Du Bois (1903/1989) introduced the concept of "double consciousness" as a "sense of always looking at one's self through the eyes of others" and suggested that there are different perspectives of influence and power to consider besides our own (p. 3). As well, fear, ignorance, and cultural misconceptions throughout history have contributed to academic performance anxiety, known as "stereotype threat" (Steele & Aronson, 1995), as well as other negative attitudes such as "misandry" (Ferguson, 2000), the hatred of boys and men, especially boys and men of color.

Some educators simply avoid or ignore students in K–12 and postsecondary classrooms to avoid conflict or discomfort with unfamiliar cultures (Gay, 2000). Others proudly announce that they do not see color, culture, race, or ethnicity, unaware of their perpetuation of "color-blind racism" (Bonilla-Silva, 2005), which fails to acknowledge the individuality or racial and cultural heritage that defines these ethnic and cultural groups. Today, these conditions and behaviors are more covert and subtle, yet just as destructive to the psyche and academic performance of all students at risk (Addus, Chen, & Khan, 2007; Jones, 2001).

## The Paradigm Shift

Superintendents, principals, and assistant principals in K–12 programs often possess an Ed.D., as do directors and vice presidents in student affairs divisions of higher education. These Ed.D. programs and courses tend to focus on the practice aspect of leadership rather than on coursework related to socialization. In short, the focus is on "how to manage better," not "how to be a better manager." *U.S. News & World Report* (2014) lists these ten universities as having the best Ed.D. higher education programs in the country:

1. University of California (Los Angeles)
2. University of Michigan (Ann Arbor)
3. Pennsylvania State University (University Park)
4. University of Southern California (Los Angeles)
5. Michigan State University (East Lansing)
6. University of Pennsylvania (Philadelphia)
7. Vanderbilt University (Nashville)
8. University of Georgia (Athens)
9. Indiana University (Bloomington)
10. Harvard University (Cambridge)

These Ed.D. Programs were examined to determine the extent of their relevance to culture, ethnicity, gender, nationality, and other sociological factors that support social justice education. The majority of these programs consisted of coursework focused on program evaluation, education policy, governance, leadership, and research methods.

Most doctoral programs require 60 to 72 units beyond the bachelor's degree. This equates to a program total of 15 to 24 courses, depending on the institution and credit value (3 or 4 credits per course). On average, there were only two courses at each institution that were described as being culturally relevant based on the assessment of our research panel of experts for this study. Some of the course titles were Diversity and Equity in Education, Seminar in Special Topics: Theory, Diversity and Leadership, Culture/Power/Subjectivities, and Diverse Students on the College Campus. Many of these Ed.D. programs had only one culturally relevant course, while other programs in the top ten had none. Even with two courses at 4 units each, that's a maximum of 8 units from a total of 60 to 72 units, depending on the institution. This implies that between 11% and 13% of Ed.D. courses offered in the top ten programs in the nation relate to, teach, or practice some aspect of cultural relevancy when nearly 50% of the population are people of color (U.S. Census, 2014), 3.5% are part of the LGBT community (Gates, 2011), and at least half are women. These percentages and disparities further suggest a need for a cultural intervention that an intercultural Ed.D. might provide.

Harvard University first offered the Ed.D. in 1920 (Perry, 2012a, 2013). However, the Ed.D. was discontinued and enrolled its last cohort in the fall of 2013 in favor of the recently developed Doctor of Education Leadership (Ed.L.D.) and a traditional Ph.D. in education (Basu, 2012). Harvard administrators state that this will "strengthen the education school's ties to other parts of the university," yet neither of these terminal degrees incorporates additional coursework reflective of cultural pluralism.

The University of Southern California (USC) recently revised one of its Ed.D. programs to emphasize urban education and blended learning options, components that acknowledge culture and current education trends. However, the focus is on K–12 education, not postsecondary education (Marsh & Dembo, 2009). USC does have a higher education Ed.D.; however, it offers a limited culturally relevant curriculum. The University of Massachusetts offers an Ed.D. in social justice education, which focuses on social justice and culture. However, as an interdisciplinary education doctorate, the program lacks leadership, program assessment, or policy-related courses typically associated with an Ed.D., making this degree resemble the Ph.D. in sociology of education.

In some cases, Ed.D. programs have been established at schools that only recently granted doctoral degrees and are seeking to expand their academic offerings.

Some of the less reputable programs are referred to as "cash cows" (Ramirez, 2009) because of their relative lack of academic rigor, inadequate program design, and questionable qualifications of some faculty. While Ph.D. students often do not work and usually qualify for fellowships, Ed.D. students typically *do* work as educators and are more likely to apply for expensive school loans (Draut, 2009)—thus the term "cash cow." These are but a few of the factors that have contributed to the tension between the Ph.D. and the Ed.D. that has been the focus of the Carnegie Project on the Education Doctorate (CPED). The CPED is currently working with over 50 institutions to redesign the Ed.D. "to make it a stronger and more relevant degree" (Perry, 2012a, 2013).

## METHODS

A focus group approach (Edmunds, 1999; Marshall & Rossman, 2011) was used for this study in order to provide the best environment for shared critical dialogue (Babbie, 2010) regarding the development of a culturally relevant Ed.D. and its applications in higher education. Participants from three different communities or regions within California were selected by an expert panel of scholars and administrators in postsecondary education and sociology of education and were comprised of 20 men and 22 women from culturally, ethnically, academically, linguistically, religiously, and economically diverse backgrounds. Three in-depth comprehensive research questions were devised by the expert panel to be discussed and answered with recommendations by each focus group as a means of developing a conceptual foundation for an intercultural education doctorate. The questions and responses are detailed in the research findings below.

All participants were graduate students in good academic standing who were enrolled either in Ed.D. programs (28) or Ph.D. programs in education (14) and were divided into five focus groups: two from the Sacramento region, two from the Los Angeles region, and one from the Orange County/Anaheim region. The purpose of the study was explained in detail, and participation was 100% voluntary. Personal identities and specific educational institutions were kept confidential, and confidentiality agreements were provided and signed prior to participation.

Focus group sessions took place at various facilities for approximately 45 minutes of open discussion in response to the three study questions developed by the expert panel of scholars and administrators. Each session was recorded, transcribed, coded, and recoded thematically. Further data analysis involved the use of member checking and methodological triangulation in order to achieve trustworthiness (Marshall & Rossman, 2011).

# RECOMMENDATIONS

The focus groups provided a wide array of responses and feedback related to the need for and development of a culturally relevant Ed.D. Many of the conditions and experiences described in the literature, such as disproportionate graduation rates (Ginder et al., 2014; U.S. Department of Education, 2011), the gender gap (Hawkins, 1996; Lopez & Gonzalez-Barrera, 2014), and the growing minority demographic (Lopez & Fry, 2013), were discussed. There were also topics among the focus groups that were not evident in the literature, such as the growing utilization of technology and the emphasis on activism as part of social and cultural engagement. The following are the recommendations of the participants for the foundation of an intercultural educational doctorate.

**Question 1:** What are your recommendations for improving academic support and academic engagement for students in Ed.D. programs?

- Respecting and valuing the opinions and experiences of students
- Providing regular and timely feedback on academic progress
- Relying less on lectures and more on student participation and engagement
- Establishing a student committee that shares input in their program
- Providing students with flexible options for completing assignments
- Providing opportunities for student teaching or co-teaching

**Question 2:** What are your recommendations for improving research and leadership skills for students in Ed.D. programs?

- Teaching all students the basics of both qualitative and quantitative research
- Teaching all students basic coursework in educational leadership and policy studies
- Requiring all students to develop a portfolio/syllabus for a course they want to teach
- Working directly with students toward gaining conference presentation experience
- Teaching students how to develop and submit a manuscript for a publication

**Question 3:** What are your recommendations for improving social awareness, social engagement, and interculturalism for students in Ed.D. programs?

- Utilizing scholars and lecturers from other fields such as sociology or women's studies
- Becoming actively involved with community organizations and social advocacy groups
- Volunteering time or support at A.A. and N.A. meetings, homeless shelters, and cultural centers

- Encouraging both faculty and students to utilize a culturally critical approach to teaching and learning
- Incorporating technology, distance learning, and social media to minimize the digital and cultural divide

## COURSEWORK EXAMPLE FOR AN INTERCULTURAL ED.D. PROGRAM

Based on the feedback from the participants in the focus groups, an example of a culturally diverse and comprehensive Ed.D. program was developed. Unlike the top ten Ed.D. programs listed by *U.S. News & World Report* (2014), the courses developed for the intercultural Ed.D. include a minimum of nine courses that are culturally relevant and/or diverse and that promote the values of equity and social justice engagement. The intercultural Ed.D. would be a 3-year program with participants enrolled full-time and attending year-round, including summer semesters. Though it incorporates technology, it is not a blended program.

This schedule requires enrollment of three courses per semester at three units/credits per course. In order to minimize the risk of student "burnout" or overload, the participants from this study recommend that all students in the program meet with their academic advisor twice a month, even if only to "check in" and make sure that they are "on track." This also improves rapport and contributes a sense of caring often desired among marginalized students (Gay, 2000; Howard, 2008; Ladson-Billings, 1995; Noguera, 2001, 2008). This also helps to minimize the risk of students becoming overwhelmed and going astray without proper guidance and support (Engberg, 2004). The expected result would be that students also maintain a sense of confidence and experience lower levels of anxiety (Abouserie, 1994). This process also provides more immediate feedback for faculty and administrators, resulting in better assessments and program evaluations (Villegas & Lucas, 2002).

## Course Sequence: Three Years Including the Dissertation

This program consists of 60 units of study, three units or credits per course, three semesters per year, and full-time enrollment.

### YEAR 1

**Semester 1 (Fall)**

EDD 700 Quantitative Research Methods I

EDD 705 Equity, Diversity, and Culture in Postsecondary Education

EDD 710 Psychosocial Development and Andragogical Learning Approaches

**Semester 2** (Spring)

EDD 715 Quantitative Research Methods II—Research Tool 1

EDD 720 Critical Theories, Praxis, and Reform in Higher Education

EDD 725 Community College Culture and Governance

**Semester 3** (Summer)

EDD 730 Qualitative Research Methods I

EDD 735 Writing for Presentations and Publications

EDD 740 Multicultural Leadership in K–12 Education

# YEAR 2

**Semester 4** (Fall)

EDD 745 Qualitative Research Methods II—Research Tool 2

EDD 750 Technology, Distance Learning, and Diversity in Education

EDD 755 Culturally Relevant Leadership in Higher Education

**Semester 5** (Spring)

EDD 760 Seminar in Ethics, Policy, and Law in a Pluralistic Society

EDD 765 Culturally Relevant Curriculum Development and Socio-Constructivist Instruction

EDD 770 Program Development, Assessment, and Evaluation for Diverse Populations

**Semester 6** (Summer)

EDD 775 Literature Review Development

EDD 780 Intercultural Seminar in Preparing Future Faculty

EDD 785 Dissertation Proposal Development and Defense

# YEAR 3

**Semester 7** (Fall)

EDD 790 Dissertation Development I

Semester 8 (Spring)

EDD 795 Dissertation Development II

Semester 9 (Summer, if needed)

EDD 800 Independent Study—Dissertation Development III

## CONCLUSIONS

Arguments persist regarding the differences between the Ph.D. and the Ed.D. (Aiken & Gerstl-Pepin, 2013; Neumann, 2005), even though both terminal degrees are research based. One such argument is that the Ph.D. is designed for theoretical purposes, while the Ed.D. focuses on applied research, an approach associated more with practitioners than with theorists (Reardon, 2013). Future scholars, researchers, and administrators possessing an intercultural Ed.D. are likely to be practitioners of social justice because of the emphasis on culturally critical engagement such as that recommended in this study.

Regardless of existing controversies, there are several well-known scholars with Ed.D.s who are graduates of reputable institutions, such as Lisa Delpit (Harvard, 1984), Linda Darling-Hammond (Temple, 1978), Sonia Nieto (Massachusetts, 1975), and Michael Apple (Columbia-Teachers College, 1970). There are a number of celebrities outside the field of education as well, such as Jill Biden, the wife of Vice President Joe Biden (Delaware, 2007); Betty Shabazz, widow of Malcolm X (Massachusetts, 1975); Bill Cosby (Massachusetts, 1976); and Camille Cosby, married to Bill Cosby (Massachusetts, 1992). Even retired N.B.A. legend Shaquille O'Neal earned an Ed.D. from Miami's Barry University in 2012 (Hiestand, 2012).

Though the Ed.D. has undergone reconstruction (Marsh & Dembo, 2009; Perry, 2012a, 2013; Wergin, 2011), been lauded by celebrities (Hiestand, 2012), and sometimes been targeted for elimination (Perry, 2012b), it appears that it is here to stay. Institutions such as Harvard, the University of Massachusetts, and the University of Southern California have already revamped their education doctorate programs to reflect the demands of their respective student populations and the changing education market. Based on these trends, as well as on the results and recommendations from this study, the development and implementation of an intercultural Ed.D. seem not only practical but possibly inevitable, given the ever-changing demands of a culturally complex society.

## REFERENCES

Abouserie, R. (1994). Sources and levels of stress in relation to locus of control and self-esteem in university students. *Educational Psychology, 14*, 323–331.

Adams, J. (2000, November 18). *The G.I. Bill and the changing place of U.S. higher education after World War II*. Paper presented at the meeting of the Association for the Study of Higher Education, Sacramento, CA.

Addus, A., Chen, D., & Khan, A. (2007). Academic performance and advisement of university students: A case study. *College Student Journal, 41*(2), 316–326.

Aiken, J., & Gerstl-Pepin, C. (2013). Envisioning the EdD and the PhD as a partnership for change. *Planning & Changing, 44*(3/4), 162–180.

Aiken, J., Salmon, E., & Hanges, P. (2013). The origins and legacy of the Civil Rights Act of 1964. *Journal of Business & Psychology, 28*(4), 383–399.

Alexander, M. (2012). *The new Jim Crow: Mass incarceration in the age of colorblindness*. New York: New Press.

Aud, S., Hussar, W., Kena, G., Bianco, K., Frohlich, L., Kemp, J., & Tahan, K. (2011). *The condition of education 2011* (NCES 2011–033). Washington, DC: U.S. Department of Education, National Center for Education Statistics.

Babbie, E. (2010). *The basics of social research* (5th ed.). Belmont, CA: Wadsworth/Thomson Learning.

Banks, J.A. (1981). *Education in the 80's: Multiethnic education*. Washington, DC: National Education Association.

Banks, J.A. (1999). *An introduction to multicultural education*. Boston: Allyn and Bacon.

Bartley, N.V. (2007). Looking back at Little Rock. *Arkansas Historical Quarterly, 66*(2), 112–124.

Basu, K. (2012, March 29). Ending the first Ed.D. program. *Inside Higher Ed*. Retrieved from: http://www.insidehighered.com/news/2012/03/29/country%E2%80%99s-oldest-edd-program-will-close-down

Beachum, F. (2009). Part I: Multiple lenses of democratic leadership. Chapter 2. Culturally relevant leadership for complex 21st-century contexts. *The Sage handbook of educational leadership* (2nd ed., pp 27–35). Thousand Oaks, CA: Sage.

Bell, D.A., Jr. (1973). *Race, racism and American law*. Boston: Little, Brown.

Bonilla-Silva, E. (2005). Racism without racists: Color-blind racism and the persistence of racial inequality in the United States. *Educational Studies, 38*(2), 177–179.

Burns, C. (2011). *Fact sheet: LGBT discrimination in higher education financial aid: Assistance should be allocated on need, not sexual orientation*. Washington, DC: Center for American Progress.

Carson, E., & Golinelli, D. (2013). *Prisoners in 2012: Trends in admissions and releases, 1991–2012*. Washington, DC: U.S. Department of Justice.

Casas, J.F., & Ryan, C.S. (2010). How Latinos are transforming the United States: Research, theory, and policy. *Journal of Social Issues, 66*(1), 1–10.

Clark, K.B. (1965). *Dark ghetto: Dilemmas of social power*. Hanover, NH: Wesleyan University Press.

Crenshaw, K.W., Gotanda, N., Peller, G., & Thomas, K. (Eds.). (1995). *Critical race theory: The key writings that formed the movement*. New York: New Press.

Delgado, R., & Stefancic, J. (2001). *Critical race theory: An introduction*. New York: New York University Press.

Dewey, J. (1938). *Democracy and education: An introduction to the philosophy of education*. New York: Macmillan.

Draut, T. (2009). Debt-for-diploma system. *New England Journal of Higher Education, 23*(3), 31–32.

Du Bois, W.E.B. (1989). *The souls of Black folk*. New York: Penguin. (Original work published 1903)

Edmunds, H. (1999). *The focus group: Research handbook*. Chicago: NTC Business Books.

Engberg, M.E. (2004). Improving intergroup relations in higher education: A critical examination of the influence of educational interventions on racial bias. *American Educational Research Association, 74*(4), 473–524.

Ferguson, A. (2000). *Bad boys: Public schools in the making of Black masculinity.* Ann Arbor: University of Michigan Press.

Freire, P. (1970). *Pedagogy of the oppressed.* New York: Continuum.

Fry, R. (2009). *College enrollment hits all-time high, fueled by community college surge.* Washington, DC: Pew Research Center.

Gates, G.J. (2011). *How many people are lesbian, gay, bisexual, and transgender?* Los Angeles, CA: Williams Institute.

Gay, G. (2000). *Culturally responsive teaching: Theory, research, and practice.* New York: Teachers College Press.

Ginder, S., Kelly-Reid, J., & Mann, F. (2014). *Postsecondary institutions and cost of attendance in 2013–14; Degrees and other awards conferred, 2012–13; and 12-month enrollment, 2012–13: First look (provisional data)* (NCES 2014–066rev). Washington, DC: National Center for Education Statistics. Retrieved from http://nces.ed.gov/pubsearch

Green, T.M. (2008). *The racial academic achievement gap.* Online submission. Retrieved from ERIC database. ED500218.

Grodsky, E., Warren, J., & Felts, E. (2008). Testing and social stratification in American education. *Annual Review of Sociology, 34,* 385–404.

Groves, H.E. (1951). Separate but equal—the doctrine of *Plessy v. Ferguson. Phylon, 12*(1), 66–72.

Harro, B. (2000). The cycle of socialization. In M. Adams, W.J. Blumenfield, R. Castaneda, H.W. Hackman, M.L. Peters, & X. Zuniga (Eds.), *Readings for diversity and social justice: An anthology on racism, anti-Semitism, sexism, heterosexism, ableism, and classism* (pp. 79–82). New York: Routledge.

Hawkins, B. (1996). Gender gap. *Black Issues in Higher Education,* 1320–1322.

Hiestand, M. (2012). Shaq adds yet another title: Ed.D. *USA Today.*

Hillstrom, L. (2009). *The Voting Rights Act of 1965.* Detroit, MI: Omnigraphics.

Howard, T.C. (2008). Who really cares? The disenfranchisement of African American males in pre-K–12 schools: A critical race theory perspective. *Teachers College Record, 110*(5), 954–985.

Jones, L. (2001). *Retaining African Americans in higher education: Challenging paradigms for retaining Black students, faculty, and administrators.* Sterling, VA: Stylus.

Ladson-Billings, G. (1995). Toward a theory of culturally relevant pedagogy. *American Education Research Journal, 35,* 465–491.

Ladson-Billings, G. (2006). From the achievement gap to the education debt: Understanding achievement in U.S. schools. *Educational Researcher, 35*(7), 3–12.

Ladson-Billings, G., & Tate, B. (1995). Toward a critical race theory of education. *Teachers College Record, 97,* 47–67.

Lambert, L. (1995). *The constructivist leader.* New York: Teachers College Press.

Lopez, M., & Fry, R. (2013). *Among recent high school grads, Hispanic college enrollment rate surpasses that of Whites.* Washington, DC: Pew Research Center.

Lopez, M., & Gonzalez-Barrera, A. (2014). *Women's college enrollment gains leave men behind.* Washington, DC: Pew Research Center. Retrieved from http://www.pewresearch.org/fact-tank/2014/03/06/womens-college-enrollment-gains-leave-men-behind/

Lynch, M., & Engle, J. (2010a). *Big gaps, small gaps: Some colleges and universities do better than others in graduating African-American students.* College Results Online.

Lynch, M., & Engle, J. (2010b). *Big gaps, small gaps: Some colleges and universities do better than others in graduating Hispanic students.* College Results Online. Retrieved from http://files.eric.ed.gov/fulltext/ED514356.pdf

Marsh, D., & Dembo, M. (2009). Rethinking school leadership programs: The USC Ed.D. program in perspective. *Peabody Journal of Education, 84*(1), 69–85.

Marshall, C., & Rossman, G. (2011). *Designing qualitative research*. Los Angeles: Sage.

Neumann, R. (2005). Doctoral differences: Professional doctorates and PhDs compared. *Journal of Higher Education Policy & Management, 27*(2), 173–188.

Noguera, P. (2001). Racial politics and the elusive quest for excellence and equity in education. *Education and Urban Society, 34*(1), 18–41.

Noguera, P. (2008). *The trouble with Black boys*. San Francisco, CA: Jossey-Bass.

Patten, E. (2014). *On equal pay day, key facts about the gender pay gap*. Washington, DC: Pew Research Center. Retrieved from http://www.pewresearch.org/fact-tank/2014/04/08/on-equal-pay-day-everything-you-need-to-know-about-the-gender-pay-gap/

Perez, A., & Hirschman, C. (2009). The changing racial and ethnic composition of the US population: Emerging American identities. *Population & Development Review, 35*(1), 1–51.

Perry, J. (2012a). To Ed.D. or not to Ed.D.? *Phi Delta Kappan, 94*(1), 41–44.

Perry, J. (2012b). What history reveals about the education doctorate. In M. Macintyre Latta & S. Wunder (Eds.), *Placing practitioner knowledge at the center of teacher education: Rethinking the policies and practices of the education doctorate* (pp. 51–72). Charlotte, NC: Information Age.

Perry, J. (Ed.). (2013). *The education doctorate: A degree for our time*. Special issue of *Planning & Changing, 44*(3/4), 113–126.

Ramirez, E. (2009, March 25). What you should consider before education graduate school. *U.S. News & World Report.*

Reardon, R. (2013). Towards best practice in ethics education for scholarly practitioners of leadership: An undistorted view of reality. *Planning & Changing, 44*(3/4), 286–307.

Rothenberg, P.S. (2005). *White privilege: Essential readings on the other side of racism* (2nd ed.). New York: Worth Publishers.

Steele, C.M., & Aronson, J. (1995). Stereotype threat and the intellectual test performance of African Americans. *Journal of Personality and Social Psychology, 69*(5), 797–811.

Taylor, J.E. (2012). *Freedom to serve: Truman, civil rights, and Executive Order 9981*. New York: Routledge.

Toldson, I.A. (2012). Editor's comment: When standardized tests miss the mark. *Journal of Negro Education, 81*(3), 181–185.

U.S. Bureau of Labor Statistics. (2012). *Current population survey*. Chart 1: Unemployment rate for African Americans, Hispanics and Whites. Washington, DC: U.S. Bureau of Labor Statistics.

U.S. Census Bureau. (2011). *Statistical abstract of the United States, 2012*. Washington, DC: U.S. Census Bureau.

U.S. Census Bureau. (2014). *State & county quickfacts*. Retrieved from http://quickfacts.census.gov/qfd/states/00000.html

U.S. Congress. (2008). *Higher Education Opportunity Act* (Public Law 110–315).

U.S. Department of Education, National Center for Education Statistics. (2011). *Digest of education statistics, 2010*. (NCES 2011–015). Washington, DC: National Center for Educational Statistics.

U.S. Department of Labor, Bureau of Labor Statistics. (2011). *Unemployment rates by race and ethnicity, 2010*. Washington, DC: Bureau of Labor Statistics, U.S. Department of Labor. Retrieved from http://www.bls.gov/opub/ted/2011/ted_20111005.htm

*U.S. News & World Report*. Education. (2014). *Best graduate schools; Higher education administration*. Washington, DC: Author. Retrieved from http://usnews.com/best-graduate-schools/top-education-schools/higher-education-administration-rankings?int=9a2b08

Usher, R. (2002). A diversity of doctorates: Fitness for the knowledge economy. *Higher Education Research and Development, 21*(2), 143–153.

Villegas, A.M., & Lucas, T. (2002). *Educating culturally responsive teachers: A coherent approach.* Albany: State University of New York Press.

Wergin, J. (2011). Rebooting the EdD. *Harvard Educational Review, 81*(1), 119.

Wilson, R. (2007). The new gender divide. *Chronicle of Higher Education, 53*(21), A36–A39.

Wise, T. (2011). *White like me: Reflections on race from a privileged son: The remix.* Berkeley, CA: Soft Skull Press.

# CHAPTER TWENTY-TWO

# Bridge Building

## Can Ed.D. Program Redesign Connect Social Justice Scholars and Practitioners?

*Cynthia J. Macgregor and Michele Smith*

## INTRODUCTION

The academy of scholarship and the real world of practice are disparate lands with their own native peoples. Differences between these people can be found in the forms and styles of communication and are perpetuated by the nature of their socialization systems. The most vexing of educational problems should be addressed by scholars and practitioners, but how will the chasm between these people be bridged? A growing movement within Ed.D. programs proposes to build a leadership bridge between scholar and practice worlds known as the "scholarly practitioner" (CPED, 2014a). Ed.D. redesign includes the dissertation in practice (DIP) as the capstone project (CPED, 2014a) and viewing research problems as problems of practice (Archbald, 2008; Osterman, Furman, & Sernak, 2014; Willis, Inman, & Valenti, 2010). Can the Ed.D. redesign build leadership bridges between the academy and school leaders to address long-standing social justice challenges?

This chapter will explore the nature of the chasm between the worlds of scholar and practitioner (Murphy, 2014a), including differences in publications, communities of learners, languages, advanced degrees, and views of research problems. Connecting researchers and practitioners through the Ed.D. redesign promises to produce a new frontier of educational leaders equipped with an array of skills and knowledge for resolving pervasive problems of educational inequity. Such program changes are consistent with Brown's (2004) call for leaders who "foster successful, equitable, and socially responsible learning and accountability practices for all students" (p. 80). New understandings of leadership and redesigns of such programs have sparked much-needed debate with regard to the knowledge base, course offerings, and foundational purpose of educational leadership programs (Donmoyer, 1999; English, 2000; Murphy, 1999). AERA and UCEA conferences "have identified social justice as a new anchor for the entire profession, servant leadership as a new metaphor, and equity for all as a new mantra" (Brown, 2004, p. 80).

Given the nature of the separate worlds of theoreticians and school leaders, what additional bridge building, beyond Ed.D. redesign, is needed to connect scholars and practitioners? This chapter will reconsider the nature of the divide between these worlds (Bartunek & Rynes, 2014) and provide insights into important next evolutions of the scholarly practitioner movement. With social justice leadership as a guiding principle for this movement, there is the offer of hope to "address and eliminate marginalization in schools" (Theoharis, 2007, p. 223).

## SOCIAL JUSTICE LEADERSHIP

Before exploring the specific nature of Ed.D. redesign and the potential for bridge building between scholar and practitioner for social justice, it is first essential to provide a foundation. This foundation, by necessity, includes definitions of social justice and social justice leadership. Furthermore, such exploration of strenuous redesign and bridge building based on social justice is an outgrowth of social justice leadership in schools. Finally, the consideration of social justice leadership includes an examination of where and how this topic is being considered by scholars and practitioners.

### Defining Social Justice Leadership

For leadership scholars, Furman (2012) asserted that a common understanding of social justice focuses "on the experiences of marginalized groups and inequities in educational opportunities and outcomes" (p. 194). Such focus includes "issues of race, class, gender, disability, sexual orientation, and other historically and currently marginalizing conditions" (Theoharis, 2007, p. 223). With origins in critical theory, a growing body of literature throughout education and other social sciences has advocated for leaders and scholars to address these pervasive societal disparities.

Theoharis (2007) provided a definition of social justice leadership that expands on the definition of social justice. For him, a definition of social justice leadership "centers on addressing and eliminating marginalization in schools" (p. 222). Such school leaders would make issues of social justice the focal point for their "advocacy, leadership practice, and vision" (Theoharis, 2007, p. 223). Social justice principals, examined by Theoharis, enacted social justice leadership through a "remarkable commitment to equity and justice" (p. 231). These leaders were found to sustain social justice work by "raising student achievement, improving school structures, re-centering and enhancing staff capacity, and strengthening school culture and community" (p. 231). Furman (2012) echoed this definition of social justice leadership by identifying these "transformative activists" as "committed and persistent" (p. 196). Social justice leadership "goes beyond good leadership" (Theoharis, 2007, p. 251).

Social justice leaders can be differentiated from "good leaders" in multiple ways. Good leaders work to build connections and coalitions that support the success of all students, including sub-publics (Theoharis, 2007). They speak of success for all students and support a variety of programs for diverse learners (p. 252). Good leaders work to empower staff, build a collective vision of a great school, and provide professional development in best practices. In addition, good leaders use data to understand the realities of the school, recognize that children have individual needs, and work long and hard to make a great school. Beyond good leadership, social justice leaders "place significant value on diversity" and extend "cultural respect" (p. 252). These leaders end "segregated and pull-out programs that prohibit both emotional and academic success for marginalized students" (p. 252). As well, Furman (2012) labelled social justice leaders as "inclusive and democratic" (p. 196).

More than just using data for educational decisions, social justice leaders see "all data through a lens of equity" and "demand "that every child will be successful" (Theoharis, 2007, p. 252). The professional development provided by social justice leaders extends beyond best teaching practices and strives to "make sense of race, class, gender, and disability" (p. 252). With such a tall order for school leaders, the "perfect social justice leader or the perfect social justice school does not exist" (McKenzie et al., 2007, p. 114). Even in schools making significant strides toward success for all students "not every single student in these schools is high achieving, though that is the goal" (p. 114). In schools being led by social justice leaders, "virtually all students...are learning at high academic levels," and persistent patterns of differences are absent (Brown, 2004, p. xvii).

## The Need for Social Justice Leadership

Only a brief, persuasive platform is needed to support the societal need for social justice leaders. The need for such leaders has been well established throughout the educational literature (Brown, 2004; Furman, 2012). The "importance of social justice leadership in K–12 schools is widely recognized" (Furman, 2012, p. 194). The high-stakes accountability of recent federal and state mandates for school performance have increased student testing but have yielded limited or mixed benefits for student achievement (Malen, 2011). For marginalized populations, the achievement "gaps are persistent, pervasive, and significantly disparate" (Brown 2004, p. 79). Given this "disturbing reality, courageous, transformative leadership is needed" (Brown, 2004, p. 96).

The conversation about social justice leadership may be widespread, but it is taking place in two different groups of educational experts with little shared conversation between them: the scholars and practitioners of educational leadership. Capper, Theoharis, and Sebastian (2006) identified and reviewed 72 scholarly articles and book chapters addressing social justice leadership. These sources included special issues of *Educational Administration Quarterly* and the *Journal of School Leadership*. Extensive scholarly conversation has focused on the preparation of school leaders and the redesign of such programs (Brown, 2004; Capper et al., 2006; Guerra, Nelson, Jacobs, & Yamamura, 2013; Jean-Marie, Normore, & Brooks, 2009; McKenzie et al., 2007; Theoharis, 2007). Such consideration of social justice leadership is also prevalent at conferences of the University Council for Educational Administration (UCEA) (McKenzie et al., 2007). Practitioners are having separate conversations about accountability pressures regarding achievement for subgroups (Malen, 2011). Less obvious in the literature is a strong and shared conversation about social justice leadership between scholars and practitioners.

## SCHOLAR AND PRACTITIONER DIVIDED

In order to explore the nature of a shared conversation between practitioners and scholars, it is helpful to use Bruffee's (1999) concept of a knowledge community in which members of both groups "construct and maintain knowledge in continual conversation with their peers" (p. xi). As well, to Bruffee (1999), "knowledge is a social construct, a consensus among the members of a community of knowledgeable peers" (p. xiv), and such communities are maintained through conversation, spoken and written, and result in "walls of words" (p. 6) at their boundaries. Communication within a knowledge community is considered "standard discourse...negotiation among members of a community of knowledgeable peers" (Bruffee, 1999, p. 70). Also called "normal discourse," such communication "occurs within established knowledge communities whose standards are unquestioned" (Bruffee, 1999, p. 143). Knowledge communities develop a shared language, and "speaking that language fluently defines membership in the community" (p. 153). In the following section, the knowledge communities of educational scholar and educational practitioner will be explored, thereby laying the foundation for understanding the challenges of communication between their worlds.

The world of educational scholars represents the knowledge community of professors and degree programs in education. Such scholars communicate with

BRIDGE BUILDING | 297

each other at educational research conferences and through peer-reviewed education journals. Their language is rich with theoretical jargon and abstract conceptualizations. Scholarly research is theory oriented and seeks to develop, extend, or contradict existing theories. Pressure to do research is justified by filling a gap in existing research and includes the mandate to publish new theoretically based knowledge. For the scholar, social justice is an ethical mandate, driven by hegemonic issues viewed through critical theory. Educational scholars seek to understand and to challenge the status quo of marginalization. Scholars seek to develop theoretical "tools" to explore and extend knowledge. The typical entrance credential for becoming a scholar is the Ph.D.

The knowledge community of educational practitioners includes educational leaders at various levels—from classroom teachers to school administrators to policymakers. Practitioner communication venues include professional associations and action-oriented publications. Educational practitioner language is focused on an application to real-world problems and learning through scenarios and case studies. This group's work is praxis-oriented, with pressure coming from federal and state mandates to solve real-world problems of underachieving students (U.S. Department of Education, 2001). Social justice is a federal mandate to address underperforming subgroups; sanctions or loss of accreditation are issues facing the educational practitioner. Practitioners need pragmatic tools that are clearly described and immediately applicable to practice. To practitioners, a problem is a gap in practice knowledge, or what the scholars have called a "problem of practice" (Archbald, 2008; Osterman et al., 2014; Sands et al., 2013). Educational practitioners reach the height of degree credentialing when an Ed.D. is achieved.

An important distinction between the knowledge communities of educational scholar and educational practitioner is the development of new knowledge, sometimes differentiated as research versus inquiry (Sands et al., 2013). For the scholar, the aim is generalizable knowledge; for the practitioner, inquiry is focused on decision making and informed practice (Sands et al., 2013). Scholars define problems based on the need for extending research and theory into unexplored terrain; practitioners frame problems as a need for evidence for better decisions and educational practice (Archbald, 2008; Osterman et al., 2014; Sands et al., 2013). Some scholars (Bulterman-Bos, 2008) have explored the problematic divide between the clinical (i.e., practice) form of research and the traditional "researcher" view of research, clarifying the disconnect that exists between these views.

If reflection and practice are viewed as opposite ends of a continuum, the scholars are the extreme reflectors, and the practitioners are the extreme actors. What is needed is more of a true praxis in the sense of the original Greek word, where the educational experts—practitioner and scholar—move "back and forth in a critical way between reflection and acting on the world" (Brown, 2004, p. 96). This is particularly vital for addressing social justice issues, which require "action-oriented and transformative" leadership (Furman, 2012, p. 195) informed by frameworks developed by scholars.

What counts for valid knowledge to the scholar differs from that which counts as knowledge for the practitioner. Such academic and practitioner values underlie the divided worlds of educational experts (Begley, 1999) but can also be the source of powerful creative tension (Bartunek & Rynes, 2014). Driven by a need to know for the sake of knowing, scholars might be seen as the "head" of the broader education "body." In contrast, the need to know for the sake of doing could place practitioners as the image of the "hands" of educational efforts. The common element that many practitioners and scholars share is a "heart" that cares about students. And for social justice leaders within the scholar and practitioner worlds, the marginalized and unsuccessful students are the critical focus they share.

## REDESIGN OF THE DOCTORATE IN EDUCATION (ED.D.)

A growing number of education doctorate (Ed.D.) programs are being redesigned in response to critiques about the rigor and appropriateness of such degrees. A powerful consortium of universities involved in this doctoral redesign comprises the Carnegie Project on the Education Doctorate, or CPED (CPED, 2014b). The educational professionals who are students in these programs are viewed as scholarly practitioners. Education faculty members affiliated with CPED have developed working principles, including a principle of social justice, to reenvision the doctorate in education. This new vision for the Ed.D. has included curricular redesign and new forms of capstone projects known as the dissertation in practice (CPED, 2014a).

### History of Ed.D. Redesign

Under the leadership of its original president, Dr. Lee Schulman, and with the financial support of the Carnegie Foundation for the Advancement of Teaching, CPED began in 2007. The Council for Academic Deans of Research Education Institutions (CADREI) was also supportive of the project, which began with 25 member institutions. The goal of CPED was a redesign of doctoral preparation to fit the needs of professional practitioners in education. "In September 2010, the hard work of the consortium was rewarded with a $700,000 grant from the Fund for the Improvement of Post-Secondary Education (FIPSE)" (CPED, 2014c, para. 1).

As of the October 2014 convening, CPED had 85 institutional members and 11 more on a waiting list for Phase Four (J. Perry, personal communication, October 22, 2014). The consortium has begun exploring research on the working principles and a recognition process to identify programs that exemplify the CPED working principles and design concepts. An affiliation with SIG 168 of AERA will provide a block of presentations at the 2015 annual meeting (CPED, 2014b). This "movement" has been gaining momentum and is actively involved in a bridging of scholarship and practice for students involved in education doctorate programs.

A prominent design concept, CPED defines scholarly practitioners as those who "blend practical wisdom with professional skills and knowledge to name, frame, and solve problems of practice" (CPED, 2014a, para. 1). The scholarly practitioners use "practical research and applied theories as tools for change because they understand the importance of equity and social justice" (para. 2). Dissemination of research is an important part of the definition, with a focus on resolving problems of practice and collaborating with university and community stakeholders (CPED, 2014a).

CPED shares six working principles, one of which emphasizes social justice. Specifically, CPED has agreed to frame the professional doctorate in education "around questions of equity, ethics, and social justice to bring about solutions to complex problems of practice" (CPED, 2014d). The goal of leadership preparation for educational equity is "to prepare future leaders who can effectively translate re-search into community-based, responsive practice, influence policy for equity and achievement, use data effectively in decision making, and organize individuals and groups to address challenges collaboratively and successfully" (Sands, Nocon, & Shanklin, 2012, p. 201). A specific example of social justice leaders would be graduates "with a practice-based doctoral degree who can actually improve urban schools in significant ways" (Sands et al., 2012, p. 209). With various research for-mats, some graduates might be trained in conducting an outcome evaluation that would assist leaders of nonprofit and community programs and agencies (Sands et al., 2012).

## Dissertation Redesign

The social justice mission can be found in leadership preparation programs at various levels, not just within the education doctorate. Research has identified programmatic elements of leadership preparation that support the development of social justice leaders (Guerra et al., 2013). These programmatic elements for preparation of school leaders have included "developing awareness of their iden-tity, reading literature that highlighted inequities in schools, participating in tough classroom conversations...and leading and implementing action research proj-ects" (Guerra et al., 2013, pp. 142–143). This emphasis on social justice can be seen throughout the CPED-inspired redesigns of the Ed.D. curriculum but most prominently in dissertation redesign.

The call for changing the Ed.D. dissertation from a traditional five-chapter format has ranged from abandoning the format entirely (Murphy, 2014b) to switching to a portfolio approach (Maxwell & Kupczyk-Romanczuk, 2009). This call for redesign has stressed the link between theory and practice (Olson & Clark, 2009), translation of research into practice (Sands et al., 2013), and a format that is practice-focused (Willis et al., 2010). Willis and fellow researchers provide a clear comparison between the traditional dissertation and a professional practice dissertation (Figures 2.1 & 2.2, p. 36; Figure 2.4, p. 41). The practice-focused dissertation includes writing that is oriented toward communicating with the public, influencing policy, designing training and educational materials, inspiring collaboration between stakeholders, and writing for dissemination to practitioners in a style of writing needed by practitioners. For CPED affiliates, the professional practice dissertation is called the dissertation in practice (CPED, 2014a).

The redesign of the doctorate in education is opening up exciting new frontiers, especially in the pragmatic benefit of doctoral research. The problem of practice orientation, combined with a social justice ethic, is bringing doctoral research into the hands of practitioners, informed by the expertise of scholars. This new generation of doctoral graduates is being evaluated according to the impact of their research on practice rather than on scholarship. The scholarly practitioner approach to doctoral education, including the practice-focused dissertation, is an important advancement in addressing persistent educational inequities.

## A NEED FOR ADDITIONAL BRIDGE BUILDING

Missing from the conversation about a dissertation in practice as capstone for the Ed.D. is a path for practitioner research to inform scholarship. There is a clear focus on benefit to practice and products that are designed for dissemination to practitioner audiences (Maxwell & Kupczyk-Romanczuk, 2009). While traditional dissertations result in scholarly publications for less than 10% of Ph.D. graduates (Willis et al., 2010), the emphasis on scholarly publications from practitioner dissertations is even more remote. This perpetuates the "marginalization of practice" in scholarly conversation (Murphy, 2014a, p. 11).

Revisiting the "knowledge community" view of educational expertise clearly reveals the bifurcated nature of scholars and practitioners in education (Bruffee, 1999). Practitioners seeking advanced degrees solicit the expertise of scholars at universities. Once granted such degrees, the practitioners return to their "real-world" knowledge community. Practitioners gather with their peers at professional conferences and read each other's thoughts in pragmatic publications. Scholars continue to convene with other scholars at research conferences and read each other's work in research journals. A bilingual conversation of scholar-practitioner was started in the redesigned Ed.D. programs for this new generation of educational leaders, but where is this conversation sustained after degree completion?

Murphy (2014a) asserts that there is no bridge between scholars and practitioners, saying that "the bridge has never been built" (p. 7). The CPED movement of doctoral redesign is building a bridge between scholars and practitioners but, as Murphy contends, "the traffic on this bridge was and is always supposed to flow from left to right" (p. 11). This one-way traffic of practitioners seeking input (and degrees) from scholars is seen even in the dissertation in practice. The impact of the redesigned doctoral research is focused on impacting practice; do the scholars have nothing to learn from this research? Traditional dissertations are renowned for collecting dust on shelves and not impacting scholarship or practice; at least the dissertation in practice is intended to impact practice. But what about the potential that practitioner research has to inform scholarship?

When knowledgeable peers communicate within their own communities, this "normal discourse" (Bruffee, 1999, p. 70) is more comfortable than when members of different knowledge communities attempt to engage in dialogue across their borders. When an academic from the land of scholars converses with a pragmatic from the land of practitioners, their dialogue is what Bruffee called "nonstandard boundary discourse" (p. 71). This atypical conversation requires "contact zones" (p. 71) in which such different perspectives are elicited. This dialogue is taking place in graduate education programs in which practitioners are seeking advanced degrees from universities. But where are such conversations sustained? The academy is focused on helping practitioners communicate with researchers (Bulterman-Bos, 2008), but who is creating an ongoing dialogue between researchers and practitioners? How can the traffic on the bridge between scholars and practitioners flow in both directions?

The focus of developing social justice leadership has thus far been on bringing "theory to practice" (Guerra et al., 2013, p. 131). This "left to right" flow is also evident in the value of impact on practice for the dissertation in practice. The temporarily bilingual "scholarly practitioner" is engaged in research while completing a CPED-influenced Ed.D. This scholarly informed research is intended to impact practice but is not designed to inform scholarship. The focus of leadership preparation programs has been on translating research into practice (Sands et al., 2013), but who translates practice into research?

Furthermore, the scholarly practitioner typically has no ongoing professional development enriched by theory from scholars. Practitioners who receive doctoral degrees typically remain within their practice-oriented knowledge community. Meanwhile, scholars continue to participate in research conferences and publish in scholarly journals. Where does an ongoing conversation between scholars and practitioners take place?

The connection between scholars and practitioners for social justice provided in the CPED-influenced redesign of doctoral education is just the first step in bridge building between these expert groups. The practice-oriented dissertation needs to include a focus on informing scholarship, not just improving practice. Scholars need to engage in ongoing dialogue with practitioners so that theories and research designs can advance in ways that contribute meaningfully to improved practice. In so doing, the tacit knowledge of practice can contribute to knowledge creation with scholars (Nonaka, 1994). Graduates of these redesigned Ed.D. programs need ongoing professional development that supports communication with scholars. A temporary intersection of scholars and practitioners during graduate education is necessary, but not sufficient, to unravel the pervasive problems of inequitable educational practices.

## CONCLUDING REMARKS AND CALL TO ACTION

The crucial first step to crossing knowledge community boundaries is to "overcome resistance" to doing so (Bruffee, 1999, p. 12). Scholars and practitioners are more comfortable within their respective lands speaking their native languages. But the disparities in educational outcomes for marginalized students should compel experts of practice and experts of theory/research to work together in meaningful and sustained intellectual communities. These communities of experts are forming in temporary arrangements to provide redesigned doctoral education for practitioners, culminating in dissertation research intended to impact practice. With social justice as an essential principle, these dissertations have the potential to make important advances in providing equitable education (Osterman et al., 2014). Ed.D. redesign can be the beginning of a merger of expertise between scholars and practitioners to address social justice issues.

Creating and sustaining intellectual community requires more than a transitory intersection of diverse thinkers. Such intellectual community requires creating ongoing spaces in which research and ideas can be aligned with a shared purpose (Walker, Golde, Jones, Buschel, & Hutchings, 2008). These conversations could be created within current conference venues, but would the cross-pollination of practitioner and scholar contributions actually occur, given the separate professional affiliations so embedded in their respective worlds? Addressing issues of social justice could certainly provide a shared purpose, a "heart" that joins scholar and practitioner, but how do the "hands" and "heads" of these expert groups remain connected outside of doctoral redesign for practitioners?

What is needed is for scholars and practitioners to find ways to meet in the middle of a bridge that both work to build. This "meeting in the middle of the bridge" could be in the form of networked improvement communities (Dolle,

Gomez, Russell, & Bryk, 2013), similar to the R&D functions within industry. A bilingual community of scholars and practitioners could flourish in "shared spaces"—perhaps in conferences or publications. Increasing the presence of scholars at practitioner conferences and practitioners at scholarly conferences could be facilitated through opportunities for meaningful and mutually respectful dialogue across knowledge community boundaries. Scholars and practitioners need to become bilingual—to learn to communicate in the language of the other. The research of scholarly practitioners needs to be disseminated in publications read by other practitioners *and* in publications read by scholars.

The unmet educational needs of marginalized students can be the driving force for scholars and practitioners to join hands in unfamiliar and uncomfortable ways. Ed.D. redesign is not sufficient to join scholars and practitioners for social justice, but it is an essential first step. In redesigned Ed.D. programs, practitioners are learning the language of scholars and conducting research that impacts educational practice. Next, practitioner research needs to inform scholarship. Ideally, emerging intellectual communities will provide sustainable intersections of scholars and practitioners.

## REFERENCES

Archbald, D. (2008). Research versus problem solving for education leadership doctoral thesis: Implications for form and function. *Educational Administration Quarterly, 44*(5), 704–739. doi:10.1177/0013161X07313288

Bartunek, J.M., & Rynes, S.L. (2014). Academics and practitioners are alike and unlike: The paradoxes of academic-practitioner relationships. *Journal of Management, 40*(5), 1181–1201. doi:10.1177/0149206314529160

Begley, P.T. (1999). Academic and practitioner perspectives on values. In P. Begley & P. Leonard (Eds.), *The values of educational administration* (pp. 53–80). London: Falmer Press.

Brown, K.M. (2004). Leadership for social justice and equity: Weaving a transformative framework and pedagogy. *Educational Administration Quarterly, 40*(1), 77–108.

Bruffee, K.A. (1999). *Collaborative learning: Higher education, interdependence, and the authority of knowledge.* Baltimore, MD: The Johns Hopkins University Press.

Bulterman-Bos, J.A. (2008). Will a clinical approach make education research more relevant for practice? *Educational Researcher, 37*(7), 412–420.

Capper, C.A., Theoharis, G., & Sebastian, J. (2006). Toward a framework for preparing leaders for social justice. *Journal of Educational Administration, 44,* 209–224.

Carnegie Project on the Education Doctorate (CPED). (2014a). *Design concept definitions.* Retrieved from http://cpedinitiative.org/design-concept-definitions

Carnegie Project on the Education Doctorate (CPED). (2014b). *Consortium members.* Retrieved from http://cpedinitiative.org/consortium-members

Carnegie Project on the Education Doctorate (CPED). (2014c). *History of the initiative.* Retrieved from http://cpedinitiative.org/about/history

Carnegie Project on the Education Doctorate (CPED). (2014d). *Working principles*. Retrieved from http://cpedinitiative.org/working-principles-professional-practice-doctorate-education

Dolle, J.R., Gomez, L.M., Russell, J.L., & Bryk, A.S. (2013). More than a network: Building professional communities for educational improvement. *National Society for the Study of Education, 112*(2), 443–463.

Donmoyer, R. (1999). The continuing quest for a knowledge base: 1976–1998. In J. Murphy & K. Seashore-Lewis (Eds.), *Handbook of research in educational administration* (pp. 25–43). San Francisco, CA: Jossey-Bass.

English, F. (2000). A critical interrogation of Murphy's call for a new center of gravity in educational administration. *Journal of School Leadership, 10*(6), 445–463.

Furman, G. (2012). Social justice leadership as praxis: Developing capacities through preparation programs. *Educational Administration Quarterly, 48*, 191–229. doi:10.1177/0013161X11427394

Guerra, P.L., Nelson, S.W., Jacobs, J., & Yamamura, E. (2013). Developing educational leaders for social justice: Programmatic elements that work and need improvement. *Education Research and Perspectives, 40*, 124–149. Retrieved from http://erpjournal.net/?page_id=2978

Jean-Marie, G., Normore, A.H., & Brooks, J.S. (2009). Leadership for social justice: Preparing 21st century school leaders for a new social order. *Journal of Research on Leadership Education, 4*, Article 1. Retrieved from http://www.ucea.org/jrle

Malen, B. (2011). An enduring issue: The relationship between political democracy and educational effectiveness. In D.E. Mitchell, R.L. Crowson, & D. Shipps (Eds.), *Shaping education policy: Power and process*. New York: Routledge.

Maxwell, T.W., & Kupczyk-Romanczuk, G. (2009). The professional doctorate: Defining the portfolio as a legitimate alternative to the dissertation. *Innovations in Education and Teaching International, 46*(2), 135–145.

McKenzie, K.B., Christman, D.E., Hernandez, F., Fierro, E., Capper, C.S., Dantley, M., González, M.L., Cambron-McCabe, N., & Scheurich, J.J. (2007). From the field: A proposal for educating leaders for social justice. *Educational Administration Quarterly, 44*, 111–138. doi:10.1177/0013161X07309470. Retrieved from http://eaq.sagepub.com/content/44/1/111

Murphy, J. (1999). *The quest for a center: Notes on the state of the profession of educational administration*. Columbia, MO: University Council for Educational Administration.

Murphy, J. (2014a). *Insights about the profession: Questionable norms and the marginalization of practice*. Retrieved from http://cpedinitiative.org/june-2014-convening-presentation-resources

Murphy, J. (2014b). *Presentation at 2014 CPED convening*. Retrieved from http://vimeo.com/106278991

Nonaka, I. (1994). A dynamic theory of organizational knowledge creation. *Organization Science, 5*(1), 14–37.

Olson, K., & Clark, C.M. (2009). A signature pedagogy in doctoral education: The leader scholar community. *Educational Researcher, 38*, 216–221. doi: 10:3102/0013189X09334207

Osterman, K., Furman, G., & Sernak, K. (2014). Action research in Ed.D. programs in educational leadership. *Journal of Research on Leadership Education, 9*(1), 85–105.

Sands, D., Fulmer, C.L., Davis, A., Zion, S., Shanklin, N., Blunck, R.L., Leech, N.L., Tzur, R., & Ruiz-Primo, M.A. (2013). Critical friends' perspectives on problems of practice and inquiry in an Ed.D. program. In V. Storey (Ed.), *Redesigning professional education doctorates* (pp. 63–80). New York: Palgrave Macmillan.

Sands, D., Nocon, H., & Shanklin, N. (2012). Leadership for educational equity: Opportunities and tensions of a new doctorate in education. In M. Latta & L. Wunder (Eds.), *Placing practitioner knowledge at the center of teacher education: Rethinking the policies and practices of the education doctorate* (pp. 199–213). Charlotte, NC: Information Age.

Theoharis, G. (2007). Social justice educational leaders and resistance: Toward a theory of social justice leadership. *Educational Administration Quarterly, 43*(2), 221–258.

U.S. Department of Education. (2001). *NCLB executive summary*. Retrieved from http://www2. ed.gov/nclb/overview/intro/execsumm.html

Walker, G.E., Golde, C.M., Jones, L., Buschel, A.C., & Hutchings, P. (2008). *The formation of scholars: Rethinking doctoral education for the twenty-first century*. San Francisco, CA: Jossey-Bass.

Willis, J., Inman, D., & Valenti, R. (2010). *Completing a professional practice dissertation: A guide for doctoral students and faculty*. Charlotte, NC: Information Age.

# CHAPTER TWENTY-THREE

# The Ed.D. Program in Educational Leadership

## Applying Principles of Human Appreciation

*Arnold Danzig and Elaine Chin*

## INTRODUCTION

In 2007, California approved legislation that allowed California State University (CSU) campuses to offer independent doctoral programs in educational leadership. To date, 14 CSU campuses have moved through the approval process and implemented programs. This chapter describes the processes and organizing principles by which the most recent of the CSU doctoral programs were prepared, approved, and implemented as the first independent or free-standing doctoral program on this campus. In doing so, the chapter presents a case study of the doctoral program from planning through implementation and admission of the first cohort of students.

## OBJECTIVES/PURPOSES

The purpose of the chapter is to describe the rationales and underlying principles that informed program development and implementation of the recently launched (2014) Ed.D. program at San José State University (SJSU). This descriptive case study connects some of the ethical principles in Vickers's (1965/1995) work on human appreciation and judgment, which are based in human appreciation, a term that Vickers (1965/1995) employed to more deeply explain the judgments and actions of leaders and policymakers. To understand and explain praxis, Vickers introduced the notion of the "human appreciative system," one in which instrumental behavior (action) is informed by human values and reality judgments. The case study explores what is gained by connecting principles related to human appreciative systems with underlying assumptions and beliefs that are part of the SJSU doctoral program. It examines basic assumptions that were applied in the planning and implementation of a newly implemented Ed.D. program in educational leadership.

## THEORETICAL FRAMEWORK: CONNECTING LEADERSHIP THEORY AND PRACTICE

The alignment of program philosophy, curricular design, pedagogy, and degree nomenclature draws from both university learning goals and the enabling California legislation for the Ed.D. program. Lee Shulman and his fellow researchers suggest that doctoral students in education differ from those in the arts and sciences or engineering because most of them had careers before pursuing the doctorate (Shulman, Golde, Conklin-Bueschel, & Garabedian, 2006; Young, 2006). The Ed.D. and other professional degrees (e.g., Juris Doctorate or Doctor of Nursing Practice) are degrees that focus on practice-based research and are targeted to professions in which the applications of theory are explored simultaneously with the challenges of "real-world" problems (Shulman et al., 2006).

### Human Appreciative System

Vickers (1965/1995) drew upon a long career in public service to understand how human judgment and personal knowledge are applied by leaders and policymakers in selecting or modifying courses of action. He used the term "appreciative system" to explain how human beings locate themselves and find meaning in the social world. Appreciative systems allow humans to discriminate figure from ground, forest from trees, and signal from noise to create and alter organized patterns with subtlety, theme, and variation and to provide the opportunity to harmonize disparate ideas and mute difference with selective inattention. Appreciation lies at the heart of the human experience, from the level of individual consciousness to the level of culture (Vickers, 1965/1995).

Human appreciation is the noticing of signals, the developing of a sense that something is wrong or that something needs to be changed before anything is seemingly wrong, and then changing one's actions, changing the course or destination (Vickers, 1965/1995). The human appreciation system balances conflicting social and technical demands in ways that are fundamentally different from inputs into a mechanical system; it requires a combination of explicit and tacit understanding of the institution, people, and external environment, something that comes partly from experience and partly from a careful understanding of how prior experience shapes the decision maker's actions/process in reaching a decision (Vickers, 1965/1995). According to Vickers, appreciative systems are more than subjective processes in one's head; they are relational, intersubjective processes that involve communicative interaction with others. In this view, the appreciative system is one's ability to locate patterns in complexity and to shift one's choice of pattern according to varying criteria and interests.

Others have also recognized the importance of focusing on the values that leaders bring to their judgments and decision making. Heifetz (1994) suggests that the important tasks that leaders accomplish largely concern "adaptive" strategies rather than technical solutions designed to "fix" the problem. Adaptive work involves defining the problem and assessing potential solutions and implies learning on the part of everyone involved. The implied leadership approach includes (1) respecting conflict, negotiation, and diversity; (2) increasing community cohesion; (3) developing norms of responsibility taking, learning, and innovation; and (4) keeping discomfort bearable (Heifetz, 1994, p. 26).

Scharmer (2009) suggests that leadership involves *appreciative inquiry*, which is about paying attention, in ways that reconfigure the focus and structure of collective action. The act of leadership involves transforming old patterns of thought, emotion, and intention by (1) opening the mind (through appreciative inquiry); (2) opening the heart (gateway to sensing self and others, not reacting emotionally); and (3) opening the will (opening up to one's higher self and letting go of old intentions and identities). In these views, leadership is less about controlling the situation or others and more about freeing oneself in a way that changes past patterns and actualizes future possibilities. The making of appreciative judgments depends on the presence of a caring bond between self and others, between subject and object. This bond can be between two people, between person and thing (as in artist and canvas), or among members of a group, organization, or society. These conceptions of human learning and human appreciation are embedded in the leadership framework that was applied in the San José State University Ed.D. program in educational leadership.

## Human-Centered Leadership

The educational leadership framework discussed in this chapter is also informed by the idea that leadership and judgment are embedded in an appreciation of learners and learner-centered settings (Danzig, Blankson, & Kiltz, 2007; National Academy of Sciences, 2004). This approach implies a change in the source of inspiration for education leaders, one that is intended to motivate leaders and followers to extend and improve their practices through commitment to themselves as learners through self-reflection and change (Black & Murtadha, 2007; Danzig, 2009; Danzig et al., 2007; Leithwood, Seashore Louis, Anderson, & Wahlstrom, 2004; Pont, Nusche, & Moorman, 2008). This framework highlights the need to change the commitments of educational leaders from a command-and-control approach to a more broadly defined ethical responsibility associated with inquiry into human-centered systems. The perspective combines Vickers's insights regarding the human appreciative system with contemporary approaches to leadership studies that focus on real-life experiences explored through case studies, stories, and narratives within a professional community of learners (Atkinson & Maslin-Ostrowski, 2002; Danzig, 2009; Spillane & Seashore Louis, 2002).

The philosophy, curricular design, and pedagogy for the Ed.D. program in educational leadership are embedded in the leadership and administrative standards for practitioners presented in the Interstate School Leaders Licensure Consortium standards (Educational Leadership Policy Standards: ISLLC, 2008), as well as standards for the preparation of school administrators taken from the Educational Leadership Constituent Council (National Policy Board for Educational Administration, 2011) and the California Professional Standards for Educational Leaders (CPSEL).

These guidelines advocate for educational leaders who will have the ability and capacity to (1) provide optimal leadership for the education of all stakeholders in diverse organizational settings, (2) examine current educational practices and policies from a variety of relevant leadership and organizational theoretical perspectives, (3) demonstrate effective communication skills, (4) engage in scholarly research and use a variety of data to inform decision making and planning for instructional improvement, (5) identify and solve complex problems in education, and (6) lead and facilitate the professional development of self and others in the educational organization. Soon after the Ed.D. program proposal was approved, San José State University joined the Carnegie Project on the Education Doctorate (CPED), a consortium of 87 institutions of higher education with educational doctoral programs. CPED articulates six working principles for the education doctorate that also informed the implementation of the SJSU doctoral program and its commitment to practice. The education doctorate

1. Is framed around questions of equity, ethics, and social justice to bring about solutions to complex problems of practice.
2. Prepares leaders who can construct and apply knowledge to make a positive difference in the lives of individuals, families, organizations, and communities.
3. Provides opportunities for candidates to develop and demonstrate collaboration and communication skills to work with diverse communities and to build partnerships.

4. Provides field-based opportunities to analyze problems of practice and use multiple frames to develop meaningful solutions.
5. Is grounded in and develops a professional knowledge base that integrates both practical and research knowledge, that links theory with systemic and systematic inquiry.
6. Emphasizes the generation, transformation, and use of professional knowledge and practice. (Carnegie Project on the Education Doctorate, 2009)

## Achieving Top of Form

Overall, the nexus of human-centered leadership principles and the human appreciation system undergirds the development of the Ed.D. at SJSU. This case study connects the theoretical framework with the program designers' professional practices, which consider human judgment and decision making to be the core of leadership preparation and development. As a way of understanding the values and commitments that informed the development and implementation of the Ed.D. program, the authors reflect on their own experiences in program development and implementation.

## DEAN'S REFLECTION ON THE IMPLEMENTATION OF THE PROGRAM

ELAINE CHIN

In reflecting on the 4-plus years I devoted to creating and launching the Ed.D. program in the Lurie College of Education at San José State, I have come to understand how Vickers's human appreciation systems theory captures the complexities of how such activities are accomplished in complex organizations. At the time I engaged in this work, the theory of leadership that I drew on is the framework developed by Bolman and Deal (2008) and refined for higher education by Bolman and Gallos (2011).

What Vickers's theory helped me to "appreciate" is the difference between tactics or strategies and deeper ethical commitments grounded in my understanding of the interdependent relationships necessary for educational institutions to thrive. My work as a leader is also informed by my training and background in the study of literature, anthropology, professional education, and my work as a teacher in American public K–12 schools. In the rest of this reflection, I describe how strategies helped me initiate and gain support for the program. But it was my ethical commitment to education as a public good, my appreciation of a communitarian ideal, that determined the direction in which I led the program at critical junctures in its development.

## Strategy and Tactics: Structural, Human Resource, and Political Terms

At the time I began my term as dean in 2009, San José State University, like many public institutions in California, was in the midst of massive spending cuts. The state's financial crisis disrupted all levels of schooling. It was not an ideal time to launch new academic programs, much less an expensive one like the doctoral program. In my previous role as associate dean of the Lurie College of Education, I became aware of resistance from key thought leaders in the college to the opening of the Ed.D. program. Faculty and administrators outside the college who had reviewed it expressed skepticism about the original design of the program's various curricula. Given the financial exigencies and lack of political support for the proposed Ed.D. program at that time, I halted further development of the program in order to give the college time to reassess its program offerings, garner support across the campus for the program, and develop a sustainable financial base for offering the Ed.D.

The decision about whether to continue with the Ed.D. was also complicated by the history of its approval by the state legislature. Since 1960, the state's public higher education institutions were guided by the California Master Plan. The plan established the charter for each type of postsecondary institution in the state. The California State Universities (CSU) were designed to be comprehensive institutions; their mission was to develop the state's workforce and to offer baccalaureate and master's degrees only. Doctoral-level training existed only within the University of California campuses, although provisions were made for CSU campuses to partner with UC campuses in offering joint doctorates. When Chancellor Charles Reed argued for the ability of CSUs to offer an independent doctoral program, it was with the understanding that CSU doctoral programs would be not research-oriented, Ph.D. programs but practice-oriented doctorates designed to advance professional practice through education and professional development. It was a political coup for Chancellor Reed when the legislature changed the charter for the CSU in 2005.

The CSU system asked each campus to determine whether it had the capacity to offer the Ed.D., with the implicit understanding that the 14 largest campuses in the 23-campus system would eventually offer the doctorate. The Ed.D. programs would be rolled out in three successive waves, with approximately four or five of the largest campuses comprising each one of the waves. SJSU was slated to be part of the second wave of offerings. Despite the considerable challenges to the campus and college, it was not politically possible for SJSU, the founding campus for the CSU system, to withdraw from its original commitment to offer the Ed.D. There was also considerable pressure from the local community for SJSU to provide an Ed.D. program.

As was true for the other CSUs offering the Ed.D., SJSU needed to draw upon faculty from colleges outside the Lurie College of Education to teach and advise in the program. This design meant that a strong, well-respected director would be required to lead it. The faculty member who had held that position left SJSU for another university; retirements by other senior faculty at that time also led to the loss of many who had worked on the original design of the program. Launching the Ed.D. would require hiring a new director, rebuilding the faculty within the college, reconnecting with faculty from across campus who had lost interest in continuing to build the Ed.D., and garnering the necessary political and financial support from campus leaders.

A key complicating factor was instability in the leadership of the university. During the 4 years in which I led the creation of the Ed.D., the campus was headed by three presidents and three provosts. There was turnover in other key administrative positions as well. Changes in key leadership sometimes had the positive effect of allowing me to reframe and redefine the issues related to the Ed.D. program, but other changes meant that crucial allies were lost, along with individuals who could have facilitated the design and implementation of any new academic program. It became increasingly clear to me that success in launching the Ed.D. would depend on my developing relationships with individuals on campus who occupied various positions and who possessed varying levels of power and authority.

## Creating the Cultural Frame for the Ed.D. Program

No outstanding academic program is possible without faculty commitment and expertise. From its inception, faculty conceived this program to be an all-university endeavor, one that would draw on the expertise of faculty in other colleges with relevant knowledge and skills and that would be located outside the walls of an existing department. The upside of such an approach is that the program does not depend on existing faculty in a college or department to provide all of the instruction and advisement; one can draw on the best and brightest from anywhere in the university. The downside, however, is that no existing organizational unit "owns" the program. Given this organizational reality and the absence of a faculty director, it became very much the dean's responsibility to champion, advocate for, and transform faculty ideas and desires into an actual program. While faculty worked on conceptualizing the program, I spent time building coalitions with other deans and associate vice presidents across the campus to support the Ed.D. program. Departments in other colleges were reluctant to release faculty to teach in the Ed.D. without adequate compensation—an expensive proposition when the majority of these faculty were the most senior and highest paid in each college. Without support from the other deans, a cross-college Ed.D. program would not be possible.

## Moving Beyond Strategies and Tactics: What Was Really at Stake?

Looking back on the process of conceptualizing the program, I now see that decisions I made at critical junctures were driven not by the strategies I had adopted but by an overarching commitment to the communitarian ideals implicit in Vickers's human appreciative system framework. What was needed to create a meaningful Ed.D. program was an overarching framework that transcended the principles embedded in the state and national standards that typically circumscribe programs for school leaders. I can best illustrate this point with the following example.

My original plan had been to link the Ed.D. with the Executive Master's in Business Administration (MBA) program offered by the Lucas College of Business at SJSU. Joint MBA/Ed.D. programs were being attempted at other institutions such as Rice University, the University of Michigan, Stanford University, and the Curry School of Education at the University of Virginia. To my knowledge, no comprehensive public university had attempted such a joint program. I believed that the preparation of the Ed.D. students would be enhanced by their taking courses in finance and management found in MBA programs, which differed in orientation from courses covering similar topics in education doctoral programs. We were fortunate that the director who was hired for SJSU's program, Dr. Arnold Danzig, conceived of the Ed.D. program as one informed by Vickers's systems framework and that focuses on the appreciation of learners and learner-centered settings. It is clear to me now, in ways that I did not foresee originally, that my personal commitments to public education arise from an appreciation of the interconnectedness of public institutions and the communities they serve.

## PROGRAM DIRECTOR'S REFLECTION: APPLYING VICKERS'S FRAMEWORK TO THE ED.D. PROGRAM

ARNOLD DANZIG

After spending the past 12 years at Arizona State University, I came to San José State in July 2013 with the goal of creating a new doctoral program in educational leadership. Initially, my energies were spent on writing the Ed.D. proposal, which included developing a curriculum for the program, and bringing interested faculty together to write the relevant course syllabi. In addition to writing and revising the Ed.D. proposal, the challenge was to promote the program within and outside the Lurie College of Education and shepherd the proposal through the many levels of campus, university, and external review required to launch the program with "the first fifteen" students in summer 2014.

The proposal went through multiple revisions, with feedback from individuals and relevant committees at the college, university, and CSU-system levels. After many levels of campus review, the proposal was approved by the San José State University president in early December 2013 and by the California State University chancellor's office in February 2014 and received final accreditation approval from the Western Association of Schools and Colleges (WASC) at its February 2014 meeting.

The proposal itself followed a template provided by the CSU system and WASC accreditation, which included 4 sections: (1) institution and program needs, (2) program descriptions, (3) evaluation of program effectiveness, and (4) resources. An additional 31 appendixes were attached to the proposal, including syllabi for all 16 new courses, which required separate college- and campus-level reviews and approvals. The time to prepare the curriculum and initial syllabi was short (2 months), and program faculty members continue to meet to reach a consensus about the core curriculum for the Ed.D. program and the initial iteration.

The values embedded in the doctoral program were based on the idea that educational leaders serve in learner-centered systems in which inquiry, learning, and human care are central values. The inspiration for these themes came from my work as principal investigator of a $1.8 million U.S. Department of Education School Leadership Grant that I led from 2002 to 2006 (Danzig, 2009; Danzig et al., 2007). Bringing together administrators from four urban school districts, the grant connected research on educational leadership, conceptual frameworks for understanding the administration of teaching and learning, and the craft knowledge of participating administrators. I had also worked extensively with school administrators on the use of story and narrative as a way for educational leaders to build community based on collaboration and shared decision making (Danzig, 1999a, 1999b).

The importance of human care also drew on my experience as the father of a multiply handicapped daughter (Danzig, 2012) and the learning that resulted from seeking integrated services to meet her needs. These experiences shaped my commitment to an enlarged role for school leaders based on schooling as a public good in which leadership is networked and dispersed and charged with successfully educating all students. The values implied by these commitments played out in a number of ways, including (1) recruitment and selection of students, (2) courses and program sequence, (3) international experience, and (4) faculty advisement.

## Recruitment and Selection of Students

The program aimed at recruiting a diverse cohort (15 students) in the early stages of their administrative careers, with leadership experience in their schools and districts. Along with other typical admissions requirements (transcripts, writing samples, letters of recommendation), students were asked to write a narrative detailing their educational and career goals, including a discussion of challenges that they faced as educators, as well as challenges facing education locally, nationally, and globally. This allowed for consideration of one's life story as part of the data used by faculty to make admissions decisions. A decision was also made not to require the GRE for admissions, based on the view that the GRE was not a good predictor of success in doctoral programs, needlessly restricted the applicant pool, and undervalued the importance of diversity.

The commitment of the doctoral program to practice recognized that working educators would be able to devote more time during the summers and less time during the busy school year. Classes were scheduled to begin with an intensive 6-week summer session on campus, and students enrolled in three classes that met 3 days per week, 8 a.m. to 5 p.m. During the school year (fall and spring semesters) students enrolled in two courses each semester, with classes scheduled for 3 weekends (1 weekend in any given month) and 1 evening per week.

## Program of Study

The program was designed to be completed in nine semesters over 3 years. The following core areas of study, as well as 16 courses, were developed and approved:

Educational Leadership and Education Policy (4 courses/12 units)
EDD 510: Educational leadership: Theory and practice
EDD 512: Leadership, complexity, and systems thinking
EDD 515: Leadership, diversity, and culture
EDD 535: Education policy, equity, and school reform

Organizational Behavior and Adult Learning (3 courses/9 units)
EDD 511: Leadership for learner-centered schools
EDD 520: Organizational behavior and change in education
EDD 522: Communication for educational leadership

Contexts for Educational Leadership (4 courses/12 units)
EDD 530: Assessment, testing and evaluation: Contexts and implications for change
EDD 536: Politics of education and financing of schooling
EDD 540: Education and leadership in global context
EDD 585: Field studies in global context

Research Methodology: Tools for the Scholar-Practitioner (5 courses/15 units)
EDD 501: Quantitative analysis in educational research
EDD 502: Qualitative methods in educational research
EDD 591A: Proseminar I: Doctoral studies and research in education
EDD 591B: Proseminar II: Doctoral studies and research in education
EDD 591C: Proseminar III: Doctoral studies and research in education

Dissertation (12 units)
EDD 599: Dissertation

The doctoral program draws on expertise from the Lurie College of Education as well as from campus units outside the college. Three courses in particular—on organizational behavior, communication, and leadership and complexity—are taught by professors from other colleges (business, social sciences, and engineering). The program also includes five research courses in the research block including three research proseminars. The initial proseminar was taught during the first summer of the program by two internationally renowned scholars, David Berliner and Gene Glass, who were charged with setting the culture for what it means to pursue a doctoral degree in education. Both are former presidents of the American Educational Research Association and members of the National Academy of Education. Their new book, *50 Myths & Lies That Threaten America's Public Schools* (Berliner & Glass, 2014), was the jumping-off point for the cohort. The second summer includes a required global education component including a 2-week experience outside the United States in which students will meet with education policymakers and leaders, visit schools, and participate in education-related activities.

Ed.D. students progress through three general stages of the program. In Stage 1, they will complete coursework and field experiences in areas related to leadership theory and practice, organizational and adult learning, and contexts for leadership and schooling. During the second summer session (Stage 2), they will participate in an international field experience that includes lectures by international experts, school visits, and visits with representative school and government officials, and possible participation in language-related instruction. During Stage 2, students will complete educational research courses and doctoral research seminars designed to build applied research skills, culminating in the comprehensive exam/pre-proposal and a dissertation proposal.

The comprehensive examination was not intended as a recall examination of material first introduced and taught during coursework. Instead, it was viewed more as a preliminary literature review in which students would meet with their respective faculty chair and dissertation committee and craft a research question and literature review to support an initial inquiry into the question(s) posed. The comprehensive exam would then become part of the dissertation proposal, which in turn would become part of the dissertation itself. The final year of the program (Stage 3) will involve dissertation research, with individual mentoring from the dissertation advisor and doctoral committee. This final year includes preparing and defending the dissertation proposal, collecting and analyzing data, writing up findings and conclusions, and a final oral defense of the dissertation.

## Dissertation

At the time of this writing, alternative formats for the dissertation—or what some are calling a dissertation in practice (DIP)—are being considered at San José State

University. These alternative models include jointly authored dissertations, thematic dissertations, problem-solving dissertations, as well as the traditional dissertation format. Regardless of approach or format, the dissertation is expected to contribute to an improvement in educational professional practices or education policies generally or in the context of a particular education institution. It will evidence originality, critical and independent thinking, appropriate form and organization, and a rationale for the examined research problem.

## PRELIMINARY RESULTS AND FINDINGS

The Ed.D. Program in Educational Leadership was launched at San José State University in the summer of 2014. From a pool of 43 applicants, 15 students were initially granted admission into the program, one of whom declined the offer. An additional two students who had been placed on the waiting list were then accepted into the program.

Demographically, the cohort includes 12 women and 4 men. Of the 16 students in the cohort, 5 are principals, 2 are assistant principals, 4 are directors (educational services, special education, diversity), 3 are teacher leaders (department chairs, coaches), and 2 are students working in higher education institutions. Fifteen of the 16 students work in public institutions, and 1 student serves in a private school. The ethnic breakdown of the cohort is 1 African American student, 2 Asian American students, 7 Hispanic students, and 6 White students. Geographically, the students work in schools located in Santa Clara, Santa Cruz, and Monterrey counties and serve in mostly urban settings.

It is still too soon to know how well the stated values and commitment of educational leadership for human care systems are articulated in the coursework or in the research projects that will be identified by students over the coming semesters. The extent to which students are fully aware of the meanings implied by leadership for human care and how these commitments play out in practice will be the source of future research on the program.

## CONCLUSION

Research on the important factors in leadership programs for teachers and school leaders in urban, high-needs schools suggests the importance of (1) essential core beliefs and values; (2) behaviors that focus on student learning, interactions and relationships, instruction, and accountability; and (3) learning designs that promote collaboration and collegiality. Research also indicates that school leadership is an important determinant of school effectiveness and student achievement

(Darling-Hammond, LaPointe, Meyerson, Orr, & Cohen, 2007; Davis, Darling-Hammond, LaPointe, & Meyerson, 2005; Leithwood, Harris, & Hopkins, 2008). This newly established Ed.D. program in educational leadership at San José State University has been designed as a response to the California Educational Code for the offering of the doctoral degree as well as best practices embraced by doctoral programs in educational leadership as proposed by the University Council for Educational Administration (Darling-Hammond et al., 2007). The doctoral program provides research-based coursework and field experience and uses pedagogical approaches for effective instruction to maximize learning and to accommodate the diverse learning needs of participants. One additional objective of the doctoral program is, therefore, to recruit and prepare a more diverse group of leaders for the San José region's diverse educational institutions and student population. "Unless the state makes appropriate investments in student access, college-going, and degree attainment, the next generation of young adults will be less educated than previous generations and this lower level of educational attainment will have a draconian effect on the health and welfare of California" (CPEC, 2010, p. 2).

## REFERENCES

Atkinson, R., & Maslin-Ostrowski, P. (2002). *The wounded leader: How real leadership emerges in times of crisis.* San Francisco, CA: Jossey-Bass.

Berliner, D.C., & Glass, G.V. (2014). *50 myths & lies that threaten America's public schools.* New York: Teachers College Press.

Black, W., & Murtadha, K. (2007). Toward a signature pedagogy in educational leadership preparation and program assessment. *Journal of Research on Leadership in Education, 2*(1). Retrieved from www.ucea.org/jrle_2007_2_1

Bolman, L.G., & Deal, T.E. (2008). *Reframing organizations: Artistry, choice and leadership* (4th ed.). San Francisco, CA: Jossey-Bass.

Bolman, L.G., & Gallos, J. (2011). *Reframing academic leadership.* San Francisco, CA: Jossey-Bass.

California Postsecondary Education Commission (CPEC). (2010, March). *Ready or not, here they come: Projections for public higher education, 2009–2019.* Retrieved from http://www.cpec.ca.gov/completereports/2010reports/10–01.pdf

Carnegie Project on the Education Doctorate. (2009). *Definition of and working principles for EdD program design.* Retrieved from http://cpedinitiative.org/working-principles-professional-practice-doctorate-education

Carnegie Project on the Education Doctorate. (2014). Retrieved from http://cpedinitiative.org/

Danzig, A. (1999a). How might leadership be taught? The use of story and narrative to teach leadership. *International Journal of Leadership in Education: Theory and Practice, 2*(2), 117–131.

Danzig, A. (1999b). The use of stories in the preparation of educational leaders. *International Studies in Educational Administration, 27*(1), 11–19.

Danzig, A. (2009). Learner-centered leadership: A new perspective for the preparation and professional development of school leaders. In M. Khiner & I. Saleh (Eds.), *Transformative leadership and educational excellence: Learning organizations in the information age.* Rotterdam, The Netherlands: Sense Publishers.

Danzig, A. (2012). Don't ask, don't tell, don't pay: Services for children with severe and chronic disabilities. In M. Strax, C. Strax, & B. Cooper (Eds.), *Kids in the middle: The micro politics of special education* (pp. 123–140). Lanham, MD: Rowman & Littlefield.

Danzig, A., Blankson, G., & Kiltz, G. (2007). A learner-centered approach to leadership preparation and professional development. In A. Danzig, K. Borman, B. Jones, & W. Wright (Eds.), *Learner-centered leadership: Research, policy, and practice* (pp. 51–72). Mahwah, NJ: Lawrence Erlbaum.

Darling-Hammond, L., LaPointe, M., Meyerson, D., Orr, M.T., & Cohen, C. (2007). *Preparing school leaders for a changing world: Lessons from exemplary leadership development programs.* Stanford, CA: Stanford Educational Leadership Institute, Stanford University.

Davis, S., Darling-Hammond, L., LaPointe, M., & Meyerson, D. (2005). *School leadership study: Developing successful principals (Review of research).* Stanford, CA: Stanford Educational Leadership Institute, Stanford University.

Educational Leadership Policy Standards: ISLLC, 2008. (2008). Washington, DC: Council of Chief State School Officers.

Heifetz, R. (1994). *Leadership without easy answers.* Cambridge, MA: Harvard University Press.

Leithwood, K., Harris, A., & Hopkins, D. (2008). Seven strong claims about successful school leadership. *School Leadership and Management, 28*(1), 27–42.

Leithwood, K., Seashore Louis, K., Anderson, S., & Wahlstrom, K. (2004). *Review of research: How leadership influences student learning.* University of Minnesota Center for Applied Research and Educational Improvement; University of Toronto Ontario Institute for Studies in Education Commissioned by The Wallace Foundation. Retrieved from http://cehd.umn.edu/CAREI/Leadership/ExecutiveSummary.pdf

National Academy of Sciences. (2004). *How people learn: Brain, mind, experience, and school: Expanded edition.* Washington, DC: National Academy Press.

National Policy Board for Educational Administration. (2011, November). *Educational leadership program recognition standards.* Retrieved from http://www.ncate.org/LinkClick.aspx?fileticket=zRZI73R0nOQ%3D&tabid=676

Pont, B., Nusche, D., & Moorman, H. (2008). Making leadership an attractive profession. In *Improving school leadership, Volume 1: Policy and practice* (pp. 157–191). Retrieved from www.sourceoecd.org/9789264044678

Ravitch, D. (2013). *Reign of error: The hoax of the privatization movement and the danger to America's public schools.* New York: Alfred A. Knopf.

Scharmer, O. (2009). *Theory U: Leading from the future as it emerges.* San Francisco, CA: Berrett-Koehler.

Shulman, L.S., Golde, C.M., Conklin-Bueschel, A., & Garabedian, K.J. (2006). Reclaiming education's doctorates: A critique and a proposal. *Educational Researcher, 35*(3), 25–32.

Spillane, J., & Seashore Louis, K. (2002). School improvement processes and practices: Professional learning for building instructional capacity. In J. Murphy (Ed.), *The educational leadership challenge: Redefining leadership for the 21st century* (pp. 83–104). Chicago, IL: University of Chicago Press.

Stake, R. (1997). Case study methods in educational research: Seeking sweet water. In R. Jaeger (Ed.), *Complementary methods for research in education* (pp. 401–414). Washington, DC: AERA.

Stake, R. (2010). *Qualitative research: Studying how things work.* New York: Guilford Press.

Vickers, G. (1995). *The art of judgment: A study of policy making.* Thousand Oaks, CA: Sage. (Original work published 1965)

Young, M.D. (2006). The M.Ed., Ed.D., and Ph.D. in educational leadership. *UCEA Review, 48*(2), 6–9.

# CHAPTER TWENTY-FOUR

# An International Survey of the Professional Ed.D. Program

## Leading Reflective Research and Communities of Practice

*Carla DiGiorgio*

## INTRODUCTION

The professional doctorate has sprung up in many countries for many context-driven reasons (Fenge, 2009). The Ph.D., or Doctor of Philosophy, was originally intended to qualify those already expert in a field of study to teach others; in this sense the degree followed work and study rather than creating an opportunity for them to develop. In the years since, the Ph.D. has come to represent an apprenticeship toward expertise in a particular field of knowledge. Sociologist Pierre Bourdieu (Bourdieu & Passeron, 1977) categorized knowledge as cultural capital, born of education and access to that education from parents trained in similar cultural environments and thus interested in passing on that knowledge opportunity to their children.

In terms of research (often pure) and subsequent knowledge creation (Perry, 2014), the field of academia has had its own purpose. Teaching and service have supported the recruitment of future academics to carry on the tradition of knowledge creation for its own sake. Although academics contribute much to the overall substance of society through their work, their primary goal is not to work in the professions (such as education, health, and so on), although many come from these professions and are keenly aware of their distinct fields of knowledge. In this scenario, Ph.D. students of the past came to their studies ready to learn to do research and to write and teach about a particular area of study for the rest of their careers.

In the last 20 years, however, many fields have looked to a new type of doctorate to recognize and prepare students to be leaders in their professional fields (Kot & Hendel, 2012). The goal of these doctorates is to build skills and knowledge for the purpose of changing the workplace rather than moving to a new workplace in the university. Doctorates in many professions have been developed to fill the need for more knowledgeable leaders: medicine, many health professions, engineering, and education and social work, to name a few, have designated professional doctorates as the highest degree in the field for working professionals (Kot & Hendel, 2012).

## THE TRADITIONAL PH.D.

Besides being focused on pure research and teaching at the university level, Ph.D. programs have been perceived as having other unpleasant elements that professional doctorates were intended to avoid (Loxley & Seery, 2012). Ph.D. programs often leave the student alone to work through a problem that may or may not have applied use for the workplace. The focus is often on theory development or elaboration rather than practical problem solving. Ph.D. students are often left to their own devices, and many do not complete the degree. Programs, especially research-based ones, are often unstructured in that students work closely with supervisors, and the community of learners and scholars may be less extensive than one would desire.

Bourdieu and Passeron (1977) described the setting of academia as one with its own habitus and rules of the field. There is a hierarchy of power in which Ph.D. students gradually gain expertise and esteem as they complete their research and prove that they are worthy of membership in the academic community through increasing access to social and professional opportunities at the university and then into conference and partnered university environments outside one's home department. Upon successfully defending their thesis, students become members of the community of scholars, thereby making their previous membership in other professions secondary. The primary employer is now the academy, and one spends one's days working to build knowledge and sharing it with the next generation of Ph.D. students. The cycle continues.

On the other hand, professional doctorates (Ed.D.s) have been developed to allow students an opportunity to formulate their own questions—and to answer them—in a way that, upon entrance, respects their expertise and work experience in the field of their profession (Costley & Lester, 2012). Because faculty have less expertise in this type of problem solving than the professions themselves, they, too, have had to change their approach from one of apprenticeship and teacher-directed learning to one of facilitation and group-oriented learning, where the learners provide as much support to each other as the professor does to them. The notion of community of practice developed by Wenger (1998) and others would not have been known to Bourdieu in his research, but it does reflect a postmodern approach to research that acknowledges the ambiguity attached to certainty of knowledge and right or wrong answers.

Postmodernism reflects an acknowledgment that there are many valid perspectives on the same data, depending on one's background, experience, or beliefs. This also applies to research methodology. Two researchers can have the same research question, but depending on their background, philosophy, or understanding of their own research setting (usually related to their workplace), the methodology and outcome of the research may be quite different—yet just as "valid."

The limits of research methodology have been lifted, and although many still discriminate and subscribe to some methods more than others, there is an openness to including oneself in the research as a reflective researcher would (Perry, 2014). It is very important today to recognize and state one's own biases and goals in doing research. In the past, research was not good research unless it was kept at arm's length from the researcher. The bias of the researcher was not supported as part of the research. In professional doctorate work, research is done in order to facilitate better practice in the researcher's professional field. The research setting is the work setting. This makes research seem more doable and useful for doctoral students. They appreciate doing their work in conjunction with a cohort of other students, despite the frequent presence of students from various fields in programs such as leadership. Programs are often more structured along timelines so that students can continue in their programs while working full time. Their research and writing are broken into several parts, often consisting of research, reflection, problem solving, and goal setting. They present to their peers on a regular basis, and the assessment of their progress is tied to these diverse activities. In the Ph.D., assessment is often tied only to the coursework and final thesis. The presence of formative assessment in the professional doctorate allows students to keep track of their progress and to make adjustments early on so as to not leave the high-stakes assessment to the end of the degree.

## THE PROFESSIONAL DOCTORATE (ED.D.)

Notwithstanding the Ph.D., the doctorate of education (Ed.D.) is the most commonly awarded professional doctorate (Kot & Hendel, 2012). I would like to focus on the evolution of this degree in North America, Australia, and the UK, as these locations have seen the most development. In North America, the United States and Canada have different histories of Ed.D. program development. In the United States, the Ed.D. has been quite diversified (Kot & Hendel, 2012). In the last 10 years, the Carnegie Foundation—through the Carnegie Project on the Education

Doctorate—has funded research and planning to bring together representatives from many universities across the country to streamline their programs and address issues of definition. As a result, many universities are sharing their successful approaches and listening to student feedback to improve programs and increase the number of student completions.

Many professional doctorates worldwide have evolved in response to governmental policies espousing the development of capital for both professionals and the fields in which they work. The connection between research and improved capital and living for individuals and society through industry development has resulted in many universities using the Ed.D. as an opportunity to address shortfalls in society's schools and student performance. The societal problems that exist in schools have been the focus of many school leaders, and questions related to improving student performance, improving teaching, and improving access to education for students of all kinds have been promoted by government as areas that will, it is hoped, result in improved practice on the part of teachers and improved performance on the part of students, which is thought to lead to better access to work in the future. Innovation in research is tied to improved prosperity for society as a whole. Whereas universities used to have free rein in terms of their research, governments are now tying monetary support to areas of study and student progress that pay dividends for the economy (Kot & Hendel, 2012). As a result, areas such as science and technology have been seen as more profitable areas of research and have thus received more government funding.

This move toward an economic drive behind university development is a change from Bourdieu and Passeron's (1977) description of the field of academia, but it does reflect their theory that social structures reflect the values that society places on them. The change in universities to a more entrepreneurial profile reflects the situation they now face—that is, more universities fighting for less money. The choices that researchers make with regard to their work reflect their ability to get funding. This is a change from earlier times, when academics were free to explore their areas of interest, and freedom and independence of scope were central to one's identity as a researcher and scholar. Now the professional doctorate allows one to retain a dual identity—both a professional and an academic one (Costley & Lester, 2012). The complexity of this dual identity makes for some interesting ethical dilemmas, although it does recognize the reality of doing research in the workplace. However, the usefulness of the research in some fields may disqualify many topics that would previously have applications only after becoming theory in the university setting. The isolation of academia in the past allowed for arm's-length separation and served to avoid the temptation to sell out to industry in the way that research today feels tempted to do.

The lack of support for social sciences as opposed to science and technology reflects a perception that the latter areas bring more prosperity to society (Kot &

Hendel, 2012). Nevertheless, the social sciences have been mandated to explore ways to improve student learning. The ambiguity associated with postmodern approaches to research has made research in areas such as social work and education even more complicated. The context specificity of individual studies renders many of them unable to be generalized to other settings. However, the popularity of the professional doctorate in education reflects the support for this melding of practice and theory.

Bourdieu and Passeron (1977) would say that practice naturally arises from social structures and vice versa, as people act according to their habitus and the rules of the field in which they work. Thus the approaches that professions take reflect their own particular traditions of practice. It is difficult to change practices, yet research in their field allows society to see what exists and then work to change what needs to be changed. Bourdieu argued that nothing short of a crisis in the field would change the norms of practice, yet every day professionals and leaders see the limitations of policies and practices that limit what can be done to improve the lives of people living in those settings.

The Carnegie Project on the Education Doctorate has set as its goal the identification of programs and approaches that encourage students to take risks, to ask questions, and to undertake research that tries to change the status quo in order to improve practice and overall student learning (Kot & Hendel, 2012). This requires that doctoral students understand the theories and methodologies that are appropriate for them to use as jumping-off points for their work. They need to know what has been done before and to understand the requirements of the systems in which they work in order to implement change (Costley & Lester, 2012). This involves an understanding not only of the theory of their field of study but also an understanding of change theory, leadership skills, research methods, and cultural differences in global contexts. They need to appreciate the nature of their systems of work in relation to others in other places. In order to compare and learn from others, they also need to understand the relationship between home and school, society and education, culture and language. This wide perspective is necessary in order to be able to focus on a specific context and to do it justice. Knowledge of one's own work environment allows one to recognize one's identity and that of the group (Fenge, 2009).

## ACTION RESEARCH

Many doctoral programs have encouraged students to use an action research methodology (Zambo & Isai, 2012). Action research involves setting out a question for one's own workplace, trying out a strategy for solving this problem, and then assessing whether the strategy worked. Often this is repeated through several cycles to refine the strategy and reflect on its outcomes. This research approach is suited to professional doctoral students, as it allows them to apply acquired knowledge to their own workplace. Topics can be chosen to address specific needs of the student. Results are directly applicable to the workplace and can inform the student's professional work in a direct way. Results also directly influence the learners in the classroom or other setting in the case of education.

Some may believe that such research projects are less likely to be published. However, Costley and Lester (2012) found that, on average, these research-as-practice and synthesis projects produced the strongest outputs in terms of their impact on practice and, more surprisingly, dissemination. Some projects not only made a substantial, direct impact in their fields but also resulted in quite impressive catalogues of professional and academic publications. On balance, the more conventional research projects not only had less practical impact but also resulted in fewer published outputs (p. 263).

The fact that many who pursue professional doctorates are top educators in at least the middle of their careers supports the notion of giving them the freedom to decide how they want to direct their own doctoral journeys (Loxley & Seery, 2012). Many Ph.D. students have not yet worked in the field, having come directly from bachelor's and master's degree programs. Professional doctoral students, in contrast, have usually worked for several years in their field, and this is often a requirement for entrance into the program. They may need more support in the area of research training, but their awareness of the goal of the research and its outcome and application are more developed than those pursuing Ph.D.s in many cases.

The impact of professional doctoral students' work has the potential to influence the field of education in a broad way. Because professional doctoral students are connected socially to a large network of educators, their work has the potential to go beyond traditional methods of academic dissemination. Working with educators on a daily basis allows the work of these leaders to affect many teachers and students in learning settings, as well as fellow doctoral students. Bourdieu related the importance of social capital in transferring information and values from one person to many (Bourdieu & Coleman, 1991). As well, professional doctoral students, because of their membership in academic and professional circles, are aware of the tensions apparent in practice versus theory and can address these conflicts in their research. This results in a more realistic and deep understanding of the realities of education in the field and can lead to more useful policy recommendations and practices as outcomes (Fenge, 2009).

## FACULTY CHANGES IN THE UNIVERSITY

The habitus of university professors has traditionally been one in which they worked in higher education but not for it (Perry, 2014). As a result, in their pursuit of individual interests, many professors were disconnected from the real world of education. In the case of professional doctoral programs, faculty are forced to recognize the habitus of professional students and adapt their teaching and supervisory approaches to ensure that these students are successful. This has meant that the role of the professor in professional doctoral programs has become more facilitative, as well as providing more support in the area of research methodology. Much of the power traditionally situated in the professor because of his or her knowledge base is now distributed evenly between professor and students(s). As the cohort model results in a community of learners in the doctoral classroom, members of the group are able to support themselves through the wide knowledge base they already command as professionals in the field. They may need support in recognizing the theory and ethics behind what they do on a daily basis. However, they are able to relate this to their ongoing work in a way that previous Ph.D. students may not have, or may not have been encouraged to.

Bourdieu stated that changing the status quo requires a major shift in thinking about the field, and this has happened in the postmodern approach to education and society in general (Grenfell & Kelly, 1999). The idea of a positivist approach to research has taken a back seat to a much broader array of possibilities in terms of research in the social sciences. Although in some countries the governmental approach to education has become more focused on economics and standardized assessments, teachers and researchers have adopted a liberal approach to understanding the effects of these approaches to students and school systems in general. This conflict between government and economic policies, coupled with an awareness of the effects of policy on practice, has resulted in much resistance on the part of educators to following the neoliberal mandate.

The need for research to illuminate reality and provide options for change is all the more necessary in such an environment. Educators in doctoral programs want to influence the field in a positive way. There is a need to be open to a broad array of possibilities in terms of choice and approach to research. However, in undertaking their own research, all students need to be aware of the history of research and practice. This is a key role for professors—to be able to guide and facilitate discussion regarding how to read the literature and to be able to intelligently choose methodologies for research that will inform practice in the most useful way possible (Zambo & Isai, 2012).

Such faculty work requires that faculty themselves relinquish some of their power to students in taking leadership roles in the university classroom as well as the workplace (Zambo & Isai, 2012). In this case, the guardianship of knowledge is shifting from the university to the world of work. Faculty must be able to work in both environments. This shift would be more complex than that specified by Bourdieu in discussing separate fields of education in terms of tertiary education versus K–12 education (Bourdieu & Passeron, 1977). The range of K–20 now used in the education system acknowledges that the range of levels has come together and no longer separates postsecondary education from K–12. This melding of traditionally separate fields requires that faculty understand the field of education in schools and be able to communicate and work with teachers in the K–12 system.

Further, professional doctoral students are required to be "opinion leaders" and change agents, according to Perry (2014). Opinion leaders are able to influence others' attitudes on an ongoing basis. This is helpful in schools in that a leader can facilitate change by supporting the educators who are initiating that change, thereby influencing others who may not be as open to it. Change agents can bring new ideas to the workplace by being aware of the need for change, developing a rapport with fellow workers, motivating interest in change, trying a new approach and changing the behavior of others, following through with implementation of the change, and encouraging change to be a renewable process for themselves and others. Often opinion leaders and change agents can coexist in workplaces, supporting each other to make change happen.

In the university, these roles can also take place in the renewal of programs such as the professional doctorate (Perry, 2014). Deans of education can be the opinion leaders who support change agents (such as professors) in adopting new practices and programs (such as the professional doctorate). Without the support of leaders, change cannot be sustained. In the case of traditional Ph.D. programs, the dominant culture needed to change to accommodate a new professional doctorate. There has been resistance to this program, and some have felt that it is not as rigorous because it lacks the thesis requirement, or perhaps because of the practical nature of the program. Traditionally, Ph.D. programs have separated themselves from practical application, and their habitus has prided itself on the theoretical nature of their work. However, the valuing of the professional doctorate has resulted from the coming together of faculty—such as those in the Carnegie Project in the United States—to define the way in which the professional doctorate is going to make itself distinct and valuable to the university and to the education system.

Perry (2014) analyzed processes of professional doctorate implementation during and following the Carnegie collaboration among universities in the United States. Some universities were successful in taking the suggestions that emerged from the Carnegie discussions and applying them to their own faculties as a result of leadership on the part of professors. In order to be successful, such leadership required the support of deans and universities; as Bourdieu would explain, the legitimate power rested in the leadership of the university or the faculty, and there was resistance to change. The leadership of professors in changing the approach of faculties did not constitute formal power, as they were not in formal leadership positions and were not in supervisory roles over their fellow professors. Therefore, formal and informal leaders had to work together to implement change at the grassroots level within faculties to enable the professional doctorate to be successful for students. There was a balance between opinion leaders and change agents that reflected Bourdieu's understanding of the process of change.

Opinion leaders such as deans needed to be supportive but not get directly involved in the change process. Change agents led the change process from within the faculty ranks, and this allowed change to be collegial and democratic rather than top-down. Change agent professors used their social and cultural capital to influence their fellow colleagues to entertain changes in their attitudes and practices. Colleagues trusted the expertise of their change agent leaders and recognized when those leaders made suggestions that rang true to their own ways and attitudes. There were also pragmatic reasons for professors to entertain new ways of teaching and approaching students. These new ways were successful in that they met students halfway and allowed them to be leaders in their own work. This benefitted both professors and students and resulted in more students completing their doctorates, which in turn affected professors' careers in a positive way.

The valuing of this new degree has been gradual and incremental, due to the resistance to change described by Bourdieu (Kot & Hendel, 2012). But because universities needed a way to respond to the needs of students, and because in many cases the response has resulted in positive outcomes for students and schools, the change has been welcomed by many. The previous lack of direction in developing a new approach to professional doctorates has been legitimized somewhat by defining the degree on a national level (as in the case of the United States) and by working collectively with the capital of many faculty and leaders to change policy from within the system.

Traditionally, the notion of universities has not been an economic one, and the resistance to adopting this approach has come from a longstanding idea that, for knowledge to grow unhindered by the politics of the day, university and state should be separate (Perry, 2014). This notion of free thought, speech, and writing is central to the power of intellectuals in a society. However, connecting knowledge to its source—as in the case of education—leads to a more realistic and useful application of that knowledge to the recipients and actors of learning, the learners themselves.

The evolution of the professional doctorate has invited faculty and students to reimagine their place in the twenty-first century as dual-role educators and learners. The idea of lifelong learning is appropriate for faculty as well as for educators and students. Pressure to respond to economic needs to connect research to policy and practice is not inherently a bad thing, as it forces us to recognize the usefulness of the academy in leading change in the world to better the lives of people in general. Participating in the discussion is more helpful than retreating to a hermitage, and this latter approach is inappropriate for the field of education. Looking at one's own practice is a contested and potentially conflict-ridden exercise, but it pays dividends to do so in an integrity-filled way. This activity can pay off for faculties of education, and they can be leaders of the practice for all other university faculties as well.

Many participants in professional doctorates have appreciated the community of practice as an opportunity to resist the competitive atmosphere of many workplaces and environments these days. As one student said in a study by Loxley and Seery (2012):

> One of the things I would put a note in about is: we are a reasonable mature group. Some are younger...most are in a phase in life and are less concerned, if you like, about the rat-race and the competition element. We do not have the competition element, we are supportive of each other. (p. 11)

## CONCLUSION

Perhaps the ultimate benefit of the process of professional doctorate (Ed.D.) programs in universities is the notion that students, because they are not in positions of competition, are able to develop at their own pace, in an environment that models the ones we would like to see in the workplace and the real world for students. Notions of cooperation supporting individual growth are at the center of an ideal education, yet—as Bourdieu would say—the world is a competitive place. A win-win situation is not as common as we would like in our society, yet it is ideal for educators and students throughout life. Perhaps the development of the professional doctorate will allow universities to connect more genuinely with the world in a way that combines faculty's teaching skills with students' leadership in their own workplaces, resulting in a win-win for all involved.

## REFERENCES

Bourdieu, P., & Coleman, J.S. (1991). *Social theory for a changing society*. Boulder, CO: Westview Press.

Bourdieu, P., & Passeron, J.-C. (1977). *Reproduction in education, society and culture*. London: Sage.

Costley, C., & Lester, S. (2012). Work-based doctorates: Professional extension at the highest levels. *Studies in Higher Education, 3*(3), 257–269.

Fenge, L. (2009). Professional doctorates—a better route for researching professionals? *Social Work Education, 28*(2), 165–176.

Grenfell, M., & Kelly, M. (Eds.). (1999). *Pierre Bourdieu: Language, culture and education: Theory into practice*. Bern and New York: Peter Lang.

Kot, F.C., & Hendel, D.D. (2012). Emergence and growth of professional doctorates in the United States, United Kingdom, Canada and Australia: A comparative analysis. *Studies in Higher Education, 37*(3), 345–364.

Loxley, A., & Seery, A. (2012). The role of the professional doctorate in Ireland from the student perspective. *Studies in Higher Education, 37*(1), 3–17.

Perry, J.A. (2014). Changing schools of education through grassroots faculty-led change. *Innovations in Higher Education, 39,* 155–168.

Wenger, E. (1998). *Communities of practice: Learning, meaning and identity.* Cambridge: Cambridge University Press.

Zambo, D., & Isai, S. (2012). Lessons learned by a faculty member working in an education doctorate program with students performing action research. *Educational Action Research, 20*(3), 473–479.

# CHAPTER TWENTY-FIVE

# Professional Scholarship in an Ed.D. Program

## Research and Writing for Real-World Contexts and Community Impact

*Tara L. Shepperson and Jessica Hearn*

## INTRODUCTION

This chapter presents a model developed by instructional faculty while teaching research courses in a practitioner doctoral program requiring a dissertation. A directive of practitioner doctorates is that candidates extend research into professional realms. Arguments center on the value of research in seeking solutions to problems or implementing improvements in what Schön (1987) described as the "swampy lowland" of real-life settings. Practitioner programs have been criticized for research that works *on* a problem, but fails to have students work *within* a situation (Lester, 2004).

The literature is rife with arguments favoring action research or program overhauls for dissertations set in practice (Amrein-Beardsley et al., 2012; Olson & Clark, 2009; Young, 2014; Zambo, 2011). We agree with the calls for actionable research, connection with practice, and community benefit, and that these arguments fuel valuable discussion and thought. For most doctoral faculty, however, dissertations of practice must be measured against the academic traditions in which they work. At a regional university in the south-central United States, graduate students, many of them first-generation college-goers, entered an educational leadership doctoral program with a strong resolve to address social justice concerns in their rural communities. These practitioners responded positively to framing research as problem solving but still sought the research know-how necessary to complete a dissertation (Perry & Imig, 2008).

Drawing on our experience teaching a newly redesigned course in research and proposal writing, we propose a series of activities that frame research learning in such a manner as to not only inculcate the doctoral student into research habits of mind but also provide increasing levels of autonomy and ownership for their own research. Based on course materials and instructor and student reflections, we recommend a quality for teaching and learning that helps students gain demonstrable research skills that lead to dissertations of practice that ultimately benefit local communities.

Instructional faculty in practitioner programs are challenged to balance advanced research learning with the need for transferable skills applicable to varied educational fields. Criticisms that have been levelled against educational doctorates focus on the misalignment of teaching theoretical and generalizable methods to practitioners who seek real-world solutions to existing school problems. A national focus on reforming programs presents an interesting backdrop but little direct assistance to faculty who guide professional educators through doctoral programs that remain traditional in structure but actually seek to prepare students to become researchers for real-world change.

A six-credit course on research and writing is detailed from the perspective of the two-instructor team and doctoral students who participated. Outcomes of the pilot course indicated that instructors must take the long view of dissertation research, giving students progressively more ownership and gradually relinquishing control to them. The result will be students who are skilled enough to complete advanced research, but at the same time also committed to making a difference in their profession and communities.

## BACKGROUND

Doctorates for working professionals have become increasingly common since the early 1990s. Most popular in education, social and health services, and public policy, these doctorates blend academic theory and real-world practice to enhance professional knowledge and practice. Professional doctorates aim to integrate academic and professional knowledge in new ways by connecting scholarship and professional contexts that explore real-world problems (McLeod, 1999; Wergin, 2011). Most often, students continue to work while in school and generally produce a culminating original piece of research related to professional practice in their field (ESRC, 2014). Preferred methodologies include action research and program evaluation that are fundamentally different from traditional dissertations or theses designed by apprentice "professional researchers" rather than those who work in the field as "researching professionals" (Bourner, Bowden, & Laing, 2000).

## EDUCATION PRACTITIONER DOCTORATE

In the United States, professional practice doctorates in education have a history of cross-purposes and unclear outcomes. Both Ph.D. and Ed.D. education degrees were established early (Columbia in 1892 and Harvard in 1921, respectively). Either degree might train superintendents, future university faculty, researchers, or community college leaders (Perry, 2014). This has resulted in programs with neither research nor practical content rigor. Since 2000, a national debate has been underway, as exemplified in Levine (2005) and others who recommend that terminal education degrees be eliminated in favor of administration degrees akin to the Masters of Business Administration (Shulman, Golde, Bueschel, & Garabedian, 2006).

## DISSERTATION IN PRACTICE

The confused state of terminal degrees led the Carnegie Foundation for the Advancement of Teaching to undertake several studies. One group reviewed Ph.D. programs in six disciplines, including education (Walker, Golde, Jones, Bueschel, & Hutchings, 2008). Another initiated the Carnegie Project on the Education Doctorate (CPED), which sought to redesign practitioner programs to highlight research about educational practice (CPED, 2010). Debates over the education doctorate led to recommendations that an Ed.D. should result from a "dissertation in practice" based on inquiry into a problem of practice that generates actionable results (Archbald, 2008; Willis, Inman, & Valenti, 2010). Considered transformative (see Grogan, Donaldson, & Simmons, 2007), key elements of this practical dissertation are that it should include authentic learning that involves community and group interaction, critical problem solving, and application of theory to real-world situations (Wellington & Sikes, 2014; Wenger, McDermott, & Snyder, 2002). The process places doctoral candidates outside the academic ivory tower, where their research may directly benefit the community.

## THE STUDY

In departments of educational leadership, adult students often arrive from varied professions and academic disciplines. This student mix may be most intense in departments with several concentrations within single programs. These students benefit from structured programs that provide meaningful academic study and practical application. Both Shulman's (2005) argument for a signature pedagogy, or characteristic methods for teaching and learning, and Golde's (2006) support for socializing influences that inculcate students into the discipline may be especially worthwhile for programs that attract professionals from multiple arenas.

## Problem Statement

The value of a scholarly dissertation for practitioners has been widely questioned, especially when the end product is neither situated in nor useful to real-world practice (Murphy & Vriesenga, 2005). Those who seek reforms support learning that is less wed to academic conventions. Practitioners are part-time students, busy with career, family, and coursework, and with looser affiliations to the university (Deem & Brehony, 2000). As a result of having one foot in practice and the other in academia, practitioners bridge both worlds and seek knowledge useful for contemporary practice. Their goals are to increase professional expertise. Generalizations and intellectual thought are secondary to realistic plans that improve operations on the ground.

A growing number of recently redesigned programs specifically focus on action research or other methods that encourage active engagement and improved practice within schools. Program goals most often relate to the identification and resolution of educational problems for the promotion of social justice (Ball & Forzani, 2007). Many programs have not yet gone through official redesigns and therefore face internal conflict within universities that favor established research methods and dissertations. Prevailing formats, demand for tradition, and lack of awareness of discipline-specific differences often lead university authorities to eschew requests for nontraditional education dissertations.

Such was the case for the doctoral faculty in this study. They found themselves teaching students interested in preparing dissertations focused on local contexts and concerns while needing to produce traditional proposals and five-chapter dissertations. This chapter is not an empirical study of course results so much as a presentation of the activities and processes of learning during a two-part research course. Faculty members concentrated on providing step-by-step experiences by which students gained academic knowledge and functional capacity to implement and write about their own inquiries. These were rooted in local context and educational problem solving but also fulfilled the customary requirements of the department and university. Reflections recorded during and after the course provide insights into effective elements of the course and specifically the relationship of course activities to student academic and intellectual growth.

## Statement of Purpose

This chapter presents a conceptual and pedagogical model embedded into a recently developed graduate course organized to promote research and writing for doctoral students preparing to undertake dissertation research. Courses were designed to consider the needs of working professionals in the program, many of whom lived in rural locations in Central Appalachia. The course addressed the need to build the academic and research capacity of part-time students, at the same time honoring their desire to engage in research within community contexts. As well, instructors recognized a need to socialize students into the customs of academic scholarship and to develop student capacities for effective research and communications. The following questions provided guidance for the teaching and learning activities.

(1) How can instructors scaffold research learning to build skills and efficacy for student research?
(2) What challenges do students face in understanding the academic traditions and expectations of doctoral dissertation work?
(3) How might students and instructors work together to overcome barriers and ensure that students have the skills and efficacy for successful dissertations?
(4) How do instructors and students conform to academic dissertation traditions yet develop research projects that engage local communities?

## The University and Surrounding Region

The regional comprehensive university is located on the western edge of Central Appalachia, an area that includes the largely rural areas of southern Virginia, West Virginia, and the eastern half of Kentucky and Tennessee (Appalachian Community Fund, n.d.). The university has a history of stewardship in a 22-county region that is one of the poorest and least educated sections of Appalachia where, on average, just over 12% of adults earn a bachelor's degree, and 28% of adults over age 25 do not have a high school diploma. These figures point to acute economic and social problems in many rural areas of Appalachia brought on by decades of the boom-and-bust extraction industry, declining agriculture, generational poverty, and historic isolation. The result fosters a stereotype of Appalachia as a place of natural beauty and strong cultural heritage but also entrenched poverty and backwardness (Eller, 2008).

## Program and Student Characteristics

In August 2008, the educational leadership department officially began a new doctoral program focused on addressing its mixed urban and rural service area and attracting students from nearby metropolitan areas, small towns, and rural areas. The first cohorts included mainly school administrators, central office staff, and teachers in nearby districts. University, community and technical college, criminal justice, and social services professionals quickly diversified the program in terms of ethnicity, home community, and professional interest. In its first 7 years, the program served 171 students who generally continued to live and work in their communities, attending classes at night, on weekends, and online. Although official data have not been collected, anecdotes indicate that many of the doctoral students, especially those from rural locations, were first-generation college students.

## Methods of Investigation

Overall, the chapter attempts to understand the worth of a new research course to the students who participate. It requires that instructors assess how teaching is working, and, more broadly, it suggests changes to improve the doctoral program and ensure the quality and character of dissertation research. The study contains many of the same features of what Allwright (2003) defines as exploratory practice (EP), which is a form of action research concerned with researching and adjusting teaching (Burns, 2005). The study presents an example of instructor-initiated research that emphasizes teaching processes and learner outcomes.

The processes of collecting and analyzing data from the course follow those ascribed to action research, a process "whose purpose is to gain greater clarity and understanding of a question, problem or issue" (Stringer, 2007, p. 19). As is typical of action research, the instructors had only broadly defined questions focused on review and reflection of how best to teach students the skill sets and sense of self-sufficiency that would help them select topics and organize investigations for dissertation research. As Wei (2011) notes, action research is highly reflective and is useful in helping teachers improve practice (Cohen, Manion, & Morrison, 2007). It also provides room for other vested parties (including the students themselves) to have a voice in the interpretation of the experience. Interpretations of the course included instructor reflections on class activities but also student viewpoints as expressed in assignments, informal responses, and midpoint and end-of-course surveys.

## THE COURSE

For several years, the educational leadership department required that doctoral students take only one advanced research course beyond the two introductory quantitative and qualitative inquiry courses. This advanced course was to be completed after other course requirements had been fulfilled and before entering dissertation preparation. Ongoing review of student progress indicated that few students were prepared to progress from doctoral student to candidate or student researcher after only one course that was essentially designed to assist with proposal writing. Rarely were students able to complete all aspects of a proposal in one 15-week course. As a result, a two-part pilot course was designed for students nearing the end of their second year to help bridge the learning gap from instructor-directed coursework to student-directed dissertation writing and research. The goal of the course was to team-deliver the pilot course as one of the last chances at seat time for students before moving on to highly individualized dissertation research.

The course was designed so that the two instructors worked together. Thematic information and discovery activities were integrated across the two sections. Both faculty members participated in online video conferencing and face-to-face sessions and provided unified instruction and feedback throughout the semester. Nearly all students registered for both sections, though they were not required to do so. Even students who did not sign up for the full six credits ended up working on lessons and participating in activities that were designed for the merged sections.

At first, students were familiarized with the dissertation process. They learned about university and dissertation requirements, reviewed examples of dissertations, and read research articles with differing methodological approaches. Students also were asked to consider purposes for research, including their own, and to examine literature on problems in practice to develop questions for study. They were even asked to complete a Gantt chart that graphed hours on task, benchmarks events, and calculated time to completion. Students were tutored on the use of library databases, literature management and archiving techniques, and strategies for skimming articles for relevant content. Student journals and discussions revealed that the participants appreciated the approach that began with the end in sight, so that they came to understand what, for most of them, was previously an unclear process.

Literature suggests that perennial issues with writing often prevent many candidates from completing their dissertations (Hendricks & Quinn, 2000; Lillis & Turner, 2001). The course sought to meet that challenge and to debunk a commonly held notion that there is a "strict demarcation between collecting data, or doing research, and the writing of this material" (Torrance & Thomas, 1994, p. 107). Students were asked to complete near-weekly writing assignments on portions of the proposal. It was hoped that the integrative nature of inquiry, writing, reflection, and comprehension would be incorporated into student routine. As the course progressed, assignments that helped students gain understanding and confidence about the process were phased out as students undertook drafting, reviewing, and rewriting sections on their own. By the end of the course, most students had not only delineated topics, questions, and contexts in which studies would take place but had also drafted written components ready for discussion with chairs and committees.

## PROGRESSIVE SKILLS DEVELOPMENT

The course was organized in progressive steps in which students were guided through increasingly complex and self-directed assignments in order to complete a draft research proposal. Key to doctoral success is the notion of efficacy, or the ability of individuals to perceive that they have the ability to successfully complete difficult tasks (Bandura, 1989). Efficacy is not innate; rather, it is learned through individual histories of attempts, successes, and failures (Pajares & Johnson, 1996; Schunk, 1995). Students from underrepresented populations or those who do not have strong models to emulate or suffer under weaker mentoring and support mechanisms are more likely not to overcome the struggles inherent in doctoral study (Gardner, 2008).

That was the incentive for designing the research course as an iterative process that resembles the domains of instruction listed in the research skill development (RSD) framework (Willison & O'Regan, 2007). The RSD framework represents multiple stages in a research process whereby students are asked to conduct, reflect, synthesize and analyze, and apply and communicate different aspects of research. These processes can be learned along a continuum that ranges from highly instructor-directed to mostly student-directed. The goal, over the course sequence, was for the instructors to provide the right balance of direction and support combined with challenges to students to begin to take control of their own research processes. This is particularly imperative for doctoral students who, in order to successfully complete a dissertation, must reach high levels of autonomy in conducting their research. The RSD framework delineated the major learning activities of the course.

## Embark and Clarify

The course opened with readings and exercises explaining the purpose of the course and doctoral dissertation research in general and providing examples of dissertations similar to what the students would themselves complete. Early weeks focused on helping students refine their topics and research questions. Students compiled past assignments and used elements from those as beginning points. Discussions about selecting topics centered on problems of practice and future employment goals and focused on already existing areas of interest that usually related to community or career.

## Find and Generate

Essential to doctoral work is the ability to find existing information to inform new research. A major emphasis of the literature review portion of the course was to provide students with tools for searching literature, managing sources, and organizing references for later use. Although students were in their second year of doctoral work, several had not explored the full potential of online library search engines. The resource librarian developed an online tutorial, and students were assigned specific tasks to increase familiarity and comfort so they could self-select sources, find information, and collect and save references. Research included a continuing discussion of research methods and a consideration of the appropriateness of different approaches. Students began to generate written sections including topics, main arguments, and problem and purpose statements.

## Evaluate and Reflect

Critical evaluation is essential in scholarship to determine the credibility and applicability of information. Student activities focused on learning to scan, read, and critically analyze existing information for its value to their own research. At the same time, students began to exchange work with other students and to discuss instructor feedback. The processes were designed to enhance students' ability to review peer work, other sources, and, at the same time, more critically reflect on their own.

## Organize and Manage

At this stage, students were collecting and organizing existing literature as well as developing a description and initial justification for their proposed study. Students were asked to combine large amounts of information and synthesize it in a manner providing meaningful interpretation to support hypotheses or themes emerging in their proposals.

## Analyze, Synthesize, and Apply

In general, students were now able to analyze and synthesize material and to identify gaps in the literature. Many students were working independently organizing introductions, literature reviews, and methods sections. Up to now, the activities had been very focused on identifying and describing specifics of the proposed study. Now, students were asked to intellectually step back from their topic and ensure that their study was placed within the broader picture of relevant policy, sociocultural, economic, or even methodological contexts. It was especially important that students be able to articulate the value of the research to real-world situations.

## Communicate Knowledge, Processes, and Awareness

Although written communication was central throughout the course, near the end of the semester, students congregated in person and were asked to outline their progress in an oral presentation to showcase their understanding of broader context, ability to use specialized terminology, and competence at clearly communicating the goals of their proposed research and its connection to regional and/or professional needs. A written proposal draft was also required, written in a scholarly and understandable manner, organized using dissertation guidelines, and formatted in keeping with the publishing conventions of the education field.

## Features and Reflections

As the course developed, it became increasingly clear to the instructors that the original advanced research or proposal-writing course was designed in accordance with the tradition of a dissertation that would be constructed by a lone doctoral candidate working alongside a content expert in his field. In reality, this doctoral program is becoming populated by an increasingly diverse range of educational professionals who deserve support and a level of preparation that will not only allow them to complete a research study but also prepare them to develop a project that aligns with their professional position and involves them in their community. This type of research is hands-on and place-specific, and quite different from a dissertation completed in a vacuum. As a result, the instructors came to realize that the course must offer training for rigorous and meaningful research in students' own communities and among their professional peers. Knowledge acquisition had to come not from didactic teaching but rather through methods that guided students toward growing self-reliance.

## Ongoing Feedback

A major component of the course was constant feedback by both instructors and students. Because feedback was integral to the teaching and learning process, an electronic teaching platform, journal discussions, electronic cloud sharing, Internet-based video sessions (accessible at home or in the office, or even by smartphone), and face-to-face classes were all used to ensure both formal and informal spaces for communication and sharing. Each module, each step in the course, included means to respond and revise materials, ask questions, and comment. It was hoped that the many avenues for formal and informal feedback provided students with ways to measure where they started, how far they had come, what they were doing well, and where they needed to focus attention (Konold, Miller, & Konold, 2004; Murray & Kujundzic, 2005).

Straub (1997) suggests that although ongoing exchange and feedback is time consuming, it is valuable because instructors are able to transition from their conventional role as judge and critic to a more dynamic stance as coach and fellow investigator. It was hoped that transparency and connection would enhance a sense of community, familiarize students with the give and take of scholarly feedback, clarify expectations by giving examples of doctoral research, and increase students' analysis of their own work (Caffarella & Barnett, 2000). The end result seemed to be an increased understanding of what constitutes doctoral-level work and comfort with critical review and revision to reach it, as indicated by these student comments:

(1) "I have learned to accept and use the critiques of my writing."
(2) "I was least prepared for critically reviewing my own work."

## Academic Efficacy and Autonomy

Instruction was designed so that students would continue their efforts and transfer knowledge to their ongoing research. Academic skills developed directly from those course activities that promoted written communication, information gathering, and research development. It was believed that students would be able to transfer those skills to future research and writing and thereby improve their chances of successful dissertation completion (Kruger & Zechmeister, 1999). Additionally, instructors and students noted that other skills interwoven into the learning activities, such as new uses of technology and graphing and presentation skills, were beneficial to students.

To move doctoral students into roles as researchers, instructors sought to provide a learning environment in which doctoral students progressively gained efficacy to perform operations that often frustrate and slow those undertaking the lonely task of writing a dissertation. Many students initially needed frequent contact and explicit instruction, an indication that previous preparation had limited them to prescribed or highly structured inquiry. To get them to appropriate doctoral levels of rigor and competence, instructors undertook a progressive process that increased student-centered responsibility for their work. Ability to complete and self-regulate their own studies, however, demanded not only the acquisition of knowledge but also experience, exposure, and opportunity for trial and error (Little, 2007). Many students wrote that the course provided just those experiences that are meaningful to future success:

(1) "As far as writing the dissertation itself, I needed guidance."
(2) "I learned to look at other dissertations and critique them."
(3) "I thought I was ready, but I was mistaken, I had a sizable amount of literature but no real topic."
(4) "The entire process has been beneficial, development of planning and research tools."
(5) "I had some ideas about what I wanted to do, but did not have a clear plan on how to approach any section at all."

## Socialization

Dissertation research and writing is a powerful learning and socializing episode for a doctoral student. It has traditionally served as an apprenticeship for future scholarly pursuits. Even for nonacademic practitioners, the process acculturates students to the practices and values of the learning community. Vygotsky (1978) theorizes that the human mind uses social interactions, situations, and activities to learn and develop agency, or the motivation to undertake specific actions. In this case, students constructed and developed agency through active participation and engagement in the proposal-writing process, the formal and informal learning they gained as a result of the varied activities, and the ongoing support they experienced for their individual research (Wenger, 1998). As a result, students expressed a greater understanding of what it means to be a doctoral student:

(1) "I have learned that there are greater expectations in the doctoral program that are not present in other graduate/masters programs."
(2) "I had some ideas about what I wanted to do but did not have a clear plan on how to approach any section at all."
(3) "I have grown so much in the many aspects of being a doctoral student—I understand the process of the proposal and have worked very hard to compile a very good rough draft."

## Community and Professional Engagement

Community engagement generally refers to community-university partnerships that involve research and other operations (Beaulieu, 2002). Reforms in educational doctoral programs call for practitioners to experience on-the-ground research involving actual problems of practice (Andrews & Grogan, 2005; Evans, 2007). Scholars who are focused on social justice concerns have also recommended culturally responsive methodologies that are place-conscious and emphasize capacity building for communities, something that leaves the local community stronger as a result of the partnership (Johnson, Thompson, & Naugle, 2009).

Strong professional obligation or a sense of place influenced students' doctoral research, leading them to seek solutions to issues associated with career or community (Budge, 2006; Reiter, Katz, Ferketich, Riffin, & Paskett, 2009). For example, a Japanese-language instructor was interested in how language learning could increase local students' cross-cultural competencies. An outdoor recreation instructor wanted to understand ethical decisions regarding group and individual uses of natural areas. A budget administrator wanted to test the implications of performance-based funding in higher education. A technical college coordinator sought to enhance dual credit offerings for vocational high school students.

Other students indicated an interest in issues of access and equity. Several African American students were concerned about the legacy of racism and the lack of opportunity for persons of color in Appalachia. Others sought to increase career opportunities for women and young people in the region.

## CONCLUSIONS AND COMMENTS

This chapter has presented arguments from the perspective of two instructors of a pilot educational leadership Ed.D. course in research and writing. Preparation of educational leaders has attracted national attention as doctoral programs are redesigned with a focus on practical application and relevant, in-the-schools research. In our case, we agreed with the notion of research in context. Our students were similarly vested in completing dissertation research around issues related to their careers and communities. This seemed particularly meaningful, since (a) many of our students were first-generation college-goers, (b) all lived or worked in economically distressed Central Appalachia or with minority student populations, and (c) as practitioners, their dissertation research would be a natural outgrowth of their professional practice.

Our primary duty was to ensure that students developed the research and writing skills to conduct meaningful research. The research skills development framework was not initially used to construct the class but was subsequently found to follow the sequence of the course. The technique of literature review was taught by having students first understand systematic ways to search, skim, take notes, and archive sources. Students also learned how to narrow scope, synthesize literature, analyze findings, and use literature to inform their own research. Advanced research included a review of major methodologies and associated epistemologies but also careful scaffolding of ways to think about and develop dissertation topics and questions that would lead to meaningful research relating to careers, communities, and problems of practice. Students were asked to integrate writing into each learning module, and they had continual opportunities to discuss, review, and reflect with instructors and peers on their progress.

This six-credit course was originally designed to better integrate research and writing skills development so that students could gain ownership and efficacy over their own dissertation proposals. Student responses to the course varied. Some felt lost and ill at ease, at least initially. Many students commented that the course seemed significantly ratcheted up compared to previous courses. At the same time, many students also reflected that they gained necessary skills. Not only did most students feel they were more equipped to research and write a proposal; they also frequently commented on contextual and informal knowledge gain, such as how to manage time, organize literature, or select committee members.

It has been repeatedly stated that the practitioner Ed.D. should reflect the goals of its students. Whereas traditional doctorates are designed for future academics and researchers, practitioner doctorates are designed to build the capacity of individuals who work in specific real-world contexts. One thing that was apparent from teaching this pilot research class is that research and writing skills are necessary and appropriate content to teach. If our goal is to guide doctoral research so that it makes immediate, positive differences in local educational settings, it is important that the actions of that research are conducted with the highest rigor, so that outcomes from the research are similarly of the highest quality. For those of us who teach in programs with a broad or shifting complexion of students, it may be most important to consider what scholarship, what skills, and what habits of mind our newly minted doctors of practice should have as they take leadership roles in their institutions and communities.

## REFERENCES

Allwright, D. (2003). Exploratory practice: Rethinking practitioner research in language teaching. *Language Teaching Research, 7*(2), 113–141.

Amrein-Beardsley, A., Zambo, D., Moore, D.W., Buss, R., Perry, N.J., Painter, S.R., Carlson, D.L., Foulger, T.S., Olson, K., & Puckett, K.S. (2012). Graduates respond to an innovation educational doctorate program. *Journal of Research on Leadership Education, 7*(1), 98–122. doi: 10.1177/1942775112440630

Andrews, R., & Grogan, M. (2005). Form should follow function: Removing the Ed.D. dissertation from the Ph.D. straight jacket. *UCEA Review, 46*(2), 10–13.

Appalachian Community Fund. (n.d.). About Central Appalachia. Retrieved from http://www.appalachiancommunityfund.org/html/aboutcentralA.html

Archbald, D. (2008). Research versus problem solving for the educational leadership doctoral thesis: Implications for form and function. *Educational Administration Quarterly, 44*(5), 704–739.

Ball, D.L., & Forzani, F.M. (2007). What makes education research "educational"? *Educational Researcher, 36*(9), 529–540.

Bandura, A. (1989). Social cognitive theory. In R.Vasta (Ed.), *Annals of child development. Vol. 6: Six theories of child development* (pp. 1–60). Greenwich, CT: JAI Press.

Beaulieu, J. (2002). *Mapping the assets of your community: A key component for building local capacity.* Retrieved from http://srdc.msstate.edu/publications/227/227_asset_maping.pdf

Bourner, T., Bowden, R., & Laing, S. (2000) Professional doctorates: The development of researching professionals. In T. Bourner, T. Katz, & D. Watson (Eds.), *New directions in professional education.* Maidenhead, BRK, UK: Open University Press.

Budge, K. (2006, December). Rural leaders, rural places: Problem, privilege, and possibility. *Journal of Research in Rural Education, 21*(13). Retrieved from http:/jrre.psu.edu/articles/21-13.pdf

Burns, A. (2005). Action research: An evolving paradigm? *Language Teaching, 38*(2), 57–74.

Caffarella, R.S., & Barnett, B.G. (2000). Teaching doctoral students to become scholarly writers: The importance of giving and receiving critiques. *Studies in Higher Education, 25*(1), 39–52.

Carnegie Project on the Education Doctorate. (2010). *Working principles for the professional practice doctorate in education.* College Park, MD: CPED.

Cohen, L., Manion, L., & Morrison, K. (2007). *Research methods in education* (6th ed.). New York: Routledge.

Deem, R., & Brehony, K.J. (2000). Doctoral students' access to research cultures—are some more unequal than others? *Studies in Higher Education, 25*(2), 149–165.

Eller, R.D. (2008). *Uneven ground: Appalachia since 1945.* Lexington: University Press of Kentucky.

ESRC. (2014). *Economic and social research council, United Kingdom.* Retrieved from www.esrc.ac.uk

Evans, R. (2007). Comments on Shulman, Golde, Bueschel, and Garabedian: Existing practices is not the template. *Educational Researcher, 36*(6), 553–559. doi:10.3102/0013189X07313149

Gardner, S.K. (2008, March). Fitting the mold of graduate school: A qualitative study of socializing in doctoral education. *Innovation in Higher Education, 33*, 125–138. doi: 10.1007/s10755-008-9068-x

Golde, C.M. (2006). Signature pedagogies in doctoral education: Are they adaptable for the preparation of educational researchers? *Educational Researcher, 36*(6), 344–351. doi: 10.3102.0013189X07308301

Grogan, M., Donaldson, J., & Simmons, J. M. (2007). Disrupting the status quo: The action research dissertation as a transformative strategy. In C.A. Mullen, T. Creighton, F.L. Dembowski, & S. Harris (Eds.), *The handbook of doctoral programs in educational leadership: Issues and challenges* (pp. 76–89). Houston, TX: NCPEA Press.

Hendricks, M., & Quinn, L. (2000). Teaching referencing as an introduction to epistemological empowerment. *Teaching in Higher Education, 5*, 447–457.

Johnson, J., Thompson, A., & Naugle, K. (2009). Place-conscious capacity-building: A systemic model for the revitalization and renewal of rural schools and communities through university-based regional stewardship. *Rural Society, 19*(2), 178–188.

Konold, H.E., Miller, S.P., & Konold, K.B. (2004). Using teacher feedback to enhance student learning. *Teaching Exceptional Children, 36*(6), 64–69.

Kruger, D., & Zechmeister, E. (1999, August). *A skills-experience inventory for undergraduate psychology majors.* Poster session presented at the annual meeting of the American Psychological Association, Boston.

Lester, S. (2004). Conceptualizing the practitioner doctorate. *Studies in Higher Education, 29*(5), 1–11.

Levine, A. (2005). *Educating school leaders.* Washington, DC: The Education Schools Project. Retrieved from www.edschools.org.

Lillis, T., & Turner, J. (2001) Student writing in higher education: Contemporary confusion, traditional concerns. *Teaching in Higher Education, 6*(1), 57–68.

Little, D. (2007). Language learner autonomy: Some fundamental considerations revisited. *Innovation in Language Learning and Teaching, 1*(1), 14–29.

McLeod, J. (1999). *Practitioner research in counselling.* London: Sage.

Murphy, J., & Vriesenga, M. (2005). Developing professionally anchored dissertations: Lessons from innovative programs. *School Leadership Review, 1*(1), 33–57.

Murray, M., & Kujundzic, N. (2005). *Critical reflection: A textbook for critical thinking.* Québec, Canada: McGill-Queen's University Press.

Olson, K., & Clark, C.M. (2009). A signature pedagogy in doctoral education: The leader-scholar community. *Educational Researcher, 38*(3), 216–221. doi:10.3102/0013189X09334207

Pajares, F., & Johnson, M.J. (1996). Self-efficacy beliefs in the writing of high school students: A path analysis. *Psychology in the Schools, 33*, 163–175.

Perry, J.A. (2014, Winter). The CPED argument: A counter-response. *UCEA Review, 55*(1), 22–24.

Perry, J.A., & Imig, D.G. (2008, November/December). A stewardship of practice in education. *Change*, 42–48.

Reiter, D.L., Katz, M.L., Ferketich, A.K., Riffin, M.T., & Paskett, E.D. (2009, Summer). Appalachian self-identity among women in Ohio Appalachia. *Journal of Rural Community Psychology*, *12*(1). Retrieved from http://www.marshall.edu/jrcp/ve12%20n1/reiter%20jrcp.pdf

Schön, D.A. (1987). *Educating the reflective practitioner*. San Francisco, CA: Jossey-Bass.

Schunk, D.H. (1995). Self-efficacy and education and instruction. In J.E. Maddux (Ed.), *Self-efficacy, adaptation, and adjustment: Theory, research, and applications* (pp. 281–303). New York: Plenum.

Shulman, L.S. (2005). Signature pedagogies in the professions. *Daedalus*, *134*(3), 52–59. doi:10.1162/0011526054622015

Shulman, L.S., Golde, C.M., Bueschel, A.C., & Garabedian, K.J. (2006). Reclaiming education's doctorates: A critique and proposal. *Educational Researcher*, *35*(3), 25–32. doi:10.3102/0013189X035003025

Straub, R. (1997). Students' reactions to teacher comments: An exploratory study. *Research in the Teaching of English*, *31*, 91–119.

Stringer, E.T. (2007). *Action research* (3rd ed.). Thousand Oaks, CA: Sage.

Torrance, M., & Thomas, G. (1994). The development of writing skills in doctoral research students. In R.G. Burgess (Ed.), *Postgraduate education and training in the social sciences* (pp. 100–120). London: Jessica Kingsley Publishers.

Vygotsky, L.S. (1978). *Mind in society: The development of higher psychological processes*. Cambridge, MA: Harvard University Press.

Walker, G.E., Golde, C.M., Jones, L., Bueschel, A.C., & Hutchings, P. (2008). *The formation of scholars: Rethinking doctoral education for the twenty-first century*. San Francisco, CA: Jossey-Bass.

Wei, Y. (2011, June). *Understanding students' learner autonomy through practitioner research*. Unpublished doctoral thesis, University of Warwick, UK. Retrieved from http://wrap.warwick.ac.uk/38507/1/WRAP_THESIS_Wei_2011.pdf

Wellington, J., & Sikes, P. (2006). A doctorate in a tight compartment: Why do students choose a professional practice doctorate and what impact does it have on their personal and professional lives? *Studies in Higher Education*, *3*(6), 723–734.

Wenger, E. (1998). *Learning in communities of practice*. Cambridge: Cambridge University Press.

Wenger, E., McDermott, R., & Snyder, W.M. (2002). *Cultivating communities of practice*. Boston, MA: Harvard Business School Press.

Wergin, J. (2011). Rebooting the Ed.D. *Harvard Educational Review*, *81*(1), 119–139.

Willis, J., Inman, D., & Valenti, R. (2010). *Completing a professional practice dissertation*. Charlotte, NC: Information Age.

Willison, J., & O'Regan, K. (2007, December). Commonly known, commonly not known, totally unknown: A framework for students becoming researchers. *Higher Education Research and Development*, *26*(4), 393–409.

Young, M.D. (2014, Winter). From the director: Start with doctoral degree outcomes. *UCEA Review*. Retrieved from www.ucea.org

Zambo, D. (2011). Action research as signature pedagogy in an education doctorate program: The reality and hope. *Innovation in Higher Education*, *36*, 261–271. doi:10.1007/s10755-010-9171-7

# Stepping Up

## Tribal College Leadership and the Ed.D. Program

*Sweeney Windchief*

## INTRODUCTION

Leadership in Tribal Colleges and Universities (TCUs) is a unique endeavor. These institutions work within contexts that legitimize formal education but are separate from mainstream institutions in that they have different stakeholders, unique missions, and intensified fiscal challenges. The literature identifies the need for highly specialized and practical leaders, something that could be addressed by a well-tailored Ed.D. The need for strong, sustained, visionary leadership is grounded in the individual communities that TCUs serve and is fundamental to their success (Stein & Eagleeye, 1993). Comprehensively, this dictates a complex role for TCU leaders who are best served by an Ed.D. degree. A unique cultural context is to be considered when seeking a TCU leader. As stated by Moltz, "Finding a new college president is never easy, but it is especially difficult for a tribal college when its board strongly prefers to tap someone who is not only Native American but also a member of its affiliated tribe" (Moltz, 2010, para. 2).

This statement raises two critical questions. First, where will future TCU leaders come from? Second, what will potential TCU leaders need to know in order to thrive for upcoming generations? The purpose of this chapter is to address these questions. Throughout the discussion, the author uses American Indian, Native American Indian, Indian, and Indigenous people to refer to populations whose relatives have lived in North America for millennia, although there are debates in the larger Indian community about identity claims (Jaimes, 1992;

cited in Brayboy & Deyhle, 2000). When considering "Issues of Access, Diversity, Social Justice, and Community Leadership," American Indians (AI) are the least represented in higher education of any racial/ethnic category (Shotton, Lowe, & Waterman, 2013). Given the history of AIs and education, this chapter promotes a carefully constructed Ed.D. program.

## A HISTORY OF TRIBAL COLLEGES
## AND UNIVERSITIES (TCUS)

Diné College, founded as Navajo Community College in 1968, was the first tribal college established by the Navajo Nation to provide an education based on a cultural foundation. Together, the early TCUs founded the American Indian Higher Education Consortium (AIHEC) in 1972 to establish common standards that continue to support the development of new TCUs. By 2014, the number of accredited TCUs serving American Indian communities had grown to 37 (see Figure 26.1).

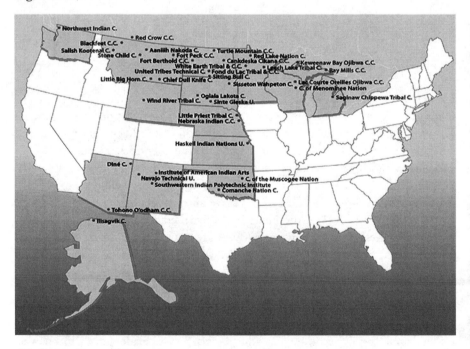

Figure 26.1. Accredited tribal colleges and universities (TCUs) in 2014.

As a result of federal law, TCUs receive some funding through the U.S. government. (U.S. Congress, 1978). Additional funding comes from the American Indian

College Fund (AICF), whose goal is to support Native students who choose to pursue a college education. In order for institutions to qualify as TCUs, they must meet three criteria: (1) they must be tribally chartered; (2) a majority of their board members must be American Indians; and (3) the majority of students must be members of federally recognized tribes. In 1994, Congress assigned land-grant status to TCUs (Phillips, 2003), which enables them to apply for equity funding, provides access to research and extension programs, and makes them eligible for other infrastructure grants and loans offered by federal agencies. This is important because only 5% of TCU students (at most) can afford to attend college without financial assistance. As a result, and to keep higher education accessible in tribal communities, TCUs strive to keep tuition costs affordable for their students. The number of students enrolled in TCUs has more than doubled in the past 30 years, and the number of degrees those students have earned has doubled in the last 25 years (American Indian College Fund, n.d.).

## TRIBAL COLLEGE LEADERSHIP: A UNIQUE ENDEAVOR

The academic literature regarding TCUs repeatedly identifies the need for highly proficient, specialized, and realistic leaders. Strong, sustained, visionary leadership that is well grounded in individual communities is crucial for TCUs to succeed in their intended role as very distinctive and culturally grounded institutions (Pavel, Inglebret, & Banks, 2001). The importance of community-held practices such as multigenerational involvement, the regeneration of traditional languages, traditional epistemologies, and reciprocal and participatory research are not lost in the modern era, and they are the very programs that make tribal colleges unique (Barnhardt, 1991). This is supported by Schuyler Houser, who states:

> Tribal colleges have faced an exceptionally tough set of managerial issues, issues which lie at the heart of the processes of economic and community development. Each tribe which has founded a college has its own ways of getting business done, its own styles and methods of management. (Houser, 1991, p. 13)

TCUs have unique students who respond to epistemological stances that are community centered rather than competitive. TCUs are considerate of family structure and relationships and are interested in maintaining cultural integrity specific to the American Indian communities that they serve. Many activities are consistent with traditional American Indian calendars rather than typical academic calendars, which can be problematic when creating articulation agreements with non-TCU institutions (Finley, 1997). Nonetheless, many TCUs establish relationships with larger 4-year and doctoral-granting institutions through articulation agreements, including dual admissions agreements that, for all intents and purposes, are designed to facilitate the transfer of a variable percentage of TCU students to partner institutions.

The literature supports the idea that the successful development of TCU leaders will include the expansion of AI spiritual and community values and of collective responsibility (McLeod, 2002). Historically, the leaders of these institutions were risk takers who travelled across the boundaries between tribal communities and Euro-American dominant culture in their positions of leadership (Phillips, 2005). McLeod's suggestions offer new insights into bicultural community knowledge and function (2002). For example, he describes TCU leaders as having a holistic interconnectedness with a wide variety of Euro-American and tribal issues. In other words, TCU presidents and their leadership teams are servant-leaders who are apt to lead by sharing responsibility with the community as well as with faculty and staff and in ways that more closely align with traditional AI values than the repressive postcolonial structure of predominantly White institutions (PWIs).

Pragmatically speaking, Stein and Eagleeye (1993) recognized many of these virtues of TCU leadership and, in creating future tribal leaders, included leadership skills such as "political savvy" (p. 33) that could potentially be developed through experiences known in Washington, D.C., as lobbying skills. They go on to explain that sustainable peer networking is often facilitated through mentorship that emphasizes tribal culture, succession planning, the ability to work within tight budgets, and other considerations as necessary for TCU leadership. Furthermore, the literature helps developing TCU leaders to consider themes of bicultural accountability, as defined by Whitinui and Macfarlane (2012), which in this case includes the ability to inspire community connectedness, political confidence, and fiscal ingenuity. Recent media focus has centered on fundraising events, grant awards, the impact of federal cuts, the ability to operate on already-stretched budgets, and equitable access to funding (see, for example, Lee, 2013; KUMV.com, 2013; *Char-Koosta News*, 2013; and *Devils Lake Journal*, 2013), demonstrating that the multiple themes that arise in TCU professional jurisdictions could be addressed effectively in Ed.D programs.

## AN ED.D. IN TRIBAL COLLEGE AND UNIVERSITY ADMINISTRATION

Empirical evidence shows that the Ed.D. and the Ph.D. are similar in some ways and dissimilar in others. Andersen's 1983 study found that the similarities include (1) the amount of work required beyond a bachelor's degree, (2) residency requirements, (3) the time allowed for preparation and defense of the dissertation, (4) the maximum time permissible for completion of the degree, and (5) a prohibition against correspondence course work. On the other hand, the majority of Ph.D.

programs required coursework outside the field of education to include an emphasis on research, while Ed.D. programs imposed such a requirement less often. Regarding the Ed.D., there were also substantial differences in terms of solving a practical problem through a capstone project as a substitute for a fundamental research study.

Moving beyond graduate degree comparisons, Osguthorpe and Wong (1993) offer compelling evidence delineating the Ed.D. as a professional degree:

> [P]rofessions are not academic disciplines, but rather fields that draw on a variety of disciplines to prepare their degree recipients for the profession. Thus research in the professions should focus on application rather than theory. And because the Ph.D. has its roots in theoretical research, the Ed.D. is a more appropriate designation for education graduates. (p. 56)

This position maintains that future TCU leaders would be better served by an Ed.D. that teaches pragmatic competencies in alignment with TCU needs than by a Ph.D. that is focused on research. Conceptually, just as a Ph.D. can be tailored to use specific theories, methods, and hermeneutics in the construction of a dissertation, an Ed.D. could be constructed using targeted skill development to facilitate a program that would best benefit future TCU leadership.

Difficulties related to TCU leadership development and succession are apparent in the turnover of leadership and in the financial concerns and are complicated by the diversity of managerial methods that are unique to different American Indian and Alaska Native communities. By combining the literature and the author's own research, we arrive at a pragmatic solution for the efficacious development of TCU leadership. Responses to the question "What will potential TCU leaders need to know in order to thrive in the next 35 years and beyond?" must be recognized as crucial in establishing a path for TCU success. Though there are leadership programs tailored to the needs of American Indians that include community and K–12 leadership, at the time of this writing, there was no higher education program or credential in the country that addresses the specific needs of TCU leaders outside of terminal grants awarded by the U.S. Department of Education's Fund for the Improvement of Postsecondary Education. The creation of a program that is both sustainable and reflective of community needs depends upon the direction of current and past TCU leaders and stakeholders.

The intent of this chapter is to explore pragmatic Ed.D. program development with a specific focus on TCU leadership, including TCU stakeholder consensus. If, indeed, the previously mentioned leadership qualities are necessary, TCU stakeholders and leaders are needed to develop appropriate Ed.D. coursework and academic programming. The following inquiry is presented to inform scholar-practitioners about program development that empowers students to step into TCU leadership positions with a clear understanding of their multiple roles and the various community/educational contexts.

## Research Method and Design

The methodologies chosen for a study investigating TCU leadership include a combination of community-based participatory research (CBPR) protocols (Burhansstipanov & Schumacher, 2005) and Indigenous research methodologies (IRMs) (Wilson, 2001). These methods were chosen specifically because, in combination, (1) they allow for research to be done in a way that protects Indigenous cultural integrity; (2) they incorporate researchers, participants, and beneficiaries who are Indigenous people; and (3) these approaches recognize and embody tribal sovereignty and tribal self-identification. This is particularly important given the population whose lives contribute to and potentially benefit from this chapter.

## Community-Based Participatory Research

Community-based participatory research (CBPR) presents numerous methods for successfully conducting research. This approach emphasizes community involvement in each step of the research process and allows for community members to become part of the research team, thus highlighting respect and cultural awareness, and is responsive to the communities being researched. Essentially, CBPR puts into place an action plan and shares results at every level, giving ownership back to the community. The literature states that CBPR gives the opportunity for communities to "generate their own knowledge" (St. Denis, 1992, p. 52). A critical reflection on the current CBPR literature reveals an assumption of success with a research model and conceivably lacks realistic approaches in building trust and developing relationships within the targeted communities. Because most of the literature reviewed uses deficit-model thinking and assumes a non–Native researcher, this research includes aspects of Indigenous methodologies in research.

## Indigenous Research Methodologies

In the literature on Indigenous methodologies, several components support Indigenous community knowledge. These methodologies are mindful of knowledge transmission within the context of tribal communities and maintain that cultural protocol is paramount and contextually dependent. This approach suggests that Indigenous researchers need to consider where their own values and belief systems intersect with the research and are respectful of involving traditional Indigenous processes in the planning, gathering of data, and analysis. It is also relationship centered. "They came. They saw. They named. They claimed" (Smith, 1999, p. 80) is the antithesis of Indigenous research methodologies. According to Bowechop and Erikson (2005), "non-native colleagues may be successfully involved in these strategic interventions by allowing tribes to determine the research objectives and ensuring a truly collaborative nature throughout the research process and structure" (p. 271).

Incongruences between CBPR and IRM were harder to uncover than congruencies. However, a focus on empirical measurement, the assumption of a non-Native researcher, and less community involvement was characteristic in CBPR. This literature served to establish the foundation for the inquiry used in this chapter.

## Procedure

The individuals who were examined in this inquiry were stakeholders at TCUs who attended the American Indian Higher Education Consortium (AIHEC) national conference in 2003. Respondents included TCU presidents and vice presidents, administrators, students, and faculty. A structured dialogue process was implemented based on "The Wisdom of the Peoples Forum" (Christakis & Bausch, 2006, pp. 111–114), and procedures were selected in a way that aligned with the AIHEC conference and were explained to the respondents. The process included three fundamental rules: (1) in order to implement a broad range of perspectives, the process was dependent upon group participation; (2) The structure implemented in the process was necessary to avoid cognitive overload; and (3) the framework of the process centered on the common goal of "developing future TCU leaders."

After the procedures for the structured dialogue were established, the participants were asked this triggering question: "Regarding future TCU leaders: What will they need to know to be successful?" Participants responded by listing skills and competencies that they viewed as necessary for TCU leaders. The research team captured and immediately posted responses in front of the room for all participants to examine. If responses were unclear, participants were prompted to clarify them. This process was repeated until the participants offered no more contributions.

The stakeholders were given the opportunity to individually mark the four most important contributions made. As a result of this activity, the researchers captured responses and were able to establish consensus about which of these were most valued in terms of TCU leader preparation. In the interest of research integrity, the participants were informed of the outcomes and asked if the responses were indeed the most essential leadership skills and traits. The results were essential in the development of an Ed.D. program that addresses the needs of TCU stakeholders.

## RESULTS

The results of the structured dialogue process were supportive of the literature and of how TCUs are experienced by the stakeholders themselves. The responses offered are shown here and numbered only for ease of reference, not to suggest hierarchy.

1. TCU leaders need to make data-driven decisions based on their own institutional research data.
2. TCU faculty need to be accessible to tribal communities.
3. TCU leaders need to create more collaborations that reach beyond the local college to include the community and other institutions of higher learning.
4. Relationships need to be improved between the Tribes and the TCUs.
5. Leaders need to be flexible to change, think outside of the box, and try new things.
6. TCU leaders need to be concerned with Native nation building.
7. Leaders should understand that with great authority comes great responsibility.
8. Leaders need to implement "place-based" curriculum and educational projects.
9. Leaders should exhibit emotional intelligence.
10. Leaders should understand community trends and social issues.
11. Leaders need to be cognizant of community mental health issues.
12. Leaders need to develop an awareness of the contemporary issues impacting student matriculation.
13. Leaders must have an awareness of current and future funding guidelines and practices.
14. TCU leaders need to increase the number of American Indian faculty members teaching at their institutions.
15. Leaders need to develop programs that support student resilience in transferring to non-tribal institutions.
16. Leaders must know who they are in a cultural context within the local Indigenous community as well as outside that community.
17. TCU leaders must develop an awareness of global, federal, state, and local politics.
18. It is key for TCU leaders to know the college personnel.
19. TCU leaders need to be able to reform the institution's curriculum to reflect pertinent skills needed in both the local community and outside.
20. TCUs need to develop homegrown leaders [who are] conscious of community needs.

21. TCU leaders need to utilize community resources, including the elders and the young people.

22. TCU leaders should be transparent regarding the college with the community.

The overall themes that emerged with the most support included *community collaboration*, *native nation building*, *cultural connection*, and *student support* (see Figure 26.2).

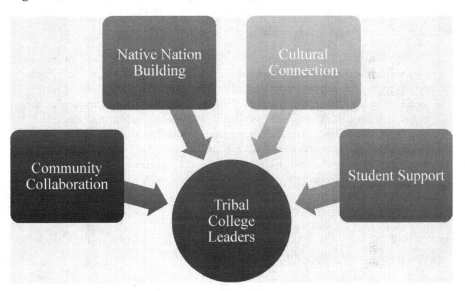

Figure 26.2. Tribal college leader responsibilities.

## RECOMMENDATIONS

In the construction of a TCU leadership development program, these themes are to be used to encourage the development of an Ed.D. program that is responsive to TCU stakeholder needs. The information below addresses these concerns and is offered to center Indigenous communities in TCU leadership development.

### Community Collaboration and Cultural Connection

Cultural connection in the context of TCUs entails not only accommodating community-held practices but also contributing and thereby addressing cultural disparities that are too often overlooked in mainstream, or non-Indian, society. This includes participation in community cultural events by providing space where traditional ceremonies can take place. Faculty, staff, and students are often members of traditional societies that participate in ceremonies and should utilize institutional resources and space for ceremonial practices if they are indeed holding true to the mission of AIHEC institutions. While this may seem a breach of ethical practice at non-Native institutions, spiritual philosophies and beliefs are entrenched in all facets of Indian life (Benally, 1992; Van Hamme, 1996) to include educational institutions. Though pertaining to an Akwesasne, K–12 context, cultural integrity in educational administration is addressed by Agbo (2001) in a way that is useful for TCU leaders:

> Among other things that we documented, we noted that administrators should know and understand the culture of the community and be sensitive to the wishes, hopes, and fears of the Mohawk community members. They should provide continual cultural orientations in locations that have cultural significance for new and experienced teachers (cultural orientation to continue throughout the year) and during these orientations teachers should be exposed to sacred and significant locations in the community. They should respect Mohawk ceremonies and lead the school—students and staff—to respect the needs for attending the ceremonies and administrators should encourage students to attend community ceremonies. They should understand and appreciate the Mohawk worldview of time, space, and patience and also understand and espouse Mohawk values of group harmony, respect for nature, respect for the elderly, and sharing. (p. 36)

This quote supports the need for TCU leaders to implement culturally attuned leadership and place-based curriculum.

Academic literature shows that place-based curriculum helps students with indigenous knowledge and ways of knowing to discover the relationship of traditional knowledge to modern sciences and social studies (Lipka & Mohatt, 1998; Sorensen, 2002). TCUs seem to be a natural fit for the implementation of these phenomena, a process which is wholly dependent upon the support of Indigenous people. As noted in Pewewardy and Hammer (2003), budding TCU leaders must learn to combine Indigenous knowledge in their roles as professionals to lead institutions that are beneficial to indigenous communities. Riggs (2005) makes this connection when talking about field-based education and Indigenous knowledge in geoscience by stating: "One of the most powerful teaching strategies in an indigenous context is the use of the local field environment, especially on lands that have been occupied and managed by indigenous people for generations" (p. 311). This quote provides a cultural basis for TCU leaders to employ local people and use natural resources to work toward the theme of Native nation building.

Native nation building includes *economic development, the integration of traditional tribal culture and custom*, and *contemporary leadership*. Tribal sovereignty and self-direction are to be implemented if leaders are indeed concerned with Native nation building. As supported by Jorgensen (2007), this includes the autonomy to employ tribal community in its institutions, making use of community principles and priorities. The concept of Native nation building includes administrators being simultaneously conscious of *cultural integrity* and *professional integrity*. Consequently, an Ed.D program focused on TCU leaders would concentrate on institutional accreditation, albeit in a way that is culturally congruent. This is no easy task, given that TCUs are evaluated by criteria originating in the dominant society. Regional accreditation agencies, for instance, might expect a college to appear, structurally and organizationally, like their impression of a college, whether it is located in a major urban area or on a rural reservation (Houser, 1991). Luckily, AIHEC is supportive and has identified the goal that TCUs attain full accreditation from their respective sanctioning organizations. According to Stein (1999), by 1998, 27 of the 31 TCUs had gained accreditation. Further, he noted that the four that had not gained accreditation were very close to achieving that goal.

## Fiscal Matters

TCUs are more reliant on the government to provide resources than their non-Native counterparts. Therefore, TCU leaders will carry this burden and responsibility as their predecessors have done. Part of the professional skillset to be taught as part of an Ed.D. for TCU leaders includes developing an understanding of federal policies and methods of lobbying congressional offices. Presentations from federal agencies and members of Congress would be beneficial, and students should take part in meetings with their respective congressional representatives in order to influence federal decisions that impact TCUs and to assure their continued operation (Stein & Eagleeye, 1993).

Essential to TCUs and their success is *substantive grant procurement*. In the past, some TCUs were able to establish agreements with existing state institutions. This connection with 4-year, bachelor's degree-granting institutions for some TCUs has been historically necessary, because tribal colleges as 2-year schools could not qualify on their own for federal research grants, which are limited to 4-year colleges. Nonetheless, as land-grant institutions, collaborative grants can be complicated, and TCU leaders will better serve their institutions if they understand this process. Nichols and Kayongo-Male (2003) had a respondent describe what collaborations can look like between TCUs and larger 4-year institutions.

I'll tell you a story. I was working with [a state university] on a…grant. They wanted to meet and talk about it. So we got together and they had the whole thing written. And do you know how much out of $200,000 the tribal college was getting? $10,000 a year. I said, "Why did you ask us here?" "Why did you waste our time?" I asked them if any of them would be willing to work for $10,000 a year. Dead silence. And about then, they brought in lunch and I'm thinking, "Oh no, here I am eating their food and I've just laid down the law." But after lunch they said, "Would you like to rewrite the grant?" I said, "Absolutely—for 1/3 of the funding." So you sort of learn. You learn what works. You learn how to work together. (p. 16)

As such, TCU leaders would benefit from a class that teaches the ins and outs of grant applications and procurement, and that can be more readily accepted as part of an Ed.D. program. as opposed to a research-based Ph.D. program.

## Student Resiliency

As indicated in the structured dialogue, student resiliency is of great concern to TCU stakeholders. Students attending TCUs have special needs that include childcare, transportation, financing, and emotional and academic support. Several TCUs have answered these needs by offering services through grants and student support programs (Stein, 1992; cited in Krumm, 1995). These unique student needs require TCU leaders to understand and develop fiscal competencies as they relate to TCU administration.

In order to support students, funding opportunities for TCUs have also expanded, with support from organizations such as the U.S. Department of Agriculture, the Tribal Colleges Endowment Fund, Tribal College Education Equity Grants, the Tribal College Research Grants Program, as well as through private foundation grants. This support has helped overcome a host of obstacles, including a chronic lack of funding, dilapidated facilities, and the low income and poor academic preparation of many TCU students.

According to Cunningham and Parker (1998), TCUs lack the ability to raise local revenues to support higher education institutions. The status of the reservations as federal trust territory prohibits levying property taxes, which are a revenue source for most community colleges. TCUs receive little or no funding from state governments, and states are not required to fund TCUs because most are located on Indian land. Due in large part to the absence of direct state or local support, TCUs receive approximately two thirds the amount of government funding per full-time equivalent student that is received by public community colleges.

## Bicultural Accountability and Interconnectivity

Learning and employing *bicultural accountability and interconnectivity* can be defined as incorporating elements of both customary and contemporary American Indian principles into education. These concepts confirm the importance of individual culture in learning activities (LeBrasseur & Freark, 1982). Because an Indigenous person may contribute to a traditional ceremony one day and attend classes in a graduate program the next, scholars who advocate for Indigenous context recommend that Indian students experience real-world examples of the complex reality that represents American Indian culture (Butterfield, 1983). American Indian Ed.D. learning must include American Indians as contemporary peoples *linking traditional values with successful involvement in contemporary space* (Van Hamme, 1996), including learning the real-world skills of *grant procurement, successful lobbying, Native nation-building, and cultural congruence* within a specific community context. Each native community is different. The successful leader will not humor stereotypes but will understand that particular needs will be delineated by the community itself and subsequently served by the TCU.

## TCU Leader Mentorship

Mentoring is a process that tends to the refinement of students who are working toward becoming authorities in a professional atmosphere. Mentoring serves to shape students' leadership stance, helps by introducing them to professional networks, and supports them in avoiding professional pitfalls that could derail their careers. Thus, successful mentoring is an integral part of leadership development and is an essential part of a successful Ed.D. program. In contrast to conventional doctoral programs wherein the faculty serve as the primary mentors, an Ed.D. program in TCU leadership would do well to employ a current TCU leader to serve as a primary mentor, with secondary mentoring responsibilities being assumed by faculty members. The primary mentor could (1) provide the impetus for a student to matriculate into the program, (2) become a member of the student committee facilitating professional skill development, and (3) potentially create a connection between a specific TCU and the doctoral degree-granting university.

It is the author's supposition that an Ed.D. program in TCU leadership could be developed to serve tribal communities most successfully by incorporating community-specific ways of being, learning, teaching, and doing. The development of pragmatic skills related to the procurement of financial resources is necessary to support programs that reflect community needs. Finally, in an effort to best serve these institutions and to meet the needs of both the community and the accreditation agencies, future TCU leaders will need to learn bicultural accountability and interconnectivity.

## REFERENCES

Agbo, S. (2001). Enhancing success in American Indian students: Participatory research at Akwesasne as part of the development of a culturally relevant curriculum. *Journal of American Indian Education, 40*(1), 31–56.

American Indian College Fund (ACIF). (n.d.). *TCU timeline.* Denver, CO: ACIF. Retrieved from http://www.collegefund.org/content/tcu_timeline

Andersen, D.G. (1983). Differentiation of the Ed.D. and Ph.D. in education. *Journal of Teacher Education, 34*(3), 55–58.

Barnhardt, R. (1991). Higher education in the Fourth World: Indigenous people take control. *Canadian Journal of Native Education, 18*(2), 199–231.

Benally, H.J. (1992). Spiritual knowledge for a secular society. *Tribal College, 3,* 19–22.

Bowechop, J., & Erikson, P.P. (2005). Forging indigenous methodologies on Cape Flattery: The Makah Museum as a center of collaborative research. *American Indian Quarterly, 29*(1), 263–273, 353–354.

Brayboy, B.M., & Deyhle, D. (2000). Insider-outsider: Researchers in American Indian communities. *Theory into Practice, 39*(3), 163–169.

Burhansstipanov, L., & Schumacher, S.C.S.A. (2005). Lessons learned from community-based participatory research in Indian country. *Cancer Control: Journal of the Moffitt Cancer Center, 12*(supp. 2), 70.

Butterfield, R.A. (1983). The development and use of culturally appropriate curriculum for American Indian students. *Peabody Journal of Education, 61,* 49–66.

*Char-Koosta News.* (2013, September 5). Confederated Salish and Kootenai tribes appeal to U.S. Congressman Steve Daines. Retrieved from http://www.charkoosta.com/2013/2013_09_05/CSKT_meets_with_Steve_Daines.html

Christakis, A.N., & Bausch, K.C. (2006). *How people harness their collective wisdom and power to construct the future in co-laboratories of democracy.* Greenwich, CT: Information Age.

Cunningham, A.F., & Parker, C. (1998). Tribal colleges as community institutions and resources. *New Directions for Higher Education, 102,* 45–56.

*Devils Lake Journal.* (2013, September 3). ND tribal colleges use grants to train workers. Retrieved from http://www.devilslakejournal.com/article/20130903/NEWS/130909866/1001/NEWS?rssfeed=true

Finley, V. (1997). Designing a cultural leadership program. *Tribal College, 9*(2), 19–22.

Houser, S. (1991). Building institutions across cultural boundaries: Indian colleges use traditional management skills to plan for the future. *Tribal College, 2,* 11–17.

Lee, T.H.. (2013, September 9). Feds consider axing Pell Grants: Tribal college students lose most. *Indian Country Today Media Network.*

Jaimes, M.A. (Ed.). (1992). *The state of Native America: Genocide, colonization, and resistance.* Boston, MA: South End Press.

Jorgensen, M. (Ed.). (2007). *Rebuilding native nations: Strategies for governance and development.* Tucson: University of Arizona Press.

Krumm, B.L. (1995). *Tribal colleges: A study of development, mission, and leadership.* ERIC Document Reproduction Service No. ED 404 064.

KUMV.com. (2013). *Conference focuses on Native American students.* Williston, ND: KUMV.com.

LeBrasseur, M.M., & Freark, E.S. (1982). Touch a child–they are my people: Ways to teach American Indian children. *Journal of American Indian Education, 21,* 6–12.

Lipka, J., & Mohatt, G.V. (1998). *Transforming the culture of schools: Yup'ik Eskimo examples.* Mahwah, NJ: Lawrence Erlbaum.

McLeod, M. (2002). Keeping the circle strong: Learning about Native American leadership. *Tribal College Journal, 13*(4), 10–13.

Moltz, D. (2010, March 25). Transition at a tribal college. *Inside Higher Ed.* Retrieved from https://www.insidehighered.com/news/2010/03/25/tribal

Nichols, T.J., & Kayongo-Male, D. (2003). The dynamics of tribal college-state university collaboration. *Journal of American Indian Education, 42*(3), 1–24.

Osguthorpe, R.T., & Wong, M.J. (1993). The Ph.D. versus the Ed.D.: Time for a decision. *Innovative Higher Education, 18*(1), 47–63.

Pavel, D.M., Inglebret, E., & Banks, S.R. (2001). Tribal colleges and universities in an era of dynamic development. *Peabody Journal of Education, 76*(1), 50–72.

Pewewardy, C., & Hammer, P.C. (2003). Culturally responsive teaching for American Indian students. *ERIC Digest.* Clearinghouse on Rural Education and Small Schools (EDO-RC-03–10), Charleston, WV.

Phillips, J.L. (2003). A tribal college land grant perspective: Changing the conversation. *Journal of American Indian Education, 42*(1), 22–35.

Phillips, J.L. (2005). Developing leaders for the 21st century. *Tribal College Journal of American Indian Higher Education, 17*(2), 28–29.

Riggs, E.M. (2005). Field-based education and indigenous knowledge: Essential components of geoscience education for Native American communities. *Science Education, 89*(2), 296–313.

Shotton, H.J., Lowe, S.C., & Waterman, S.J. (2013). *Beyond the asterisk: Understanding Native students in higher education.* Sterling, VA: Stylus.

Smith, L. T. (1999). *Decolonizing methodologies: Research and indigenous peoples.* Zed Books.

Sorensen, B. (2002). The community-based education model: Bringing validity to education and careers. *Winds of Change, 17*(4), 60–62.

St. Denis, V. (1992). Community-based participatory research: Aspects of the concept relevant for practice. *Native Studies Review, 8*(2), 52–74.

Stein, W. (1999). Tribal colleges: 1968–1998. In K. Swisher & J. Tippeconnic (Eds.), *Next steps: Research and practice to advance Indian education* (pp. 258–269). Charleston, WV: Clearinghouse on Rural Education and Small Schools.

Stein, W., & Eagleeye, D. (1993). Learned leadership: Preparing the next generation of tribal college administrators. *Tribal College, 5*(2), 33–36.

U.S. Congress. House. (1978). P.L. 95–471 Tribally Controlled Community College Assistance Act of 1978, 95th Congress, 2d Session.

Van Hamme, L. (1996). American Indian cultures and the classroom. *Journal of American Indian Education, 35*(2), 21–36.

Whitinui, P., & Macfarlane, A.H. (2012). *Indigenizing the disciplines in post-graduate studies: Self-determining Indigenous ways of knowing across the disciplines.* Paper presented at the American Educational Research Association Annual Meeting, Vancouver, BC, Canada, April 13–17, 2012.

Wilson, S. (2001). What is an indigenous research methodology? *Canadian Journal of Native Education, 25*(2), 175–179.

# CHAPTER TWENTY-SEVEN

# The Doctorate in Educational Leadership for Social Justice

## A Decade of Impact at Loyola Marymount University

*Jill Bickett, Karie Huchting, Ernest Rose,*
*Mary K. McCullough, and Shane P. Martin*

## INTRODUCTION

The Ed.D. in Educational Leadership for Social Justice at Loyola Marymount University (LMU), the sole doctoral program at LMU, is a program based on Ignatian principles and focused on preparing transformative leaders for educational settings. Though our program is young—we mark our tenth anniversary this year—we have learned and grown in the building and operationalizing of an Ed.D. at our Jesuit and Marymount institution. By way of a careful review of program history, philosophy, design, and assessment, the purpose of this chapter is to share the unique perspective of an Ed.D. program rooted in leadership and social justice and to provide data that probe the alignment of the program with its goals.

Providing clarity around the meaning, purpose, design, and assessment of the practitioner's doctorate in education has recently been taken on by the Carnegie Project on the Education Doctorate (CPED), an organization that refers to itself as a "knowledge forum on the Ed.D." (CPED, 2014a). This organization has the potential to become one of the most important change agents in defining and transforming the Ed.D. for the twenty-first century. In an effort to describe its mission and invite others into the work that it spearheads, CPED has provided a framework around which it describes its history and the resources and ideas necessary for authentic change in an Ed.D. program. This framework, "Reclaim, Reframe, Redesign, and Research & Development" (CPED, 2014d), will be the framework around which this chapter is developed.

First, we will "reclaim" our history by providing a brief outline of our Ignatian roots and their relationship to the mission and goals of the university. Here we will also describe the successes and challenges that were met in the planning and design of the program prior to having any student enrollment. In the "reframe" section of the chapter, we will drill down on the Ed.D. mission, goals, and learning outcomes, as well as their alignment with the CPED's definition and working principles of the professional doctorate. The "redesign" section will describe the change initiatives that we have undertaken throughout the course of the program, as well as the assessment process that drives that transformation. Finally, the "research & development" segment, though ongoing throughout the program, will focus on research that we have completed around the efficacy of the program and offer an analysis of future program change that we see as necessary. The CPED framework results in a cycle of continuous improvement, a process that Loyola Marymount has engaged in since the inception of the program.

## RECLAMATION: A LEGACY OF LEADERSHIP FOR SOCIAL JUSTICE

As one of 28 Jesuit colleges and universities in the United States, Loyola Marymount University follows an almost 475-year-old model of "heroic leadership" initiated by St. Ignatius of Loyola (Lowney, 2003). This model is followed throughout the university and integrated into our Ed.D. program as well. The mission of LMU is "the encouragement of learning, the education of the whole person, the service of faith and the promotion of justice." To operationalize this mission, doctoral students study the four pillars of the Jesuit leadership model early on in the program. These four pillars—self-awareness, ingenuity, love, and heroic ambition—fit well in the context of these modern times, just as they did when the Jesuits were a small "start-up company" in 1540 A.D. (Lowney, 2003; Rose, 2007). A brief description of the four pillars of Jesuit leadership follows.

### Self-Awareness

This is the understanding of one's own strengths, weaknesses, values, and world-view. An increasing number of authors on leadership have stated the need for greater self-awareness among leaders (Mezirow, 1991; Shields, 2011, 2013). Many of us know through our own experiences what it is like to work for leaders who have little understanding of what they do well and not so well. On the other hand, leaders who communicate positive morals and values and understand their place well beyond an immediate task can inspire team members to push themselves to levels of excellence beyond any previous performance.

## Ingenuity

Ingenuity refers to the confidence, innovation, and adaptation to engage an ever-changing world. The Jesuits came of age at a time when many previously held truths were being shattered by scientific discoveries. But, unlike many of their contemporaries, they embraced verifiable discoveries and grew in the confidence that most challenges had discoverable solutions if one worked hard enough and was open enough to new possibilities. The Jesuits referred to this attitude as "indifference." This did not mean a lack of caring or commitment; rather, cultivating the attitude of indifference enabled Jesuits to move away from provincialism and attachment to long-held beliefs (Lowney, 2003). With an attitude of indifference, it is possible for leaders to train a more focused eye on using new ideas and avoiding risk-averse notions about innovation.

## Love

Love is the unfailing faith to support others in becoming successful. In deemphasizing competition among Society of Jesus members, St. Ignatius formed a powerful team in which everyone pulled together to accomplish the goals of the order. Rather than jealously fighting for their own positions, the Jesuits were told to put aside their own ideas and to support the strategies of others that had a better chance of success (Lowney, 2003). In modern times, Pedro Arrupe, S.J., a former superior general of the Society of Jesus, said, "Fall in love, stay in love, and it will decide everything" (cited in *Finding God in All Things*, 2009). Thus, we believe that men and women are at their best when working with and for others in a climate of honest support, affection, and care.

## Heroic Ambition

Heroic ambition refers to an uncompromised commitment to an initiative such that one considers it a pursuit of perfection. The foundation of heroic ambition is the Jesuit's dedication to *magis*, which in Latin means *more*—as in, give all you can to the work at hand and then commit yourself to doing more to make it better than has been done before (Lowney, 2003). According to Lowney (2003), heroic ambition contributes equal parts dreamer and pragmatist. Thus, heroic leaders do not wait for the big challenges to present themselves; rather, they tackle the opportunities at hand and create the highest-quality solution.

These four pillars of Jesuit leadership create a formation for our doctoral students. We expect of them and they expect of themselves more than just the identification of challenges. The expectation is to find the right questions and to collaborate with others to co-create successful solutions to the important challenges and problems in their educational and community environments.

## HISTORY OF THE LOYOLA MARYMOUNT
## UNIVERSITY ED.D. PROGRAM

The Ed.D. program enrolled its first cohort of students in 2004, 7 years after the first planning sessions took place. The name of the doctorate, "Educational Leadership for Social Justice," was intentionally chosen for its alignment with the mission and vision of our Jesuit and Marymount University. The additional wording "for Social Justice" is unique to our program and clearly delineates our purpose in educating leaders who are committed to advocacy for equity and access. It distinguishes us from other doctoral programs that have framed their degrees around such areas as curricular leadership or educational administration.

The program was designed by the faculty to bring educational leaders from all contexts—Catholic, traditional public, charter, and nontraditional educational organizations—to the table in a cohort model of approximately 18 students per year. The small cohort size and variety in leadership provides a space for educational leaders to engage in dialogue with colleagues from different contexts. Alumni speak often of the learning that occurred not only because of the content delivered in the program but also because of the rich diversity of voices they encountered throughout their study. For example, one graduate shared:

> In my current organization, I've spent a lot of time being insular and hearing from very, very like-minded folks. So, the first thing I appreciated about the program was the cohort model and the diversity of the cohort because I was able to see a variety of perspectives about similar issues but see them from many different angles.

The program is a 3-year course of study that includes a culminating dissertation focused on educational leadership for social justice. Courses provide students the opportunity to explore aspects of leadership as they intersect with social justice in educational settings. The curriculum also includes a research and writing strand embedded in the coursework to accommodate student completion of the dissertation in the 3-year timeline. Students are encouraged to select their dissertation topic early in the program, choose a dissertation chair, and focus on a problem of practice within their educational context. During their second year, students participate in coursework and dissertation seminars in an effort to scaffold the research and dissertation-writing process to maximize their success. The third year is dedicated solely to analyzing data and writing the dissertation.

To be admitted to the Ed.D. program, prospective students must participate in a rigorous screening process. In order to be eligible to apply, students must provide (1) evidence of a master's degree from an accredited institution; (2) documentation of a GPA of 3.5 or higher in their master's degree; (3) current GRE scores; (4) a current resume; (5) three letters of recommendation; and (6) a written statement of purpose that outlines their rationale for application to an Ed.D. with particular emphasis on leadership for social justice, possible topics of study for the dissertation, and career aspirations.

After a careful screening of the application materials, including a review by professors from the School of Education, qualified applicants then advance to the interview round, where students participate in group interviews. The group interviews help faculty assess collaboration skills essential to the cohort model.

Once all of the applicant data have been collated, they are included in a decision matrix, which is then reviewed by the doctoral committee and the dean of the School of Education. Students comment that the personal nature of the admissions process, the interaction with future cohort members, and the presence of doctoral professors throughout the process are important factors in their decision to select the LMU doctoral program.

## PROGRAM REFRAMING WITHIN THE TRADITION OF ST. IGNATIUS

Grounded in the Ignatian tradition, the School of Education's conceptual framework is the foundation for the learning outcomes of the program. The conceptual framework articulates the professional dispositions for educators who will respect, educate, advocate, and lead (REAL). Respect is defined as the ability to connect theory and practice while integrating leadership and social justice. In this way, respect includes the ability to advocate for equity and diversity in educational contexts. Educate is understood as a commitment to a high-quality education for all students. Advocate is defined as preparing leaders to critically engage in complex issues within the field of education while demonstrating a commitment to social justice. Lead is understood as encouraging the development of moral and ethical leaders who meet the needs of all students in pre-K–20 public and private educational systems. As the founder of the program often shares with students, the goal of the Ed.D. program is to engage leaders to adopt the mindset that "under my watch, no one is marginalized" (M. McCullough, personal communication, 2014).

The doctoral program learning outcomes, which are derived from this framework, are as follows. As educational leaders, Ed.D. graduates will be able to

- identify and analyze the economic, political, legal, and sociocultural context of education;
- engage in inquiry and research to promote inclusive excellence in schools and/or society;
- articulate the ways in which theory and research influence the development of personal leadership praxis; and

- advocate for the transformation of educational and community settings into just and equitable learning environments.

With our recent membership in CPED, we find that our program aligns with all of CPED's working principles of the professional practice doctorate in education, but especially in our commitment to "equity, ethics, and social justice to bring about solutions to complex problems of practice" (CPED, 2014b) and in our preparation of leaders who "can construct and apply knowledge to make a positive difference in the lives of individuals, families, organizations and communities" (CPED, 2014b), both of which are program strengths that many alumni employ after graduation.

Specifically, graduates discuss how they are able to connect theory and practice and make recommendations for equity, ethics, and social justice through an engagement with research. One female graduate shared her story of starting out as a volunteer for a college access program in South Los Angeles for students who are underrepresented in higher education. Because of her doctoral studies, she was offered the position of curriculum instruction specialist. "Every day I get to work hand-in-hand with students and parents who come from the community that I have always wanted to serve. Every day I feel like I am making a difference." She went on to describe her ability to impact the program and the lives of students by applying the research skills she acquired in the doctoral program, saying:

> With my dissertation, for example, I studied the program where I am employed and I had a series of recommendations that didn't always bring to light the most favorable parts of the program. The program was very open to hearing my recommendations and my suggestions as a researcher to benefit the program. And just this year we've already started brainstorming on interventions that will, in the long run, help our students succeed once they get to college.

Another graduate also spoke of his ability to address complex issues at his school by sharing research with his colleagues. He related how his school site is "now more aware of data-driven decision making" rather than relying on subjective opinions. And a female graduate stated, "I am able to see things through the lens of a researcher and I am confident in sharing my ideas and recommendations, which is something that has come as a result of my doctoral degree."

## ED.D. PROGRAM REDESIGN IN THE SPIRIT OF CONTINUOUS IMPROVEMENT

The change initiatives undertaken by the doctoral program are based on a philosophy of continuous improvement. Specifically, the program engages in assessment processes to measure student satisfaction and the program's learning outcomes.

These annual assessment measures include surveys, focus groups, exit interviews, and supervisor interviews. In these data, we have found evidence to suggest that our graduates are transformed to lead their educational communities for social justice (Huchting & Bickett, 2013). For example, supervisors indicated that students were better prepared to be advocates for the voiceless, to be more adamant about equity in programming, and to be more impassioned about access for all to educational opportunities and supports.

Structures also exist within the School of Education to promote continuous improvement and redesign. For example, a doctoral program faculty committee meets on a monthly basis throughout the year to discuss the program's curriculum and development, students' progress, and outreach from the university to the surrounding community. Further, we have agreed upon a cycle of external and internal dissertation review. Recently, we tasked doctoral faculty members with reviewing randomly assigned LMU published dissertations. Using an agreed-upon rubric, faculty reviewed approximately 15 dissertations and came to important conclusions about student needs and process modifications for the dissertation. Also included in this process was an external review of our published dissertations, which included five faculty from outside the university who—again, using an agreed-upon rubric—evaluated and commented on the quality of our published dissertations. This, too, proved to be very fruitful for our continuous improvement initiative.

As a result of these combined efforts to continually assess the program, specific changes have been implemented over the past 10 years. Although some changes in the program were made in the early years that involved class meeting times, course resequencing, and additional dissertation support, the first major review took place in Year 5 of the program and was initiated by the dean of the School of Education. This retooling came in the form of a task force that focused closely on two things: the core content of the curriculum and the capstone project or dissertation.

As the program progressed, faculty felt that there had been an unintentional shift away from the two-pronged focus—leadership and social justice—that was to be the center of every class. Some argued that classes had become focused on either leadership or social justice, but not on both. Thus the task force passed this resolution:

> The program is committed to the integration of theory and practice in the context of leadership for social justice. Thus leadership and social justice are integrated concepts. While specific courses may emphasize one area more than the other, for the purposes of this program they should always be action oriented and solution based. Thus, courses in leadership should always include a focus on social justice issues and courses in social justice should always have a focus on leadership. (LMU, 2010)

The second major change in the program that was a result of the doctoral task force was a reconstruction of the notion of the dissertation experience. Some faculty wanted to move away from the constraints of emulating the Ph.D. and the notion of the five-chapter dissertation. The intention was to encourage more practice- and/or project-based dissertations that might not fit neatly into the five-chapter mold. Thus, the task force shifted the focus to professional practice, decided on the necessary elements of the dissertation, and left open the requirements of chapters or structure of the document. Instead of requiring a chapter-based project, the task force agreed on required elements for each dissertation. The required elements are the following:

- Use of leadership for social justice as a focusing lens
- Literature review/knowledge base
- Research question
- Acknowledgment of lens or theoretical framework
- Methodology
- Rationale/contextual analysis
- Findings/evidence
- Recommendations for practice (LMU Doctoral Task Force, 2010)

Faculty agreed that there must be consistency across projects and a reference to the impact on professional practice in every dissertation.

The work of the task force brought us closer to the design concept definition of the dissertation experience as recommended by CPED. CPED encourages a "dissertation in practice" (CPED, 2014c), which is defined as "a scholarly endeavor that impacts a complex problem of practice" (CPED, 2014c). However, though our task force adopted this language, adoption and implementation are two different things. There is still work to be done in this area, as we continue to emphasize the importance of the focus on the practitioner/scholar and our commitment to the principles of CPED.

## RESEARCH AND DEVELOPMENT

Research on the Ed.D. program in leadership for social justice has focused on the efficacy of the program in engaging educators to lead in their educational contexts through the lens of social justice. This research has led to several conference presentations and publications, including a descriptive book chapter (Huchting & Bickett, 2012) and a journal article documenting student transformation (Huchting & Bickett, 2013). The data described below highlight evidence from exit interviews that capture the students' voices in describing three core areas of the program: social justice, leadership, and program improvement. The doctoral program committee reviews these snapshots regularly and engages in dialogue about potential changes to the program.

## Social Justice

While the title of the program embeds the fundamental concept of *social justice*, and while it is likely that students apply to this program because of their interest in and alignment to this core concept, evidence suggests that our students transform their conceptual understanding of social justice during the program. For example, a male student of color described social justice in education this way:

> At first I saw it more of a religious term…it was a ministry term. [Now] it's sensing injustice. Education can be a vehicle for change and advancement for everybody, regardless of economic background, race, and ethnicity. Everyone deserves an equal chance and it's an educator's responsibility, especially the leader, to make sure that it is available to all students.

A female student of color shared that:

> Social justice in terms of education to me means equal access to quality instruction, access to adequate materials, access to adequate facilities, all of that. So a leader for social justice must bring about change and make a difference. A leader for social justice promotes change, promotes access, and promotes equity.

## Leadership

Throughout the Ed.D. program, students are encouraged to think about what being a leader truly means. Across most exit interviews, we hear evidence of student transformation in that students often share that they "found their voice" or were able "to speak up" when faced with unjust issues in their educational context. The notions of advocacy and confidence appeared across the data. Interestingly, many students, when asked about their view of leadership, discussed leadership as leadership *for social justice* and articulated that this type of leadership is related to being a change agent. One student shared that "Leadership for social justice is creating the awareness of need for change." Another offered: "Leadership for social justice is a call to action. It's a call to challenge the status quo." These ideals of leadership seemed to be more important to students than status. During an exit interview, a student reflected on obtaining the Ed.D. degree:

> I think the initial allure was the idea of having an Ed.D., just having the degree. I expected it to change me, but I was focusing more on how much work it was going to take, not so much the benefit afterward. I take that back, not the benefit, the *responsibility* afterward.

Additionally, student views of leadership broadened to include leadership from any position rather than just positions of authority. Students discussed collaborative leadership styles rather than hierarchical leadership:

> Before I was in the program, I thought there were certain archetypes—that is, if you wanted to be a leader you needed to be a principal or vice principal or superintendent, a leading figure in an educational environment. Through the program, I've seen that leadership means being able to make decisions on behalf of students and with students and families so that their opportunities are expanded, so they are able to choose their own pathway....

## Program Improvement

Based on our recent involvement with the Carnegie Project on the Education Doctorate, we now see a need for program modification that will align us more closely with the CPED design concept definitions and working principles. Though conceptually our program aligns well with the CPED principles and design, as indicated earlier, implementing some of these elements continues to be challenging. We have work to do in embedding collaborative initiatives with community partners, operationalizing the dissertation in practice, and continuing to develop true laboratories of practice.

However, using our new knowledge base from the CPED initiative and research data that we have collected from our own alumni, we continue to engage in dialogue about program improvement and future program changes. We are in Year 2 of a School of Education strategic plan that includes several specific initiatives about the doctoral program, some of which include developing funding initiatives for greater scholarship support for doctoral students. Further, we have commissioned a task force to discuss the content of the current methods courses with an eye toward the appropriate placement and depth necessary for qualitative, quantitative, and mixed-methods instruction. In addition, we have formed an alumni council with representatives from each of the graduated cohorts. The alumni council will provide additional voices about program efficacy in the field while presenting opportunities for graduates to share experiences with current students.

## CONCLUSION

Since its inception 10 years ago, the Loyola Marymount University doctoral program in educational leadership for social justice has grown and changed, recently graduating its 100th student. Change has come as a result of a continuous improvement cycle informed by research and student data. Most significantly, students continue to affirm the importance of the program for their own personal growth as well as their professional development, culminating in a decade of heroic impact for the doctorate in educational leadership for social justice at Loyola Marymount University.

## REFERENCES

Carnegie Project on the Education Doctorate (CPED). (2014a). [Home page]. Retrieved from http://cpedinitiative.org/

Carnegie Project on the Education Doctorate (CPED). (2014b). *Definition of and working principles for the education doctorate.* Retrieved from http://cpedinitiative.org/definition-and-working-principles-edd-program-design

Carnegie Project on the Education Doctorate (CPED). (2014c). *Design concept definitions.* Retrieved from http://cpedinitiative.org/design-concept-definitions

Carnegie Project on the Education Doctorate (CPED). (2014d). *Research & resources.* Retrieved from http://cpedinitiative.org/research-resources

*Finding God in all things: A Marquette prayer book.* (2009). Milwaukee, WI: Marquette University Press.

Huchting K., & Bickett, J. (2012). Preparing school leaders for social justice: Examining the efficacy of program preparation. In C. Boske & S. Diem (Eds.), *Global leadership for social justice: Taking it from field to practice.* Bingley, UK: Emerald Publishing.

Huchting, K., & Bickett, J. (2013). Inspired to lead: Two years of evaluation data from a Jesuit Ed.D. program for educational leadership in social justice. *Jesuit Higher Education: A Journal, 2*(2), 28–40.

Lowney, C. (2003). *Heroic leadership: Best practices from a 450-year-old company that changed the world.* Chicago, IL: Loyola Press.

Loyola Marymount University. (2010). *Final report: Doctoral taskforce on doctorate in educational leadership for social justice.* Unpublished manuscript.

Mezirow, J. (1991). *Transformative dimensions of adult learning.* San Francisco, CA: Jossey-Bass.

Rose, E. (2007). *Chief academic officer's convocation address.* Los Angeles, CA: Loyola Marymount University.

Shields, C.M. (Ed.). (2011). *Transformative leadership: A reader.* New York: Peter Lang.

Shields, C.M. (2013). *Transformative leadership in education: Equitable change in an uncertain and complex world.* New York: Routledge.

# CHAPTER TWENTY-EIGHT

# Whose Knowledge Counts in an Ed.D. Program?

## Building Diverse Relationships to Illuminate Opportunities and Challenges

*Christopher Burke and Truman Hudson, Jr.*

## INTRODUCTION

In this chapter, we share our reflections on the development of the Ed.D. program in metropolitan education at the University of Michigan-Dearborn (UM-D). The chapter provides insights into our individual and collective development as members of the academic community during the process. As an African American male student (Dr. Truman Hudson, Jr.) and a European American male faculty member (Dr. Christopher Burke), we believe that the first aim of the program is to seek and attract professionals who aspire to impact and transform urban communities. Our vision for the program includes broadening the definition of education to include acts of public pedagogy (Giroux, 2003; Sandlin, Schultz, & Burdick, 2010), refocusing outcomes to include social justice (Apple, 1996), and aiming to develop a program that empowers us to act as change agents in the local community. We believe that this vision can only be enacted by valuing and centering the experiences of students as a source of knowledge and by intentionally cultivating relationships as part of a learning community. It was this shared belief that attracted both of us to the program.

Building on the student-centered framework, we believe the program cultivates and promotes a practical research orientation and a praxis-based knowledge and skill set as defined by Freire (1971). Additionally, the doctoral program's focus on working with and for engaged professionals promotes active reflection and action in the world, with the goal of transforming those communities to which we belong. While we articulate and share this focus as the mission of the Ed.D.

program, the lack of full commitment by all of the stakeholders has resulted in the doctoral program not meeting all of its stated goals. Our critical reflection shares the ways in which we were both successful and challenged in our efforts to influence the program's development, norms, and outcomes.

Through the use of self-study methodology (Berry, 2008), we examine our own experiences as members of the program in order to explore the alignment between our individual and mutual expectations and programmatic outcomes. Self-study allows us to assess the program, its development, policies, and structures in terms of its impact on us as individuals and to further theorize our experiences. We base our reflections on critical incidents as we remember them throughout the development of our relationship in the first 5 years of the program. Truman was a member of the first cohort in the Ed.D. program. He was admitted to the program before it was fully approved by the Higher Learning Commission and the university's Board of Regents. He entered the program with professional experience in aiding nonprofit, for-profit, and governmental agencies in identifying and securing funding for new and existing programs. Truman also served as an adjunct with two local colleges. His work focused on community building through the collective impact framework.

Chris was one of five faculty members responsible for the planning phase and helped to develop the first set of courses for the program. In the second year, he became codirector for the program. His research interests focus on issues of social justice and community engagement as a tool for cultivating K–12 student science agency. This chapter reflects on the relationship that developed between the two of us as student/advisor and, ultimately, collaborating colleagues. Our reflection highlights how the goals for the program developed and evolved. Grounded in these experiences, we identify recommendations for actions that would increase the program's fidelity to Freire's construct of praxis (1971).

## INITIAL GOALS OF THE ED.D. PROGRAM

When the program was conceived in 2009, the proposal identified three distinct yet overlapping foci as essential characteristics for the next generation of educational leaders.

### Engagement with the Community

Leaders who are engaged with the community are firmly rooted in everyday educational contexts. They recognize that they are a part of—not apart from—the community that provides many types of educative experiences (informal as well as formal). Engaged educational leaders build community partnerships that are responsive to the educational needs of the local clientele.

## Transformational Leadership

Transformational leaders in education enact equitable and just practices in order to achieve organizational change that will facilitate the learning of all students. These individuals possess the motivation and skills to be leaders who are eager to meet the challenges faced by our region's schools. Transformational leaders are able to make the connection between theory and practical problem solving to assist planned change in pre-K–12 and community college settings.

## Scholarly Practice

Scholarly practitioners blend theory and practice. This viewpoint is based upon the idea that theory and practice are linked and that research knowledge should be rooted within the context of authentic problems faced by practicing educators. Integrating theory and practice will allow graduates to understand and implement the best evidence-based approaches needed to address the current issues in education (see Figure 28.1) (School of Education, UM-Dearborn, 2008).

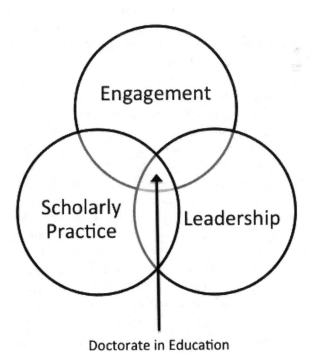

Figure 28.1. Preferred location of program elements in the Doctorate of Education (Ed.D.).

The stated goals of the program establish the importance of serving professionals who aspire to impact and transform urban communities by valuing and centering their experiences as a source of knowledge through intentionally cultivating relationships as part of a learning community. Through this process, the program promotes a practitioner's research orientation and a praxis-based knowledge and skill set (Freire, 1971). By developing a program focused on supporting and learning with professionals who are engaged with their communities in the metropolitan area, the program promotes active reflection and action on the world with the goal of transforming it through one's networks, influence, and decision making. In addition, our approach is intended to model an inclusive perspective on community building and a pro-social approach to individual development as it is rooted in one's professional work and identity.

## STRUCTURES ENACTED TO REALIZE OPPORTUNITIES

Over the course of our experience in the program, there were efforts by both faculty and students to enact structures that would support the realization of these goals. In reflecting on the different actions taken, it is clear that both Truman and Chris see centering the students' experiences and fostering trusting relationships among faculty and students as essential to achieving these goals. We envision these goals as being embodied in the passion and drive shown by the candidates during the deliberate application process, which seeks out students who can articulate their research interests in relationship to issues that arise from their professional experiences. For example, Truman brings an extensive background working with nonprofits, particularly with helping community-based organizations develop the human capital of their community. His commitment to trying to connect these efforts to empowering kids and schools was evident in work in and outside the classroom. His commitment to effecting change is grounded in his personal and professional experiences.

Like Truman, other doctoral students bring with them years of experience that provide them with insights into what happens in schools, how kids are engaged, and the complexities that made education difficult and an ongoing struggle. Further, his approach is grounded in lived experiences that provide insight into how others can engage, empower, and transform students, families, and communities. These experiences are the basis of students' professional funds of knowledge (Barton & Tan, 2009; Moll, Amanti, Neff, & Gonzalez, 1992), which can inform classroom discourse and be a space for making sense of the scholarship on education that we are studying. It also provides a valuable space for critiquing the questions on which current scholarship and research are focused.

Truman's and the other students' experiences create space to critique the academic canon, the types of questions asked, what counts as evidence, and how any research findings are interpreted, analyzed, and discussed. In our respective roles as faculty and doctoral student, a trusting, collaborative relationship emerged that shifted both the origins of and the gaze at the epistemological underpinnings of our discussions and the aims of our research. Furthermore, our relationship empowers each of us to assume greater authenticity in developing growth mindsets (Dweck, 2006).

As a faculty member and codirector of the Ed.D. program at UM-D, Chris, in collaboration with other faculty members, seeks to enact structures and practices that draw on and maximize the students' experiences as strengths and assets that provide significant and distinctive knowledge sources. By focusing on relationships as a central dimension of the implementation of the program and by centering students' professional experiences as a source of knowledge, the doctoral students' professional work provides the essential context for students' meaning-making and the immediate application of the theoretical constructs (Kaser & Halbert, 2009). Further, the vision for centering the professional learning that emerges from a dialogic process among faculty and doctoral students is intended to impact our collective understanding of knowledge construction, honoring multiple voices from the field, and traditional modes of learning in the academy. In this way, the program is building relationships among faculty and doctoral students in a way that levels the power dynamics at times, a process that does not often occur organically (especially in a commuter program) without intentionally creating new spaces for dialogue.

Relationships that extend beyond the typical course structures and purposes are promoted by instituting a coffee hour before class in order for faculty and students to stop in and visit informally. The coffee hour provides faculty and students with a transition time between other competing demands on their time and energy. For many doctoral students who come to campus after full and energy-draining days in school settings or other organizations, the conversations over refreshments are a chance to relax, exchange personal experiences, and regroup before going to class. For faculty, coming to the coffee hour from meetings or other classes allows them to step away from other demands and reconnect with students on a personal level.

In the third year, we initiated discussion sessions with visiting scholars for the doctoral students. These events created opportunities for doctoral students to visit in unstructured sessions and allowed them to interact and direct conversations. Finally, while the program does not mandate cohorts in order to provide flexibility for working professionals, we encourage students to progress through the program as a cohort as much as possible. In our efforts to promote and support community, we also sponsor events that build relationships with colleagues among various cohort groups and years.

In class, we aim to establish a climate that promotes relationship building, dialogue, and valuing of students' professional experience and work. Early on, we articulate class norms for difficult or challenging conversations to encourage the sharing of complex ideas within safe, trusting, and collaborative learning environments. This list of class norms is posted and revisited in subsequent courses. Students are also asked to work in pairs to prepare for class discussions and on an initial research project using an inquiry, project-based learning approach. Finally, we promote peer editing in class for all papers in order to develop students' critical editing skills and practice in providing and receiving constructive feedback about their ideas and writing.

Truman, along with other students, had a voice in advocating and establishing structures to access the potential of the community. For example, the students' requests for establishing a writing group to support their academic progress was honored by faculty. In an effort to ensure that the students' aims were met, Chris established a biweekly voluntary writing group that became a safe and trusting space for students to focus on developing relationships and sharing professional learning, personal life happenings, challenges, and successes. Outside of the typical graduate course with formalized instruction and evaluation practices, the writing group serves as a space for socializing that regulates and often stimulates students' progress and maintains their resilience in the program. Further, by focusing on these activities, behaviors, and structures, we cultivate relationships as part of a learning community that allows students to draw on the insight and expertise of their peers and faculty in ways that support them professionally and within their progression in the program.

## STRUCTURAL BARRIERS ROOTED IN
## HISTORICAL WAYS OF BEING

While the activities described above were grounded in the belief that students' funds of knowledge were an essential resource and that the program needed to bridge students' field experience in education and draw on their insights as a tool for critiquing and revisioning the field, Chris and other faculty members oftentimes operate through a framework of privilege. This privilege, which is associated with their race, class, gender, and prior academic experience, influences the planning and development of the program. For example, the doctoral planning committee began the development phase of the program by identifying a series of courses that reflect what they believe to be essential content.

While the required 16 courses are designed to help students develop an understanding of the existing state of research and scholarship and are viewed as essential in supporting the development of students' competencies in core subject areas, the approach marginalizes students' knowledge and experiences and privileges the academic canon. In practice, the courses end up directing the students away from the interests and questions that they brought to the program and focus them instead on issues that the faculty see as essential and interesting in the field as defined by current research. Moreover, because the faculty's design of the program lacks a student voice, students' ability and credibility in identifying and framing worthwhile issues for study is marginalized.

The initial focus on the existing canon of academic scholarship also raises the issue of who defines what counts as knowledge and whose knowledge counts (Apple, 1996) within course curriculum, classroom discussions, literature reviews, dissertation work, and praxis. In the academy, knowledge is valued when it is collected in specific ways—that is, if it has been peer reviewed and is recognized as legitimate in the canon. The specific ways in which certain knowledge is regarded and the expectations for formalized language structures within the academy serve as gatekeeping mechanisms when students do not already possess such knowledge and skills from their previous educational and professional experiences. Further, by beginning with an a priori curriculum, we are not adhering to the third tenet of the program and assuming a praxis perspective on developing students' research orientation and research practices.

In many ways it is the observance of these traditionally norming expectations for language use and practice that mutes the contributions of multiple and diverse knowledge sources and professional experiences of doctoral students who come from and serve communities in the metropolitan region, where other types of knowledge, language expertise, and experience are privileged (Banks, 1993). The presence of norming techniques concerning appropriate or legitimate knowledge sources and language that are used to socialize doctoral students into the academy often creates some degree of tension. When code switching, many of the students dislocate their experiences as irrelevant during the initial phase of their doctoral program.

The standard for what is accepted as scholarly work in the academy and the expectation for "peer review" is also problematic. Who counts as a peer for peer review? In helping students learn to complete a literature review, we find that learning to identify articles that count as scholarly and worthy of inclusion in the literature review means looking for peer-reviewed articles. While the peer review process is identified as a tool to ensure the meritocracy of scholarship, it often masks personal networks of scholars that reinforce hegemonic structures.

Requiring students to identify peer-reviewed articles exclusively creates a circle in which those inside the academy are the ones who are asked to review and approve the texts that are considered valuable knowledge. Students who do not have the recognized credentials are not accepted as reviewers, a practice that further marginalizes their experiences and insights into the profession. These structures keep separate the academic networks that are used to define what counts as important knowledge and the students' professional networks, which we believe are essential facets of authentic and legitimate tools for making meaning in the program. The same issue emerges with the requirements for identifying seminal texts in order to cite the authors who are recognized in the field as originators of theory and frequently members of the academy and, not so inconsequentially, also often belong to the White, male, European demographic. Although students are encouraged to be reviewers for journals and conferences, many of these positions have gatekeepers who inhibit student engagement in the process. Moreover, the requirement of having prior experience in the academy oftentimes causes students to opt out of the peer-review process.

The post-coursework part of the program is seen as the appropriate space for students to draw on their personal, professional, and academic experience to define their own scholarship and scholarly voice. During this phase, we found that the points of evaluation (qualifying exam, proposal defense, and dissertation defense) are measured based on the work's fidelity to the academic peer review standard and the student's ability to locate the work within that framework. Hence, the qualifying exam serves as a single point of evaluation in which students are asked to demonstrate their knowledge of the academic canon.

As currently structured in the program, a successful proposal evaluates a student's ability to frame her professional questions and problems in acceptable research methodologies as defined by Cresswell (2009), the methods text used at UM-Dearborn. For the final dissertation defense, students are required to adequately locate their professional understanding within the academy. Chris sees this sequence of structures as a process that works to help students connect the questions and issues that emerge from their professional experience with the existing academic conversation taking place in the literature. Truman experienced this process as marginalizing his professional experience, silencing his questions, and privileging dominant academic discourses.

In our reflection on the experience, we note that the foregrounding of the coursework and the high-stakes accountability of the qualifying exam and proposal serve to push the connection to Truman's professional experience and networks to the very end of the program, when they have less impact and value on the meaning-making process. Like Truman, many students struggled to fit studies that addressed complex issues grounded in their personal experience into a clinical structure for a study as defined by Cresswell (2009).

## MEDIATING STRUCTURES THROUGH
## PERSONAL RELATIONSHIPS

Many of the barriers that the program structure creates are mediated and mitigated through an emphasis on personal relationships and trust established over time, such as the one that emerged between Truman and Chris. Chris acted as an advocate and a mentor for Truman within the academy. Truman opened up his professional networks and encouraged Chris to collaborate with him outside the academy. Both of them regularly extended their own social and cultural capital in order to support the other.

Truman's research and its location within the academy were continually negotiated. The ongoing tension that occurred, while valued, aroused feelings of mistrust for what was perceived as disingenuous academic jousting. It was only through the extended history of mutual caring that Truman and Chris were able to overcome the insecurity that was created by the process. This ultimately led to a dissertation that did not address Truman's initial question: How do you teach African American boys economics in ways that empower them to be successful in higher education? A new question emerged from the process: How does an economics teacher's intentional action of embedding Bronfenbrenner's Ecological Systems framework into instruction influence students in the margins? The resulting dissertation focused on the issue of what it meant to center student voice and experience in the curriculum development process, a question that both Chris and Truman saw as a valuable contribution to the field and one that furthered their thinking about praxis.

## PERSONAL AND PROFESSIONAL GROWTH

Our personal identities influence our assumptions and expectations for our relationship. Through our critical reflection on them throughout the development of our collegial and personal relationship, we were able to see how these identities both enhanced and obstructed our understanding of the work we aspire to do. As we worked together over a 5-year period, the relationship required time and extended interactions in order to allow the work to be negotiated. In order for our relationship to develop to the point where we were able to achieve the goals of the program, we had to develop trust with one another. The trust provided us with a solid foundation for bridging the gap between the academy and the community. It also required personal and professional growth from both of us. We each played a central role in cultivating this growth in each other. Ways in which we grew are reflected in the following commentary.

**Chris:** I have come to recognize that I have continually benefitted from being inside the academic network without ever really realizing that I am. I grew up in a multigenerational doctoral family that can be traced to the 1800s with a great-great-grandfather completing a Ph.D. program in the sciences. While I worked outside of the university, I was always a part-time student until I got a job as a faculty member. This insider status meant that I never had to pay attention to or develop professional networks; I found that I easily fit into existing networks. Working with Truman pushed me to recognize the networks that I am part of and to be intentional about leveraging the capital from my networks to support his research and grant-funded project.

**Truman:** Entering the doctoral program, I was a successful family man, businessman, civic leader, mentor, and educator with a myopic perspective on how systems impacted human development. My prior knowledge of integrating theory and praxis in many educational and community economic development projects throughout the states of Michigan and Ohio aided me in maneuvering the rigors of academe. While my capital and network pre-doctoral studies were of great value, the rigors of the academy extended my research methodologies and theoretical lens. Due in part to the research and investigation training I received in the doctoral program, and the guidance of Chris, my original plan of study shifted from a focus on teaching economics to students in the margins to understanding how my intentional actions in the classroom influence student development.

Working with Chris promoted new thought that pushed boundaries, created new networks and base, and extended my areas of interest. Post-dissertation, through my publications and presentations at national conferences, I have gained a voice in the academy and am pivoting closer to my professional goals. Due in part to Chris's mentoring and coaching, I have secured grant support for my research on student voice in economic instruction and have developed a student-centered curriculum.

## RESTRUCTURING TO CENTER THE PROFESSIONAL
## AND THE PERSONAL

As a result of our collectively and individually reflecting on our relationship and experiences that developed through the Ed.D. program, we believe that two recommendations can be made for rethinking the structure of the program. First, the program needs to identify ways to more clearly and routinely center and value the passion, professional experience, and questions that the students bring to the program. One recommendation is to restructure the sequence of students' progression in the program and to foreground the development of their research question prior to the coursework rather than placing this phase after coursework. By reordering these two significant stages of the program, we could better focus on developing students' ability to develop and practice their critical reflective skills about their professional learning and experiences and thus be better prepared to engage in critical reflection about their scholarship as it emerges.

The second recommendation is to enhance students' levels of responsibility in reviewing and evaluating each other's work. Instead of requiring students to persuade or convince the three faculty that make up their committee that their work is ready to move forward, they would need to convince a quorum of their peers that their work was acceptable and significant. We are advocating that the peer-review process be expanded to include not just the faculty, but their colleagues and stakeholders in the community as well. With this recommendation, we are actively challenging the current practice of faculty retaining all of the authority for legitimizing students' progress and work as "good enough" and demonstrate an adherence to the second tenet of the program, "transformational leadership." In order to develop metropolitan leaders, our program can better recognize the value of developing peer-to-peer communication skills that rely on one's ability to provide critical reflection and feedback in high-stakes, public forums.

In the first stage of the program, students would enroll in symposiums that focus on helping them develop an understanding of different methods of research, reviewing the literature, and writing a proposal. At the end of the first year, students would have to produce a research prospectus that outlines the topic for a study and a justification as to why it would be of value. In order to be reviewed, a group of faculty and students must nominate the proposal. Faculty, students, and community members would then approve the proposal during a public symposium. In the second year, the student would complete coursework that was identified as being supportive and important background information. He or she would also take supplementary research courses that support the development and piloting of research methods. A final research proposal would be developed at the end of this year of work that would again need to be approved by faculty and students.

Our intention in restructuring the program is to change the structural focus in ways that center on and privilege students' professional experiences and networks in an effort to make them more central to the process. However, we recognize that these changes alone will not transform the process of trying to bridge the gap between the experiences of the academy and those of the professional community. This work still needs to take place within personal relationships. These relationships need to be intentionally nurtured, and both students and faculty need to be encouraged to be critically self-reflective in the process.

## REFERENCES

Apple, M.W. (1996). *Cultural politics and education*. London: Open University Press.

Banks, J.A. (1993). The canon debate, knowledge construction, and multicultural education. *Educational Researcher, 22*(5), 4–14.

Barton, A.C., & Tan, E. (2009). Funds of knowledge and discourses and hybrid space. *Journal of Research in Science Teaching, 46*(1), 50–73.

Berry, A. (2008). *Tensions in teaching about teaching: Understanding practice as a teacher educator*. Dordrecht, The Netherlands: Springer.

Cresswell, J.W. (2009). *Research design: Qualitative, quantitative, and mixed methods approaches* (3rd ed.). Thousand Oaks, CA: Sage.

Dweck, C. (2006). *Mindset: The new psychology of success.* New York: Random House.

Freire, P. (1971). *Pedagogy of the oppressed.* New York: Continuum.

Giroux, H.A. (2003). Public pedagogy and the politics of resistance: Notes on a critical theory of educational struggle. *Educational Philosophy and Theory, 35*(1), 5–16.

Kaser, L., & Halbert, J. (2009). *Leadership mindsets: Innovation and learning in the transformation of schools.* New York: Routledge.

Moll, L.C., Amanti, C., Neff, D., & Gonzalez, N. (1992). Funds of knowledge for teaching: Using a qualitative approach to connect homes and classrooms. *Theory into Practice, 31*(2), 132–141.

Sandlin, J., Schultz, B., & Burdick, J. (Eds.). (2010). *Handbook of public pedagogy: Education and learning beyond schooling.* New York: Routledge.

School of Education, University of Michigan–Dearborn. (2008) *Doctorate in Education (Ed.D.) degree proposal.* Dearborn, MI.

# CHAPTER TWENTY-NINE

# Issues of Superintendent Preparation in Disadvantaged Areas

## Considering the Usefulness of the Educational Doctorate (Ed.D.)

*Chris Willis and Kay Brocato*

## INTRODUCTION

Could equity emerge without excellent leadership? This ever-vexing question persists in American public education without reason. We know that disadvantaged populations have historically suffered from lack of access to resources that bring about academic success. It logically follows, then, that excellent leadership is a resource that matters. The extent to which quality school superintendent leadership matters still has not been empirically examined well enough over time to offer direct quantitative links between the quality of superintendent and student academic performance. Still, literature proliferates in the field, with enough evidence to determine that the more that excellent leadership is accessible, the better the probability for excellent academic outcomes for students, teachers, and school communities (Murphy, Moorman, & McCarthy, 2008; Waters & Marzano, 2006; Young & Creighton, 2002). Further, recent work by the Carnegie Project on the Education Doctorate (Ed.D.) shows that educational leaders with an Ed.D. are better prepared to be stewards of their schools and communities (Zambo, 2011).

For the past 25 years, American public schools have been scrutinized by communities and the government in an attempt to improve operations and student outcomes (Elmore, 1996; Gross, 1978; National Association of Secondary School Principals, 1996; National Commission on Excellence in Education,

1983; Newmann & Wehlage, 1995; No Child Left Behind Act of 2001, 2002). More recently, that pressure has been focused on the improvement of student test scores. Researchers have demonstrated that when demographic differences and teacher impacts are factored out of the academic performance equation, quality of school facility and district leadership do have an impact on student performance (Byrd, Slater, & Brooks, 2006; Waters & Marzano, 2006). As a result, a new method of preparation for educational leaders is being suggested (Murphy et al., 2008). New educational leadership preparation plans are of utmost importance in supplying a pool of effective leaders to schools in disadvantaged areas. One example of the difficulty in supplying such leaders nationwide is described in this analysis.

Revamped preparation programs for educational leaders are addressed from a variety of perspectives in the research and accountability literature. One model focuses on the impact that program graduates should have once they are working in the field and calls for the preparation of high-impact leaders who encourage schools to address social justice issues, demonstrate higher-quality instruction, and provide evidence of high-quality student learning. In what Wiggins and McTighe (2001) call a backward design, educational leadership programs across the country were challenged to develop instructional and field experiences to specifically address those three components. A retooling of the accreditation process of educational leadership preparation programs brought on a modernization and institutionalization process across the nation. Varrati, Tooms, and Thomas (2006) discussed how an Ed.D. program was redesigned in response to new NCATE and ELCC standards, while Levine (2005) called for the complete elimination of the Ed.D. as a preparation option. Emerging now are Ed.D. programs seeking more payoff for leader candidates. Action research engagement and rich, embedded fieldwork are more the norm in current programs seeking to impact and improve learning conditions for children. Rooted in the new practices of leadership preparation is the stuff of schools researcher-practitioner action with intent to deeply impact schools (Zambo, 2011; Zambo & Isai, 2013). Clearly, current phases of school leader preparation are rooted in the practice of leadership within schools.

The purpose of this study was to examine the issue of leadership preparation levels in a highly disadvantaged region of the United States in order to determine whether lack of access to and poor quality of leadership preparation programs may be perpetuating educational inequity. The study includes a quantitative analysis of existing data to determine if there is any significant relationship between the preparation levels of school district superintendents and school performance in one disadvantaged state, Mississippi. Implications from this analysis highlight the need for specific kinds of Ed.D. programs that emphasize the science underlying the practice of leading schools and the school community.

# REGIONAL LANDSCAPE OF SUPERINTENDENT PLACEMENT AND LICENSURE

In order to contextualize the Mississippi dilemma, a description of the southern region of the United States educational leadership preparation landscape is helpful. Among the Southern Regional Education Board (SREB) states, only three elect superintendents. During the 1990s, the practice of electing school superintendents became limited to just Alabama, Florida, and Mississippi (Southern Regional Education Board, 2000). These three states also have licensing procedures for superintendents that are linked to allowing for the elected district leader status. Neither a unique certification nor a unique degree for the school district superintendent exists in these states, wherein a single type of license is issued that allows individuals to serve in an administrative capacity within a school district. The minimum level of education required for this license is a master's degree.

Every other SREB member state provides different certification requirements for becoming a principal than becoming a superintendent. Nationwide, Arkansas, Delaware, Maryland, North Carolina, South Carolina, and Virginia all require additional graduate-level coursework beyond the master's degree in educational administration to become a superintendent. This additional education may come in the form of a specialist degree, a doctoral degree, or simply a collection of additional graduate-level hours that are not directly applied to a degree program. In general, these states have required at least 30 hours past the master's degree for superintendent positions.

The states of Kentucky, Oklahoma, Texas, and West Virginia have a minimum requirement of a master's degree, but the degree must be certified by the state as a specialized program for the preparation of school superintendents. In these instances, the states have separate programs that lead to principal licensure or superintendent licensure. With the exception of Tennessee, the SREB states can be separated into two groups. One group holds superintendent elections and has no requirement for specialized superintendent training through the licensure process. The other group does not elect superintendents, and every state has specialized, separate licensure programs that focus on the preparation of superintendents.

The process of electing local school superintendents is currently a uniquely southern phenomenon. Georgia and Tennessee—which at the time were the states with the largest number of elected superintendents—enacted laws in the 1990s requiring that all superintendents be appointed by the local school board. By the fall of 2000, the number of elected superintendents in the United States had dropped from 341 to 154. That year, Mississippi became the state with the most elected superintendents, 69 (Southern Regional Education Board, 2000). Since that time the number of elected superintendents in the state has decreased to 63, but Mississippi still maintains a higher number of elected superintendents than either Alabama or Florida, the only other states that use a superintendent election process.

## THE CASE OF MISSISSIPPI

The state of Mississippi is largely rural and overwhelmingly impoverished, and these disadvantaged conditions are so widespread that the entire state is classified as such. In regard to the rural nature of Mississippi, the 2000 census showed that Mississippi had the fourth-highest percentage of people living in rural areas in the United States. While states such as Montana,.Idaho, and Alaska have a much lower population per square mile, those populations are mostly centered in defined urban clusters. For example, the 2000 census figures show that Mississippi had a population density of 60.6 people per square mile. Idaho, in contrast, had a density of 15.7 people per square mile (U.S. Census Bureau, 2010a), and is thus more rural. However, if the percentage of the population living in urban clusters is examined, the picture is reversed. Idaho had two thirds of its population in these clusters, compared to less than half (48.8%) of the Mississippi population (U.S. Census Bureau, 2010b). In addition, the 2010 census showed that Mississippi had the second-lowest population density of states east of the Mississippi River. These specific metrics establish that, as a state, Mississippi is clearly disadvantaged by the fact that its population is so heavily rural.

Mississippi can also be readily described as impoverished. The 2010 census figures indicated that the state had the highest levels of poverty in the United States and was second only to Washington, D.C., in childhood poverty (U.S. Department of Agriculture, 2010). In Mississippi, 22.4% of the population was found to live in poverty. An even greater percentage of the children in the state, 32.4%, fell into the impoverished category. Only 6 of 82 Mississippi counties had a poverty rate lower than 17% (U.S. Department of Agriculture, 2010). As a state, Mississippi had the lowest median household income in the United States (U.S. Census Bureau, 2009) and thus can be clearly characterized as among the most rural and impoverished states in America.

### Mississippi Superintendents

When considering the district superintendency preparation path and role in Mississippi, two public policies are relevant. First, Mississippi administrative licenses are tiered by educational level. The tiered licenses affect how the holder is paid but have relatively no impact on the level of administrative position the individual is authorized to hold. The minimum education level that an individual must complete to obtain an administrator's license is a master's degree in educational leadership. This license is known as a double A (AA) initial administrator's license. If an individual completes an educational specialist (Ed.S.) or doctorate (Ph.D. or Ed.D.) program, he or she would receive a AAA or AAAA license accordingly.

For each of these higher levels of education, the individual would be eligible for increased pay, but no difference exists among the types of administrative positions these various licenses allow the holder to seek. The result is that an individual with the lowest possible level of education and preparation required to obtain an administrative license is eligible for any administrative position along the continuum, ranging from the entry-level assistant principal to superintendent. At the start of the 2011–2012 school year, 50% of the superintendents in the state of Mississippi held AA licenses. In other words, half of the districts in the state were managed by leaders whose highest level of educational attainment was the entry-level master's degree. But this licensure-preparation phenomenon describes only part of the challenge for ensuring quality school superintendents in Mississippi.

As stated earlier, Mississippi, Alabama, and Florida are the only states in the country where a portion of the state's district superintendents are chosen through the general election process. In Mississippi, such elections take place every 4 years. In 2007, 65 school district superintendencies were determined by election. For the next election cycle—in 2011—this number was reduced to 63. This reduction was the result of one district undergoing a change from having an elected superintendent to having an appointed one and one district being abolished by the state because of poor academic performance. If this abolished district is improved in the next 4 years, the community will return to electing a superintendent. In the remaining 86 districts in the state, determining superintendent leadership requires that the local school board engage in a search, interview, and hiring/appointment process.

Local school boards in Mississippi may consider superintendent candidates who meet two basic requirements. First, the individual must hold a valid Mississippi administrative license. Second, the individual must reside within the boundaries of the district. Such requirements are fairly standard across the nation. The first is a basic standard for working within any public school setting. To fill nearly any school staff position, an individual must hold the required licensure. This requirement is the same for all certified positions within a school district, from superintendent to classroom teacher, and even other paraprofessional positions such as bus driver, teaching assistant, and so on. The second requirement for candidacy is a basic American standard for nearly any elected position. In most elections, a candidate must maintain residency in the community represented by the elected officeholder. Herein lies an additional challenge to educational leadership equity: the state's rural nature limits access to quality leaders within the boundaries of some of the most disadvantaged school districts in the state.

## Access to Ed.D. Programs

Mississippi has fifteen public and private universities with education preparation programs. Of these universities, only seven grant doctoral degrees in educational leadership; the other eight offer the master's as the most advanced degree for education professionals and scholars. Of the seven doctoral-granting institutions, six of them offer a Doctorate of Education, or Ed.D. degree. Degree options for educational leaders through traditional brick-and-mortar campuses, as well as online universities, should mean that access to degree-granting programs is not a concern for educators in Mississippi. Also important to note is the logical assumption that when individuals who have earned a doctorate are elected to the position of school superintendents, their earned degree would likely be a doctorate in education, though this is not part of any requirement or policy.

## METHODOLOGY

### Questions on School Leader Preparation

It must be stated that this research does not attempt to make a statement about the "effectiveness" of the examined school administrators. The focus questions of this research specifically ask the following:

- Are leadership preparation variations revealed when comparing education levels of elected superintendents and candidates for the superintendency from the Mississippi 2011 primary and general elections?
- What, if any, relationship exists between superintendent preparation levels and school district academic performance?

The state accountability system index score for the overall district was used as the correlation variable. In terms of this analysis of equitable access to high-quality school district leaders, Mississippi offers a unique perspective for school districts across the United States.

### Participant Sampling, Data Collection, and Data Analysis

Because a large number of its school districts have elected superintendents—over 40% of all districts in the state—Mississippi serves as an ideal case study. The system for licensing administrators in Mississippi allows for a good data fit for reliable and valid results. There are three levels of Mississippi school administrator licenses: (1) AA, (2) AAA, and (3) AAAA, each corresponding to the highest level of education a superintendent candidate has completed. In the state, primary and general election results reveal data identifying the education levels of the candidates who sought election in these districts. With appointed superintendents, this kind of information is not readily available for comparison; therefore, the analysis herein is limited to elected superintendents.

The data used for this study were collected through the examination of the public records of the state of Mississippi. Information regarding the primary and general election candidates and results were gathered from the Mississippi Secretary of State website. This site provides access to the reports submitted to the Secretary of State's office by each county for all positions involved in a specific election—including local school superintendent—for every type of election (primary, general, and special). These reports provided the number of candidates, their names, and any party affiliation of the candidate.

Licensure information for the current superintendents as well as the superintendent candidates was obtained through the Mississippi Department of Education (MDE) website, which contains a database of all the licensed educators in the state. Candidates' names were searched in the database in order to obtain the level of licensure each individual holds. As stated earlier, the level of license—AA, AAA, or AAAA—indicates the highest level of education the individual has completed—master's, specialist, or doctorate, respectively. A determination of doctorate types—either Ed.D. or Ph.D.—is not available. This database was also used to obtain information about each school district. The primary data examined were the aggregate poverty levels and the school accountability ratings for the districts.

## RESULTS

Results of this analysis were examined to determine whether there are leadership preparation variations revealed in Mississippi when comparing education levels of elected superintendents and unsuccessful candidates for the superintendency from the 2011 primary and general elections. This study also considered what relationship, if any, exists between superintendent preparation levels and school district academic performance.

In the fall of 2011, an election was held in Mississippi to choose school superintendents. Table 29.1 shows the highest attained education levels for all superintendents at the beginning of the 2011–2012 school year. This table provides an overall view of how the various levels of education are distributed between the elected and appointed positions.

An important result concerning level of leadership preparation found in the data on sitting superintendents is between districts that appoint and those that elect. Sixty-three percent of the districts that elect the superintendent have leaders with the minimum level of education required for the position. This percentage compares to only 40% of the districts with appointed superintendents. Similarly, proportionally fewer superintendents (14%) with the maximum level of education—the doctoral degree—hold superintendencies in districts that elect as compared to those that appoint (50%). Data regarding incumbent superintendents and the impact of the election process on the continued tenure of a given incumbent superintendent also provide a clear indication of the level of preparedness.

Table 29.1. Highest Education Level Obtained by Sitting Superintendents in Mississippi Schools, Fall 2011.

|  | Master's # (% of $n$) | Specialist # (% of $n$) | Doctorate # (% of $n$) |
|---|---|---|---|
| Elected Superintendents $n = 65$ | 41[2] (63%) | 15 (23%) | 9 (14%) |
| Appointed Superintendents $n = 83$[1] | 33[3] (40%) | 8 (10%) | 42[4] (50%) |
| Total $n = 148$[1] | 74 (50%) | 23 (16%) | 51 (34%) |

[1] One district excluded because no information was found regarding the interim superintendent.
[2] Includes 3 interim superintendents and 2 school leaders placed by the state due to poor school performance.
[3] Includes 3 interim and 1 state appointments.
[4] Includes 3 interim and 1 state appointments.

The first reported result concerns the pool of all individuals who sought to be elected to a school superintendent post in the state of Mississippi in 2011. This pool would include all the candidates that participated in the party primaries in August 2011 and those individuals who participated in the general election of November 2011. Table 29.2 shows the number and percentage of individuals running for a superintendent position distributed by the highest level of education attained.

Table 29.2. Highest Education Level Achieved by Superintendent Candidates in Mississippi Schools, Fall 2011.

|  | Master's # (% of $n$) | Specialist # (% of $n$) | Doctorate # (% of $n$) |
|---|---|---|---|
| $n = 165$[1] | 108 (65%) | 29 (18%) | 28 (17%) |

[1] Two candidates were excluded due to lack of license information.

Table 29.2 also shows the overall candidate pool of unique individuals participating in any part of the election cycle, primary or general. The most striking revelation of this table is that, of the total pool of candidates for 63 school districts, only 167 individuals were listed as candidates for the position of school district superintendent. This translates into fewer than three candidates per district on average. Other data trends show that the highest degree for 65% of the candidates was a master's degree, compared to 63% of the sitting superintendents. Similarly, 17% of the candidates held doctoral degrees, while 14% of sitting superintendents held that level of degree. The one degree level that was different between these groups was that of the Education Specialist degree. For this degree group, 23% of the sitting superintendents held a specialist degree, while only 18% of the total candidate pool held that degree.

For the number of superintendent candidates per district, the range was one to six. Seventeen districts had only one (unopposed) candidate for superintendent of their local schools. Of the districts participating in the election for a superintendent, 27% had no real choice. An additional 19 districts had the superintendent position filled through the party primary process, effectively ending the election process after the competing superintendent candidates were from a single political party. When the districts with single-party primary candidates are added to the number of districts whose race was totally uncontested, 57% of the superintendents were elected in an uncontested general election.

Mississippi, like all states, has an accountability system that categorizes schools and districts based on state standardized exam performance. The Mississippi accountability rating system had six categories at the time of this data collection: Failing, At Risk, Academic Watch, Successful, High Performing, and Star. Schools are placed in these categories based on a metric called the quality distribution index, or QDI. This index is a weighted calculation of student performance levels on the state test. In other words, the higher the percentage of a district's students scoring well (proficient or advanced) on the state test, the higher the QDI. These ratings can be used as an ordinal statistic to compare with the preparation level of the superintendents to determine whether there is a relationship between the two data sets. Toward these ends, a first type of comparison was simply to examine the distribution of preparation levels across the six categories of school performance. Table 29.3 shows the distribution of superintendent preparation across the various performance categories.

A comparison of Tables 29.3 and 29.1 reveals that superintendent preparation percentages are very similar, especially in the middle ranges of the four performance categories, which represent the vast majority of schools in the state. Such a parallel distribution would indicate that the likelihood of a statistically significant correlation between the level of superintendent preparation and school performance is very low. This is, in fact, the case. A Spearman's rank order correlation was used to determine the relationship between the superintendents' preparation levels and the district performance rating. An extremely small, statistically insignificant relationship ($r_s$ = 0.040, $P$= 0.682) was found. Without a stronger correlation, significance of formal and specific superintendent preparation can be called into question. The study now considers other factors that might have led to a lack of statistical significance in the relationship between superintendent preparation level and academic performance.

Table 29.3. Distribution of Superintendent Preparation Levels Across School Performance Categories.

| | Master's<br># (% of $n$) | Specialist<br># (% of $n$) | Doctorate<br># (% of $n$) |
|---|---|---|---|
| Star<br>$n$ = 3 | 0 (0%) | 1 (33%) | 2 (66%) |
| High Performing<br>$n$ = 24 | 12 (50%) | 3 (13%) | 9 (38%) |
| Successful<br>$n$ = 50 | 25 (50%) | 6 (12%) | 19 (38%) |
| Academic Watch<br>$n$ = 35 | 20 (57%) | 6 (17%) | 9 (26%) |
| At Risk<br>$n$ = 30 | 15 (50%) | 5 (17%) | 10 (33%) |
| Failing<br>$n$ = 7 | 2 (29%) | 2 (29%) | 3 (43%) |

## DISCUSSION: THE MISSISSIPPI CASE OF EDUCATIONAL LEADER PREPARATION

In Mississippi, school districts with elected superintendents are more often led by individuals with lower levels of education than in those districts where the school superintendent is appointed. This difference in distribution raises concerns regarding the pool of candidates available within the elected districts. The investigation of the election data—for both primary and general elections—illuminates the nature of the superintendent candidate preparedness distribution in Mississippi. Examining the aggregate pool of candidates shows that the highest educational level obtained by the candidates closely parallels the education levels of the individuals who held those positions prior to the election. Concerning the diversity of educational backgrounds of school superintendent candidates, the pool was quite limited in diversity of preparation.

In the wake of the most recent election, the children in districts with an elected superintendent are almost twice as likely to have a district leader with the minimum amount of formal education required for the position. This shift also means that over half the school districts in the state are led by superintendents with the lowest level of formal training required. Policymakers can and should address the disparity between preparedness of elected and appointed superintendents. Surely policymakers would address the lesser-prepared nature of elected superintendents if student academic performance data correlated to superintendent preparation levels. Next we examine the relationship between superintendent preparation levels and school performance.

In the face of increased deregulation of licensure and preparation requirements for superintendents across the country, Mississippi provides a unique perspective with its current minimal licensure standards (Kowalski & Björk, 2005). It would appear that when the state allows for low levels of preparation, it becomes the norm across the state. But what are Mississippi schools—and potentially those in other states that have deregulated the superintendency—missing by not requiring higher levels of preparation?

The Carnegie Project on the Education Doctorate (CPED) (2014) has developed some key working principles that focus on the importance of developing practitioners with strong field experience linked to research. These principles also focus on issues of community, poverty, and social justice. By allowing individuals with lower levels of preparation to become superintendents, the majority of Mississippi schools miss the opportunity to have district leaders with knowledge, understanding, and dispositions geared to address some of the state's greatest challenges. Even if every university in the state retooled its doctoral program to align with the Carnegie Project and successfully embodied the civic leadership traits in its Ed.D. graduates, the majority of Mississippi school children would not benefit, due to the lack of required training and preparation to engage in this work (Zambo, 2011).

## CONCLUSIONS

Two clear conclusions emerge from the data presented. First, for those districts in the sample that held elections, there was a strong probability that the superintendent would have the minimum level of education required for the position. Nearly three fourths of the examined districts that held elections have superintendents with a master's degree as their highest level of education. Second, of the many sample districts holding elections, no real choice between candidates with differing preparation levels was available. Nearly 60% of the examined districts slated only one final candidate for school superintendent.

Some implications of this data set are worth considering. First, state-level policy implications are unique for the state of Mississippi and its particular practices of licensing and electing superintendents. Electing superintendents and minimally certifying district administrators are related in ways that should be more closely examined. By using the election process for school superintendents, the state of Mississippi has sanctioned a more general—even a lesser—preparation level for school superintendents than SREB member states that do not elect individuals to this position. The diminished size of the candidate pool for elected offices of superintendent highlights the sanctioning of a more general, lesser-prepared superintendent.

If the state were to make more specific the licensure, training, or educational requirements for the superintendent position, the available pool of candidates would surely become even narrower. In some communities, the pool would likely be reduced to zero. Suppose the state mandated more training for superintendent candidates and a separate certification, as does most of the southern region. The practice of electing superintendents might need to be eliminated; in any case, it would certainly require closer scrutiny. Again, this research does not attempt to make assumptions about superintendent effectiveness around the state. However, researchers have shown that quality leadership does matter to school and student outcomes (Byrd et al., 2006; Waters & Marzano, 2006). Likewise, if the state of Mississippi wished to increase the likelihood of having effective leaders by requiring specific training/education in the area of school district administration, then the state would also need to consider the elimination of the practice of electing local superintendents.

From a broader perspective, this research raises concerns about the preparation levels of superintendents working in the most challenging districts in the country. Mississippi is uniquely positioned with its licensure practices and the use of the election process, which allows for the public examination of the candidate pools. No matter what superintendent appointing process is used in Mississippi, further examination is needed for highly marginalized areas to attract a sizable pool of highly prepared candidates for the superintendent position. Naturally, applicant pools in high-poverty areas like Mississippi will continue to be small, and candidates will continue to have lower levels of preparation until policy changes are made. Additional research about forms of superintendent preparation, recruitment, and retention of quality school leaders is needed to encourage stronger superintendent preparation in disadvantaged areas.

## REFERENCES

Byrd, J.K., Slater, R.O., & Brooks, J. (2006). *Educational administration program quality and the impact on student achievement.* Retrieved from http://files.eric.ed.gov/fulltext/ED493288.pdf

Carnegie Project on the Education Doctorate (CPED). (2014). *Education doctorate: Definition and working principles.* Retrieved from http://cpedinitiative.org/working-principles-professional-practice-doctorate-education

Elmore, R.F. (1996). Getting to scale with good educational practice. *Harvard Educational Review*, *66*(1), 1–26.

Gross, R.E. (1978, December). Seven new cardinal principles. *Phi Delta Kappan*, *60*(4), 291–293.

Kowalski, T.J., & Björk, L.G. (2005). Role expectations of the district superintendent: Implications for deregulating preparation and licensing. *Journal of Thought*, *40*(2), 73–96. Retrieved from http://0-search.ebscohost.com.maurice.bgsu.edu/login.aspx?direct=true&db=ehh&AN=17404117&site=ehost-live&scope=site

Levine, A. (2005). *Educating school leaders*. Washington, DC: Education Schools Project. Retrieved from http://www.edschools.org/reports_leaders.htm

Murphy, J., Moorman, H.N., & McCarthy, M. (2008). A framework for rebuilding initial certification and preparation programs in educational leadership: Lessons from whole-state reform initiatives. *Teachers College Record*, *110*(10), 2172–2203.

National Association of Secondary School Principals (NASSP). (1996). *Breaking ranks: Changing an American institution: A report of the National Association of Secondary School Principals in partnership with the Carnegie Foundation for the Advancement of Teaching on the High School of the 21st Century*. Reston, VA: The Association.

National Commission on Excellence in Education. (1983). *A nation at risk: The imperative for educational reform: A report to the nation and the Secretary of Education, United States Department of Education*. Washington, DC: National Commission on Excellence in Education.

Newmann, F.M., & Wehlage, G.G. (1995). *Successful school restructuring: A report to the public and educators*. Madison, WI: Center on Organization and Restructuring of Schools.

No Child Left Behind (NCLB) Act of 2001. (2002). Pub. L. No. 107–110, 115, Stat. 1425.

Southern Regional Education Board (SREB). (2000). *Focus on school district superintendents*. Retrieved from http://www.sreb.org/page/1335/00s02_focus_on_school_district_superintendents.html

U.S. Census Bureau. (2009). *Household income—distribution by income level and state: 2009*. Washington, DC: U.S. Census Bureau.

U.S. Census Bureau. (2010a). *State population—rank, percent change, and population density: 1980 to 2010*. Washington, DC: U.S. Census Bureau.

U.S. Census Bureau. (2010b). *Urban and rural population by state: 1990 and 2000*. Washington, DC: U.S. Census Bureau.

U.S. Department of Agriculture. (2010). *2010 county-level poverty rates*. Washington, DC: U.S. Department of Agriculture.

Varrati, A.M., Tooms, A.K., & Thomas, S.B. (2006). Is NCATE the answer to current criticism of educational leadership preparation programs? *Journal of Scholarship & Practice*, *3*(1), 37–43.

Waters, T.J., & Marzano, R.J. (2006). *School district leadership that works: The effect of superintendent leadership on student achievement. A working paper*. Retrieved from http://eric.ed.gov/?id=ED494270

Wiggins, G.P., & McTighe, J. (2001). *Understanding by design*. Alexandria, VA: Association for Supervision and Curriculum Development.

Young, M.D., & Creighton, T.B. (2002). *Who is framing the nation's understanding of educational leadership and practice?* Paper presented at the National Council of Professors of Educational Administration, Burlington, VT.

Zambo, D. (2011). Action research as signature pedagogy in an education doctorate program: The reality and hope. *Innovative Higher Education*, *36*(4), 261–271. doi: 10.1007/s10755-010-9171-7

Zambo, D., & Isai, S. (2013). Action research and the educational doctorate: New promises and visions. *Journal of Research on Leadership Education*, *8*(1), 97–112. doi: 10.1177/1942775112464960

# Reimagining the Education Doctorate (Ed.D.) as a Catalyst for Social Change

*David J. Siegel and Crystal R. Chambers*

The revolutionaries thought that a frontal assault could accelerate the switch from the present to the future, from black to white, from hell to heaven. The alternative is to approach problems at a tangent. That is a poet's way, and perhaps now we prefer a poet's way, to find our way around problems, to seek hybrids, alliances of opposites, impure compromises, and to be wary of the human brain's love of coherence when impure compromises may serve us best.

—Geoff Mulgan, *The Locust and the Bee* (2013)

## INTRODUCTION

The academic enterprise faces a bewildering array of stakeholder demands, including greater access, cutting-edge scientific research, regional economic development, workforce preparation, and accountability. At the same time, colleges and universities are expected to reduce costs, increase faculty productivity, hold the line on tuition, generate revenues from new sources, tap into emerging global markets, leverage the latest technologies, and realize greater efficiencies, all while providing peak learning experiences for diverse students in a climate of heightened scrutiny and diminished autonomy. External—and occasionally even internal—calls for a radically different business model grow more frequent and insistent, almost by the day (see, for example, Christensen, Horn, Caldera, & Soares, 2011; Lumina Foundation, 2013).

These and related pressures are not unique to higher education; they are, in fact, expressions of broader social issues and challenges, ones that confront other societal sectors—business, government, and nonprofits—with accelerating force. Classic "wicked problems" (Rittel & Webber, 1973), or meta-problems (Chevalier, 1966), are exacerbated by our tendency to fragment them, to address them from the perspectives of our specialized professional orientations (educator, industrialist, government official) rather than from a more holistic and integrated perspective that acknowledges social problems as enormously complex ecosystems in their own right. As the Kellogg Commission on the Future of State and Land-Grant Universities put it in a widely publicized report titled *Returning to Our Roots* (1999, p. 9), "Although society has 'problems,' our institutions have 'disciplines.'"

In this chapter we advance an argument that the education doctorate ought to be better tailored to social purpose by reorienting the education experience to prepare change agents to think and work effectively *across societal sectors* to address complex social problems. The term applied to this arrangement is *cross-sector collaboration* or *cross-sector social partnership* (Bryson, Crosby, & Stone, 2006; Selsky & Parker, 2005; Siegel, 2010), and the repertoire of understandings and competencies necessary to help it flourish suggests a different, less education-centric, approach to the Ed.D. than has been the case historically. What follows is a brief exploration of the possibilities and difficulties inherent in educating leaders for constructive engagement across sectors.

## A CLIMATE OF ESCALATING DEMAND

A detailed elaboration of forces impinging on higher education at the beginning of the twenty-first century is unnecessary; even the most casual observer can easily discern that the academy is under pervasive and growing pressure to remake itself in one image or another, depending on the interest group. A selective sample of recent reports, initiatives, and developments highlights the general trend.

1. A national college completion agenda is being fueled and funded by influential proponents, including the Lumina Foundation for Education, the Bill and Melinda Gates Foundation, The College Board, the Obama administration, and state governors. Lumina's "Big Goal" for college attainment is the most visible of these efforts: it is pushing for 60% of Americans to possess a high-quality postsecondary degree or credential by 2025. For its part, the Obama administration would like to see an additional 5 million Americans with some level of postsecondary education by 2020.

2. The National Task Force on Civic Learning and Democratic Engagement (2012)—a partnership of the U.S. Department of Education, the Global Perspectives Institute (GPI), and the Association of American Colleges and Universities (AAC&U)—has issued a national call to action to make

civic learning and democratic engagement a priority for higher education, largely in reaction to troubling indicators of civic decline in recent years.

3. It is not uncommon to hear that American higher education, like the country itself, is in crisis. This is the conclusion of Clayton Christensen and his colleagues in *Disrupting College*, a 2011 report issued by the Center for American Progress, in which the authors argue that what is needed for the delivery of high-quality and affordable postsecondary education is a healthy dose of disruptive innovation, notably in the form of online learning. Given the inordinate amount of attention that massive open online courses (MOOCs) have garnered in both the academic and popular press since 2012, it appears that we are witnessing a period of experimentation—some of it enthusiastic, some of it quite skeptical—with these and similar education innovations.

4. Not all crises in higher education are created equal; the humanities are under particular assault in an age dominated by commercialism, consumerism, and vocationalism (see, for example, Schrecker, 2011). Although the National Research Council (2012) asserts "the importance of supporting the comprehensive nature of the research university, spanning the full spectrum of academic and professional disciplines, including...the arts and humanities" (p. 6), none of its recommendations bolster this beleaguered area of academe. The humanities are not alone; other revenue-challenged fields—education, fine arts, and social work among them—are chronically vulnerable.

The prominent narrative in American higher education and among higher education systems around the world is that universities are indispensable to *economic* growth and prosperity—to the income potential of graduates, to national innovation, and to the discovery and development of commercially viable products. What we are observing in American higher education is also true of higher education systems abroad. From Europe to Australia, there has been a pronounced shift from a Humboldtian notion of the university to one that is increasingly market oriented and managed according to the logic of markets (see, for example, Krejsler, 2006). Meanwhile, as Kuttner (1999) reminds us, "much of human life cannot be reduced to a market" (p. 40), and much of the university's value to society is lost when it is reduced to a mere engine of capitalism.

## THE LARGER SOCIAL CONTEXT

As much as it seems that higher education is coming in for especially severe criticism for its failure to service various public priorities, the fact is that nearly every societal institution is laboring under the combined burden of intense social pressure and diminished public trust (Kellerman, 2012; Vail, 2008). Businesses, for example, contend with a corporate social responsibility (CSR) mandate that holds them accountable for their performance on a number of social and environmental indicators (see, for example, McElhaney, 2008), and stricter monitoring of corporate activity—enabled largely by the Sarbanes-Oxley Act of 2002—has been the norm since the large-scale scandals of the early 2000s (Enron, WorldCom, Tyco, and News Corp, to name but a few).

In the government arena, the past 5 years have been enormously challenging for state-dominated governance systems around the world, which have had to contend with economic collapse, rising social inequalities, massive technological and biophysical changes, and questions about the role and relevance of centralized bureaucracies in large-scale social problem solving. These realities have been accompanied by a pervasive and growing climate of cynicism in reaction to government corruption, incompetence, and negligence. In the United States, for example, public confidence in political institutions continues to erode in the face of ideological polarization, extreme partisanship, incivility, and corporate influence in the policymaking process. The most recent congressional job approval data reveal that only about 14% of respondents think the U.S. Congress is doing its job (Real Clear Politics, 2014).

At the same time, the unprecedented speed and scale of urban growth has led to massive increases in urban poverty, threats to natural resources, risks to public health, and a weakening of social cohesion, especially in the developing world (Cohen, 2006). Indeed, these and other challenges present an almost insuperable burden on traditional governance and management systems, which simply lack the capacity to deal with such problems and their unpredictable consequences.

Whether we are talking about unequal access to education, poverty, disease, environmental degradation, or ethnic violence, one of the common attributes referenced in discussions of these thorny issues is that they are intricately interconnected with other sets of problems. They are also agnostic with respect to boundaries. In short, they migrate across disciplinary, professional, organizational, or sectoral borders with impunity. Not surprisingly, given the scope and scale of social problems, single organizations or sectors have been largely ineffectual in their attempts—however well meaning—to "solve" such problems, which simply overwhelms the resources of independent entities.

## CROSS-SECTOR COLLABORATION

Informal networks of social actors have emerged as a viable design alternative—or supplement—to institutionalized technocracies, and their proliferation heralds a number of possibilities for theorists, practitioners, and supporters of social change. As network forms of organizing (Chisolm, 1998), open-source initiatives, copyleft licensing, "do-it-yourself (DIY)" movements in various domains (Iveson, 2013), and the sharing economy (Gansky, 2010) all serve to illustrate, there appears to be increasing interest in broadly participatory, citizen-led efforts to take greater control of the prospects for social change in ways that lead to more sustainable, resilient, self-reliant, and innovative communities and institutions. Boundaries are falling away in many areas of modern life, a phenomenon enabled in large part by technological advances that permit a new ease of assembly without the concomitant burden of institutional infrastructure and its associated costs.

Cross-sector collaboration fits neatly within this category of activity. Although cross-sector collaboration can and does refer to a whole spectrum of linkages for a variety of purposes (for example, for scientific, technological, and economic development), our primary concern is with cross-sector collaboration for the creation of *social* value. Cross-sector social partnerships, as a subset of cross-sector collaboration, are those "formed explicitly to address social issues and causes that actively engage the partners on an ongoing basis" (Selsky & Parker, 2005, p. 850). Sectors themselves are generally understood as domains of similarly oriented and organized enterprises, although there is tremendous diversity even within sectors. The three primary sectors are government, business, and the nonprofit sector (see, for example, Fosler, 2001), with higher education traditionally located in the nonprofit sector.

Collaboration within and across sectors has increased significantly over the past few decades, both in the United States and throughout the world. There has been a rapid expansion of organized voluntary activity in advanced and developing regions, leading one scholar to proclaim the emergence of a "global associational revolution" that may be to the modern era what the nation-state was to the late 1800s and early 1900s (Salamon, 2005, p. 137). The twenty-first century is forecast to be the age of organizational alliances, and collaboration already has all the force of a global social mandate (Austin, 2000). The 2002 World Summit on Sustainable Development, for example, explicitly encouraged the development of partnerships among government, business, and civil society in order to reduce poverty in developing countries.

## A CROSS-SECTOR APPROACH TO DOCTORAL EDUCATION

All indications are that the future holds even greater, more perplexing public challenges than we face at the moment, and we can reasonably expect that society's organizations will be called on to take more responsibility for them in a neoliberal era. How should we prepare our doctoral students to think about and respond to these challenges? What are the experiences that should be on offer to cultivate intercultural competence?

Our contention is that constructive engagement across sectors calls for a different model of education and a different mindset. Taking a cue from sociologist C. Wright Mills, who observed in *The Sociological Imagination* (1959) that "to understand the changes of many personal milieux we are required to look beyond them" (p. 10), we introduce a three-part framework for reimagining the education doctorate as a more potent catalyst for social change by emphasizing the development of "relational intelligence" and allied capacities. Beginning with awareness and moving on to identification and engagement, the sequence goes in the direction of a gradual loosening of institutional self-interest in favor of joint problem solving for prosocial ends.

## Awareness

Collective action for social change begins with awareness. The initial stage of development in our framework exposes students to the complexity of social problems, beginning with very basic questions such as the following:

1. What are social problems? What distinguishes a social *issue* from a social *problem*? How do different identity groups or special interest groups frame or define social problems differently, and what are the effects of these different problem framings?
2. What are the sources of social problems?
3. Who bears responsibility for addressing or solving them? How have ideas of social responsibility shifted over time?
4. How and why are various collectivities—sectors, organizations, professions—expected to address social problems?
5. How do unilateral organizational or sectoral responses both contribute to problem solving and exacerbate social problems?
6. In what ways are organizations themselves—whether universities, schools, business corporations, government agencies, nonprofit groups, or other entities—producers and propagators of social problems. In what ways, for example, is higher education complicit in the reproduction of "existing racial hierarchies" (Chesler, Lewis, & Crowfoot, 2005, p. 26) even as it promotes diversity?

One of the outcomes or consequences of exposure to social problems should be the realization that independent problem-solving efforts by sectors—or by the organizations that comprise the various sectors—often sub-optimize, if not altogether sabotage, the change process, consistent with the idea that complex public problems exceed the capacity of single actors to do very much about them. Alternative configurations of actors provide the diversity of expertise and other vital resources necessary to tackle such problems. A general introduction to collaboration theory and empirical studies of partnership dynamics will acquaint students with the following:

1. Starting conditions—environmental and organizational—that give rise to collaboration among the sectors;

2. Specific rationales and *types* of rationales (from self-interest to altruism) used by organizations to justify entry into multi-sector social alliances, as well as the ways in which the narrative process of rationale *construction* over time—not just in the initial entry stage—continues to shape the conduct and consequences of social engagement among sectors (Siegel, 2008);

3. The role that issue framing (for example, the centrality of a social issue to an organization's scope of work or the consistency of the issue with existing organizational priorities) plays in the formation and development of social partnerships;

4. The actual experience of collaboration, including (1) negotiating the terms of involvement and clarifying expectations (such as the differentiation of roles and the division of labor), (2) establishing management and governance structures, (3) building trust, (4) dealing constructively with differences (conflicting operating styles or inconsistent interpretations of shared tasks, for example), (5) attending to the cultural and symbolic aspects of collaboration, such as the use of metaphors to describe joint work, and (6) sustaining enthusiasm and commitment;

5. The ultimate difference made by cross-sector alliances (their outcomes, consequences, or effects) for (1) the social issue and its affected parties, (2) participating organizations, and (3) larger social systems;

6. Particular advantages and challenges of asymmetric contribution in cooperative systems (see, for example, Benkler, 2011), which encourages participants to "come as you are, contribute what you can";

7. The institutional difficulties of engaging in hybrid ("promiscuous, impure") forms of organizing; and

8. A continuum of partnership activity that runs from informal to formal.

## Identification

Beyond the development of awareness and understanding, how do we induce doctoral students in education to see their enterprise as "one" with other sectors for purposes of social problem solving? In other words, how do we encourage something like a common identification to take hold? This is a difficult proposition in a world where much is staked on strongly held group identities and affiliations, which tend to build cohesion, impart a sense of order, and provide meaning for their members (see, for example, Bouchikhi & Kimberly, 2003; Dutton, Dukerich, & Harquail, 1994). To be sure, the academy is rife with contests among competing tribes and territories (Becher, 1989), and on a larger cultural level, one need only look to debates over the corporatization of higher education to see that many in the "academic tribe" view their work as distinct from—even incommensurable with—that of business.

But too much time spent uncritically among one's own kind is ultimately distortive—of reality, perspective, and possibility. This is not to say that tribes, however we define or delineate them, are always perfectly uniform or even internally consistent in their values, beliefs, and behaviors; there is, of course, plenty of diversity within identity groupings, and there are numerous examples of dissent, divergence, and departure from whatever—sometimes nominal—ideological or normative orthodoxy binds a community together. The point to be made here is that tribalism breeds, among many other things, a certain insularity, a clipped and shaded view of the world, and even a disinclination to open oneself and one's community to alternative ways of thinking and being and experiencing. Tribes, in other words, can become closed—not open—systems, where priority is placed on maintaining the system, repelling external threats, and continually justifying the group's existence.

Rigid identity distinctions can lead to intergroup conflict that undermines the social engagement project. A collective identity can aid in more effective collective action to address social issues. Helpful strategies for improving intergroup relations are suggested by research findings from social psychology (Dovidio, Gaertner, & Saguy, 2009) and social identity theory (Tajfel & Turner, 1979).

For example, studies have shown that a simple substitution of in-group pronouns ("we" and "us") for outgroup pronouns ("they" and "them") when thinking about others "spontaneously activates more positive associations" (Dovidio et al., 2009, p. 5). These and similar research findings support the idea that the process of social categorization, which is the root of identity formation, can be manipulated in the interest of expanding category boundaries to make them more inclusive. Of particular interest for present purposes is a "recategorization" strategy described by Dovidio and colleagues (2009) that induces members of different groups "to conceive of themselves as a single, more inclusive superordinate group" (p. 5). Doctoral students, for example, might be reoriented to think of themselves not just as higher education leaders but as social problem solvers or stakeholders in social problems. This broader identification would permit the inclusion of members of "rival" tribes (from business, government, and nonprofits) that might prove salutary for social problems. Structured opportunities for direct, meaningful interactions with doctoral students from other disciplines, and rich encounters with representatives from industry and government, can be expected to facilitate the development of mutual understanding, trust, empathy, and solidarity.

## Engagement

The third and final stage of our model focuses on the actual experience of cross-sector collaboration in situ. The essential idea is for doctoral students in education to work together with counterparts across sectors to address an identified social problem or challenge that has relevance for all partners involved. This might take the form of an action research project, an internship, a practicum, or a similar experiential learning opportunity in which doctoral students are awarded credit for the satisfactory completion of a social engagement project that draws on the concepts and principles described earlier. Details of the project would of necessity vary by program and circumstance; some programs might be able to place students in existing multi-sector partnerships that are already well underway, whereas other programs might require students to launch such efforts from scratch. Either way, initial contact with the institution's office of community relations, corporate relations, government relations, or public affairs would be advisable in order to facilitate connections with prospective partners.

The primary objective is for students to acquire cross-sector organizing skills in support of social problem solving. They should assume complete responsibility for—or be active participants in—all aspects of the task: framing the problem, organizing the group, assigning roles, dividing labor, coordinating resources, negotiating courses of action, managing conflict, making decisions, documenting results, and so on. In the process, they will develop a more sophisticated understanding of group dynamics, including the value of diverse views and perspectives, the challenges of achieving consensus, the role of dissident opinions, how people make sense of novel or ambiguous situations, how frustration may be productively channelled, and other dynamics that are central to any collaborative activity. The faculty role during this stage is one of encouraging students to connect their field-based experiences to theoretical understandings of cross-sector collaboration developed earlier in the program. As in other pedagogies of engagement such as service learning (Jacoby & Associates, 2009), instructors (or supervisors) call attention to particular learning opportunities and help students make sense of their experience as it unfolds.

## CHALLENGES

The central challenge in moving beyond a theoretically reimagined education doctoral experience to a realized model lies in balancing the tensions of being faithful to one's core values and strengths and becoming open to change and innovation. At one extreme, we can rely on the relative intransigence of higher education institutions—their reliable form, functions, and processes since medieval times. Toward that end, we can treat doctoral education generally, and the education doctorate in particular, as a form of cultural reproduction wherein we as faculty convey to our students the canon once conveyed to us.

At the other extreme is a passion to effect change. We can expose our students to a multiplicity of perspectives and arm them with tools for critical self-reflection, but without a core sense of self and an appreciation for the incomparable position that higher education holds in society, chisels intended to shape and tweak are turned into sledgehammers that destroy. In pursuing cross-sector partnerships, we risk losing ourselves in the process of engaging an "alien" other. How the sectors can maintain their unique identities (in our case, an academic identity) while working more closely with other organizations and sectors is a question to be pondered. At stake is the possibility that close ties with other entities will homogenize us so that we become duplicative, disposable, or perhaps even obsolete one day. This is the concern articulated by Stanley Fish (2008), who cautions that, if we as academics take on the world's problems instead of sticking to our proverbial knitting, we will dilute and ultimately destroy higher education as we know it.

But universities are, among other things, social constructions, susceptible to change as society finds new uses for them and reconstitutes them on that basis. Right now, and for the foreseeable future, universities and other organizations are being asked to play a more active and direct role in ameliorating a range of social problems and injustices. The question is not whether we will answer that call but how we will do it. To fuse and not lose one's unique contribution in the meld appears to be the challenge.

## THE DIFFERENCE MADE

What looks different when this change has been made? How are students, institutions, and problems themselves altered when we widen the ambit of our concerns in educational leadership programs? The overarching bet being wagered is that by practicing the art of seeing collaborators as constituent parts of a superordinate social system whose care is our *joint* responsibility, we may become more effective stewards of the common good and better able to fulfill our obligations in the social sphere. By approaching social challenges with an appropriate sense of self and an understanding of the positionality of actors and organizations outside of one's own realm, multiple vantages and expertise can be leveraged, with a distinct possibility that the combined knowledge, skills, and abilities yielded are more valuable than the individual parts. In so doing, we may overcome our own sense of inadequacy and feelings of being overwhelmed by joining together with partners who, like us, have perspectives, tools, and resources to address social problems.

## REFERENCES

Austin, J.E. (2000). *The collaboration challenge: How nonprofits and businesses succeed through strategic alliances*. San Francisco, CA: Jossey-Bass.

Becher, T. (1989). *Academic tribes and territories: Intellectual enquiry and the cultures of disciplines*. Buckingham, UK: Open University Press.

Benkler, Y. (2011). *The penguin and the leviathan: How cooperation triumphs over self-interest*. New York: Crown Business.

Bouchikhi, H., & Kimberly, J.R. (2003). Escaping the identity trap. *MIT Sloan Management Review*, *44*(3), 20–26.

Bryson, J.M., Crosby, B.C., & Stone, M.M. (2006). The design and implementation of cross-sector collaborations: Propositions from the literature. *Public Administration Review, 66* (special issue), 44–55.

Chesler, M., Lewis, A., & Crowfoot, J. (2005). *Challenging racism in higher education: Promoting justice*. Lanham, MD: Rowman & Littlefield.

Chevalier, M. (1966). *A wider range of perspectives in the bureaucratic structure*. Ottawa, ON, Canada: Commission on Bilingualism and Biculturalism.

Chisholm, R.F. (1998). *Developing network organizations: Learning from practice and theory*. Reading, MA: Addison-Wesley.

Christensen, C.M., Horn, M.B., Caldera, L., & Soares, L. (2011). *Disrupting college: How disruptive innovation can deliver quality and affordability to postsecondary education*. Washington, DC: Center for American Progress.

Cohen, B. (2006). Urbanization in developing countries: Current trends, future projections, and key challenges for sustainability. *Technology in Society, 28*(1), 63–80.

Dovidio, J.F., Gaertner, S.L., & Saguy, T. (2009). Commonality and the complexity of "we": Social attitudes and social change. *Personality and Social Psychology Review, 13*(1), 3–20.

Dutton, J.E., Dukerich, J.M., & Harquail, C.V. (1994). Organizational images and member identification. *Administrative Science Quarterly, 39*(2), 239–263.

Fish, S. (2008). *Save the world on your own time*. Oxford, UK: Oxford University Press.

Fosler, R.S. (2001). *Working better together: How government, business, and nonprofit organizations can achieve public purposes through cross-sector collaboration, partnership, and alliances*. Washington, DC: Independent Sector.

Gansky, L. (2010). *The mesh: Why the future of business is sharing*. New York: Portfolio Penguin.

Iveson, K. (2013). Cities within the city: Do-it-yourself urbanism and the right to the city. *International Journal of Urban and Regional Research, 37*(3), 941–956.

Jacoby, B., & Associates. (2009). *Civic engagement in higher education: Concepts and practices*. San Francisco, CA: Jossey-Bass.

Kellerman, B. (2012). *The end of leadership*. New York: HarperCollins.

Kellogg Commission on the Future of State and Land-Grant Universities. (1999). *Returning to our roots: The engaged institution*. Washington, DC: National Association of State Universities and Land-Grant Colleges.

Krejsler, J. (2006). Discursive battles about the meaning of university: The case of Danish university reform and its academics. *European Educational Research Journal, 5*(3–4), 210–220.

Kuttner, R. (1999). *Everything for sale: The virtues and limits of markets.* Chicago, IL: University of Chicago Press.

Lumina Foundation. (2013). *America's call for higher education redesign: The 2012 Lumina Foundation Study of the American public's opinion on higher education.* Indianapolis, IN: Lumina Foundation.

McElhaney, K.A. (2008). *Just good business: The strategic guide to aligning corporate responsibility and brand.* San Francisco, CA: Berrett-Koehler Publishers.

Mills, C.W. (1959). *The sociological imagination.* Oxford: Oxford University Press.

Mulgan, G. (2013). *The locust and the bee: Predators and creators in capitalism's future.* Princeton, NJ: Princeton University Press.

National Research Council (2012). *Research universities and the future of America: Ten breakthrough actions vital to our nation's prosperity and security.* Washington, DC: National Academies Press.

National Task Force on Civic Learning and Democratic Engagement. (2012). *A crucible moment: College learning and democracy's future.* Washington, DC: Association of American Colleges and Universities.

Real Clear Politics. (2014). *Congressional job approval.* Retrieved from http://www.realclearpolitics.com/epolls/other/congressional_job_approval-903.html

Rittel, H.W.J., & Webber, M.M. (1973). Dilemmas in a general theory of planning. *Policy Sciences, 4*(2), 155–169.

Salamon, L. (2005). Globalization and the civil society sector. In S. Hewa & D.H. Stapleton (Eds.), *Globalization, philanthropy, and civil society: Toward a new political culture in the twenty-first century* (pp. 137–152). New York: Springer.

Schrecker, E. (2011). The humanities on life support. *Academe, 97*(5), 47.

Selsky, J.W., & Parker, B. (2005). Cross-sector partnerships to address social issues: Challenges to theory and practice. *Journal of Management, 31*(6), 849–873.

Siegel, D.J. (2008). Framing involvement: Rationale construction in an inter-organizational collaboration. *Journal of Further and Higher Education, 32*(3), 221–240.

Siegel, D.J. (2010). *Organizing for social partnership: Higher education in cross-sector collaboration.* New York: Routledge.

Tajfel, H., & Turner, J. (1979). An integrative theory of intergroup conflict. In W.G. Austin & S. Worchel (Eds.), *The social psychology of intergroup relations* (pp. 33–47). Monterey, CA: Brooks/Cole Publishing Company.

Vail, J. (2008, August 25). Nonprofits need to restore trust, experts say. *Philanthropy Journal.* Retrieved from http://www.philanthropyjournal.org/news/nonprofits-need-restore-trust-expert-says

# About the Contributors

**Dr. Zarrina Talan Azizova** is a recent graduate of the Ph.D. Educational Leadership and Policy Studies/Higher Education and Student Affairs program at Oklahoma State University. During the 2012–2013 academic year, she was a recipient of the Robert B. & Maxine Kamm Distinguished Graduate Endowed Fellowship for her research and service at Oklahoma State University. Currently she teaches graduate courses in Educational Leadership/Higher Education and Student Affairs and continues to conduct her research in the College of Education, OSU. Broadly, her research focuses on diversity and inclusion issues in postsecondary education. She grounds her research in a historical, legal, and socioeconomic context of higher education access of historically underrepresented racial/ethnic minority students. Specifically, she is interested in how critical context of higher education affects graduate students' perceptions, experiences, and academic/professional socialization. By exploring doctoral students' experiences in two professional fields (STEM and agriculture), she is interested in learning possibilities, qualities, and capacities of doctoral student agency within a critical context of academia. Contact: zarrina.azizova@okstate.edu

**Dr. Jill Bickett** is the associate director of the Doctoral Program for Educational Leadership for Social Justice at Loyola Marymount University (LMU). She is a lifelong educational leader serving in Catholic secondary schools. Her research interests include single-sex education and social justice leadership. A member of the second cohort of LMU's Doctoral Program for Leadership in Education for Social Justice, she earned her Ed.D. in 2008. Her dissertation research was a case study of a Catholic female single-sex high school that explored student perspectives about leadership and service. Dr. Bickett's current research has focused on the transformation of students through social justice education. Recent publications include "Preparing School Leaders for Social Justice: Examining the Efficacy of Program Preparation," with Karen Huchting, in C. Boske & S. Diem (Eds.), *Global Leadership for Social Justice: Taking It from Field to Practice* (Bingley, UK: Emerald Publishing, 2012), and "Inspired to Lead: Two Years of Evaluation Data from a Jesuit Ed.D. Program for Educational Leadership in Social Justice," in *Jesuit Higher Education* (2013), also with Dr. Huchting. Contact: Jill.Bickett@lmu.edu

**Dr. Kay Brocato** is an associate professor in the Department of Educational Leadership and Foundations at Mississippi State University. She currently teaches courses on school culture and on planning for the diversity of learners. Kay's research focuses on innovative ways to equitably serve all students. She is the lead investigator in a study to understand the relationship between a studio learning environment and students' brain development. This project uses fMRI technologies to understand the real-time activation patterns of the brain as well as the long-term development impact on the brain. Contact: kbrocato@colled.msstate.edu

**Dr. Christopher Burke** has been an associate professor in the College of Education, Health, and Human Services at the University of Michigan (UM)-Dearborn since 2001. Dr. Burke earned his doctorate in science education from the University of Illinois at Urbana-Champaign in 2001. He is currently the codirector of the Ed.D. Program at UM-Dearborn and has worked with 17 doctoral students as either chair or a committee member in the past 5 years. Dr. Burke's research focus is on issues of equity and social justice in science education. In particular, his focus is on the school–community interactions in urban settings and how these shape student engagement and student learning. Currently he is looking at the impact of integrating school and community gardens into the curriculum on student engagement and school–community relationships and how to effectively prepare preservice teachers to integrate gardening and garden science into the curriculum. Contact: cjfburke@umich.edu

**Dr. Jioanna Carjuzaa** is an associate professor who holds a Ph.D. in multicultural, social and bilingual foundations of education from the University of Colorado-Boulder. At Montana State University, she teaches courses in education and

Native American Studies. Jioanna is grateful to serve as the co-advisor to the American Indian Council and as the facilitator for Indian Education for All, professional development opportunities for the MSU community. She was the recipient of the 2013 G. Pritchy Smith Multicultural Educator of the Year Award and is executive director of the MSU Center for Bilingual and Multicultural Education. Contact: carjuzaa@montana.edu

Dr. Crystal R. Chambers is Associate Professor of Educational Leadership at East Carolina University in Greenville, North Carolina. Dr. Chambers is a graduate of Spelman College and holds a J.D. as well as a Ph.D. in education policy from the University of Virginia. She was the 2003 winner of the American Association for Higher Education's Black Caucus Doctoral Student Award and a 2005 recipient of a research grant from the Association for Institutional Research. Dr. Chambers's published works include *From Diplomas to Doctorates: The Success of Black Women in Higher Education and Its Implications for Equal Educational Opportunities for All* (Stylus), *Support Systems and Services for Diverse Populations: Considering the Intersection of Race, Gender, and the Needs of Black Female Undergraduates*, and *Black Female Undergraduates on Campus: Successes and Challenges* (Emerald). Contact: chambersc@ecu.edu

Dr. Elaine Chin began her appointment as dean of the Connie L. Lurie College of Education at San José State University on June 1, 2009. Prior to that, she was the associate dean of the Lurie College of Education from August 2007 to May 2009. She has held a number of administrative and faculty positions, including department chair and faculty member for the Teacher Education Division in the College of Education at Cal Poly, San Luis Obispo, and faculty in the School of Education at the University of Michigan, Ann Arbor. She is a former high school English and journalism teacher. She has been active in research on alternative teacher certification programs, policies governing teacher licensure, socialization into the professions, and the development of professional expertise by novices in the fields of journalism, medicine, chemistry, and K–12 teaching. Her publications include articles and book chapters in *Educational Researcher, Written Communication*, the *Journal of Learning Sciences*, and the *International Handbook of Educational Policy*. Contact: elaine.chin@sjsu.edu

Thomas W. Christ, Ph.D., is an associate professor and chair of the education leadership doctoral program at the University of Bridgeport. He is chair of the AERA Mixed Methods Special Interest Group, a board member for the Mixed Methods International Research Association (MMIRA), and is on the editorial board for the *Journal of Mixed Methods Research*. Dr. Christ brings two decades of research experience in qualitative, quantitative, action, and mixed methods, was a school psychologist, a postsecondary program evaluator, a university research teacher, and worked on federally funded grants. His research is cross-disciplinary and includes research pedagogy; student, program, and organization evaluations; international education reform; and education leadership. He continues to promote new and innovative concepts by presenting papers and workshops about mixed methods across the United States, Canada, England, Spain, and Saudi Arabia. His publications include qualitative, mixed, and action research methodologies, postsecondary supports, technology, leadership, program evaluations, and doctoral program research. Contact: tchrist@bridgeport.edu

**Jude Soo Meng Chua, Ph.D.**, is Associate Professor of Philosophy at Policy and Leadership Studies Academic Group and Sub-Dean for Higher Degrees and Research at NIE, NTU. He is the program coordinator for the Ed.D. (Dual Award) program that IOE offers with NIE and is occasionally Visiting Academic at the IOE, London, and Visiting Research Scholar at Blackfriars Hall, Oxford. He held a visiting graduate fellowship at the Center for Philosophy of Religion (2002–2003) at the University of Notre Dame, Indiana, and worked with the eminent natural law theorist John Finnis. He is a Fellow of the Royal Historical Society (FRHistS), London, and a Fellow of the College of Teachers (FCollT), London. He won the Novak Award (Acton Institute, Michigan) for his research in economics and liberty in 2003 and is associate editor of the *Journal of Markets and Morality*. Contact: jude.chua@nie.edu.sg

**Dr. Arnold Danzig** is professor and founding director of the Ed.D. program in Educational Leadership in the Connie L. Lurie College of Education at San José State University and professor emeritus at Arizona State University, where he served as professor and associate director, School of Public Affairs/College of Public Programs at Arizona State University. Prior to that, he served as professor and director of the Division of Advanced Studies in Policy, Leadership, and Curriculum and professor of education leadership and policy studies in the Mary Lou Fulton Institute and Graduate School of Education. He has published numerous books and articles on educational leadership and education policy, including *Learner-Centered Leadership: Research, Policy, and Practice* (2007) and *School Leadership Internship* (3rd ed., 2012). His newest book, edited with Liz Hollingworth, is *Research in Learning and Teaching in Educational Leadership* (2014), a volume in the University Council for Educational Administration Leadership Series. He is also an author and editor of the American Educational Research Association's journal *Review of Research in Education*, which released the 2012 volume *Education, Democracy, and the Public Good*, and the 2014 volume *Language Policy, Diversity, and Politics in Education*. Contact: arnold.danzig@sjsu.edu

Dr. Christina (Tina) M. Dawson has served as teacher and administrator across the pre-K–graduate school spectrum. She strives for social justice, respect for diversity, and the valuing of the uniqueness of each person while creating a climate that supports risk taking, collegiality, and learning. She has been working with doctoral students for almost 20 years and has earned teaching excellence awards from Virginia Tech, Antioch, and Walden. She earned her Ed.D. at Virginia Tech. Contact: Christina.dawson@WaldenU.edu

Dr. Jocelyn Romero Demirbag serves as chair of the School for Strategic Initiatives at the Haleakala Waldorf School in Kula, Maui, Hawai'i. She is a sociologist within the field of education, having obtained her M.A. in sociology at UC Berkeley and her Ed.D. at the University of Hawai'i at Mānoa. She has worked in independent schools for almost 25 years, as well as with nonprofits and philanthropic organizations. Contact: jocelyn@waldorfmaui.org

Carla DiGiorgio, Ph.D., is an associate professor of educational psychology at Brandon University in Manitoba, Canada. She has been involved in research and teaching in the area of inclusive education for over 23 years. Dr. DiGiorgio has used the theoretical framework developed by Pierre Bourdieu to analyze various educational settings and processes, including children and adults with disabilities, gifted education and enrichment, the tenure process in universities, the francophone education system in Canada, Reggio Emilia in Italy, and the El Sistema music program. She has looked to culture, identity, and power as ways to understand learning settings, their stakeholders, and practices. She has published two books as well as many chapters, articles, and conference presentations. Dr. DiGiorgio has been the editor of the *Canadian Journal of Education* and has made several international speeches and consultations. Contact: c_digiorgio@hotmail.com

Four Arrows, aka Don Trent Jacobs, Ph.D., Ed.D., is a faculty member at the College of Educational Leadership for Change at Fielding Graduate University (FGU), formerly associate professor at NAU, and before that Dean of Education at Oglala Lakota College. He is the recipient of the Martin Springer Institute for Holocaust Studies Moral Courage Award as well as the Canadian Mid-Day Star for his activism on behalf of Indigenous Peoples. AERO selected him as one of 27 "visionary educators" for its text *Turning Points*. He is the author of 20 books, more than 40 invited chapters, and over 100 articles. His books include *Unlearning the Language of Conquest; Critical Neurophilosophy and Indigenous Wisdom; The Authentic Dissertation: Alternative Ways of Knowing, Research and Representation;* and *Teaching Truly: A Curriculum to Indigenize Mainstream Education.* See more at http://www.teachingvirtues.net. Contact: DJacobs@fielding.edu

**Dr. Kelly S. Hall** has served as research director for the largest Ed.D. program in the world at Walden University and as a member of advisory committees for two new Ed.D. programs, one at Wright State University in Dayton, Ohio, and the other at Frostburg State University in Frostburg, Maryland, where she serves as Assistant Professor of Education Professions and institutional designee to the Carnegie Project on the Education Doctorate. While serving as director of Planning, Research, and Grants at Clark State Community College, Dr. Hall has developed and taught a dozen graduate research classes delivered in a variety of formats. She has consulted with for-profit and nonprofit organizations internationally, developing strategic research and management initiatives. She holds a certificate from Harvard University's Institute for Education Management, a Ph.D. in Education Administration, an M.S. in Sociology from Illinois State University, and a B.A. in Business Marketing from Capital University in Columbus, Ohio. Dr. Hall is the author of articles about service learning and research centers in higher education and has presented globally on topics related to navigating research and grants processes. Contact: kshall@frostburg.edu

**Dr. M.D. Haque** is an assistant professor at the Doctor of Education Program in Organizational Leadership at the University of La Verne. He has an extensive background in technologies pertaining to education. His research interest lies in exploring effective pedagogies for the online and hybrid learning environment. Contact: mhaque@laverne.edu

**Jessica Hearn, Ph.D.**, is the Director of the Evaluation Center and clinical faculty member in the Educational Policy Studies and Evaluation Department at the University of Kentucky. Her doctoral concentration was in instructional leadership, and for the past 6 years, she has worked with graduate students on research and writing skills in Virginia and Kentucky. Dr. Hearn works with teacher leaders, principals, and doctoral students as they pursue degrees to make a difference where they work. She has published work examining principal preparation programs (Ed.S.), teacher use of classroom assessment practices, clinical models for teacher preparation, and teacher-candidate self-efficacy. Contact: Jessica.hearn@uky.edu

**Dr. David Henderson** is an assistant professor in educational leadership at Montana State University in Bozeman, Montana, and facilitates Courage to Teach, Courage to Lead, and Circles of Trust retreats for the Center for Courage and Renewal in Seattle, Washington. He continues to study and research the intersection of the inner life of leaders with their practice of leadership grounded in a heart striving for integrity and authenticity. Contact: david.henderson3@montana.edu

**Dr. Ann Toler Hilliard** is an assistant professor in the Department of Educational Studies and Leadership at Bowie State University in Maryland, where she teaches classes related to educational leadership, policy issues, school law, planning and evaluation, management of human resources, dissertation one/two, group dynamics, and human relations. Her research interests are instructional leadership, learning communities, professional development, teaching, learning, blended learning, and international studies. Beyond teaching, Prof. Hilliard has experience as a college and school leader in administration. She currently coordinates activities that provide professional experiences for graduate candidates seeking the opportunity to serve as school administrators at the building and district level. She holds an Ed.D. from George Washington University, an M.S. from Johns Hopkins University, an M.A.T. from Trinity University-Washington, a B.S. from Elizabeth City State University, and a Certificate for Consulting from Harvard University. Contact: draph1@juno.com

**Dr. Audrey Hovannesian** currently serves as Assessment and Student Success Coordinator for California State University San Bernardino's (CSUSB) College of Natural Sciences. She was the first CSUSB student to complete undergraduate through doctoral degree consecutively on the campus. Dr. Hovannesian's 100 Dinners Project dissertation won second place at the system-wide CSU Research Competition in 2013, and she was acknowledged as the 2012 Victor Valley Person of the Year and Soroptomist Ruby Award Nominee for the study. A K–12 teacher for 12 years, she is currently a lecturer and will be serving the CSU Chancellor's Office as the Program Director for the High Impact Practice Project funded by the Gates Foundation. Dr. Hovannesian is also a Research Fellow for the Carnegie Project on the Education Doctorate (CPED) and travels the country to strengthen Ed.D. student and alumni scholarly work. Her areas of expertise also include data visualization and teacher professional development. Utilizing these skills, she helped transform the Guam Department of Education's curriculum through the Common Core State Standards transition and delivers teacher professional development in many areas, including Depth and Complexity, Depth of Knowledge, Project-Based Learning, and Step up to Writing. Contact: ahovanne@csusb.edu

**Karen "Karie" Huchting, Ph.D.**, is an assistant professor in the Department of Educational Leadership at Loyola Marymount University. She teaches in the Doctoral Program in Leadership for Social Justice, and her area of expertise is quantitative research methodology and assessment. Dr. Huchting's scholarship centers on social justice in the educational context, and she recently published phase 3 of a longitudinal study examining the efficacy of Catholic education for students living in poverty in Los Angeles. She is currently the principal investigator of an empirical research study examining Catholic identity within a diocese in California. Her work in this area has been sponsored by grants totalling over $1 million. She is also an author of a 2014 assessment textbook, *Managing What You Measure: Effective Assessment for Catholic High School Teachers*, published by the National Catholic Education Association. Dr. Huchting serves as an editor for the *Journal of Catholic Education*. Contact: Karen.Huchting@lmu.edu

**Dr. Truman Hudson, Jr.**, president of the DEXDesign Community Development Club, L3C and BMe community manager, is a highly respected social economist and entrepreneur with 25 years' experience in developing, implementing, and evaluating educational and community economic development projects. Dr. Hudson's efforts produced over $698 million in resources for various projects. In 2013, Truman received a $20,000 BMe Leader award for his work in teaching economic literacy to youth. His current research investigates student voice, development, and engagement in economic instruction. Truman is also exploring how Black males' engagement in economics, education, and social organizations influences community and economic development. A native of Detroit and a product of its public schools, Dr. Hudson received his doctorate of education from the University of Michigan and was recognized by the Detroit Public Schools as an outstanding educator. Contact: thudsonjr@ dexteam1.com

**Dr. Whitney Johnson** earned her bachelor's degree in Mathematics at the University of Delaware, her master's degree in Mathematics at Michigan State University, and her doctorate in Teacher Education at Michigan State University. She spent 10 years preparing secondary undergraduate preservice mathematics teachers. Her current research interest is the schooling experiences of Black students in mathematics from the time of segregation to the present. She co-directed a 3-year study of how African American math teachers create a sense of purpose for their students to study Algebra I. Her article "Teaching with Speeches: A Black Teacher Who Uses the Mathematics Classroom to Prepare Students for Life" recently appeared in *Teachers College Record*. Her long-range goal is to begin a nonprofit organization that provides out-of-school learning experiences for K–12 students in the city of Baltimore. Contact: whitney. johnson@morgan.edu

**Stephanie J. Jones, Ed.D.**, has been an associate professor and program coordinator for the Higher Education Program in the College of Education at Texas Tech University since 2008. During her time at TTU, she has been instrumental in the development and implementation of the only predominantly online Ed.D.

in higher education with an emphasis in Community College Administration provided by a public university in the state of Texas. Through her leadership, the doctoral program in higher education has grown to one of the largest doctoral programs in the university. This program is successfully serving the needs across the U.S. of producing qualified leaders with the skills to solve problems in practice and to lead community colleges now and in the future. Dr. Jones currently serves on the editorial board of the *Community College Journal of Research and Practice*, is the technology editor for *Community College Enterprise*, and is an associate editor for the *Journal of Asynchronous Learning Networks*. Her current research agenda includes community colleges, distance learning, women in higher education, and organizational efficiencies and economics. Before her position at TTU, she was Associate Dean of Distance Education and Instructional Support at South Plains College, where she assisted with the administration of distance learning initiatives, dual enrollment, instructional technology, faculty development, and student support. She also served as the project director of a DOE Title V Cooperative Grant that partnered South Plains College with Amarillo College in efforts to increase community college student access to higher education through distance learning. Prior to her move into administration, she served as faculty and department chairperson of computer information systems. Before her move into academia, Dr. Jones worked in the information technology sector. Contact: stephanie.j. jones@ttu.edu

**Dr. Cheryl Keen**'s coauthored book, *Common Fire: Leading Lives of Commitment in a Complex World* (Beacon Press, 1996), and her ongoing research on the topics of emerging adulthood, diversity, service learning, reflection, and career development have been the focus of her scholarly outreach. At Walden University, she serves as core faculty in the Ph.D. in Education program and has supervised dissertation work at the Union Institute. Previously she served as dean of faculty, co-dean of students, and director of the Center for Community Learning at Antioch College and served for 15 years as senior researcher for the Bonner Foundation and several years as evaluator of the Volunteers Exploring Vocation program. Cheryl has also been the director of the New Jersey Governor's School on Public Issues and the Future of New Jersey, serving gifted high school students, and the Millicent Fenwick Research Professor for Public Issues and Education at Monmouth University. She served for several years as a faculty member in low-residency adult degree B.A. programs at Lesley College Graduate School and Goddard College. Her first professional work involved founding and coordinating the Harvard Peace and Conflict Studies Program. She holds an Ed.D. from Harvard University's Graduate School of Education. Contact: Cheryl.Keen@WaldenU.edu

**Dr. Carol Kochhar-Bryant** is professor and senior associate dean of the Graduate School of Education and Human Development at the George Washington University, Washington, D.C. For 27 years, she has developed and directed advanced graduate and doctoral leadership preparation programs, guiding the introduction of Ph.D. and professional practice doctoral programs. She consults with public school districts, state departments of education and federal agencies, and nonprofit organizations that seek to improve services and supports for children and youth with disabilities in education, employment, and independent living. She has been invited to collaborate in special education research with the World Bank and by the U.S. Department of Education to lead evaluation teams for the six Federal Resource Centers. Dr. Kochhar-Bryant is past president of the Division on Career Development and Transition of the International Council for Exceptional Children. She was born in the United Kingdom and has traveled to Israel, India, the UK, and Austria in her work. Contact: kochhar@gwu.edu

**Dr. Yew-Jin Lee** is a former high school biology teacher turned science teacher educator. He is currently the Assistant Head for Primary Science in the Natural Sciences & Science Education Department at the National Institute of Education in Singapore and was involved in teaching the Ed.D. program in previous years. He was also a visiting fellow at the Institute of Adult Learning (Singapore) and a Fulbright scholar in 2008–2009, when he researched urban science education with the City University of New York. His interests are in learning in the workplace and how expertise is developed among children and adults. Yew-Jin is on the editorial board of four science education journals and coedits the journal *Pedagogies*. Contact: yewjin.lee@nie.edu.sg

**Lerona Dana Lewis** is a Ph.D. candidate in Educational Studies at McGill University. She taught multicultural education and global education and social justice at the undergraduate level and research methods at the graduate level. Her areas of research interest are sociology of education, Black Canadian feminist thought, education in contexts of immigration, parental involvement in education in second-language contexts, and equity in education. She is also a research assistant and was the president of the Teaching Assistants Union at McGill University for 3 years. Contact: lerona.lewis@mail.mcgill.ca

**Dr. Sunny Liu** is an assistant professor at University of La Verne with several years' experience working in higher education. She teaches research methodology courses and demonstrates her knowledge in her research, committee work, presentations, and publications. She is the 2008 and 2009 research fellow for the National Summer Data Policy Institute and the 2013 U.S. Department of Education's Institute of Education Sciences (IES) What Works Clearinghouse (WWC) reviewer certification trainee. Contact: lliu2@laverne.edu

**Cynthia J. Macgregor, Ed.D.**, is a professor in the Counseling, Leadership, and Special Education Department at Missouri State University and serves as the site coordinator for the regional portion of a statewide Ed.D. program in educational leadership offered through the University of Missouri. She helped design a new dissertation format for this Ed.D. program that aligns with the working principles of CPED. With a background in psychology and adult education, she brings a non-native perspective to the challenges of pre-K–20 education. From this perspective, she sees a problematic divide between pre-K–12 and higher education, as well as a divide between practitioner and scholar that plagues many disciplines. She teaches and advises students in one of the only pre-K–20 Ed.D. programs affiliated with CPED. Her unique vantage point, combined with her pragmatic worldview, allows her to see vexing problems within education and propose novel and systemic solutions. Contact: cmacgregor@missouristate.edu

**Shane P. Martin, Ph.D.**, is an educational anthropologist by training and expert in the areas of intercultural education, cultural diversity, and the spectrum of public, charter, and Catholic schools. He was appointed dean of the Loyola Marymount University School of Education in 2005 and dean of graduate studies in 2012. Dr. Martin serves as a state commissioner to the California Commission on Teacher Credentialing and is a member of the National Council for Accreditation of Teacher Education (NCATE) Board of Examiners and California Committee on Accreditation Board of Institutional Reviewers. He is past chair of the Green Dot Public Schools Board of Directors, a member of the Teach for America Los Angeles Board, and Loyola High School of Los Angeles Board of Regents. He received the National Catholic Educational Association's (NCEA) Michael J. Guerra Leadership Award in 2005, the Catherine T. McNamee, CSJ, Award in 2009, and the Loyola High School Alumni Association's Cahalan Award in 2008. Contact: shane.martin@lmu.edu

**Mary K. McCullough, Ph.D.**, serves as the Associate Dean for Faculty in the School of Education at Loyola Marymount University. As a professor in educational leadership, Dr. McCullough served as department chair, inaugural director of the doctoral program, director of the administration program, and Faculty Senate president. Dr. McCullough earned her Ph.D. from USC in policy, planning, and administration. She has received awards as Outstanding Administrator, Outstanding Alumna, and Outstanding Graduate. Dr. McCullough was editor of the journal *Educational Leadership and Administration: Teaching and Program Development* and currently serves as editor of the *Journal of Catholic Education*. She has edited two books, including *The Just One Justices: The Role of Justice at the Heart of Catholic Higher*

*Education.* Dr. McCullough facilitated $5 million in grant processes for California Secondary Schools and served as chair for WASC accreditation. Her research areas include principalship, organizational change, generations in the workplace, and culture and climate in Catholic schools. Contact: mmccullo@lmu.edu

**Dr. Marnie O'Neill** is a Senior Honorary Research Fellow in the Graduate School of Education at the University of Western Australia. She served as dean and head of school from 2000 to 2005. She has taught across all degree levels in the school and was director of teaching in the preservice program for a number of years. Marnie coordinated the Doctor of Education program from 1998 to 2011 and was instrumental in reviewing the program in preparation for offering it in Hong Kong and Singapore. Her major responsibilities were in supervision of doctoral students in both the on-shore programs and the transnational programs in Singapore and Hong Kong. She has successfully supervised 70 HDR students, including 30 doctoral candidates, since her Ph.D. was conferred in 1995. Contact: marnie.oneill@uwa.edu.au

**Mariam Orkodashvili** has researched education and linguistic issues for more than 12 years at academic institutions. She has been affiliated with Georgian-American University, Georgia; Peabody College of Education and Human Development, Vanderbilt University; Tbilisi State University; the Parliament of Georgia; Education Research Institute, Washington, D.C.; Max Planck Institute for Social Anthropology, Halle-Saale, Germany; and Edinburgh University, Scotland. She has worked in national testing, university accreditation, bilingual education, and second-language acquisition at Tbilisi State University, Georgian-American University, and at the Parliament of Georgia. She has researched issues of linguistic universals and typological syntax; access to higher education; corruption in higher education; quality manipulation in education; education and social cohesion; shadow education and private tutoring; educational linguistics; anthropocentric analysis of reciprocity; bilingualism; cognitive neuroscience, syntax/semantics interface; relevance theory; and linguistic minimalism. Ms. Orkodashvili has published in the following journals: *Sociology of Education, European Education: Issues and Studies, Peabody Journal of Education, Immigration and Education Nexus, International Perspectives on Education and Society,* and the *Journal of Post-Soviet Demokratization.* She is the recipient of the following awards: Chevening/FCO scholarship; Muskie/U.S. Department of State scholarship; DAAD/OSI research fellowship; Carnegie fellowship; RESET/HESP/Fulbright scholarship; and an OSI international scholar grant. She has participated in a number of conferences, seminars, and annual meetings, including GRM, CIES, ASA, BSA, HGSE, AERA, ASHE, and BSA. Contact: morkoda@yahoo.com

**Dr. Carol Philips** earned her Ed.D. in human development and psychology from the Harvard Graduate School of Education. At HGSE, she codirected the Writing, Research and Teaching Center. She subsequently served as the Director of Research for doctoral programs at Walden University's College of Education, where she was involved in redesigning the college's Ed.D. program. As associate director of Temple University's Teaching and Learning Center, Dr. Phillips initiated the development of an innovative Certificate in Teaching and Learning program that combined seminars and practica and that enrolled both Temple doctoral students and faculty members throughout the area. Using the full range of delivery formats—from brick-and-mortar to hybrid to online—she has taught in institutions ranging from community colleges to universities. Her research, which has been recognized as distinguished by the American Education Research Association, currently addresses best practices in learning and teaching in higher education. Contact: Carol. Philips@WaldenU.edu

**Dr. Glenda M. Prime** is Professor of Science Education and chair of the Department of Advanced Studies, Leadership and Policy at Morgan State University in Baltimore, Maryland. In this capacity, she leads a department with an enrolment of approximately 400 doctoral students in five different specializations in education. Her primary research focuses on the impact of social and cultural contexts on student learning in the sciences. She has authored several articles in research journals, as well as three book chapters on a range of topics in science education, mathematics education, and technology education. Professor Prime has extensive experience in the graduate preparation of science and mathematics education researchers and practitioners in both national and international contexts. She holds the Ph.D. in Education from the University of the West Indies. Contact: glenda.prime@morgan.edu

**Dr. Paris T. Priore-Kim** earned a B.A. from Princeton University, an M.Ed. from the University of Hawai'i, and, most recently, an Ed.D. from the University of Hawai'i's Program in Professional Educational Practice. She is currently a dean of students at Punahou School, one of the largest K–12 independent institutions in the United States, where she has also taught social studies at the middle school level and French at the high school level. Contact: pprio-re-kim@punahou.edu

**Dr. Amanda J. Rockinson-Szapkiw** holds an Ed.D. in distance education, an M.A. in counseling, and a B.S. in education. Over the past 5 years, she has served as program chair for an online Ed.D. program. Prior to entering higher education, she served as a counselor specializing in child and adolescent disorders and trauma. Her research has focused on distance education and doctoral persistence, and she recently published the coedited book *Navigating the Doctoral Journey: A Handbook of Strategies for Success*. Dr. Rockinson-Szapkiw's development of a collaborative workspace to facilitate doctoral mentorship was recognized by Microsoft via a case study and was awarded a Campus Technology innovator award. Contact: aszapkiw@liberty.edu

**Ernest Rose** is Professor of Special Education in the Department of Educational Support Services and Professor of Educational Leadership in the Department of Educational Leadership and Administration, School of Education, Loyola Marymount University. He is director of the school's doctorate of education program in educational leadership for social justice. He teaches courses focusing on transformative leadership for school achievement, the foundations of special education, inclusion, transition, and special education research. Dr. Rose has been the director of six U.S. Department of Education-funded projects in the areas of special education and drug-free schools and communities and is currently the senior consultant for special education grants awarded from NIH and NSF to the School of Education. He has written numerous articles and book chapters on issues related to children and adults with disabilities and is the coauthor of *Growing Up: The Transition of Students with Disabilities to Adult Life*. Contact: Ernest.Rose@lmu.edu

**Dr. William G. Ruff,** an associate professor of educational leadership at Montana State University (MSU), has published more than a dozen journal articles and book chapters addressing school leadership, social justice issues, and comprehensive school reform. He was one of the founders of the Indian Leadership Education and Development (I LEAD) program and continues to play a key leadership role in the program's development as the primary investigator for the current $1.3M grant from the Office of Indian Education, U.S. Department of Education. He is also Associate Director of the Center for Bilingual and Multicultural Education at MSU. Contact: wruff@montana.edu

**Tara L. Shepperson, Ph.D.**, is an assistant professor in educational leadership and policy studies at Eastern Kentucky University, where she teaches leadership, research, ethics, and rural studies to doctoral and master's students. Her research focuses on trends that push traditional boundaries in education, including professional doctoral education, alternative schools, and collaborative dual-credit and early-entry college programs. Dr. Shepperson is interested in policy and practice that expands access, opportunity, and experiences for students, and has acted as evaluator for programs that bring new resources to education, ranging from school technology to place-based science learning. She presents and publishes regularly on innovations in pre-K–16 education and on the changing landscape of graduate leadership preparation. Contact: tara.shepperson@eku.edu

Dr. David J. Siegel is an associate professor in the Department of Educational Leadership at East Carolina University. He is the author of *Organizing for Social Partnership* (Routledge, 2010) and *The Call for Diversity* (RoutledgeFalmer, 2003) and is coeditor (with John C. Knapp) of *The Business of Higher Education* (Praeger, 2009), a three-volume set. His research on the dynamics of cross-sector collaboration has appeared in journals such as *Higher Education*, *Innovative Higher Education*, *The Journal of Higher Education Outreach and Engagement*, and *The Journal of Further and Higher Education*, and his essays on academic life and culture have appeared in *Academe*, *Liberal Education*, *The Chronicle of Higher Education*, *Diverse Issues in Higher Education*, and *About Campus*. Siegel is the recipient of Fulbright and Lumina Foundation grants. He holds a B.A. from Wake Forest University, an M.Ed. from the University of South Carolina, and a Ph.D. from the University of Michigan. Contact: siegeld@ecu.edu

Michele Smith, Ph.D., is an assistant professor in the Counseling, Leadership, and Special Education Department and serves as Coordinator for Recruitment & Marketing in the College of Education at Missouri State University. Her scholarship explores mentoring undergraduate and graduate students and new faculty with a focus on women faculty of color, women in leadership, and issues of race and gender in athletics focusing on African American men in football and basketball. She has taught diversity courses at the undergraduate and graduate levels, sports marketing at the undergraduate and graduate levels, and has worked administratively in admissions and recruitment, academic advising, and accreditation. She currently teaches and advises students in the Student Affairs in Higher Education master's program and uses her unique background and perspective to investigate historical and current issues in higher education and how these issues impact faculty and students. Contact: mdsmith@missouristate.edu

Dr. Lucinda S. Spaulding earned her Ph.D. in special education and educational psychology, her M.Ed. in special education, and her B.S. in elementary education. She is an associate professor in the School of Education at Liberty University, where she teaches advanced research courses and chairs doctoral dissertation committees. Prior to serving in higher education, she taught general and special education in New York and Virginia, as well as ESL in Japan. Dr. Spaulding is the vice president of the Virginia Federation of the Council for Exceptional Children and serves as coeditor of the association's journal. Her research interests include examining factors related to doctoral attrition and persistence, resilience in children and youth, specific learning disabilities and methods of best practice, and the history of special education. Dr. Spaulding was born and raised in Ottawa, Canada, and currently resides in Forest, Virginia, with her husband and three children. Contact: lsspaulding@liberty.edu

**Dr. Virginia Stead** earned her Ed.D. in educational administration at OISE University of Toronto in 2012. She is the 2013 founding series editor of *Equity in Higher Education Theory, Policy, and Praxis* (Peter Lang Publishing). Dr. Stead launched her series as editor of Vol. I, *International Perspectives on Higher Education Admission Policy: A Reader*, which includes essays by authors from over 30 countries, showcases her qualitative doctoral thesis, *Teacher Candidate Diversification through Equity-Based Admission Policy*, offers new insights into higher education admissions across most fields, and introduces new ways of understanding higher education policy implementation. Dr. Stead furthers her social justice agenda through graduate student mentoring, research conference symposia with her series authors (Vols. 1, 4, & 5), and the development of edited and authored books for her Peter Lang equity series. She is active within research associations such as AERA, AESA, ASHE, CIES, CSSE, CSSHE, and EAN and may seek a faculty position in 2016. Contact: virginia.stead@alum.utoronto.ca

**Michael L. Washington** is a qualitative researcher and certified life coach who specializes in social justice education, sociology of education, and adult education. He has a master's degree in educational leadership and policy studies in urban leadership. He anticipates completion of his Ph.D. in 2015, jointly at Claremont Graduate University and San Diego State University and, as a change agent, advocates for social justice and educational reform. Mr. Washington has 10 years' teaching experience in adult and correctional education and has lectured for continuing education, adult, alternative, correctional, and higher education programs. His publications and research interests include culturally relevant teaching and leadership practices, educational achievement gaps for marginalized, at-risk populations, and African American male resiliency and perseverance in postsecondary education. He has chaired sessions and presented his research at several national conferences such as the annual meeting of the American Educational Research Association (AERA), the Association for the Study of Higher Education conference (ASHE), the Ethnographic and Qualitative Research Conference (EQRC), the Universal Design for Learning (UDL) conference, the Council for the Study of Community Colleges conference (CSCC), the Adult Education Research Conference (AERC), the American Association for Adult and Continuing Education (AAACE) conference, the National Association for Multicultural

Education (NAME) conference, and the Lilly conference. Prior to commencing graduate studies, he accumulated over 25 years of professional experience in various fields such as information technology, case and social work, curriculum development, professional development, corporate training, and supervision and management. Contact: michael@themixx.com

**Dr. Chris Willis** is an assistant professor in the School of Foundations, Leadership, and Policy at Bowling Green State University. He currently teaches courses in organizational change and instructional supervision. Before coming to BGSU, Chris was an assistant professor at Mississippi State University. He also has 13 years' experience as a school administrator in Indiana. He earned his doctorate from Indiana University in educational leadership. His research focuses on school policy issues and barriers to school reform. His current research includes an examination of the policy implementation of new teacher evaluation processes in Ohio, and he is part of a large project that is using fMRI technologies to understand how innovative instructional settings impact the brain activity and development of at-risk students. Contact: wchris@bgsu.edu

**Dr. Lara Willox** is the director of the Ed.D. program in school improvement and an Assistant Professor of Learning and Teaching at the University of West Georgia. She is a teacher-educator and has been involved in the field of teaching for over 20 years. Her beliefs are centered on the importance of connecting with learners, promoting inquiry, and creating equitable educational environments for all students. Dr. Willox's research is in the area of collaborative action research, social studies education, and transformative pedagogy. She is active in the College and University Faculty Assembly (CUFA) of the National Council for Social Studies (NCSS) and served as chair of the elementary social studies special interest group. She advocates for the improvement of schools through transformative pedagogies and civic engagement while stressing that development of a transformative lens promotes greater civic engagement. Prior to completing her doctorate at UNC Chapel Hill in culture, curriculum, and change, she taught for 12 years in public elementary schools in Charlotte, North Carolina. Contact: lwillox@westga.edu

**Dr. Sweeney Windchief** is a member of the Fort Peck Assiniboine tribe in northeastern Montana and is an assistant professor in the Adult & Higher Education program at Montana State University in Bozeman. His research agenda includes Indigenous intellectualism, American Indian experiences in higher education, Tribal college leadership succession and development, and Indigenous values-based leadership. His teaching responsibilities include American Indian Experiences, Resource and Program Management in Higher Education, Law and Policy in Higher Education, Theoretical

Foundations of College Students, Critical Race Theory in Education, and Institutional Research. He is currently developing a course in Indigenous research methodologies for the purpose of expanding research capacity in American Indian communities in a culturally appropriate way. He received his Doctor of Education degree in educational leadership and policy with a focus on higher education at the University of Utah in 2011. Prior to this he served as the Assistant Dean for Diversity in the graduate school at the University of Utah, implementing pragmatic programs that serve students as well as their communities in a way that helps them maintain cultural integrity as they navigate a system that has been historically, and is currently, experienced as assimilative. Focusing on praxis and how critical race theory and various Indigenous theories are enacted and impact indigenous communities, Sweeney is motivated to help facilitate access to higher education and support students in maintaining indigenous identities. He has previously worked as Director of Fellowships and Special Programs with the American Indian Graduate Center in Albuquerque, New Mexico; in student affairs at Idaho State University in Pocatello; and as an academic advisor at the University of Montana-Missoula as a minority admissions counsellor. Contact: sweeney.windchief@montana.edu

A BOOK SERIES FOR EQUITY SCHOLARS & ACTIVISTS

# Virginia Stead, H.B.A., B.Ed., M.Ed., Ed.D., *General Editor*

Globalization increasingly challenges higher education researchers, administrators, faculty members, and graduate students to address urgent and complex issues of equitable policy design and implementation. This book series provides an inclusive platform for discourse about—though not limited to—diversity, social justice, administrative accountability, faculty accreditation, student recruitment, admissions, curriculum, pedagogy, online teaching and learning, completion rates, program evaluation, cross-cultural relationship-building, and community leadership at all levels of society. Ten broad themes lay the foundation for this series but potential editors and authors are invited to develop proposals that will broaden and deepen its power to transform higher education:

(1)  Theoretical books that examine higher education policy implementation,
(2)  Activist books that explore equity, diversity, and indigenous initiatives,
(3)  Community-focused books that explore partnerships in higher education,
(4)  Technological books that examine online programs in higher education,
(5)  Financial books that focus on the economic challenges of higher education,
(6)  Comparative books that contrast national perspectives on a common theme,
(7)  Sector-specific books that examine higher education in the professions,
(8)  Educator books that explore higher education curriculum and pedagogy,
(9)  Implementation books for front line higher education administrators, and
(10) Historical books that trace changes in higher education theory, policy, and praxis.

Expressions of interest for authored or edited books will be considered on a first come basis. A Book Proposal Guideline is available on request. For individual or group inquiries please contact:

Dr. Virginia Stead, General Editor | *virginia.stead@alum.utoronto.ca*
Christopher S. Myers, Acquisitions Editor | *chrism@plang.com*

To order other books in this series, please contact our Customer Service Department at:

(800) 770-LANG (within the U.S.)
(212) 647-7706 (outside the U.S.)
(212) 647-7707 FAX

Or browse online by series at www.peterlang.com